Japanese Language, Gender, and Ideology

STUDIES IN LANGUAGE AND GENDER
Mary Bucholtz, *General Editor*

Reinventing Identities: The Gendered Self in Discourse
    Edited by Mary Bucholtz, A. C. Liang, and Laurel A. Sutton

Pronoun Envy: Literacy Uses of Linguistic Gender
    Anna Livia

Japanese Language, Gender, and Ideology: Cultural Models and Real People
    Edited by Shigeko Okamoto and Janet S. Shibamoto Smith

Japanese Language, Gender, and Ideology

Cultural Models and Real People

Edited by
Shigeko Okamoto
Janet S. Shibamoto Smith

UNIVERSITY PRESS

2004

OXFORD
UNIVERSITY PRESS

Oxford   New York
Auckland   Bangkok   Buenos Aires   Cape Town   Chennai
Dar es Salaam   Delhi   Hong Kong   Istanbul   Karachi   Kolkata
Kuala Lumpur   Madrid   Melbourne   Mexico City   Mumbai   Nairobi
São Paulo   Shanghai   Singapore   Taipei   Tokyo   Toronto

Copyright © 2004 by Oxford University Press, Inc.

Published by Oxford University Press, Inc.
198 Madison Avenue, New York, New York 10016

www.oup.com

Oxford is a registered trademark of Oxford University Press.

Library of Congress Cataloging-in-Publication Data
Japanese language, gender, and ideology : cultural models and real people /
edited by Shigeko Okamoto, Janet S. Shibamoto Smith.
   p. cm.—(Studies in language and gender)
Includes bibliographical references and index.
ISBN 0-19-516617-5; 0-19-516618-3 (pbk.)
1. Japanese language—Social aspects.   2. Sociolinguistics.   I. Okamoto, Shigeko.
II. Shibamoto Smith, Janet S.   III. Series.

PL524.75.J36 2004
306.44'0952—dc22   2003066233

9 8 7 6 5 4 3 2 1

Printed in the United States of America
on acid-free paper

ACKNOWLEDGMENTS

We would like to express our gratitude to all the colleagues who contributed chapters to this volume. We have greatly enjoyed working with them and have learned a lot in the process. We are deeply grateful to Mary Bucholtz, general editor of the Studies in Language and Gender Series, for her insightful comments and unflagging support and encouragement, and the two anonymous reviewers for their valuable comments on the draft of each chapter. We also thank Peter Ohlin, our editor at Oxford University Press, and the Oxford University Press staff. Special appreciation must go to artist Tanno Yumiko, who generously provided the perfect visual image for the cover of this volume. On a more personal front, we want to acknowledge our husbands, Per Gjerde and David Glenn Smith, for their support and patience throughout this project. We are happy to have had such cooperative and intellectually engaged partners over the last two years.

The creation of this collection has been a long process but also an intellectually rewarding journey. There have been numerous occasions when we exchanged our views by e-mail, over the phone, or—on all-too-rare but very treasured occasions—in person. Both of us enjoyed these exchanges and have benefited enormously from this extended conversation. Our names appear in alphabetical order.

FOREWORD

The Japanese language has played a foundational role in the development of language and gender as an area of linguistic research, and the language use of Japanese women—and, increasingly, men—continues to serve as a touchstone for theoretical and empirical advances in the field. This scholarly interest in Japanese was stimulated in the first instance by the widely discussed linguistic style known as "women's language." For pioneering English-speaking feminist linguists in the 1970s and 1980s, "women's language" in the Japanese case provided a powerful illustration of the intimate relationship between gender and language, one that was seen as both like and unlike linguistic arrangements of gender in the West. Japanese was seen as different from English in having inscribed gender into its very structure, through the prescribed use of differential grammatical and lexical forms for women and men. Yet despite this tendency to treat Japanese "women's language" as alien and exotic, at the same time the linguistic situation of Japanese women was often seen as different from the circumstances of English-speaking women only in degree, not in kind. Thus "women's language" in Japan came to be examined for its potential in informing the understanding of language and gender in other societies as well.

In addition to its utility for Western feminists seeking to theorize language and gender, "women's language" has long been the object of scholarly scrutiny in Japan. Male Japanese scholars had been discussing this speech style for at least a century. In the late 1970s female Japanese linguists began to investigate "women's language" from a feminist perspective, and their findings often challenged nonfeminist perceptions of language and gender. Some researchers identified a number of fissures in what had been up until then a seamless and largely unquestioned cultural ideology of how Japanese women ought to speak. The recognition of the ideological dimension of "women's language" was a crucial breakthrough that opened up new avenues of investigation.

At the same time, feminist researchers sought to expand the range of issues examined within language and gender research in Japan. The fascination with "women's language" among both Japanese and non-Japanese had led to the tendency to overlook other crucial aspects of the relationship between language and gender, and researchers worked to bring these other topics into analytic view: issues such as the diversity of Japanese women's identities and subject positions and hence of their linguistic practices; the links between language use and linguistic ideologies related to gender; the interconnection of gender and sexuality and the linguistic aspects of sexual identity and practice; and the central but unacknowledged importance of men and masculinity in the study of language and gender. Many of these issues had begun to be addressed by feminist linguists working on other languages and cultures as well, but their investigation in the Japanese context has been especially significant in shifting scholars from a near-exclusive focus on "women's language" to the full range of issues that connect gender to language. Informed by and contributing to new strands of feminist thought within language and gender studies, *Japanese Language, Gender, and Ideology: Cultural Models and Real People* brings together an impressive group of international scholars to advance this research goal.

This volume forges bold new directions in research on the much-studied and much-misunderstood topic of "women's language" while heading out into previously uncharted territories of linguistic scholarship in Japanese. In the following pages, "women's language" receives extensive and critical attention from scholars, who historicize and contextualize the emergence and development of this style as part of a wider Japanese gender ideology. Other contributors focus on the numerous women of various classes, regions, ages, and sexualities who do not always or ever use "women's language," as well as groups of men who draw on its resources to position themselves outside of hegemonic Japanese masculinity. Still other chapters examine emergent issues of language, gender, and sexuality in Japan, including questions of scholarly and popular representations of language and gender, gendered cultural styles and practices, sexual identity and romance, and the linguistic practices of communities of speakers in a rich array of social contexts. *Japanese Language, Gender, and Ideology* includes researchers based both within and outside of Japan, and it is an especially significant achievement of the volume that it makes available in English for the first time the writings of several important contemporary feminist Japanese linguists.

The purpose of Oxford's series Studies in Language and Gender is to promote the most innovative, significant, and enduring research in the study of language, gender, and sexuality around the world. The inclusion of this volume in Studies in Language and Gender signals the continuing importance of feminist scholarship on the Japanese language as well as the contributions of this body of work in moving the field into exciting new arenas of inquiry.

CONTENTS

NOTE ON NAMING

The names of our chapter contributors and our names are listed according to Western convention, that is, with given name preceding family name, irrespective of nationality. In the text of the chapters, Japanese names are given according to the Japanese convention, family name preceding given name, with some minor exceptions where the individuals themselves have made other choices in professional contexts. Western names appear in given name–family name order. We recognize these inconsistencies, as we participate in a global economy of intellectual endeavor that incorporates numerous disparate cultures of naming.

CONTRIBUTORS

Hideko Abe — Associate Professor, Department of Foreign Languages, Western Michigan University

Orie Endo — Professor of Humanities, Faculty of Language and Literature, Bunkyo University

Miyako Inoue — Assistant Professor, Department of Cultural and Social Anthropology, Stanford University

Wim Lunsing — Free scholar based in Leiden

Claire Maree — Full-time Lecturer, Department of English, Tsuda College

Yoshiko Matsumoto — Associate Professor, Department of Asian Languages, Stanford University

Laura Miller — Associate Professor, Department of Anthropology, Loyola University

Ayumi Miyazaki — Graduate student, Graduate School of Education, Harvard University

Momoko Nakamura — Professor, Department of Economics, Kanto Gakuin University

Yumiko Ohara — Instructor, Liberal Arts Department, Hawai'i Tokai International College

Shigeko Okamoto — Professor, Department of Linguistics, California State University, Fresno

Masami Saito — COE Post Doctoral Research Fellow, Ochanomizu University

Janet S. Shibamoto Smith — Professor, Department of Anthropology, University of California, Davis

Cindi Sturtz Streetharan — Assistant Professor, Department of Anthropology California State University, Sacramento

Yukako Sunaoshi Lecturer, the School of Asian Studies, the University of Auckland, New Zealand

Rumi Washi Instructor, Institute for Japanese Studies, Nagoya Gakuin University

Sumiyuki Yukawa Professor, Faculty of Humanities, Toyama University

Japanese Language,
Gender, and Ideology

SHIGEKO OKAMOTO
JANET S. SHIBAMOTO SMITH

Introduction

I.1. Toward a new framework for Japanese language and gender studies

Models of Japanese society and culture, in particular the *Nihonjinron* 'theories on the Japanese' literature, commonly stress such attributes as homogeneity, harmony, consensus, and hierarchy, including gender stratification (Yoshino 1992, Befu 2001, Sugimoto 2003). In line with this framework, Japanese sociolinguistic practice (e.g., the use of honorifics, address terms, and indirect speech styles) as part of Japanese cultural behaviors has been described primarily based on context-independent, abstractly normative usage in Standard Japanese. Speech produced by real Japanese people in real situations that differs from that "appropriate" language use has been considered "erroneous" or "deviant," or has simply been ignored. Descriptions of Japanese female and male speech are no exception. Despite decades of intensive research into Japanese speaking practices and into Japanese "women's language" (see, e.g., Ide 1979, 1997; Shibamoto 1985; Ide, Hori, Kawasaki, Ikuta, & Haga 1986; Reinoruzu[Reynolds]-Akiba 1993), our understanding of Japanese women and men as speaking subjects still remains largely obscured by essentialized depictions of "the Japanese woman" and "the Japanese man" and their "languages"—or *joseego* 'women's language' and *danseego* 'men's language'—characterized by a number of stereotypical linguistic features held to be differentially used by "average" Japanese women or men.

These stereotypical features include broad characteristics of speech styles, such as polite, gentle, unassertive, and empathetic speech, as well as more specific features

3

(particularly in Standard Japanese) such as honorifics, self-reference and address terminologies, sentence-final particles, indirect speech acts, interjections/exclamatory expressions, and voice pitch level (see Shibamoto Smith 2003 for a summary of these features). However, we argue that "women's language" and "men's language" characterized as such are cultural constructs informed by the hegemonic ideology of language and gender—constructs that have been widely disseminated as linguistic norms in Japanese society not only through popular media but also by language policy makers and linguists like ourselves. In fact, the latter group—policy makers and linguists—seems to have had considerable influence on the former. Previous studies of Japanese language and gender have tended to focus on these normative usages without examining their implications for the real language practices of real speakers. In particular, real women and men who are not—by virtue of their age, class, regionality, sexual orientation, or other characteristics—identifiable as "average" speakers and their speaking choices, which may or may not conform to the normative usages, have effectively been erased from the record.

However, the view of Japanese as homogeneous, interdependent, and so forth has been increasingly criticized in recent years as partial and misleading, representing hegemonic ideologies as Japanese cultural behaviors (e.g., Yoshino 1992; Befu 1993, 2001; Sugimoto 2003). In order to gain a better understanding of Japanese society and culture, a growing number of researchers are now investigating diversity and heterogeneity in Japanese society. These researchers pay more attention to previously understudied sociocultural subgroups (e.g., blue-collar workers, working women, and ethnic minorities) and social situations (e.g., Weiner 1997, Eades, Gill, & Befu 2000, Sugimoto 2003). In Japanese sociolinguistics, diversity has been studied primarily in relation to differences in regional dialects. However, there is now growing awareness of the need for studying linguistic variation as it relates to social and contextual diversity that involves real Japanese people interacting in real-world situations (see, for example, Maher & Yashiro 1995, Cook 1998, Sato & Okamoto 1999, Saft 2001; see also papers presented in conjunction with Miller 1995 and Okamoto & [Shibamoto] Smith 1998). In particular, researchers on Japanese language and gender have been actively engaged in the investigation of linguistic diversity and its meaning. Since the early 1990s, there has been increasing interest in the study of within-gender variability in speech practice, in particular, "nonnormative" uses (Okamoto & Sato 1992; Smith 1992; Takasaki 1993; Okamoto 1995; Sunaoshi 1995; Inoue 1996; Ogawa & [Shibamoto] Smith 1996, 1997; Maree 1997; Matsumoto 1999; Abe 2001; Sturtz 2001). These studies necessitate consideration of the relationship between linguistic practice and ideologies—a central issue addressed in this volume.

This volume brings together studies that contribute to advancing Japanese language and gender studies in this new direction. It is also in line with the orientation of recent language and gender research in general, which cautions against essentialist approaches based on abstractions and binary oppositions of women and men, while emphasizing the importance of examining local linguistic practices of real speakers as social agents and their context-dependent and potentially multiple social and pragmatic meanings in relation to dominant gender and language ideologies (see, among others, Hall & Bucholtz 1995, Bergvall, Bing, & Freed 1996, Bucholtz, Liang, & Sutton 1999). This volume builds on and contributes to these trends. It begins with a close examination of the ideologies and cultural models that underlie our conceptions of the idealized Japanese woman and man, as these may have significant regimenting effects on speaking practices of real women and men (parts I and II); it then calls into question these very ideologies and models via a close examination of socially and ideologically diverse Japanese women and men in real verbal interactions (part III). It presents a significant move forward for Japanese language and gender studies by attempting to overcome the limitations of previous studies in several ways.

First, this volume highlights the linguistic and cultural ideologies that provide the backdrop against which Japanese men and women choose how to speak and interpret what is said. Language ideology—a rationalization of perceived language structure and use (Silverstein 1979:193)—has not in general been a serious focus of study in Japanese sociolinguistics, perhaps because it is considered to be somewhat unscientific, or a "distraction from primary and thus 'real' linguistic data," as it has been in American linguistics (Woolard 1998:11). However, as ideology has come to be recognized as a powerful shaping force on language production and interpretation generally (Kroskrity 2000) and as Silverstein (1985) illustrates for language and gender in English, we attempt to demonstrate in this volume that considering language ideology is essential to Japanese sociolinguistic research, as it serves as "a mediating link between social forms and form of talk" (Woolard 1998:3). Previous studies in Japanese language and gender have often confounded native speakers' linguistic ideology with their practice by characterizing Japanese female and male speech patterns in terms of distinct differences based on normative usages for women and men. Recognizing the importance of distinguishing language ideology and practice, this book problematizes the ideologies and cultural models that underlie our conceptions of "the Japanese woman" and "the Japanese man" as these relate to speaking practices; it considers how these ideologies and models are constructed, both historically and today, and how they relate to real Japanese women and men in real verbal interactions.

Second, the volume questions binary distinctions in social and linguistic categories such as Japanese women and men and Japanese female and male languages. Such distinctions, often taken for granted in previous studies, assume that each category is internally homogeneous, consisting of members who share characteristics distinct from the members of the other category. And the category subjected to the most scrutiny has generally been women. In contrast, this volume emphasizes the importance of examining and accounting for real language practices of both female and male speakers whose identities in one way or another position them relative to the models of the idealized average Japanese woman and man. They may fit the "normative" patterns, for reasons that are context-dependent and strategic. These uses need explanation. They may fall outside the normative models; the talk of these speakers, too, requires explanation. The chapters in this book demonstrate that both normative and nonnormative patterns of language-use-in-context should be identified and accounted for in a principled way without delegitimizing the latter use by labeling it incorrect or marginal. They show, in other words, that a sociolinguistic account of Japanese language and gender relations can encompass a much wider group of Japanese speakers—female and male—speaking in more diverse social situations than has hitherto been the case.

Third, the volume demonstrates that research on Japanese sociolinguistic phenomena cannot remain focused on static and abstract descriptions of the relationship between language and social categories. In particular, the essays here move the field away from the common but problematic assumption that one linguistic form, such as a morphological element or a pitch height, can be directly linked to a single social category, such as gender. This assumption presupposes that one chooses linguistic forms simply because one belongs to the category "woman" (or "man"). However, speakers do not automatically choose language because they belong to a particular social category. Irvine argues that the relationship between the distributions of linguistic and social forms is not straightforward; rather, it "is more productively sought in cultural ideologies of language—those complex systems of ideas and interests through which people interpret linguistic behaviors" (1998:52). In this volume, indexicality, or the relationship between linguistic expressions and social meanings, is understood, not as direct and fixed, but rather as multiple, flexible, context-dependent, and mediated by speakers' beliefs and attitudes concerning language use, which are variously influenced by hegemonic ideologies. That is, the social meanings of a particular linguistic expression may be interpreted differently, depending on the context as well as on the speaker's (or the interpreter's) beliefs about language use. For example, a particular stereotypically gendered form in Japanese (e.g., a sentence-final particle) may not necessarily be used to index the speaker's gender, although it may be interpreted as doing so by hearers. Sociolinguistic phenomena must, thus, be understood through close examination of local contexts of language uses, including ideational contexts. In addition to providing empirical analyses of diverse real speaker data, then, the volume addresses how linguistic expressions are linked to social meanings in specific contexts and attempts to account for the complex and dynamic nature of the relationship between language and gender.

Fourth, as a corollary of the third point, the volume considers the use of language in relation to the construction of identities and interpersonal relations (Wodak 1997, Bucholtz, Liang, & Sutton 1999). It examines the speaker's active involvement in language choice as a performative strategy for creating the desired social context, in particular identities and relations. Bucholtz argues that "identities, far from being given in advance for individuals to step into, emerge over time through discursive and other social practices" (1999:12). Viewing identities as multifaceted and dependent on the relational context, this volume examines language use as a series of strategic speaker choices made in the interests of creating a context-appropriate social persona. With regard to gender, language is thus seen as a resource upon which speakers as social agents draw in order to construct diverse forms of gender identities and relations. Understanding such creative use of language is possible only by recognizing the flexible and multiple relationship between language and social meanings.

Finally, this volume presents a methodological challenge to the field of Japanese language and gender as well. Reliance on introspection and survey data has been common in Japanese sociolinguistics, as noted by Shibamoto (1987), but these methodologies tend to provide information only about normative or prescriptive usages that reflect dominant linguistic and cultural ideologies. However, it is important to clearly distinguish between beliefs about how one should talk and the way one actually talks. The chapters in this volume that examine language practices (part III) utilize alternative methodologies to surveys and introspection. They all analyze actual speech data gathered in specific social contexts employing sociolinguistic or discourse analytic methods; furthermore, most analyses are supported by rich ethnographic data. Such analyses reveal a complex and dynamic relationship between language and gender that cannot possibly be envisioned by macrosociological ideologies.

These five issues are explored in the ensuing chapters, which are grouped into three parts: part I, historical and theoretical foundations; part II, linguistic ideologies and cultural models; part III, real language, real people.

I.2. Historical and theoretical foundations

Part I tackles ideological issues head-on. As mentioned earlier, one of the most notable gaps in Japanese language and gender research has been a clear distinction between ideology and practice. This distinction entails (1) a close examination of the normative ideology of language and gender and its implications in the Japanese context, (2) a thorough investigation of the historical development of gendered speech norms and their associated ideology, and (3) a principled analysis of the relation between the normative ideology and the range of real speaking practices that constitute Japanese verbal life. The chapters in part I all address one or more of these issues, starting with a critical overview of the Japanese language and gender research field and its ideological underpinnings and presuppositions (Yukawa & Saito), then proceeding to a reexamination of the ideology of women's speech and its implications for linguistic analysis and practice (Okamoto), to tracing the historical development of contemporary stereotypical "feminine" and "masculine" Japanese speech-as-ideology (Inoue, Washi), to a look at the hegemonic—and often damaging—psychosocial effects of these ideologically and culturally salient styles on oft-ignored speakers, in particular, lesbians and gays (Lunsing & Maree).

The chapters in part I provide an invaluable look back over the development of what is often called *joseego* 'women's language' in the first half of the twentieth century, both as a social narrative of appropriate behavior for Japanese women and as a story in part constructed by linguists but used more broadly for (largely exclusionary) social ends. Part I also considers how the ideology of gendered speech norms that developed over the years affects both linguistic practice and analysis. Recognizing that we researchers of language and gender ourselves are often susceptible to the hegemonic language and gender ideology, these chapters go a long way toward providing a coherent framework that takes a distinction between ideology and practice into account in investigations of Japanese speech. Part I closes with a powerful statement of the importance of this distinction for a particular group of nonnormative speakers (lesbians and gay men) struggling to find "suitable" speaking practices usable to locate themselves socially in ways that do not violate their inner sense of self.

Sumiyuki Yukawa and Masami Saito's comprehensive overview of Japanese language and gender studies in the latter part of the twentieth century and into the present traces the historical development of the field from the era of a "persistent essentialism" that relegated women and men into oppositional and internally undifferentiated categories toward constructivist frameworks that can incorporate both the dominant discourses of femininity and the real behavior of speaking women. A most welcome component of this survey is the rare chance to read in English about the pioneering work of Jugaku Akiko, whose 1979 volume, *Nihongo to onna 'The Japanese language and women'*, established a framework for language and gender research centered around the notion of *onnarashii kotoba* 'feminine speech' as a normative constraint on women's speech behavior. Yukawa and Saito delineate Jugaku's understanding of *onnarashii kotoba* as distinctive from other researchers' treatment of this concept in including not only language used *by* women but also the language used *to* women and the topics deemed suitable *for* women, all of which reveal "the workings of linguistic and cultural ideologies in the structural oppression of women." Yukawa and Saito note that while it is sometimes overlooked, Jugaku's work remains ahead of its time even today. Their chapter also reviews the work of Japanese feminists on issues concerning language and gender, in particular sexism in Japanese—valuable information that has not been readily available in English. It focuses on two groups of feminists: activists in the *uuman ribu* 'women's lib' movement in the early 1970s and feminist scholars in the 1980s and 1990s. Yukawa and Saito demonstrate that the former were concerned with oppression through language and were, in fact, engaged in "subversive linguistic practices," and call our attention to the efforts made by the latter group toward eliminating "institutionalized manifestations of gender ideologies," such as sexist representations in dictionaries, newspapers, and other print media. After documenting the Western-influenced Japanese language and gender research led by Ide and her colleagues that formed the mainstream of research into "Japanese women's language" through the 1980s and into the 1990s, the authors close their chapter by outlining new research trends aimed at clarifying the relationship between language, identity—here, gender identity—and ideology. It is a matter of some pride to us as editors that so many of the scholars mentioned by Yukawa and Saito as contributing to these new lines of research have chapters in this volume.

Shigeko Okamoto turns to a sustained examination of just those language and gender ideologies that have greatly influenced both linguistic practice and analysis in the Japanese case. Her analysis centers around the generalization that "women speak more politely than men," arguing that close examination of such generalizations is necessary in order to understand their ideological underpinnings as well as their relation to actual speaking practice. Through an extensive interrogation of the linkages between politeness, honorifics, and gender made by linguists and other researchers, on the one hand, and purveyed as social norms to the public *via* education and media, on the other, Okamoto demonstrates the remarkable consistency of messages to women that, in order to be *onnarashii* 'feminine', they should speak in ways that are gentle, polite, and refined. In the examination of actual speaking practices that follows, however, she demonstrates that there is much less consistency in the ways that women and men can be observed to speak. Okamoto then elucidates the relation between the ideological and actual by critically examining the three ideologically nonneutral assumptions that often serve as the foundation for theorizing about the nature of women's language in Japan: (1) that most or all women share the same attributes and therefore (should) use language in the same way, (2) that certain linguistic expressions, such as honorifics, are inherently polite, and (3) that speaking politely, that is, showing deference or refinement through the use of honorifics and other expressions, indexes femininity or the female gender. Her critique of these three assumptions and her reframing of them as simply one of several possible orientations toward social norms opens the door to much new empirical work on not just the diversity of language use but also diverse interpretations of variant language forms as individuals adopt, resist, or simply ignore normative statements concerning femininity and masculinity while engaging in real speaking events. Her point that femininity and masculinity manifest simultaneously at two levels, the ideological and the practical, and that the speech forms chosen may not be interpreted in the same way on both levels is pursued by the chapters in part III.

The next two chapters address the historical development of contemporary constructions of women's speech norms. They address the processes of construction and dissemination of the contemporary complex of forms in Standard Japanese that form normative *joseego* today. Miyako Inoue's chapter focuses on the modernizing period (late nineteenth–early twentieth centuries) and investigates the process by which women and their linguistic practices came to embody "the shifting boundary between tradition and modernity." Her description of language modernization, built on previous scholarship (e.g., Komori 1992, 2000), is centered around the standardization of Japanese and the development of the modern Japanese novel. It is, Inoue argues, in the dialogues and reported speech of these new novels—where women's voices were "objectified, reified, and re-presented"—that "Japanese women's language" was constructed. Inoue describes for the reader the process by which writers selected, systematized, and disseminated particular "feminine" forms, forms neither inherently feminine nor inherently refined, which, through the popular consumption of *katee shoosetsu* 'domestic novels' by a female readership, served to ascribe these forms to that new icon of appropriate or socially desirable femininity, the middle-to-upper-class Tokyo woman. This newly created language, argues Inoue, is the origin of today's "Japanese women's language." Much work remains to be done both on the specific processes by which the forms identified in her chapter came to constitute an ideology of "women's language" and on their links to earlier articulations of ideas about women and speaking practices, but Inoue's investigation into the historical process of creating a modern "Japanese language" and a "women's language" within it clearly demonstrates the importance of historicizing women's speech, of incorporating an understanding of the sociopolitical nature of the indexical process (and an appreciation of its power) into our analyses of sociolinguistic variation, and of the political potential of reported or represented speech, a topic that occupies part II of this volume.

Rumi Washi also argues for understanding "Japanese women's language," which she refers to as "female speech," as an artificial construct. In her chapter, based on an extensive survey of historical documents, she examines the relationship between language policy, in particular language standardization policy, and the education of women as it relates to "female speech" in the period between 1920 and 1945 (that is, the period before and during World War II). Washi first outlines the various strands of influence on women and their speaking practices in general during this period, then turns to a detailed investigation of one semiofficial body, the National Language Association, and its relationship to female educators. She first traces language policy developments from the 1930 founding of the National Language Association, charged with rationalizing, improving, and promoting the national language, to the establishment of a women's wing in 1939. The women's wing was established, in the words of the association's then vice president, in order to "obtain the cooperation of women in preserving and honoring the national language." The chapter then turns to the substance of that cooperation, the ideal *form* of female speech, and the process by which the contemporary complex of features that were asserted to constitute "female speech" was linked to much earlier historical forms of speech associated with women, specifically *nyooboo kotoba* 'court women's language'. Washi provides a compelling rationale for female educators to cooperate in disseminating this language construct based on the various associations of "female" or "feminine" speech styles with high social position for women under ideologies of sexual complementarity (or, put another way, of separate equality); it was only later that Japanese women were to "uncover the trick" whereby they were led to espouse speaking patterns that—far from affording them "separate but equal" status—relegated them to subordinate positions in the larger social order.

Part I closes with Wim Lunsing and Claire Maree's discussion of the implications of hegemonic gender ideologies for groups of speakers who have been marginalized by most previous research: lesbians and gays. The relation of gender to sexuality is a topic that has been largely neglected in Japanese language and gender studies. Lunsing and Maree challenge the linking of linguistic gender performance in Japanese to dominant heterosexist discourses, arguing for a need to investigate the complex relations between dominant gender norms for language use and individuals who do not participate in the associated discourse of heterosexual normativity (with its *hentai* 'queer' offshoots, the "effeminate gay man" and the "masculine lesbians"). The heart of their chapter is a poignant depiction of the struggles both gay men and lesbian women make to fit their nonnormative sexual identities with the normatively constrained choices they have for self-reference. Normative (Standard) Japanese self-referencing practices require that women and men use different sets of forms. But these gender norms are equally strongly associated with sexual orientation norms; that is, female users of feminine self-reference forms (e.g., *watashi*) are assumed to be womanly (hence, heterosexual) and male users of masculine self-reference forms (e.g., *boku*) are assumed to be manly (and therefore also heterosexual). The lingering distaste Lunsing's and Maree's consultants express for the limitations of the pronoun choices available to them makes abundantly clear the heteronormative underpinnings of Japanese language and gender ideology. Lunsing and Maree argue, however, that "prescription is never fully reflected in actual language use" and that "self-reference choice is not the result of a speaker's gender identification but a reflexive negotiative strategy" for dealing with a sense of multiple selfhood. By focusing on the intersections of gender and sexuality as speakers strive to make appropriate choices from among a set of stereotypically—that is, explicitly—gendered and implicitly sexually oriented language forms, Lunsing and Maree allow us to see, first, the implicit conflation of gender and sexuality in both linguistic and popular accounts of Japanese "gendered language" and, second, the importance of incorporating notions of negotiation and variability into our analyses of women's and men's language use.

I.3.   Linguistic ideologies and cultural models

Part II focuses on the question of how Japanese women and men are conceptualized and represented in Japanese—a particularly crucial exercise for highlighting issues of gender and language ideology. Each chapter examines how the cultural models for women and for men are produced and reproduced through the language itself—through the lexical, morphosyntactic, discursive, and performative choices made when representing women and men in print and other media.

The late twentieth century has been an important period in the reevaluation of "traditional" gender relations in Japan; it has also been a period of hypersaturation of everyday life by (multi)media presence. An understanding of the media messages Japanese women and men are receiving—about how to be adequate or attractive women or men, about how to view feminine and masculine social roles, about how to construe love and marriage—is critical to an understanding of the ongoing production, reproduction, and transformation of gender relations. Rosenberger, in an analysis of Japanese women's magazines, argues that print media have "some power over the way women categorize themselves, their wishes for self-actualization and relationship, and their sexual desires" (1995:143–144). This is, we argue, equally true for men. In a variety of ways, print and other media have the power to establish ideas about what constitutes desired femininity and masculinity with respect to personality traits, behaviors, and so on. These ideas may not always be internally coherent but can provide alternatives to the ideas provided by dominant institutions.

The close scrutiny given the representation of gendered selves in novels, magazines, television dramas, and dictionaries provided in the chapters of part II sheds new light on the role of ideological symbolic forms, forms that have the potential to produce and reproduce cultural models for women and men in the Japanese social field. Here, then, we are not concerned with the recognition that individual women and men create individual female and male personae that may be more or less stereotypically "feminine" or "masculine" but with the linguistic representation of these stereotypes and its dissemination in society. Compared to the explicit commentary on how Japanese women and men should talk detailed in part I, the linguistic representations examined in part II are more implicit. Such covert prescriptions—or "implicit pragmatics" (Woolard 1998:9)—take the legitimacy of their models for granted. Accordingly, they may be equally or even more effective in serving to regiment women and men into normative femininities or masculinities and to reinforce the hegemonic control of societal gender arrangements.

Janet S. Shibamoto Smith considers the linguistic representation of cultural models for women and men by examining Japanese romance fiction. This chapter is particularly important in bringing issues of emotionality and sexuality, especially heterosexuality, into Japanese language and gender studies. Shibamoto Smith analyzes category romance novels to see how (ideal) lovers use language with each other to convey their femininity and masculinity. Her analyses of first- and second-person references and sentence-final particles in lovers' dialogue show that heroines and heroes make extensive use of normative gendered speech styles, which may serve as references for readers—that is, real women and men—as they set about falling in love. Further, her analyses demonstrate that unlike Western romances, in which nonlinguistic attributes, particularly physical features, are emphasized in the depictions of ideal heroines and heroes, language plays an essential role in the cultural construction of heroes and heroines in Japanese romance novels. Shibamoto Smith argues that lovers' dialogue is a primary site for the expression of gender politics in these novels. Her study thus illustrates not only the complex relationship of sex and gender to language but also the role of language in constructing (the images of) gendered subject positions in a particular activity (i.e., "falling in love") through an appeal to culturally grounded semiotic practice (Kulick 2000).

But, of course, there is more to heteronormative femininity and masculinity than romance. Momoko Nakamura presents the results of her analysis of discourse constructs in two women's and two men's popular lifestyle magazines published between 1999 and 2000. Her analytic framework, a reformulation of Fairclough's (1989) model of the dialectic between social structures and discourse, gives ideologies a central mediating role. Within this framework, Nakamura asks how a specific gender identity not preestablished—or at least, not fully preestablished—in gender ideologies is "invented" in discourse practices. Her argument starts with the magazine writers' and producers' need to construct a specific identity for a specific set of targeted readers *as they are imagined to be*. Using speech styles that are, again, *imagined* to appeal to targeted readers, magazine discourse attempts to draw real young women or young men into the discursively constructed "magazine community"—and to attract, thereby, a regular subscriber and purchaser base. Nakamura's extended analysis illuminates the gender-differentiated ways that such communities are organized, how their readers are differently constructed as "participating" in the community, and how topics of fashion and the like position the members of the respective communities in gendered ways via language. It effectively shows us that several of the features stereotypically associated with female patterns of speech (exclamations, inclusive stance marked by hortatives, interactively oriented sentence-final particles) occur in the young women's magazines, while stereotypically "masculine" patterns (absence of affect indicators, imperatives, use of assertive *da* forms) occur in the young men's magazines. She closes with a discussion of the contrastive metaphors for conceptualizing fashion—FASHION AS TASK versus FASHION AS BATTLE—metaphors that themselves align differentially with gender ideologies. Her analysis provides us with a close look at how the forms implicated in ideologies of gendered language can be and are used to construct finely tuned, very specific images of femininities and masculinities suited to particular magazines and their communities of readers.

Novels, magazines, comic books, and television inundate Japanese-speaking subjects with images of "suitable" feminine or masculine behavior. The "tenets for proper female behavior" and the "behavioral paradox" that these impose on women are the focus of Laura Miller's chapter on *burikko* 'phony girl(s)'. *Burikko* is a derogatory label used to describe women whose speaking and other behavioral patterns are seen as exaggerated and false exhibitions of naïveté, innocence, and cuteness. Therein, of course, lies the "behavioral paradox": many of the prescriptions for proper female behavior—that is, the linguistic reflexes of modesty and innocence—overlap with traits commonly associated with *burikko*. Miller's chapter first presents a description of *burikko* stylistic features, then draws on various popular print and visual media sources for data on how *burikko* images are constructed using many of the same features that are part of the stereotypical "women's language." Examining media representations as well as several ethnographic cases of women performing *burikko*, Miller provides a rich analysis of the context in which the term *burikko* is used to evaluate this exaggeratedly and childishly "feminine" form of speaking and acting, that is, when and why a particular behavior is considered too "feminine." These observations demonstrate that at the same time a Japanese woman is being taught that being feminine is a desirable social trait, she also is learning that there are relatively strict limits on the performance of femininity. *Burikko* is but one of many expressions that are used to categorize and evaluate women. Miller's careful analysis of this term well illustrates how women are subject to close scrutiny of their behavior. She returns us, that is, to Inoue's point that "woman" has historically been—and, we see here, continues to be—a "regimented category," regimented in this case by the critical gaze and commentary of other members of women's speaking communities.

In the final chapter in part II, Orie Endo provides us with updated and detailed information about another regimenting force on the cultural construal of the category "woman": dictionaries. Unlike the popular texts and media productions described in the previous three chapters, dictionaries are "authoritative texts" par excellence. Endo and her associates in Kotoba to onna o kangaeru kai 'Group for Thinking about Language and Women' have been studying sexist language in dictionaries and other authoritative texts (e.g., media and governmental guidelines for nonsexist language) for over two decades. This chapter is a fine-grained analysis of the treatment of three representative derogatory expressions related to women, *onnadatera* (*ni*) 'despite being a woman', *rooba* 'old woman/old crone', and *oorudo misu* 'spinster' (lit., 'old miss') in dictionaries, on the one hand, and in newspapers and novels, on the other, clearly demonstrating the substantial lag of dictionaries compared with popular or even other "official" usage (e.g., government publications). Endo contextualizes the changes found in the use of these words in both popular and (semi)official publications (such as publishing houses' in-house guidelines for nondiscriminatory language usage)—and the unchanging treatment found in many or most of the dictionaries in her 66-volume corpus—with respect to the various strands of popular protest against discriminatory language in general, the effects of women's movements in particular, and national and local-level governmental action. She closes with an expression of regret that dictionaries—the ultimate "authoritative source" for words and their uses—have not played a more active role in re-presenting women and their roles in Japanese life.

I.4.   Real language, real people

Part III presents empirical studies of real women and men in real Japanese interactional contexts, with a primary, although not exclusive, focus on groups of speakers who are typically not studied in research on language and gender. While previous studies on (stereotypical) gender differences in speech have tended to focus on speakers of Standard Japanese, in particular, female speakers who belong to a "privileged" group, that is, middle- and upper-middle-class housewives, the speakers examined in these studies vary widely in their social attributes, such as gender and sexual orientation, region, occupation, and age; they include speakers of regional dialects (Sturtz Sreetharan, Sunaoshi), socially diverse male speakers (Miyazaki, Ohara, Sturtz Sreetharan), junior high school students (Miyazaki), women in a variety of occupations, including farm women (Abe, Ohara, Sunaoshi), and lesbians (Abe), as well as "typical" women, or middle-aged housewives in middle-class families (Matsumoto).

The chapters in part III investigate real talk produced by these diverse women and men vis-à-vis the cultural models and ideological frames discussed in parts I and II. They examine actual speech data closely with regard to the use of linguistic features that are normatively associated with gender, such as self-reference and address terminology, sentence-final particles, honorifics, (in)direct speech acts, and phonological features. The results reveal impressive variation and extensive "deviations" from normative or stereotypical usage, suggesting that "deviant" uses are meaningful choices rather than mere exceptions or anomalies. They convince us that speakers do not blindly follow dominant social norms and expectations but rather relate to them variously—by adopting them, negotiating them, contesting or resisting them, or simply disregarding them because of their perceived lack of relevance to some concrete situation—and then choose expressions that they think most appropriate for a given context. Further, speakers observed in these studies all use stereotypically gendered expressions to convey not only femininity or masculinity but also a variety of other pragmatic meanings (e.g., solidarity, relative power), suggesting that indexicality is multiple and indirect and that the interpretation of gendered expressions as feminine or masculine is not given but normative and ideological. These chapters demonstrate how individual speakers as social actors use language strategically, by making pragmatic choices that draw simultaneously on their linguistic resources and their beliefs about language use, and how such choices contribute to constructing their identities and relationships.

Yukako Sunaoshi studies women who have historically been overlooked, a group of linguistic "others," namely, female speakers of a regional dialect living in a farming community in Ibaraki Prefecture. Sunaoshi analyzes interactions of three farm women and an Agricultural Extension Adviser, matched with detailed ethnographic descriptions of the social context, which are essential in understanding these interactions. She identifies two discourse strategies—the use of Ibaraki dialect and the treatment of the farm women as the representatives of their households—as means for the adviser's solidarity building with and empowerment of farm women. The Ibaraki dialect these women use lacks the morphological, lexical, and phonological features of the normative construct "Japanese women's language," but it serves as an important linguistic resource for them in constructing their identities and relationships. Sunaoshi then asks if even the ideology of "Japanese women's language," as it is defined in terms of features of Standard Japanese, is shared by these rural women. Her study suggests that research on Japanese women's speech must consider the extent to which the dominant gender and linguistic norms are relevant to real women, especially women who are in some sense linguistic "others," and must attempt to look at their linguistic practices in their own right—a suggestion that echoes Okamoto's (chapter 2, this volume) view that it is important to consider individual speakers' apprehensions of linguistic norms for specific local contexts.

Hideko Abe deals with another group of women who have been considered linguistic "others," namely, lesbians. Based on ethnographic research, Abe analyzes two aspects of the discourse of women observed at lesbian bars in Tokyo: the use of expressions for categorizing themselves and others, such as *rezu* 'lesbian' and *futsuu* 'ordinary', and their speech styles as they relate to the use of linguistic features stereotypically associated with gender (e.g., self-reference and address terminology, sentence-final particles). Her analyses demonstrate how the speakers discursively construct their shifting identities and relations through strategic uses of these linguistic means. Particularly interesting are her observations that these women use "masculine" expressions extensively, but not exclusively, and that the same speakers shift speech styles (e.g., between the "neutral" *anta* 'you' and "masculine" *omee* 'you') depending on the context (e.g., interlocutors, speech act types). Her observations show that the speakers negotiate the dominant gender and linguistic norms and relate to them differently depending on the context and that their use of stereotypically gendered "masculine" expressions does not straightforwardly index "masculinity" (or "femininity") but rather conveys a variety of context-dependent meanings, including solidarity/distance, emotional engagement, and resistance to the dominant gender and sexual norms.

In contrast to Sunaoshi and Abe, Yoshiko Matsumoto looks at the speech of women who have been commonly assumed to use stereotypical feminine speech styles—namely, middle-aged, middle-class Standard Japanese–speaking housewives. Her analysis centers on the use of expressions that convey different stances—"forcefulness" and "delicacy"—normatively associated with "masculine" and "feminine" speech (Ochs 1993) and reveals that, contrary to the common-social stereotype, these women do not use a traditional feminine speech style exclusively but rather exhibit wide inter- and intraspeaker variation. Some of them use forceful expressions more or less than others; further, variation is observed within a single individual's utterances even in the same conversation. Matsumoto explains that forceful and delicate expressions convey various pragmatic and social meanings, such as friendship, emotion, and deference, and that women use these linguistic resources variably to construct complex and flexible personae and relationships. Thus femininity, argues Matsumoto, cannot be considered a single concept; rather, depending on speakers' social backgrounds and interactional goals, different women may negotiate traditional gender norms and constraints differently in order to construct diverse female personae.

Yumiko Ohara's chapter also addresses the question of how real speakers relate to Japanese gender and cultural norms when using language in real social situations. Ohara observes not only women but also men—four company employees—interacting in two kinds of contexts: talking with customers and talking with acquaintances or friends. Unlike the other chapters in part III, Ohara's essay examines the use of prosody, specifically voice pitch level—a feature often associated with gender. Her analysis shows that this feature, too, cannot be directly linked to the dominant gender norm. Although a high-pitched voice is normatively associated with politeness and femininity, Ohara found that the women in her study did not always use it and that men also used it at times. This, however, does not mean that the use of this feature is haphazard. Taking a closer look at her data, Ohara accounts for her findings as a reflection of the complex way that speakers treat this feature—which functions both as a linguistic resource and as a cultural constraint. That is, both women and men may use a high pitch level pragmatically as a linguistic resource to emphasize certain parts of their utterances. However, Ohara observes an intriguing phenomenon in which the female speakers, but not the male speakers, varied their pitch levels substantially across interlocutors; that is, only the women used a considerably higher pitch when speaking to customers than when talking to close friends. From this, Ohara concludes that depending on the context, women but not men may use a high pitch level according to the cultural constraint that links this feature to politeness and thence to femininity.

Ayumi Miyazaki's chapter investigates the language use of junior high school students, both female and male, based on extensive ethnographic study. Her close look at the students' use of first-person pronouns reveals a complex and dynamic process of meaning making that is "far beyond the imagination of the fixed, dichotomous picture" of the normative usage. These students adopt, contest, and continually negotiate traditional gender norms, which often brings about nonnormative uses, such as girls' use of the "masculine" pronouns *boku* and *ore*. Examining the relations among students and the subcultures within the classroom as well as the students' metapragmatic discourses about these pronouns, Miyazaki demonstrates how the students use pronouns to index a multitude of pragmatic meanings that concern not only femininity and masculinity but also levels of formality, power, and solidarity. For example, studious, pro-school girls use the "feminine" pronoun *atashi*, whereas girls who are more nonconformist use "masculine" pronouns *ore* and *boku*; many girls also prefer the nontraditional pronoun *uchi* because it is more informal and less feminine than *atashi*. Powerful boys always use *ore*, while powerless boys use *boku* when talking with powerful boys but *ore* when talking with other powerless boys or girls. These observations—possible only through sustained ethnographic study— eloquently speak of how complex the relation of gender to a linguistic form can be and how important it is to examine closely the context in which a linguistic form is used in order to understand its social meaning(s) adequately.

In the final chapter, Cindi Sturtz Sreetharan focuses on men's speech. Rather than restricting her study to speakers of Standard Japanese, Sturtz Sreetharan includes speakers of a regional dialect (Kansai, or Hanshinkan, dialect) as well. Her analyses of the use of sentence-final particles in their conversations exhibit not only individual and regional differences but also considerable "deviation" from the normative usage, which undermines the idea that there is a single "Japanese men's language." Based on her finding that all speakers used "masculine" forms relatively infrequently, Sturtz Sreetharan concludes that these men do not utilize sentence-final particles to index (traditional) masculinity (although they may resort to other means to do so). Rather, they use sentence-final particles to express a variety of pragmatic meanings; for example, "masculine," or forceful, expressions are used to signal camaraderie, authority, anger, and so on. Further, speakers of the regional dialect may avoid using forms in Standard Japanese in order to create a sense of friendliness or solidarity. Sturtz Sreetharan notes, however, that the metapragmatic discourses of these men suggest that they are capable of using stereotypical strongly "masculine" speech, depending on the context (e.g., in quarreling). Sturtz Sreetharan's chapter, in line with those by Lunsing and Maree, Miyazaki, Ohara, and Okamoto, demonstrates that men also actively engage in discursive constructions of identities and relationships and use language strategically according to their interactional goals.

The findings of the studies presented in part III together offer compelling evidence for the importance of examining the social meanings of linguistic forms used in real contexts. For example, the pronouns *boku* and *ore* are both typically characterized as "masculine" first-person. However, the meanings conveyed by these pronouns in specific contexts are far more complex than this characterization offers. For example, high school boys may use *ore* to index relative powerfulness rather than simple male speakerhood and *boku* to index relative powerlessness. High school girls may also use *ore* (or *boku*), to reject traditional femininity or to be nonconformist, but they are not indexing masculinity. Women at lesbian bars may use *ore* to establish solidarity with the interlocutor, while at the same time rejecting the dominant gender and sexual norms, but again their use of *ore* does not index masculinity. Farm women in rural areas in Tohoku may use *ore* regularly (chapter 10, this volume) as part of their regional dialect, which can serve to establish solidarity among local people. But this does not mean that they are either rejecting conventional gender and sexual norms or trying to express masculinity. The meanings of *ore* and *boku* are, we see, highly context-dependent. In like manner, the chapters in part III all demonstrate that only a close examination of language use in real contexts enables us to fully understand the complex and dynamic relationship between specific linguistic choices and their social meanings.

I.5.   Concluding remarks

The studies in this volume not only shed new light on issues of Japanese language and gender but also contribute to deepening our understanding of the complex relationship of sex, sexual orientation, and gender to language ideologies and language practices in general. This volume also serves as an illustration of new approaches to the investigation of linguistic diversity and ideology in sociolinguistic research. Attention to real Japanese women and men performing linguistic selves is long overdue; this volume provides a first exploratory look at sexed/sexing, gendered/gendering, and sexually oriented/orienting persons performing their linguistic lives against the backdrop of normative ideologies in Japan. The contributions to this volume illuminate the terms of these ideologies and trace real persons as social agents as they variously relate to their dictates, by conforming to, negotiating, resisting, openly challenging, or disregarding them. The result is a rare glimpse into the heretofore largely hidden situated linguistic practices of socially diverse Japanese women and men.

References

Abe, Hideko (2001). *Speaking of power: Japanese women and their language*. Munich: Lincom Europa.

Befu, Harumi (1993). Nationalism and nihonjinron. In H. Befu (ed.), *Cultural nationalism in East Asia: Representation and identity*, 107–135. Berkeley: Institute of East Asian Studies, University of California, Berkeley.

—— (2001). *Hegemony and homogeneity: An anthropological analysis of Nihonjinron.* Melbourne: Trans Pacific Press.

Bergvall, Victoria L., Janet M. Bing, and Alice F. Freed (eds.) (1996). *Rethinking language and gender research: Theory and practice.* London: Longman.

Bucholtz, Mary (1999). Bad examples: Transgression and progress in language and gender studies. In M. Bucholtz, A. C. Liang, and L. A. Sutton (eds.), *Reinventing indentities: The gendered self in discourse,* 3–24. New York: Oxford University Press.

Bucholtz, Mary, A. C. Liang, and Laurel A. Sutton (eds.) (1999). *Reinventing identities: The gendered self in discourse.* New York: Oxford University Press.

Cook, Haruko M. (1998). Situational meanings of the Japanese social deixis: The mixed use of the *masu* and plain forms. *Journal of Linguistic Anthropology* 8 (1): 87–110.

Eades, J. S., Tom Gill, and Harumi Befu (eds.) (2000). *Globalization and social change in contemporary Japan.* Melbourne: Trans Pacific Press.

Fairclough, Norman (1989). *Language and power.* London: Longman.

Hall, Kira, and Mary Bucholtz (eds.) (1995). *Gender articulated: Language and the socially constructed self.* New York: Routledge.

Ide, Sachiko (1979). *Onna no kotoba otoko no kotoba (Women's language, men's language).* Tokyo: Nihon Keizai Tsushinsha.

—— (ed.) (1997). *Joseego no sekai (The world of women's language).* Tokyo: Meiji Shoin.

Ide, Sachiko, Motoko Hori, Akiko Kawasaki, Shoko Ikuta, and Hitomi Haga (1986). Sex difference and politeness in Japanese. *International Journal of the Sociology of Language* 58: 25–36.

Inoue, Miyako (1996). The political economy of gender and language in Japan. Unpublished Ph.D. dissertation, Washington University, St. Louis, MO.

Irvine, Judith T. (1998). Ideologies of honorific language. In B. B. Schieffelin, K. A. Woolard, and P. V. Kroskrity (eds.), *Language ideologies: Practice and theory,* 51–67. New York: Oxford University Press.

Jugaku, Akiko (1979). *Nihongo to onna (The Japanese language and women).* Tokyo: Iwanami Shoten.

Komori, Yoichi (1992). Buntai to aidentitii (Style and identity). *Gekkan Gengo* 21(10): 48–55.

—— (2000). *Nihongo no kindai (The Japanese language in modern times).* Tokyo: Iwanami Shoten.

Kroskrity, Paul V. (ed.) (2000). *Regimes of language: Ideologies, polities, and identities.* Santa Fe, NM: School of American Research Press and Oxford: James Currey.

Kulick, Don (2000). Gay and lesbian language. *Annual Review of Anthropology* 29: 243–285.

Maher, John C., and Kyoko Yashiro (eds.) (1995). Special issue: Multilingual Japan. *Journal of Multilingual and Multicultural Development* 16(1&2).

Maree, Claire (1997). Jendaa shihyoo to jendaa no imisee no henka: Eega *Shinjuku Boys* ni okeru onabe no baai (Gender indexicality and semantic shifts in gendered meanings: The case of an onabe in the documentary film *Shinjuku Boys*). *Gendai Shisoo* 25(13): 263–278.

Matsumoto, Yoshiko (1999). Japanese stylistic choices and ideologies across generations. In J. Verschueren (ed.), *Language and ideology: Selected papers from the 6th International Pragmatics Conference,* vol. 1, 352–364. Antwerp: International Pragmatics Association.

Miller, Laura (1995). Japanese linguistic diversity. Panel presented at the 9th Annual Meeting of the American Anthropological Association, Washington, DC.

Ochs, Elinor (1993). Indexing gender. In B. D. Miller (ed.), *Sex and gender hierarchies,* 146–169. Cambridge, MA: Cambridge University Press.

Ogawa, Naoko, and Janet S. Shibamoto Smith (1996). The linguistic gendering of an alternative Japanese lifestyle: Speech variation in the gay communities of urban Japan. In R. Ide,

R. Parker, and Y. Sunaoshi (eds), *SALSA: Proceedings of the Third Annual Symposium about Language and Society—Austin*, vol. 36, *Texas Linguistics Forum*, 28–40. Austin: University of Texas, Department of Linguistics.

Ogawa, Naoko, and Janet S. Shibamoto Smith (1997). The gendering of the gay male sex class in Japan: A preliminary case study based on *Rasen no Sobyoo*. In A. Livia and K. Hall (eds.), *Queerly phrased: Language, gender, and sexuality*, 402–415. New York: Oxford University Press.

Okamoto, Shigeko (1995). "Tasteless" Japanese: less "feminine" speech among young Japanese women. In K. Hall and M. Bucholtz (eds.), *Gender articulated: Language and the socially constructed self*, 297–325. New York: Routledge.

Okamoto, Shigeko, and Shie Sato (1992). Less feminine speech among young Japanese females. In K. Hall, M. Bucholtz, and B. Moonwomon (eds.), *Locating power: Proceedings of the Second Berkeley Women and Language Conference*, vol. 2, 478–488. Berkeley: Berkeley Women and Language Group.

Okamoto, Shigeko, and Janet S Shibamoto Smith (1998). Japanese speaking choices: Real diversity meets the ideology of homogeneity. Panel presented at the 6th International Pragmatics Conference, Reims, France.

Reinoruzu [Reynolds]-Akiba, Katsue (ed.) (1993). *Onna to nihongo (Women and the Japanese language)*. Tokyo: Yushindo.

Rosenberger, Nancy (1995). Antiphonal performances? Japanese women's magazines and women's voices. In L. Skov and B. Moeran (eds.), *Women, media and consumption in Japan*, 143–169. Honolulu: University of Hawaii Press.

Saft, Scott (2001). Displays of concession in university faculty meetings: Culture and interaction in Japanese. *Pragmatics* 11(3): 223–262.

Sato, Shie, and Shigeko Okamoto (1999). Reexamination of Japanese "cooperative" communication style. In J. Verschueren (ed.), *Pragmatics in 1998: Selected Papers from the 6th International Pragmatics Conference*, vol. 2, 518–527. Antwerp: International Pragmatics Association.

Shibamoto Janet S. (1985). *Japanese women's language*. New York FL: Academic Press.

———— (1987). Japanese sociolinguistics. *Annual Review of Anthropology* 16: 261–278.

[Shibamoto] Smith, Janet S. (1992). Women in charge: Politeness and directives in the speech of Japanese women. *Language in Society* 21(1): 59–82.

———— (2003). Gendered structures in Japanese. In M. Hellinger and H. Bussmann (eds.), *Gender across languages*, vol. 3, 201–225. Amsterdam: John Benjamins.

Silverstein, Michael (1979). Language structure and linguistic ideology. In P. R. Clyne, W. Hanks, and C. L. Hofbauer (eds.), *The elements: A parasession on linguistic units and levels*, 193–247. Chicago: Chicago Linguistic Society.

———— (1985). Language and the culture of gender: At the intersection of structure, usage, and ideology. In E. Mertz and R. J. Parmentier (eds.), *Semiotic mediation: Sociocultural and psychological perspectives*, 219–259. New York: Academic Press.

Sturtz, Cindi L. (2001). *Danseego da zo! Japanese men's language: Stereotypes, realities, and ideologies.* Unpublished Ph.D. dissertation, University of California, Davis.

Sugimoto, Yoshio (2003). *An introduction to Japanese society*, 2nd ed. Cambridge, MA: Cambridge University Press.

Sunaoshi, Yukako (1995). Japanese women's construction of an authoritative position in their communities of practice. Unpublished master's thesis, University of Texas at Austin.

Takasaki, Midori (1993). Josee no kotoba to kaisoo (Women's language and social class). *Nihongogaku* 12(6): 169–180.

Weiner, Michael (1997). *Japan's minorities: The illusion of homogeneity*. New York: Routledge.

Wodak, Ruth (ed.) (1997). *Gender and discourse*. London: Sage.

Woolard, Kathryn A. (1998). Introduction: Language ideology as a field of inquiry. In P. V. Kroskrity, B. B. Shcieffelin, and K. A. Woolard (eds.), *Language ideologies: Practice and theory*, 3–47. New York: Oxford University Press.

Yoshino, Kosaku (1992). *Cultural nationalism in contemporary Japan: A sociological enquiry*. London: Routledge.

PART I

HISTORICAL AND THEORETICAL FOUNDATIONS

SUMIYUKI YUKAWA

MASAMI SAITO

Cultural Ideologies in Japanese Language and Gender Studies

A Theoretical Review

For the first two decades of its history, language and gender research could not free itself from a persistent essentialism that assumed women and men, and "women's language" and "men's language," as internally undifferentiated categories. It attempted to connect specific linguistic forms or strategies directly to the speaker's sex, theorizing women's speech style as either *dominated* by men (e.g., Spender 1980) or *culturally different* from that of men (e.g., Maltz & Borker 1982, Tannen 1990). However, in the 1990s a new theoretical framework emerged, based on recent developments in social and feminist theories and discourse-based methodologies. Influential essays by Eckert and McConnell-Ginet (1992) and Gal (1991) proposed a new approach to analyzing gender in language use, one that overcomes the essentialism of the earlier studies by focusing on cultural ideologies mediating diverse language forms and gender meanings. As Susan Gal observed, "the study of language and gender is significantly enhanced by simultaneous attention to everyday practices on the one hand, and on the other to the ideological understandings about women, men, and language that frame these practices and render them interpretable in particular social contexts, historical periods, and social institutions" (Gal 1995:180). The mandate for new research is "to analyze the hegemonic power of linguistic ideologies and the ways in which speakers attempt to parody, subvert, resist, contest, or in some way accommodate these positioned and powerful ideological framings" (Gal 1995).

The new double emphasis of the field on domination and resistance is articulated in one way or another in all the chapters in this volume, the first collection of essays to reexamine Japanese and gender from the new "third-wave language and gender research" perspective (Bucholtz 1999a:viii), which focuses on mechanisms of gender hegemony on the one hand and the construction of subversive identities on the other (see Bucholtz 1999b).

This chapter reviews the development of Japanese language and gender studies (hereafter JLGS) from this perspective. Specifically, it highlights the work of Jugaku Akiko (1979), who focused on gender ideologies and subversive linguistic practices long before Western language and gender researchers realized their central importance. Also, by attending to the metalinguistic discourse generated by linguists of different schools we hope to reveal when, how, and by whom such influential categories as "Japanese," "Japanese women's language," and *onnarashisa* '[Japanese] womanliness' were formed and sustained. In other words, our review attempts to uncover the cultural ideologies of JLGS.

1.1.   National-language studies and the construction of "Japanese women's language"

Studies of Japanese and women preceded by many decades the rise of feminism in Japan in the 1970s. Scholars in *kokugogaku* 'national-language studies' have described and cataloged features of normative women's speech style (personal pronouns, sentence-final particles, honorifics, and so on) since the beginning of the twentieth century. As nationalism and militarism increasingly took hold of the country, more and more scholars alluded to the traditional speech style of Japanese women and claimed it as part of a valuable cultural heritage that had been maintained for centuries. For example, one leading linguist wrote during World War II, "It is now being noted that the way of Japanese women is beautiful and superb, standing out from the ways of women throughout the world. Related to the way of Japanese women, Japanese women's language also seems to be a rare phenomenon in the world" (Kindaichi 1942, cited in Endo 1997:163).[1] Some argued that *nyooboo kotoba*, the distinctive register used by court ladies in and after the fourteenth century, formed the foundation of the contemporary women's speech style (cf. Washi 2000, chapter 4, this volume). These studies assumed that Japanese has a distinct women's speech style, namely, "Japanese women's language," and that all Japanese women (should) speak it. This assumption and the essentialism behind it were inherited by many strands of work in JLGS. Thus, the study of women's speech by national-language scholars has strongly influenced JLGS's course of development.

Many later national-language scholars have also played an important part in reinforcing the cultural dictates of feminine speech style (cf. Endo 1997, Nakamura 2001). They commented on emerging changes in women's speech style, denouncing them as deviant from "beautiful Japanese women's language." Their comments were very often based on stereotypes that connected women's polite and "feminine" speech style to *onnarashisa* 'womanliness' and respectability, and "unfeminine" speech style to improper upbringing. Such comments in turn fed back to commonsense beliefs, sustaining a language ideology that links a particular speech style with desirable femininity (cf. chapters 6 and 7, this volume).

1.2.   The women's liberation movement in the 1970s: Resistance to gender norms in language

It is against such a background that in the 1970s the Japanese women's movement started to recognize and act against the oppressive force of language. Many of the newly formed women's groups challenged traditional gender ideologies and called their own movement *uuman ribu* (from the English phrase "women's lib") to differentiate it from the existing women's movements for peace and democracy.

There is some evidence that the people in the Japanese women's movement, especially the women's liberation movement in the 1970s, were aware that women were generally represented in a derogatory manner and that feminine speech style forced them to speak as respectful subordinates and prevented them from forcefully asserting themselves as the equals of men. Of particular significance is the fact that many *uuman ribu* activists abandoned normative women's language and spoke in an assertive, nonpolite, and utterly "unfeminine" style. They dropped honorifics from their speech and used vulgar vocabulary like *gaki* 'hungry devils' for *kodomo* 'children', *meshi* for *gohan* 'meal', and *temee* for *anata* 'you'. Their speech style was part of an attempt to reject prescribed femininity and to revolutionize their own gendered consciousness.

The women's movement in the 1970s was also characterized by its active efforts to change sexist language practices. The written texts of some activists are scattered with remarks that show their recognition of the patriarchal value system inherent in Japanese. These remarks include the points that *ningen*, literally 'human being', practically speaking only refers to men and that conjoined phrases such as *otoko to onna* 'men and women' reflect a male-centered viewpoint because the term for men comes first. They also insisted on using the basic term *onna* to refer to women, which is often avoided because of sexual connotations, rather than the more "tasteful" alternatives *fujin* and *josee*. In 1975, the women's group, Kokusai fujinnen o kikkake ni koodoo o okosu onnatachi no kai 'The International Women's Year Action Group' was founded, consisting of Diet members, lawyers, media critics, teachers, office workers, and housewives. Their activities included a protest against a hit television commercial for instant noodle soup that promoted stereotyped gender roles. It featured a girl saying, "*Watashi tsukuru hito* 'I am the one who cooks it'," joined by a boy who yelled, "*Boku taberu hito* 'I am the one who eats it'." The commercial was discontinued because of the protest, an epoch-making event in the history of the Japanese women's movement. The group also demanded that the influential media giant NHK (Japan Broadcasting Corporation) stop using women in unimportant "assistant" roles in programs, increase the number of female staff, and refrain from using sexist words and phrases, including the notorious *shujin* 'master' for husband.

Past reviews of JLGS (cf. [Reinoruzu [Reynolds]-Akiba 1993:224, Abe 1995:651–652, Nakamura 2001:9) argue that while feminism in the West concentrated its efforts on abolishing sexism in language, feminism in Japan has paid little attention to matters of language. As we have seen, however, Japanese feminists in the early 1970s were seriously concerned with oppression through language and were engaged in subversive linguistic practices. Their recognition of the important relationship between language and hegemonic gender ideologies was to be fully articulated by Jugaku Akiko's (1979) monumental treatise on language, gender ideologies, and women's resistance.

1.3.   Jugaku Akiko's focus on ideologies and subversive practices

In *Nihongo to onna 'The Japanese language and women'*, Jugaku single-handedly provided a comprehensive theoretical framework for the study of language and gender. Nationally known for her lifelong commitment to postwar democratizing movements, she had also supported the forementioned campaign against the television commercial. Though her book was written for a general readership, it provided an outline of an extensive research program with illustrations from her 20 years of research as a distinguished scholar in national-language studies. Though the significance of the book in JLGS can be compared to that of Robin Lakoff's *Language and Woman's Place* (1975) in Western language and gender studies, it oriented later researchers more directly to the important connection between language and cultural ideologies.

The book explicates the workings of language in sustaining gender ideologies prevalent in Japanese society up to that time, with analyses of stereotyped images of women in popular songs and the cultural stock of categories, phrases, and proverbs used for criticizing women who challenge normative femininity. The core of Jugaku's theoretical framework is the idea that linguistic and cultural ideologies related to Japanese women severely constrain their behavior and ways of life. Her key concept *onnarashii kotoba* 'womanly language/speech/words' (which would ordinarily mean womanly speech style or womanly expressions), enabled her to go beyond essentialism and come to grips with gender ideologies over a decade before Western feminist linguists did so. She theorized that the concept consists of three components: (1) language designed for a female audience, (2) topics chosen for a female audience, and (3) linguistic strategies used to display that the speaker is a woman. A comparison of these components with Lakoff's (1975) definition of "women's language" as (1) women's speech style and (2) words that describe women shows why Jugaku was able to tackle the issue of hegemonic cultural ideologies while Lakoff did not go beyond gender dualism.

The first component of *onnarashii kotoba* is language used with a female audience in mind. Jugaku's quantitative study of women's magazines had revealed some distinctive stylistic features, including (1) a greater percentage of exclamatory and uncompleted sentences, which reflects a belief in women's emotionality and lack of logical thinking; (2) a smaller number of proper nouns, which implies that women are less interested than men in learning about the world; and (3) an abundant use of the second-person pronoun *anata* 'you' instead of ellipsis[2] to directly address the reader, which—being a typical feature of advertisements—treats women as if they were more susceptible to insincere seduction. These features, Jugaku argues, are part and parcel of the tendency to think of men as the norm and women as needing special consideration ("This is too difficult for women to do/understand/etc.").

The second component of *onnarashii kotoba* involves topics chosen specifically for a female audience. Women's magazines are filled with articles on fashion, home-making, and the private affairs of celebrities. Jugaku argues that this limits the range of topics women read about and discuss, which in turn provides a reason for men to look down on them.

The third and final component of *onnarashii kotoba* is linguistic strategies that serve to display that the speaker is a woman. Jugaku believes that *onnarashii kotoba* is part of the general concept of *onnarashisa* 'womanliness' or idealized femininity that regulates the thinking and behavior of Japanese women in detail. A woman's ways of doing things—from her way of walking and talking to the course of life she chooses—are subject to criticism based on alleged deviance from these norms of idealized femininity. Jugaku notes that Japanese is replete with grammatical and prosodic devices through which women can display their *onnarashisa*. However, in contrast to many of her colleagues in national-language studies, she refuses to reify "Japanese women's language." Instead of reviewing the same old linguistic devices, she emphasizes their arbitrary and intentional nature: Immersed as we are in a language like Japanese that manifests an excessive ability to leave traces of *onnarashisa* in form, she claims, we may even suffer the illusion that *onnarashisa* in speech is indispensable. However, *onnarashisa* in speech is the result of very carefully manipulating various features of Japanese to create the appearance of "natural" femininity (Jugaku 1979:22).

In light of the constructed nature of "women's language," Jugaku focuses on the subversive acts of women who challenge *onnarashisa* and *onnarashii kotoba* in spite of personal risks. She describes the linguistic practices of a group of farmers' wives (cf. chapter 10, this volume). These women were often told by their husbands and their parents to shut up and stay out of important matters. Jugaku reports how they began to speak up to solve personal and community problems. They tried to "say what is difficult to say to the person to whom it is most difficult to say it to" (1979:200) and initiated changes at home and in the community.

Jugaku further notes an interesting subversive linguistic practice emerging among schoolgirls, that is, their use of *'boku'*, a presumed sex-exclusive first-person pronoun for boys and men (cf. chapter 14, this volume). She characterizes it as a strategy by which "girls make it impossible for boys to make their masculinity salient through language," and argues that it is evidence for women's advance into men's world, deserting "the speech style that places them in a kind of safety zone" (1979:82). The book ends with a chapter on arguments between married couples, which encourages Japanese women to break their silent obedience and start changing the hierarchical gender arrangement at home.

When we look back on the history of JLGS and Japanese women's studies in the two decades after the book, Jugaku's stress on women's agency in the construction of personal and societal gender relationships is remarkable. She is as much concerned with showing Japanese women what they can do to change their life and the society as she is with revealing the workings of linguistic and cultural ideologies in the structural oppression of women. This contrasts with later JLGS and Japanese women's studies, which largely remained concerned with uncovering and protesting against prevalent sexist practices. Although *Nihongo to onna* was read quite extensively throughout the 1980s, unfortunately it had only a partial influence on the later development of JLGS. Its influence can be seen in studies of gender representation (see section 1.5) but not in sociolinguistic studies of women's speech behavior (see section 1.4). The then-emerging field of Japanese women's studies chose to distance itself from the radical feminism of the *uuman ribu* movement and turned for its source of knowledge and authority to the U.S. feminist scholarship of the day (cf. Ehara 1990). In the field of language and women, this scholarship was introduced into Japan by Ide's (1979) discussion of early Western feminist linguistics and later by Akiba Reynolds's translation of Lakoff (1975/tr. 1985) and Spender (1980/tr. 1987).

1.4. Essentialism in "women's language studies"

From the vantage point of the twenty-first century, we see that studies of sex differences in speech behavior throughout the 1980s and early 1990s failed to advance JLGS in significant ways. The reasons are both theoretical and methodological, but underlying them all is an implicit essentialism that caused the researchers to conceptualize women and men as homogeneous groups of language users.

Led by Ide, sociolinguistic studies of "women's language" and "linguistic sex differences" emerged in the early 1980s and until recently formed the mainstream of JLGS. Ide (1993) claimed that she aimed for a scientific study of the linguistic features of women's language, not motivated by feminism. She had studied sociolinguistics in the United States, but her approach did not move JLGS toward studying the actual speech of women in specific social situations. Instead, she discussed in abstract terms normative usages of Japanese women's speech assumed to be used by middle-class women in the Tokyo metropolitan area, neglecting the actual speech of women, many of whom spoke nonstandard dialects or failed to conform to normative usages for various reasons. By assuming that all Japanese women speak "women's language," she reinforced the essentialist assumption of many national-language scholars. In effect, the work of Ide and her colleagues represents part of a long period in the history of JLGS in which "women's language" was objectified or taken for granted.

Ide persistently claimed that "Japanese women's language," rather than a language of the oppressed sex as feminists tended to characterize it, displays dignity and that Japanese women have more actual power in domestic matters than men, with their husbands devoting most of their time and energy to their companies (Ide 1979, 1993). This theory neglected the hierarchical gender structure and its mechanisms of control, thereby reinforcing hegemonic gender ideologies. However, it remained influential in JLGS in the 1980s and 1990s, standing in opposition to Reinoruzu-Akiba's argument that represented the feminist camp's emphasis on male dominance and their call for degendering Japanese (e.g., Reinoruzu [Reynolds]-Akiba 1993).

As a sociolinguistic research program, "women's language studies" carried out by Ide and her colleagues had some fundamental limitations shared by many research projects in Japanese sociolinguistics. Their research typically assumed sex differences in politeness level and tried to establish such differences quantitatively with questionnaires about the participants' self-reported linguistic behavior (Ide 1979, 1990). Thus, instead of examining features of actual speech, these researchers really surveyed speakers' knowledge of and attitudes toward normative usage of language, that is, their language ideologies.

Two methodological explanations can be given for the lack of development in these sociolinguistic studies of women's speech. The first is that JLGS failed to keep up with the important shift of focus in Western feminist linguistics from pursuing abstract sex differences to examining language in the context of actual social interactions through which gender and identity are constructed. Consequently, JLGS was not able to share important new insights that eventually revolutionized language and gender studies overseas, for example, the discursive construction of identities, the inseparability of gender identity from other social identities, and differences among women. The unfortunate result was that gender dualism was retained in JLGS. Second, neither discourse analysis nor ethnography was established as a research method in sociolinguistics in Japan. Tape-recording social interactions and analyzing their details from a theoretical perspective is only now becoming part of the methodology used in JLGS in Japan. As Shibamoto [Smith] (1985:5–6) observed years ago, JLGS scholars seldom listened to real people talk in their everyday life.

1.5. Toward eliminating institutionalized manifestations of gender ideologies

In the mid-1980s, studies of the gender norms reflected in language flourished. They were carried out by feminist scholars mainly in sociology and national-language studies who had been encouraged by Jugaku's book. Their inquiries into the cultural ideologies that underlay sexist gender representations developed in the 1980s and 1990s into criticisms of various forms of institutionalized language practices.

Endo Orie and her colleagues (Kotoba to onna o kangaeru kai 'Group for Thinking about Language and Women' 1985) examined dictionaries and analyzed how women and men are represented in definitions and examples. They found that the definitions of words related to women and men present an image of men as strong, reliable, taking initiative, and influencing the course of women's lives. The images of women in these definitions were passive. They were expected to be nice and pretty. Examples in the dictionaries were found to describe men as agents of actions, whereas women tended to be depicted only in terms of appearance and sexual promiscuity. Arguing that such a stereotypical treatment of women and men reproduces asymmetrical gender arrangements, the group called for dictionaries free from sexism. Some major publishers have honored their proposal and made revisions. The group has been updating their analyses as new editions come out (chapter 9, this volume). They have also been examining Japanese textbooks from the same perspective.

Tanaka Kazuko (1993) analyzed newspaper articles and found that they reinforce a patriarchal viewpoint based on a double standard for women and men. She identified several conventional sexist practices, including (1) unnecessarily marking women ("female company president," etc.); (2) making the female subject subordiante by referring to her in relation to a man as, for example, "Yoko, the wife of a construction worker, Mori Taro," instead of just saying "Mori Yoko"; and (3) extensively using stereotypical images that depict women as emotional, considerate, devoted, and passive. Tanaka's analyses of sexist discourse strategies represent an advance over earlier feminist media criticism, which focused only on obviously discriminatory words and phrases.

Building upon her work and moving further from sexist words to sexist discourses, Media no naka no seesabetsu o kangaeru kai 'The Workshop on Gender and Media' (1991) focused on the ways media discourse constructs gender ideologies. It is noteworthy that the group not only analyzed newspaper articles and problematized sexist representations of women but also made it a rule to provide alternative expressions and repeatedly met with local newspaper reporters to discuss what could be changed in the production process to alleviate the problems. More recently, they have proposed the first guidelines in Japan for gender-equal media discourse, based on a study of media guidelines in the United States (Ueno & Media no naka no seesabetsu o kangaeru kai 1996). Their feminist guidelines are reflected in the revised versions of the reporters' guidelines issued by such news media as Kyodo News Agency and *Asahi Shimbun*, one of the leading national papers (cf. Gallagher 2001:174–175). Many other studies have been carried out that examine the asymmetrical gender ideologies manifested in Japanese and how they can be changed. Notable examples include (1) studies of the reference term *shujin* 'master' for husband (Ogino 1992, Fukuda 1993, Yamaguchi 1998), (2) gendered reference terms in general (Endo 1992), (3) Sino-Japanese characters related to women (Kawata 2000), and (4) stereotypes about female and male language use (Takeda 1990, 1991). Saito (1994) and Sasaki (1994) examined how English textbooks published in Japan reflected feminist language reform in English-speaking countries.

1.6. Reconstructing JLGS: Hegemonic ideologies and resisting identities

As was mentioned in the introduction to this chapter, a new link between recent social and feminist theories and discourse analytic approaches to identities radically transformed language and gender research in the 1990s. However, JLGS inside Japan took several years to respond to these new developments in the field in Western countries. One reason is that there was a persistent tendency to reify "Japanese women's language" and dichotomize gendered language use. For example, as late as 1998 Ide remarked in a published conversation, "In Japanese, men and women use different first-person pronouns. That proves that it has 'men's language' and 'women's language' (Ide, Keiko, & Machi 1998:35). Another reason is that Spender's (1980/tr. 1987) central message, that women as a homogeneous group are oppressed by men as a group, still formed the core of Japanese feminist thinking about the relationship between language and gender.[3]

Nevertheless, Nakamura (1993) suggested a new direction for JLGS. She argued that previous research in JLGS emphasized knowledge of language rather than language use, prescriptions rather than descriptions, and a synchronic approach rather than a diachronic approach. Such tendencies were based on the premise that linguistic studies were objective. Pointing out that Western feminist linguistics had started to question objectivism and scientism, she proposed that JLGS do the same. Nakamura's proposal notwithstanding, research along these lines did not begin until the mid-1990s.

Studies that use this new theoretical framework and new methodologies are steadily increasing in JLGS both in and outside Japan. These studies are rethinking both the concept of "the Japanese language" and the traditional view of gender. Though it has been generally taken for granted, the category of "Japanese" or "the national language" has been employed to erase linguistic heterogeneity or naturalize the boundaries between groups of people (cf. Gal & Irvine 1995, cited in Nakamura 2001:216–217). Gender has been conceptualized in binary terms, asking only how women and men speak differently. The new focus of research is the relationship between identity and ideology, that is, how, and through what linguistic practices the speaker's identity is constructed under the influence of dominant ideologies.

This renewed focus of research in JLGS has been pursued via two different approaches. The first approach traces how "Japanese" and "gender" have been conceptualized, analyzing the history of the metapragmatic discourse that has naturalized and sustained dominant ideologies. The second approach focuses on agents who have been marginalized in the earlier studies and examines the strategies with which they construct new identities in the face of hegemonic gender ideologies. The two approaches analyze, in other words, how hegemonic ideologies have been maintained and how they have been negotiated or resisted.

The first approach is represented by the work of M. Inoue (1994), Endo (1997), Nakamura (1995, 2001), and Washi (2000). Based on a previous study (Komatsu 1988) that compared colloquial sentence-final forms used in two novels published in 1813 and 1909, Inoue argues that the cultural category of "Japanese women's language" emerged in the context of Japan's early modernization in the late nineteenth century, when "state formation and industrialization rapidly advanced and both language and women's role came to be articulated as 'national issues'" (Inoue 1994:322). She observes: "The construction and dissemination of women's language is closely linked to the construction and dissemination of the doctrine of 'good wife and wise mother' and to the larger political project of the consolidation of the nation-state" (1994:325).

Endo (1997) documents the role played in this process by linguists, educators, and government officials, citing many of their comments on women's language use. Integrating Inoue's and Endo's perspectives, Nakamura (2001) examines metapragmatic discourse on women's language use throughout Japanese history. She concludes: "What is most important about all these comments on women's language use over several hundred years is not what they specifically encouraged or discouraged about women's language use, but the maintenance of the concept of 'women's language' itself" (2001:210). As she has argued in *Kotoba to feminizumu 'Language and feminism'* (1995), the category of "women's language" leads us to believe that there are characteristic features common to all Japanese women's language use. Thus, the category on the one hand helps to keep women in submissive silence and on the other hand seduces them into using the stereotypical feminine speech style, which most likely protects them from criticism.

Washi (2000) specifically focused on the function performed by the discourse in national language studies that connected "women's speech" to *nyooboo-kotoba*, the register of women who served in Japan's imperial court in the fourteenth century and later. As was mentioned earlier, national-language scholars repeatedly claimed that Japanese women's speech styles had its origin in this register. *Nyooboo kotoba* consists of lexical items substituting for ordinary words for foods, clothes, kitchen utensils, and so fourth. Scholars argued that its use represented refined demeanor and displayed the privileged status of the speaker (see Shibamoto [Smith] (1985: 29–31) and Abe (1995:653–654) for descriptions of *nyooboo kotoba* in English). Washi examined the discourse of these scholars and concluded that it naturalized such concepts as "Japanese," "the national language," and "women's speech." Considering that "Japanese" or "the national language" was created as a means of culturally integrating the country into a modern state (cf. Lee 1996), Washi argues that the discourse of these national-language scholars performed the functions of justifying a state centralized around the emperor and of mobilizing women to adhere to its prescriptions of their own accord as "good" subjects of the imperial state (see also chapter 4, this volume). Washi rightly emphasizes the necessity of looking closely for regional and class-related differences among "the Japanese language" and "Japanese women," instead of conceptualizing them as internally undifferentiated categories.

Let us now turn to some of the studies that constitute the second approach, which focuses on how groups of people who had been neglected in past JLGS construct their identities while coping with hegemonic gender ideologies. Okamoto Shigeko's work on speech style overcomes many of the methodological problems of previous sociolinguistic studies in JLGS. Okamoto and Sato (1992) tape-recorded conversations between women and analyzed the sentence-final forms used by women of different age-groups. They found that young women used far fewer stereotypically feminine forms (e.g., *wa*, *nano*, *kashira*) and more forms that had been regarded as "masculine" (e.g., *zo*, *da*, *dayo*). Okamoto (1995) analyzed the pragmatic meanings of young women's speech styles in specific social contexts, revealing that their "unfeminine" speech styles, which had been neglected as "exceptions" in previous studies, are actually chosen strategically according to multiple social variables (e.g., age, marital and occupational status, degree of intimacy, formality level of the situation) in order to communicate desired pragmatic meanings and to construct identities and relationships. Her work highlights the variability of the actual language behavior of Japanese women and shows that "Japanese women's language" is not reality but ideology.

Another researcher within this approach, Ohara (1992), measured the pitch level of bilingual Japanese female and male students when they spoke Japanese and English. She found that female students but not male students spoke at a significantly higher pitch when they spoke Japanese than when they spoke English. Her finding suggests that this aspect of women's speech behavior, which had tended to be considered wholly biologically determined, is actually influenced by historical and cultural conditions. That is to say, Japanese women choose to speak at a higher pitch under the influence of a gender ideology that says it is desirable for women to speak in a high voice (see also chapter 12, this volume). Ohara suggests that the same group of women speak English at a lower pitch because they are freed from the influence of Japanese gender ideologies when they speak English.

Other studies focus on how gender ideologies influence the language use of understudied groups, especially those with nonnormative sexualities or genders. Ogawa and Shibamoto Smith (1997) examined personal pronouns and sentence-final particles used by a gay couple in a documentary film and analyzed the relationship between their speech patterns and gender identities. Similarly, Maree (1997) focused on different first-person pronouns used in a film about transvestites who lived in Shinjuku, Tokyo. Her analysis showed that those terms of self-reference (as well as their nonuse) were strategically chosen according to contextual features like the topic of the conversation and the nature of relationships and that they represented the performance of new identities different from those of heterosexual men.

Integrating "the third-wave language and gender research" perspective with critical discourse analysis (CDA), Saito (2001) reexamined media discourse on the women's liberation movement in Japan. Although previous studies had stressed that the movement was marginalized by the media, she pointed out that this view had been influenced by a research framework that was exclusively committed to exposing the mechanisms by which the media maintained hegemony. Her feminist CDA showed that the media was not a monolith and that some media discourse actually constructed subversive gender identities.

1.7. Conclusion

The past decade has seen a burgeoning general academic interest in the workings of cultural and language ideologies in the course of Japan's modernization. Work such as Lee (1996) and Komori, Kono, and Takahashi (1997) has shed light on how constructs such as "Japanese," "the national language," and "Standard Japanese" were deployed as Japan developed into a modern imperial state and how linguists took an active part in their deployment. In the future, JLGS is expected to strengthen its efforts to reveal the historical processes through which gender and language have been constructed and sustained.

At the same time, a greater number of studies need to be done to further uncover linguistic practices in which speakers negotiate and subvert dominant gender ideologies. The studies should focus on groups of people who have been marginalized in Japanese society, attending carefully to how gender interacts with ethnicity, class, generation, and sexual orientation in those practices. Blue-collar workers, speakers of regional dialects, the social outcasts or *burakumin*,[4] transgendered speakers, ethnic minorities such as the Ainu and Koreans, and other minority populations need to be studied. In view of the fact that JLGS itself has long played a part in maintaining the damaging concept of "Japanese women's language" and in colluding in the exclusion and marginalization of women and minorities, it is particularly important for the sound future development of JLGS that it now reexamine its own theoretical frameworks and methodological assumptions.

Notes

1. All translations from the Japanese originals are ours.

2. In Japanese sentences, personal pronouns are often deleted when they are obvious from the context, for example, from the use of honorifics.

3. Introductions to Western language and gender studies published in the 1990s by influential leaders of Japanese women's studies and JLGS give a false impression that it is exhausted by the work of Lakoff (1975/tr.1985) and Spender (1980/tr.1987); (Ide 1993, Reinoruzu [Reynolds]-Akiba 1993, Sakamoto 1993, Ehara 1994, Inoue 1999). It is significant that Cameron (1985/tr. 1990) and Nakamura (1995), which reflected later developments in Western feminist linguistics, were not paid due attention for many years. This reflects the fact that Japanese feminists had long been comfortable with Spender's simplistic view that all men dominate all women. The more current history of language and gender research abroad was not made available in Japanese until recently. See Yukawa (1998) and Nakamura (2001).

4. The exclusion and oppression of these people can be traced back to the thirteenth century, when some occupations were regarded as impure according to Buddhist and Shintoist thinking. Discrimination against these groups continues today.

References

Abe, Hideko (1995). From stereotype to context: The study of Japanese women's speech. *Feminist Studies* 21(3): 647–671.

Bucholtz, Mary (1999a). Series foreword. In M. Bucholtz, A. C. Liang, and L. A. Sutton (eds.), *Reinventing identities: The gendered self in discourse*, vii–viii. New York: Oxford University Press.

——— (1999b). Bad examples: Transgression and progress in language and gender studies. In M. Bucholtz, A. C. Liang, and L. A. Sutton (eds.), *Reinventing identities: The gendered self in discourse,* 3–24. New York: Oxford University Press.

Cameron, Deborah (1985). *Feminism and linguistic theory.* London: MacMillan. [= 1990, trans. Momoko Nakamura, *Feminizumu to gengo riron (Feminism and linguistic theory).* Tokyo: Keiso Shobo.]

Eckert, Penelope, and Sally McConnell-Ginet (1992). Think practically and look locally: Language and gender as community-based practice. *Annual Review of Anthropology* 21: 461–490.

Ehara, Yumiko (1990). Feminizumu no nanajuunendai to hachijuunendai (Feminism in the 1970s and 1980s). In Y. Ehara (ed.), *Feminizumu ronsoo: Nanajuunendai kara kyuujuunendai e (Feminism from the 1970s to the 1990s),* 2–46. Tokyo: Keiso Shobo. [= 1993, Japanese feminism in the 1970s and 1980s, *U.S.-Japan Women's Journal English Supplement* 4: 49–69.]

——— (1994). Josee to hyoogen (Women and representation). In Y. Meguro (ed.), *Jendaa no shakaigaku (Sociology of gender),* 38–44. Tokyo: Hoso Daigaku Kyoiku Shinkokai.

Endo, Orie (ed.) (1992). *Josee no yobikata daikenkyuu (Research on how women are addressed).* Tokyo: Sanseido.

——— (1997). *Onna no kotoba no bunkashi (A cultural history of Japanese women's language).* Tokyo: Gakuyo Shobo.

Fukuda, Mayumi (ed.) (1993). *Shujin to yuu kotoba (The expression shujin).* Tokyo: Akashi Shoten.

Gal, Susan (1991). Between speech and silence: The problematics of research on language and gender. In M. di Leonardo (ed.), *Gender at the crossroads of knowledge: Feminist anthropology in the postmodern era,* 175–203. Berkeley: University of California Press.

———— (1995). Language, gender and power: An anthropological review. In K. Hall and M. Buchettz (eds.), *Gender articulated: Language and the Socially Constructed Self*, 169–182. New York: Routledge.

Gallagher, Margaret (2001). *Gender setting: New agendas for media monitoring and advocacy*. London: Zed Books.

Ide, Sachiko (1979). *Onna no kotoba, otoko no kotoba (Women's language, men's language)*. Tokyo: Nihon Keizai Tsushinsha.

———— (1990). How and why do women speak more politely in Japanese? In S. Ide and N. H. McGloin (eds.), *Aspects of Japanese women's language*, 63–79. Tokyo: Kuroshio.

———— (1993). Sekai no joseego, Nihon no joseego: Joseego kenkyuu no shintenkai o motomete (Women's language of the world, women's language of Japan: Searching for new developments in women's language research). *Nihongogaku* 12(6): 4–12.

Ide, Sachiko, Ochiai Keiko, and Tawara Machi (1998). Zadankai: Kotoba ni miru josee (Roundtable talk: Portrayal of women in words). In T. J. Zaidan (ed.), *Kotoba ni miru josee (Portrayal of women in words)*, 13–40. Tokyo: Kureyon House.

Inoue, Miyako (1994). Gender and linguistic modernization: Historicizing Japanese women's language. In M. Bucholtz, A.C. Liang, L. A. Sutton, and C. Hines (eds.), *Cultural performances: Proceedings of the Third Berkeley Women and Language Conference*, 322–343. Berkeley: Berkeley Women and Language Group.

Inoue, Teruko (1999). Nichijoosee no naka no jendaa to sekushuaritii (Gender and sexuality in everyday practices). In Kokuritsu Fujin Kyooiku Kaikan Joseegaku Jendaa Kenkyuukai (ed.), *Joseigaku kyoiku/gakushuu handobukku (Handbook of women's studies)*, 160–165. Tokyo: Yuhikaku.

Jugaku, Akiko (1979). *Nihongo to onna (The Japanese language and women)*. Tokyo: Iwanami Shoten.

Kawata, Fumiko (2000). *Onna to yuu moji, onna to yuu kotoba (Characters and words for women)*. Tokyo: Akashi Shoten.

Kindaichi, Kyosuke (1942). Joseego to keego (Women's language and honorifics). In K. Kindaichi (ed.), *Kokugo kenkyuu (A study of the national language)*, 293–315. Tokyo: Yakumoshorin.

Komatsu, Hisao (1988). Tokyogo ni okeru danjosa no keesee: Shuujoshi o chuushin to shite (The form of gender differences in Tokyo dialect: Centering on the sentence-final particles). *Kokugo to Kokubungaku* 65(11): 94–106.

Komori, Yoichi, Kensuke Kono, and Osamu Takahashi (eds.) (1997). *Media, hyooshoo, ideorogii: Meiji sanjuunendai no bunka kenkyuu (Media, representation, and ideology: Cultural studies on the Meiji thirties)*. Tokyo: Ozawa Shoten.

Kotoba to onna o kangaeru kai (The Group for Thinking about Language and Women) (1985). *Kokugo jiten ni miru josee sabetsu (Sexism in dictionaries)*. Tokyo: Sanichi Shobo.

Lakoff, Robin (1975). *Language and woman's place*. New York: Harper and Row. [1985, trans. Reynolds Akiba Katsue, Tokyo: Yushindo.]

Lee, Yeounsuk (1996). *"Kokugo" to yuu shisoo (Ideology called "kokugo" [the national language])*. Tokyo: Iwanami Shoten.

Maltz, Daniel, and Ruth Borker (1982). A cultural approach to male-female miscommunication. In J. Gumperz (ed.), *Language and social identity*, 196–216. Cambridge: Cambridge University Press.

Maree, Claire (1997). Jendaa shihyoo to jendaa no imisee no henka: Eega *Shinjuku Boys* in okeru onabe no baai (Gender indexicality and semantic shifts in gender meanings: The case of an *onabe* in the documentary film *Shinjuku Boys*). *Gendai Shisoo* 25(13): 262–278.

Media no naka no seesabetsu o kangaeru kai (The Workshop on Gender and Media) (1991).

Media ni egakareru josee zoo (*Portrayals of women in the newspapers*). Toyama: Katsura Shobo.

Nakamura, Momoko (1993). Gengogaku no 'kagakuteki' gensoku no jissen ni taisuru feminisuto no hihan (A feminist critique of the "scientific" principle of linguistics). In K. Reinoruzu [Reynolds] Akiba (ed.), *Onna to nihongo* (*Women and the Japanese language*), 67–95. Tokyo: Yushindo.

—— (1995). *Kotoba to feminizumu* (*Language and feminism*). Tokyo: Keiso Shobo.

—— (2001). *Kotoba to jendaa* (*Language and gender*). Tokyo: Keiso Shobo.

Ogawa, Naoko, and Janet S. Shibamoto Smith (1997). The gendering of the gay male sex class in Japan: A preliminary case study based on *Rasen no Sobyoo*. In A. Livia and K. Hall (eds.), *Queerly phrased: Language, gender, and sexuality*, 402–415. New York: Oxford University Press.

Ogino, Miho (1992). "Shujin" no koogengaku: Nihongo ni okeru otto no koshoo ni tsuite (Why do Japanese women call their husbands "shujin"?). *Joseegaku Nenpoo* 13: 11–24.

Ohara, Yumiko (1992). Gender-dependent pitch levels: A comparative study in Japanese and English. In K. Hall, M. Bucholtz, and B. Moonwomon (eds.), *Locating power: Proceedings of the Second Berkeley Women and Language Conference*, 469–477. Berkeley: Berkeley Women and Language Group.

Okamoto, Shigeko (1995). "Tasteless" Japanese: Less "feminine" speech among young Japanese women. In K. Hall and M. Bucholtz (eds.), *Gender articulated: Language and the socially constructed self*, 297–325. New York: Routledge.

Okamoto, Shigeko, and Shie Sato (1992). Less feminine speech among young Japanese females. In K. Hall, M. Bucholtz, and B. Moonwomon (eds.), *Locating power: Proceedings of the Second Berkeley Women and Language Conference*, 478–488. Berkeley: Berkeley Women and Language Group.

Reinoruzu [Reynolds]-Akiba, Katsue (1993). Gengo to seesa no kenkyuu (The study of sex differences in language). *Nihongogaku* 12(5): 224–234.

Saito, Masami (1994). Sabetsugo gari de wa nai gengo kaikaku: eego kyookasho, eewa jisho ni miru (Language reform in English textbooks and dictionaries). *Hyuuman raitsu* 78: 40–49.

——(2001). Feminizumu riron ni yoru hihanteki disukoosu bunseki no tenkai: Uuman ribu undoo no media gensetsu o jiree to shite (Feminist critical discourse analysis: A study of the media discourse of the "women's lib movement" in Japan). Unpublished Ph.D. dissertation, Ochanomizu University.

Sakamoto, Kazue (1993). Kotoba kaidai (Introduction: Language). In S. Kato, K. Sakamoto, and K. Sechiyama (eds.), *Feminizumu korekushon III* (*Feminism collection III*), 322–326. Tokyo: Keiso Shobo.

Sasaki, Eri (1994). Habikoru josee sabetsu to "kokusaijin" no yukue: Chuugaku eego kyookasho no jittai to kongo no kadai (Sexism in English textbooks: How could Japanese possibly survive in the "internationalized" world?). *Joseegaku* 2: 121–139.

Shibamoto, Janet S. (1985). *Japanese women's language*. New York: Academic Press.

Spender, Dale (1980). *Man made language*. London: Routledge and Kegan Paul. [1987, trans. Reynolds Akiba Katsue, *Kotoba wa otoko ga shihai suru: Gengo to seesa* (*Man controls language: Language and sex difference*). Tokyo: Keiso Shobo.]

Takeda, Haruko (1990). Gengo seesa no sutereotaipu: "Imada Yuuko" e no shikisha no komento o yomu (Stereotyped images of women's writing: Reading the comments on the letters to "Imada Yuko"). *Joseegaku Nenpoo* 11: 28–39.

—— (1991). Gengo seesa no sutereotaipu (Gender differences in language use). *Joseegaku Nenpoo* 12: 53–62.

Tanaka, Kazuko (1993). Shimbun ni miru koozooka sareta seesabetsu hyoogen (Sexist expressions in the newspapers). In K. Reinoruzu [Reynolds], Akiba (ed.), *Onna to nihongo* (*Women and the Japanese language*), 97–122. Tokyo: Yushindo.

Tannen, Deborah (1990). *You just don't understand: Women and men in conversation.* New York: Morrow.

Ueno, Chizuko, and Media no naka no seesabetsu o kangaeru kai (The Workshop on Gender and Media) (eds.) (1996). *Kitto kaerareru seesabetsugo: Watashitachi no gaidorain* (*Nonsexist guidelines for Japanese mass media*). Tokyo: Sanseido.

Washi, Rumi (2000). *Nyooboo kotoba* no imisayoo: Tennoosee, kaisoosee, and sekushuaritii (The political function of *nyooboo kotoba*: Symbolizing the imperial system, class consciousness, and sexuality). *Joseegaku Nenpoo* 21: 18–35.

Yamaguchi, Michiyo (1998). Honyaku no naka no "shujin" ("Shujin" in translation). *Joseegaku Nenpoo* 19: 36–42.

Yukawa, Sumiyuki (1998). Kotoba to jendaa to kenryoku no kakawari ni semaru (Exploring language, gender, and power). *Joseegaku* 6: 135–160.

2

SHIGEKO OKAMOTO

Ideology in Linguistic Practice and Analysis

Gender and Politeness in Japanese Revisited

Language ideology plays an important role in affecting both linguistic practice and analysis. Defining linguistic ideologies as "any sets of beliefs about language articulated by the users as a rationalization or justification of perceived language structure and use," Silverstein (1979:193) stresses that in scientific studies of language one must distinguish ideology from actual language use. Woolard and Schieffelin (1994) and Bergvall (1999) emphasize the importance of examining the dominant, or hegemonic, ideology and its relationship to specific linguistic practices. In this chapter, I consider the role of ideologies in linguistic practice and analysis with a focus on the Japanese case, especially issues concerning gender and politeness in Japanese.

In language and gender research, it has commonly been claimed that, women generally speak more politely, indirectly, and cooperatively and use more standard linguistic forms and prescriptively correct grammar than men (e.g., Trudgill 1972, Lakoff 1975, Brown 1980, Holmes 1995). However, as noted by Eckert and McConnell-Ginet (1999) and others, such generalizations about gender differences always encounter exceptions in any community. At the same time, they cannot be easily dismissed as simple overgeneralizations or stereotypes. For they seem often to relate to dominant gender norms and expectations in society and may affect actual language practices and their interpretations in some way, although exactly how is not well understood. It is thus important to reexamine these generalizations as to what they represent, in particular, their normative and ideological aspect, and how they relate to actual language practices. A close examination of these questions requires us to recognize the plurality of social meanings, for it is here that we begin to understand the origins of diversity and change in language practice.

As a case in point, this chapter considers the generalization that women speak more politely than men. I examine this generalization in relation to the use of Japanese honorifics—an important means of expressing politeness. In the ensuing sections I first discuss how the relationship between honorifics, politeness, and gender has been treated by researchers (section 2.1) and the general public (section 2.2), both of whom participate in the construction of linguistic norms and expectations in Japanese society. I then look at some examples of actual honorific uses by both women and men (section 2.3), and finally, I reconsider the relationship between language, politeness, and gender in an attempt to account for the diversity in linguistic practice of Japanese women and men (section 2.4). Before moving to section 2.1, however, a brief description of the Japanese honorific system is in order.

Japanese honorifics are usually divided into two major categories: the so-called *taisha keego* 'addressee honorifics (AH)' and *sozai keego* 'referent honorifics (RH)'.[1] Referent honorifics are further subdivided into three types: the so-called *sonkee-go* 'respectful words' (RH/R), *kenjoo-go* 'humble words' (RH/H), and *bika-go* 'beautification words' (RH/B; see, for example, Minami 1987). Addressee honorifics are said to be used to show deference toward the addressee. Among referent honorifics, *sonkee-go* and *kenjoo-go* are used to show deference toward the person being talked about by "elevating" that person, her or his belongings or action (in the case of *sonkee-go*) or by "lowering" another person (usually, the speaker), her or his belongings or action (in the case of *kenjoo-go*).[2] *Bika-go* are used for making the utterance sound "refined" or "elegant."

For example, in example (1), the title *sensee* 'professor' and the auxiliary verb *o-V-ni nar* are both referent honorifics or, more specifically, *sonkee-go*; and the form *-mash* is an addressee honorific. In example (2), the prefix *o-* in *o-nimotsu* is a referent honorific, or *sonkee-go*, the form *o-V-sh* is a referent honorific, or *kenjoo-go* in this case, and the form *-mash* is an addressee honorific. In example (3) neither a referent nor an addressee honorific is used.

(1) *Tanaka-<u>sensee</u>   ga kore o <u>o-</u> kaki-<u>ni nar-</u> <u>i</u>mash-ita.*
    Tanaka-Prof.RH/R SM this OM   write-RH/R   AH-Pst

    'Professor Tanaka wrote this'.

(2) *Watashi ga sensee no <u>o-</u>   nimotsu o <u>o</u>-moch-<u>ish-imash</u>-ita.*
    I   SM prof. GN RH/R luggage OM carry-RH/H-AH-Pst

    'I carried the professor's/your luggage (for him/you)'.

(3) *Tanaka ga kore   o   <u>ka-ita</u>.*
    Tanaka SM this   OM   write-NRH/R-Pst.NAH

    'Tanaka wrote this'.

Note that the referent and the addressee may or may not be the same person. For example, in example (2) the speaker may be talking to a professor about the professor's own luggage or that of another professor. In the former interpretation, the referent and addressee honorifics are both used toward this person, but not in the latter.

(4) *Q-yasai*   *mo* *tabe-te*.
    RH/B-vegetables   also eat-NRH/R-GD

    '(Please) eat the vegetables, too'.

The prefix *o-* in *o-yasai* in example (4) is a referent honorific, but it is a *bika-go* and not a *sonkee-go*. The use of *bika-go* has been linked to stereotypical femininity.

2.1. Previous studies on gender and politeness in Japanese

One of the most commonly noted gender differences in Japanese is that women generally speak more politely than men (e.g., Ogino, Misono, & Fukushima 1985, Niyekawa 1991, [Shibamoto] Smith 1992, Kawanari 1993, Shigemitsu 1993). Suzuki (1993:148), for example, states that the essence of "women's language" is women's concern about politeness. Likewise, Ide notes that "among various features which make women's speech feminine, politeness in speech stands out in Japanese" (1990: 63). Based on these observations, it has also been claimed that women's language, or polite speech, indexes femininity or the female gender (Ide 1993, Suzuki 1993). There are a number of linguistic devices for making utterances polite (e.g., honorifics, indirect speech acts, hedges, reactive tokens, and sentence-final particles), but the complex system of honorifics is considered particularly important. It is commonly claimed that Japanese women tend to use more honorifics and formal expressions than Japanese men, thereby making their speech more polite than men's (e.g., Ogino, Misono, & Fukushima 1985, Ide 1990, Niyekawa 1991, Kawanari 1993). Shibatani (1990:374), for instance, notes that "more than anything, the politeness in women's speech derives from the higher frequency of the use of the honorific forms." Similarly, Sugimoto (1997:235) asserts that women's language has its own unique structure and that this uniqueness derives from the use of honorifics.

There are a number of different explanations for the claim that women speak more politely than men by using honorifics and other linguistic devices: (1) biologically determined traits, such as gentleness (Sugimoto 1997); (2) their relatively lower social status (Ide 1982; Reynolds 1985, 1990); and (3) their social roles, or their association with domains that require "sociable/civil" interactions (Ide 1990). It is further argued that women, lacking their own status in society, tend to be more concerned about appearance and thus use honorifics, or polite language, to indicate that they are refined, or members of a higher social class (e.g., Ide 1982, 1990; Reynolds 1985).

While many of these previous studies suffer from methodological weaknesses by relying on self-report surveys and researchers' introspections (see also Shibamoto 1987, chapter 1, this volume), their findings—in particular, the results of self-report surveys—are nonetheless interesting in that they seem to reveal certain normative expectations for women's and men's speech, although to what extent these expectations affect actual language practice is unclear. Ide (1990), for example, reports that when participants were asked to assess the politeness levels of different linguistic forms expressing the same meaning "When do you go?" women gave lower levels of politeness than men for almost all forms. Ide (1990:67) notes that "thus, to express the same level of politeness, a woman has to use a politer linguistic form than a man would." Kawanari (1993) reports that when participants were asked what request forms they would use in hypothetical situations, women generally gave more indirect and polite expressions, which contained more honorific expressions (see also Ogino, Misono, & Fukushima 1985). These studies suggest that at the level of language norms, it is undeniable that women are expected to speak more politely than men, using more honorifics and other formal or indirect expressions. Two major questions at hand are how and why this prescriptive norm is promulgated in Japanese society and how it relates to actual language practices. I discuss the first question in section 2.2, and the second in sections 2.3 and 2.4.

2.2. Gender and honorifics: Norms and expectations

As noted by a number of studies (e.g., Miller 1996, Wetzel 1994, Okamoto 1999), in Japanese society the importance of using "correct" honorifics to express politeness is emphasized through various means, in particular, through education and media. For example, Kokugo-shingikai, a Japanese government council on the national language, recommends in its 1996 report that schools continue to improve teaching children appropriate honorifics according to their developmental levels. There are also numerous books, magazine articles, and other materials on how to use honorifics "correctly," which suggests that knowledge of honorifics is not evenly distributed in the society and that many native speakers aspire to acquire it, because they consider it linguistic capital for improving their social status (Miller 1996). Wetzel (1994) reports that in a subjective reaction test users of honorifics were judged to be more intelligent, more educated, and more capable than nonusers. These observations suggest that many Japanese associate the use of honorifics with higher class status, education, intelligence, and other prestige factors.

Politeness and honorifics are thus considered important for both women and men. However, as noted earlier, there is a difference in expectations. That is, there is a belief among many Japanese that women should speak more politely than men, using honorifics and other formal expressions. Media, as well as education at home and school, seem to play an important role in promoting this idea, as illustrated in the following excerpt from a self-help book for women, titled *Kashikoi hito ni narinasai: Utsukushiku ikitai anata ni 'Be a wise woman: To you who want to live beautifully'*:[3]

> It is often said that young women nowadays—whether they are students or working women—cannot use honorifics well. . . . I sometimes hear female teachers use the same language as male teachers. . . . Even in a democratic society, it's natural that there are differences in ways of talking based on sex differences, because men and women have different vocal cords. . . . But women dare to use men's language. Are they ignorant or lazy, or are they making foolish efforts not to be dominated by men? . . . Not knowing honorifics is embarrassing. Parents and teachers should teach that [to children] by showing good models. . . . Even today, . . . when I see such people [people who use proper and polite language], I'm impressed by their good upbringings. (Tanaka 1986:29–33, translated from the Japanese original)

The book, by a well-known woman writer, has been widely read and was reprinted 73 times between 1986 and 1995. The author assumes in this passage that gender differences in speech are both biologically and socially based and that it is natural that women speak women's language and men speak men's language. She then emphasizes that women should use honorifics properly, assuming that honorifics are an important part of women's language; those women who do not use honorifics properly should be socially sanctioned, receiving negative evaluations, such as ignorant, lazy, and improperly brought up.

There are numerous books that specifically teach women how they should speak in order to become attractive and beautiful, as illustrated by the following book titles.

> *Suteki na anata o tsukuru: Josee no utsukushii hanashi-kata* 'To make yourself nice: Women's beautiful ways of speaking' (Suzuki 1989)
> *Onna no miryoku wa hanashi-kata shidai* 'Women's attractiveness depends on how they speak' (Kanai 1994)

These how-to books usually contain a section on how to use honorifics "correctly"— the ability is presented as essential for a sophisticated woman, or *kotoba-bijin* 'language beauty', as illustrated by the following section heading in one of these books: "Keego o kichin to hanasu koto ga bijin no jooken desu" 'Using honorifics properly is an indispensable condition for a "beautiful woman"' (Kanai 1994). In his book on women's beautiful speech, Suzuki (1989), a television announcer and best-seller writer, recommends that married women speak politely to their husbands, using honorifics (see also chapter 6, this volume):

> When a man is asked [by his wife, using honorifics] *Nanji-goro o-kaeri ni naru no* 'What time will you come back?', he feels her gentleness, good upbringing, and reserved elegance. . . . [At parties, etc.] men are very worried about the impressions their wives' ways of speaking give about their educational levels. (Suzuki 1989:130–32, translated from the Japanese original)

These how-to books thus promote the notion that women's attractiveness depends on their appearance (beauty), which is in part determined by their good upbringing and education, including the knowledge of honorifics.

There are also many books on how to write letters, which usually refer to gender differences in styles. One good example is a pair of books on letter writing—one for women and the other for men (Ohashi 1994a, b). Written by the same male author, these two books provide many sample letters in female and male versions. Compared to the male versions, the female versions are normally longer and written with more curvy (rather than straight-lined) handwriting, using more honorifics, as shown in examples (5a) and (5b), taken from Ohashi (1994a, b).

(5a) (a sample letter; from a man to his nephew, congratulating him on his engagement)
    Masaki-kun, konyaku-shita soo da   ne. Omedetoo. Sore to naku
      RH/R   NRH/R   NAH   NAH
    kanjite wa ita   kedo, konna ni hayaku to wa bikkuri-suru yara
      NAH

odoroku yara, nan to itte o-iwai no kotoba o okur-oo ka. . . .
        RH/B   NRH/H-NAH

'Masaki, I heard that you got engaged. Congratulations! I had a feeling [that you might], but I'm very surprised that it came so fast. What kinds of congratulatory words shall I give you'?

(5b)   (a sample letter; from a woman to her nephew, congratulating his marriage engagement)
Haruki-san, go-konyaku omedetoo-gozaimasu. Saikin no anata no
    RH/R RH/R   AH
yoosu kara sore to naku kanjite wa i- mashita ga, konna ni hayaku
                         AH
konyaku to wa bikkuri-suru yara odoroku yara, nan to itte o-iwai no
                                     RH/B
kotoba o okur- imashoo ka. . . .
    NRH/H-AH

'Haruki, congratulations on your engagement! I had a feeling [that you might] from the way you have been behaving recently, but I'm very surprised that you got engaged so fast. What kind of congratulatory words shall I give you'?

Examples (5a) and (5b) have similar content and are both addressed to younger persons. But they differ in that (5b) is more formal and contains more honorifics than (5a). In addition, the suffix *-kun* is used in (5a), but a more formal suffix, *-san*, is used in (5b).

Further, popular culture materials, such as films, television dramas, novels, and cartoons, often show female characters, especially middle-aged women in the middle and upper-middle classes, using more honorifics than male characters. For example, in one of the most popular television drama series, *Wataru seken wa oni bakari* 'Making it through', two main characters, both middle-aged women in middle-class families, use honorifics toward their husbands, but not vice versa. Similarly, in the comic strip *Nono-chan*, which appears daily in a major newspaper (*Asahi Shimbun*) in Japan, honorifics are often used nonreciprocally from one of the main female characters to her husband.

As these examples demonstrate, the belief that women should use more honorifics, or polite language, than men is widely promoted as a behavioral norm in Japanese society. Further, they suggest that the use of honorifics is linked not only to gender but also to class status in that it is treated as a sign of good upbringing and education by many how-to books and is particularly associated with the speech of middle- and upper-middle-class female roles in popular culture materials.

It seems that the link between polite speech, women, and a higher class status has long been promoted and sustained as a behavioral norm for women in Japanese society. Endo (1997) points out that it was during the feudal Edo period (1603–1868), a period in which the ruling classes were greatly influenced by Confucian philosophy, that the importance of disciplining women began to be emphasized, as illustrated by the emergence of many books that taught women's virtues and stipulated detailed rules of conduct for women, including prescriptions for speech. Endo (1997) notes that these prescriptions instructed women to speak gently, politely, and in a refined manner and offered many specific example expressions related to *nyooboo kotoba*—a language used among court ladies-in-waiting since the fifteenth century (see also Sugimoto 1997). That is, the speech of women in higher social echelons was thought to be polite, gentle, and refined and hence to be emulated by all women. At the same time, this emphasis on the use of proper language suggests that many women, in particular women in the lower classes, did not use such language, as indicated by the speech styles of women in commoners' classes represented in novels written at the time (Endo 1997, Sugimoto 1997).

Upon the termination of the feudal period in 1868, the notion of "proper" women's language came to be resituated in the context of modern Japan, in which the education of women was considered an important part of the development of Japan as a modern nation-state. Prescriptions of ideal Japanese women, or *ryoosai kembo* 'good wife and wise mother', were disseminated through various channels (e.g., textbooks, magazines). These prescriptions often included instructions about speech, which recommended that women speak gently, politely, and in a reserved and refined manner (Endo 1997). At this time, the importance of establishing Standard Japanese as the national language was emphasized and Tokyo-go 'Tokyo language', or the speech of the educated, or middle-class, Tokyoites, was promoted through education to become Standard Japanese (Lee 1996). Media also contributed to its promotion. In this regard, it has been noted that distinct gendered speech styles as part of the (presumed) speech of the educated class in Tokyo were disseminated particularly through their representations in novels (Komori 2000, chapter 3, this volume), although it is unclear to what extent such speech styles were perceived by ordinary Japanese women and men, particularly those living in regional Japan, as models for their own speech.

Washi (2000, chapter 4, this volume) observes that the use of "proper" women's language was encouraged through media (e.g., radio, books, newspapers), especially before and during World War II in the context of rising nationalism, and that *nyooboo kotoba* was often given as a model language. For example, in 1935 linguist Yoshida Sumio gave a radio lecture on women's language in which he said that because gender differences in speech are biologically based, women's language has always been *yuubi* 'gentle and elegant', containing honorifics, indirect expressions, and the like, as illustrated by *nyooboo kotoba*. Similarly, in a 1936 radio lecture on women's language, Hoshina Koichi, an expert on national language policies, said that while there is little gender difference in the speech of the lower and working classes, women in higher classes, or women with proper demeanor, generally use honorifics, or polite and decent language, like *nyooboo kotoba* (Washi 2000). These examples also illustrate the active involvement of scholars in the construction of societal norms for women's speech.

The foregoing discussion is by no means intended to suggest that *nyooboo kotoba* (or any other specific speech variety) is the origin of "normative" women's speech. Rather, it shows that *nyooboo kotoba* as an index of femininity and class status played an important symbolic role in the ideological construction of women's speech. Specific speech forms regarded as models for women's speech in contemporary Japanese are, of course, quite different from *nyooboo kotoba*. In fact, it is questionable if there is a set of agreed-upon model speech forms in contemporary Japanese. (See section 2.4 for further discussion.) The hegemonic ideology that attempts to regulate women's speech may also have had different practical implications and importance in different historical contexts. However, the belief that women should speak politely, gently, and in a refined manner as women in higher social strata did seems to have continuously played a key role in the history of the norm construction for women's speech.

2.3. Variability in the use of Japanese honorifics in conversations

The notion that women should speak more politely than men is thus widely promulgated in Japanese society. However, it may not have a universal effect on women (or men). Examinations of actual language use show wide intragender differences as well as intergender similarities. In this essay I illustrate these cases, drawing examples mainly from a number of recent studies.

With regard to variation in women's speech, both Dunn (1996) and Okamoto (1996) report that in our research older women used more honorifics than younger women. For example, in my earlier study, which examined dyadic conversations of 10 college students and 10 middle-aged women, the older women generally used referent honorifics much more than the younger subjects (65% vs. 12% of the relevant tokens; see Okamoto 1996 for examples). The same kind of variation was observed in the use of the referent, beautification honorific prefix *o-*. That is, older women used this prefix more than younger women—e.g., *o-shooyu* 'soy sauce', said by an older woman, versus *kane* 'money', said by a younger woman. These age-group differences may also involve differences in roles.

As mentioned earlier, how-to-books on letter writing recommend the use of honorifics, particularly by women. It has also been noted that in letters one is likely to use honorifics even toward persons one knows well (e.g., Minami 1987). My analysis of personal letters, which were collected by Yasuda Wakako in 1999, shows that unlike older people (40–60), younger people (18–24), both women and men, generally do not use honorifics when they write to people they know well. This contrast is illustrated by example (6), a letter from a female college student to her friend, which uses no honorific, and example (7), a letter from a 59-year-old woman to her younger sister, which uses both addressee and referent honorifics.

(6) *Watashi wa itsumo nagara genki da yo. Shimpai kakechat-ta kedo,*
                                NAH   NRH/H-NAH

    te wa naot- ta   yo.
        NAH

    'I'm fine as always. I made you worry, but my hand is cured now'.

(7) *Wakaba no utsukushii kisetsu desu. Sono go x-san o-kagen ikaga*
                          AH   RH/R

    deshoo ka. Totsuzen no koto de odoroki mashita.
    AH   AH

    'It's a season of beautiful new green leaves. How is X since then? It was sudden and I was caught by surprise'.

There are also wide individual differences in speech within the same age-group. For example, in my 1996 study two women in the older age-group used referent honorifics and the prefix *o-* much more frequently than the others and one woman hardly used them at all (see also chapter 13, this volume, for variable honorific use among middle-aged women). This variation may be related to differences in speakers' social backgrounds and their attitudes toward honorific use. Moreover, the nonuse of honorifics by subjects when they spoke to their friends does not indicate lack of knowledge. Rather, it seems strategic, for when I interviewed subjects in person, they spoke in formal style, using both referent and addressee honorifics.

Another example of variation in women's use of honorifics comes from my observation of salespersons in two kinds of retail places in the Kansai area, two major department stores and two large marketplaces, each housing more than 150 small shops. According to the canonical rule, a salesperson is expected to use honorifics toward customers. In fact, in the department stores both female and male salespersons used high levels of honorifics most of the time. However, vendors in the two marketplaces, including women, often did not use honorifics toward the customers at all. Example (8) illustrates the use of honorifics by a female salesperson at a department store and example (9) the nonuse of honorifics by a female vendor (see also Okamoto 1997).

(8) *Irassha- imase. Doozo goran   kudasa- imase.*
     RH/R   AH   RH/R   RH/R   AH

     'Welcome. Please take a look at them'.

(9) *Koobe-niku yasui yo yasui yo, negittara maketok-u yo.*
     NAH   NAH   NRH/R NRH/H-NAH

     'Kobe beef, it's cheap; it's cheap. If you haggle, we will make it cheaper'.

Similarly, Abe (chapter 11, this volume) observes that employees at lesbian bars often speak to their customers without honorifics.

Turning now to men's speech, despite the generalization that men use fewer honorifics than women, there seem to be many situations in which men use honorifics extensively. It is commonly said that lower status persons use honorifics to higher status persons. This seems to apply to men as well as women. For example, as mentioned earlier, I observed that male salesclerks at department stores used high levels of honorifics for customers in the same way as female salesclerks, as illustrated in example (10):

(10) (Waiter, at a coffee shop in the department store in Kyoto)
     O-sara no hoo o-sage-shite—yoroshii desu ka.
     RH/B   RH/H   RH/B   AH

     'Would it be all right if I took away your plate?"

The frequent use of honorifics by male salespersons may be related to their roles. Takahashi (1996) noted that male instructors on television cooking shows generally used very formal and polite speech styles, while female instructors showed more variation. The speech of male instructors included many instances of the beautification honorific prefix *o-*, as in *o-yasai* 'vegetable', *o-ajimi* 'tasting', and *o-suimono* 'soup', as well as referent and addressee honorifics, as illustrated in example (11), taken from Takahashi (1996).

(11)   *Suton to otoshi te shimaw-areru no ne. Koron to ireru to osshatta desho.*
                    RH/R N-AH   RH/R   AH

    'You chop it up and you said you dump them in'.

Further, it is often said that in hierarchical situations honorifics are often used nonreciprocally, from the powerless to the powerful (e.g., Niyekawa 1991). However, reciprocal uses are quite common. For example, I observed that some customers, both women and men, reciprocated honorifics, especially addressee honorifics, to salespersons, while others did not. In example (11), the speaker, a male cooking instructor in his midfifties, used honorifics toward his young female assistant. In example (12), the speaker, a male supervisor (in his early sixties), reciprocated honorifics to the addressee, a newly hired female subordinate (in her late forties; see also Okamoto 1999).

(12)   *Maa, ano kongo iroiro kyooryoku-shite itadaku to omo-imasu node . . .*
                                         RH/H   AH

    'Well, I think I will be asking for your cooperation in various [matters] in the future, so . . .'

2.4.   Rethinking the relationship between honorifics, politeness, and gender

As demonstrated earlier, the use of honorifics by Japanese women and men is diverse and does not necessarily conform to the normative expectation. How can we account for this diversity? Does the norm play any role? How does each speaker understand the norm in specific contexts? I address these questions in this section by considering the use of honorifics seen earlier vis-à-vis three ideologically nonneutral assumptions that often accompany generalizations and prescriptions about gender and linguistic politeness.

2.4.1.   Social and contextual diversity and the use of honorifics

As seen in sections 2.1 and 2.2, in both scientific descriptions and nonacademic prescriptions about politeness and gender, women and men are commonly treated as constituting homogeneous categories. That is, the reasons that Japanese women "should" speak more politely than men, using honorifics and other linguistic devices, are explained on the basis of shared attributes, such as biologically determined traits (e.g., gentleness), women's relatively lower social status, their social roles, or their desire to look better (e.g., refined, a member of a higher class). These arguments are comparable with the accounts given by a number of researchers (e.g., Trudgill 1972, Lakoff 1975, Brown 1980) for the women's greater use of standard, or prestigious, polite linguistic forms in English and other languages (see James 1996 for a critical review on this topic). They may contribute to highlighting gender inequalities in language and society, but their focus on gender differences may also serve to support and perpetuate the stereotypical gender dichotomy, because they are all based on the following assumption (see also Cameron 1988, Bucholtz 1999, Nakamura 1995, among others, for relevant discussions).

Assumption 1: Most women, if not all, share the same attributes (e.g., biologically determined traits, social inferiority, social roles, concerns about appearance) and therefore (should) use language in the same way.

However, the examples seen in the previous section as well as the findings of the chapters in part III of this volume and many other recent studies on gender and language (Hall & Bucholtz 1995, Bergvall, Bing, & Freed 1996, and Bucholtz, Liang, & Sutton 1999, among others) suggest otherwise.

Counterproposal 1: Not all women (or men) share the same attributes: they are socially diverse with regard to age, role, status, and other factors; their conversational contexts also vary widely with regard to interlocutor, setting, and so on. As a consequence, not all women (or men) may speak in the same way.

Thus, for example, it is difficult to apply an abstract claim of gender difference in linguistic politeness to the fact that the interactional styles of female vendors are much less formal than those of male salesclerks at department stores or to the variability in speaking or writing styles among women of different ages. These examples indicate that the use of honorifics needs to be examined in relation to social and contextual diversity that involves individual speakers, because in addition to gender, a variety of other factors also seem relevant. For example, as indicated in the foregoing discussion, female students' less frequent use of honorifics may be (indirectly) related to their age, role, type of interlocutor, setting, and other aspects of the social context.

However, while it is important to consider multiple factors for the use of honorifics, this does not mean that if one can identify all the relevant factors, one can predict the use of honorifics (see also Cameron 1990 and Eelen 1999 for critical discussions of correlational studies). This is because it is speakers as social agents, and not contextual features, that ultimately determine the use of honorifics and also because different individuals may have different attitudes toward honorific use and associated ideologies and hence may interpret and use honorifics differently. I consider this issue in the following two subsections.

2.4.2.   Honorifics and politeness:
Ambiguities of linguistic expressions

As mentioned earlier, honorifics are considered to be one of the most important linguistic features that make women's speech polite. This characterization is often based on the following assumption.

Assumption 2: Certain linguistic expressions, such as honorifics and other formal or indirect expressions, are inherently polite.

Assumption 2, also shared by many previous studies of politeness in general (e.g., Leech 1983, Brown & Levinson 1987), regards certain expressions (e.g., honorific expressions) as polite and others (e.g., nonhonorific expressions) as not (or less) polite, independently of any context.

It may correspond to the commonsense ideology of politeness and influence the interpretation of honorifics in a significant way. Yet I argue that the interpretation of honorifics is not unitary. I present this argument as Counterproposal 2.

Counterproposal 2: Certain linguistic expressions, such as honorifics and other formal or indirect expressions, are not inherently polite; their interpretations may vary among individuals as well as across contexts, depending on the (ideologically based) criterion used for evaluating them in specific contexts.

The reasons for this variability are (1) that politeness is a matter of evaluations of social conduct vis-à-vis what is understood by the evaluator as the norm (see also Eelen 1999), (2) that the same person may assume different norms for different situations, and (3) that the understanding of norms may vary among individuals. As discussed by Eelen (1999), politeness should be viewed as involving moral judgments rather than as an objective system of rules, strategies, or principles that is assumed to govern speakers' behavior. It is thus important to examine how and why such judgments are made. Addressing this question requires an examination of the language ideologies that underlie one's apprehension of what the linguistic norms are.

One interprets (non-)honorific expressions as polite or impolite against some criterion or what one understands as the norm. However, the same person may use different criteria for evaluating specific linguistic choices in different situations. For example, regarding the use of honorifics, what is considered appropriate may not be the same for vendors at marketplaces and salesclerks in department stores. Thus, the nonuse of honorifics by vendors toward their customers may be perceived not as rude but as a sign of friendliness and hence suitable for the speaker's role as vendor. Similarly, Abe (chapter 11, this volume) observes that when employees at lesbian bars speak to their customers without honorifics it is often an attempt to establish solidarity. Thus, the lack of "expected" honorifics may not necessarily be considered rude. Analogously, if one believes that women should speak more politely than men, one may interpret the (im)politeness level of the same linguistic form differently depending on the gender of the speaker. Accordingly, even if women's speech includes a higher level of honorifics than men's, this may not make the former more polite than the latter (see also Ogino, Misono, & Fukushima 1985 and Reynolds 1990).

Further, the understanding of norms themselves may vary among individuals due to differences in their attitudes toward honorifics and politeness. For example, as mentioned earlier, although it is often assumed that honorifics are used nonreciprocally between unequals, reciprocal uses are quite common. In fact, nonreciprocal uses based on a hierarchical relationship seem to be decreasing in modern Japanese, while reciprocal uses based on the degree of solidarity are increasing (e.g., Inoue 1989, Bunkacho 1996). These synchronic and diachronic variations suggest the existence of different ideologies about honorific uses, which in turn may bring about different interpretations (e.g., polite, aloof, rude) of the same honorific or nonhonorific form.

We sometimes encounter native speakers who express differing views about honorifics. For example, a 68-year-old man, in a letter to the *Asahi Shimbun* newspaper (March 3, 1996), criticizes schoolteachers who address students by name without the honorific suffix *–san*. He believes that these teachers are not polite and that they should reciprocate honorifics to students to reduce the hierachical distance. In response, a 20-year-old female student expressed disagreement in the same newspaper (March 10, 1996), saying that she felt closer to the teachers who did not use *–san* than to those who used it. Thus, she does not consider the teachers' nonuse of honorifics impolite. The two writers express virtually opposite views.

Earlier, we saw examples (11) and (12) in which male higher status persons reciprocated honorifics to lower status persons. Some people, like the 68-year old man mentioned earlier, may interpret these reciprocal uses as the speakers' attempts to show respect for lower status persons and to reduce the vertical distance. However, others, like the student who responded to the 68-year-old man's opinion, may interpret them as a sign of (horizontal) distance or unfriendliness. Similarly, some customers may perceive vendors' nonuse of honorifics toward them as rude, but others may not, because they have different expectations about honorific uses.

Thus, honorific and nonhonorific expressions cannot be assessed as polite or rude independently of the context and the speaker's ideas about politeness. Accordingly, one cannot characterize women's speech as more polite than men's in the abstract simply because the former is presumed to contain more honorifics than the latter.

2.4.3.   Politeness and *onnarashisa* 'womanliness' revisited

The normative expectation that women should speak more politely than men also implies that polite speech indexes femininity or the female gender. For example, how-to books instruct women to speak politely, because it can make them appear attractive as women or make them *onnarashii* 'womanly'. Reynolds asserts that "the notion that women should behave *onnarashiku* 'as expected of women' is still predominant. Thus, Japanese women talk submissively and politely, just as always" (1990:129). Suzuki (1993) notes that in order for a woman to maintain her identity as a woman, she must choose expressions within the socially expected women's language, which Suzuki characterizes in terms of concerns about politeness. These studies recognize the notion of *onnarashii* language as a behavioral constraint, but they also seem to essentialize its effect on women's speech without problematizing the link between particular speech styles (e.g., polite speech) and femininity. This in turn may contribute to perpetuating dominant gender norms.

As pointed out by Jugaku (1979), although Japanese women's behavior seems to be constrained considerably by the notion of *onnarashisa* 'womanliness', it does not seem to have a universal effect on all women at all times (see also chapter 1, this volume). In a self-report survey, one of the questions Takasaki (1993:170) asked of her informants was: "Do you sometimes control your speech, thinking that since you are a woman, you should speak *onnarashiku*, using honorifics, being reserved, and speaking in a refined way?" In response, the majority answered that they try to speak *onnarashiku* depending on the situation. This answer indicates that they do not try to speak *onnarashiku* all the time, and quite a few informants said they try not to do so. The answers also varied widely, depending on the respondent's occupation and educational level (see Takasaki 1993 for details). The notion of *onnarashii* language thus cannot be ignored in accounting for women's speech (cf. Nakamura 1995), but its ideological underpinnings and its relation to real language practices need to be examined more closely.

Let us first consider why polite speech is regarded as feminine. As implied by Reynolds's statement and Takasaki's question cited earlier, the answer to this question concerns what is expected of (ideal) women, namely, such traits as submissiveness, deference, and refinement, which are assumed to be expressed through polite speech. In other words, underlying the common claims about polite speech and femininity seems to lie the following assumption.

> *Assumption 3*: Speaking politely, or showing deference and refinement through the use of honorifics and other formal or indirect expressions, indexes femininity or the female gender.

Ochs (1993) claims that the relationship between linguistic features and certain contextual information, such as gender and status difference, is mediated and constituted through the pragmatic meanings of linguistic features, such as affective stances, social acts, and social activities. Assumption 3 illustrates this interpretive duality: honorifics and other formal or indirect expressions are assumed to index politeness, or deference and refinement, which is in turn interpreted as indexing femininity or the female gender. However, this construal cannot be taken for granted. Rather, it prescribes the ideal form of femininity in terms of politeness, involving not only gender arrangements that assume heterosexuality but also class stratification. Assumption 3 thus derives from the Japanese hegemonic ideology of language, gender, and class. As a mediating link between forms of talk and social structure (Woolard & Schieffelin 1994), this ideology provides a basis for construing honorific expressions as *onnarashii*.

It is to be underscored, however, that the hegemonic ideology of politeness and *onnarashisa* is not likely to be shared by everyone at all times. As discussed by Briggs, "contestation is a crucial fact of how particular ideologies and practices come to be dominant" (1998:249). Different, often competing, beliefs about politeness and femininity may impart different social meanings to the same linguistic forms. Assumption 3 does not consider, for example, the possibility that femininity may be conceptualized and expressed differently by women of different ages and social strata. Further, it may not be applied to all situations. Accordingly, the use of honorifics, or polite speech, may not always be perceived as *onnarashii* (see also chapter 8, this volume, for a discussion of how the same linguistic performance may or may not be perceived as genuinely feminine). Sunaoshi (personal communication) was told by her Korean students on multiple occasions that, in Korean, formal speech, including the use of honorifics, sounds stiff and is used more by men, while informal speech indexes femininity. Although it is unclear whether this interpretation is typical among Koreans, its contrast with the interpretation of polite speech in Japanese as *onnarashii* illustrates the subjective and arbitrary nature of the link between a particular speech style and femininity (see also Keenan 1974). In other words, the interpretation of femininity crucially depends on how its relation to linguistic forms is ideologically conceived. I therefore counter Assumption 3 as follows.

> *Counterproposal 3*: Speaking politely, or showing deference and refinement through the use of honorifics and other formal or indirect expressions, may not necessarily index femininity or female gender; its interpretation depends on the (ideologically based) criterion one uses for the evaluation of women's speech in specific contexts.

This proposal is illustrated by the age difference in the use of referent honorifics seen earlier. Older women's greater use of honorifics could be an indication that they are more affected by the normative expectation. That is, for them honorifics may serve as an expression of *onnarashisa*. At the same time, however, young women's less frequent use of honorifics may not be interpreted as unfeminine. When talking with a friend about a higher status person in the latter's absence, one may not use honorifics for the absent person because the formality expressed toward the referent may be taken as a sign of distance toward the addressee. Young women's nonuse of honorifics may be a reflection of this concern and not an attempt to speak in an unfeminine manner. In a similar vein, female vendors' nonuse of honorifics may not be perceived as unfeminine, if it is interpreted as a sign of friendliness. However, some may perceive the nonuse of honorifics both by young women and by vendors as unfeminine.

Similarly, the frequent use of honorifics by male salesclerks at department stores and male cooking instructors on television is not likely to be construed as efforts to speak like women; rather, it seems to be intended to make their speech fit their roles and the setting. Likewise, the use of honorifics by the male supervisor toward a female subordinate in example (12) may be an attempt to present himself as an egalitarian person. Although previous studies on politeness have emphasized women's concerns about their image, these examples suggest that men as well as women are concerned about how they want to appear to others and use language strategically (see also chapter 15, this volume, for a discussion of men's linguistic prowess).

In sum, to what extent polite speech, or the use of honorifics, is interpreted as *onnarashii* depends on the criteria one uses in specific contexts. Important to consider in this relation are the contexts in which regional dialects are spoken. For example, female speakers of regional dialects are sometimes evaluated as rough and unrefined (Miyake 1995), that is, as not *onnarashii*. The reference point in this evaluation seems to be stereotypical women's speech in Standard Japanese. However, speakers of regional dialects may not share such an evaluation. For example, speakers of dialects that have few honorifics (Inoue 1989) may resort to the use of Standard Japanese honorifics, particularly in relatively formal situations. However, one may choose not to do so, if one wished to establish solidarity with the interlocutor who speaks the same dialect (see chapter 10, this volume). In such a case, the nonuse of honorifics by women does not seem to be considered an unfeminine behavior, at least by the speakers themselves. This is not to suggest that female speakers of regional dialects are not affected at all by the normative expectation that women should speak more politely than men. Many of them may be affected by it but may express politeness differently from the dominant norm. In the academic literature, the so-called Japanese women's language is usually characterized in terms of Standard Japanese features or the (presumed) speech of middle-class women in Tokyo. However, speakers of regional Japanese may not understand prescriptions such as "Speak *onnarashiku*" only in terms of features of Standard Japanese. It needs to be investigated to what extent societal norms, such as "Speak *onnarashiku*"and "Speak politely," are linked to Standard Japanese or, to put it differently, to what extent scientists' focus on Standard Japanese has contributed to the construction of a narrow societal norm for women's speech informed by the hegemonic ideology of class, gender, and region.

2.5. Conclusion

Although honorifics (and other formal and indirect expressions) in Japanese are often linked to politeness and *onnarashisa*, I have argued that such a link is not inevitable but rather is based on the Japanese hegemonic ideology of language, gender, and class. I have further argued that both linguistic politeness and *onna-rashisa* involve evaluations of speech vis-à-vis what one thinks of as the norms for specific situations. The hegemonic ideology of politeness and *onnarashisa* is widely promulgated in Japanese society and may considerably affect one's conception of the norms. As a mediating link between language and social structure, this ideology provides a basis for the interpretation of honorifics as polite and *onnarashii*, which in turn contributes to the maintenance of social inequality in regard to gender and class. However, my analysis suggests that what is understood as the normative usage may not always be the same. It may vary among individuals and across time; it may also differ depending on the context. Accordingly, honorifics may not always be perceived as polite and *onnarashii*. Individuals negotiate the dominant ideology and may or may not adopt it; they choose expressions strategically based on what they think are most appropriate for specific situations.

The complex indexical process analyzed in this chapter demonstrates that it is important not only to distinguish language ideology and practice in linguistic analysis but also to appropriately assess the role of ideologies in the interpretation of social meanings of linguistic forms used in specific contexts. In particular, it illustrates the importance of considering diversity in the interpretation and use of language as related to variability in individuals' apprehension of speech norms for local contexts.

Notes

I would like to thank Akesha Baron, Sarah Benor, Mary Bucholtz, Misao Okada, Devyani Sharma, and Yukako Sunaoshi for their valuable comments on the earlier versions of this chapter. Special thanks go to Janet Shibamoto Smith, my coeditor, and Sumiyuki Yukawa, who have continuously provided me with numerous valuable comments, suggestions, useful information, and encouragement.

1. The following abbreviations are used for different types of (non-)honorific forms: AH = addressee honorific; RH/R = referent honorific-respectful word; RH/H = referent

honorific-humble word; RH/B= referent honorific-beautification word; NRH = nonreferent honorific; and NAH = nonaddressee honorific. Other abbreviations used in this study are: AUX = auxiliary; GD = gerundive form; GN = genitive marker; N = noun; OM = ojbect marker; Pst = past tense; Q = question marker; SM = subject marker; and V = verb.

2. In the case of verbal expressions, *sonkee-go* are used for the action of the subject referent and *kenjoo-go* for that of the object (or nonsubject) referent.

3. The word *hito* usually means "person," but it is translated here as "woman" because it was written with the Sino-Japanese characters women (usually read as *josee*) but accompanied by interlinear *kana* syllabary characters that gave its pronunciation as "hito."

References

Bergvall, Victoria L. (1999). Toward a comprehensive theory of language and gender. *Language in Society* 28(2): 273–293.

Bergvall, Victoria L., Janet M. Bing, and Alice F. Freed (eds.) (1996). *Rethinking language and gender research: Theory and practice.* London: Longman.

Briggs, Charles L. (1998). "You're a liar—you're just like a woman!" Constructing dominant ideologies of language in Warao men's gossip. In B. B. Schieffelin, K. A. Woolard, and P. V. Kroskrity (eds.), *Language ideologies: Practice and theory,* 229–255. Oxford: Oxford University Press.

Brown, Penelope (1980). How and why are women more polite: Some evidence from a Mayan community. In S. McConnell-Ginet, R. Borker, and N. Furman (eds.), *Women and language in literature and society,* 111–139. New York: Praeger.

Brown, Penelope, and Stephen C. Levinson (1987). *Politeness: Some universals in language usage.* Cambridge: Cambridge University Press.

Bucholtz, Mary (1999). Bad examples: Transgression and progress in language and gender studies. In M. Bucholtz, A. C. Liang, and L. A. Sutton (eds.), *Reinventing identities: The gendered self in discourse,* 3–24. New York: Oxford University Press.

Bucholtz, Mary, A. C. Liang, and Laurel A. Sutton (eds.) (1999). *Reinventing identities: The gendered self in discourse.* New York: Oxford University Press.

Bunkacho (1996). *Kokugo-shingikai hookokusho 20 (National Language Council report 20).* Tokyo: Okurasho Insatsu-kyoku.

Cameron, Deborah (1988). Introduction. In J. Coates and D. Cameron (eds.), *Women in their speech communities: New perspectives on language and sex,* 3–12. London: Longman.

——— (1990). Demythologizing sociolinguistics: Why language does not reflect society. In J. E. Joseph and T. J. Taylor (eds.), *Ideologies of language,* 79–93. London: Routledge.

Dunn, Cynthia (1996). The construction of identity in conversation: An intergenerational comparison. Paper presented at the 5th International Pragmatics Conference, Mexico City.

Eckert, Penelope and Sally McConnell-Ginet (1999). New generalizations and explanations in language and gender research. *Language in Society* 28(2): 185–201.

Eelen, Gino (1999). Ideology in politeness: A critical analysis. Unpublished doctoral dissertation, University of Antwerp.

Endo, Orie (1997). *Onna no kotoba no bunkashi (Cultural history of Japanese women's language).* Tokyo: Gakuyo Shobo.

Hall, Kira, and Mary Bucholtz (eds.) (1995). *Gender articulated: Language and the socially constructed self.* New York: Routledge.

Holmes, Janet (1995). *Women, men and politeness.* London: Longman.

Ide, Sachiko (1982). Japanese sociolinguistics: Politeness and women's language. *Lingua* 57: 357–385.

———— (1990). How and why do women speak more politely in Japanese? In S. Ide and N. H. McGloin (eds.), *Aspects of Japanese women's language*, 63–79. Tokyo: Kuroshio.

———— (1993). Sekai no joseego, Nihon no joseego: Joseego kenkyuu no shintenkai o motomete (Women's language of the world, women's language of Japan: Searching for new developments in women's language research). *Nihongogaku* 12(6): 4–12.

Inoue, Fumio (1989). *Kotobazukai shinfuukee: Keego to hoogen (New views on ways of speaking: Honorifics and dialects)*. Tokyo: Akiyama Shoten.

James, Deborah (1996). Women, men and prestige speech forms: A critical review. In V. L. Bergvall, J. M. Bing, and A. F. Freed (eds.), *Rethinking language and gender research: Theory and practice*, 98–125. London: Longman.

Jugaku, Akiko (1979). *Nihongo to onna (The Japanese language and women)*. Tokyo: Iwanami Shoten.

Kanai, Yoshiko (1994). *Onna no miryoku wa hanashi-kata shidai (Women's attractiveness depends on how they speak)*. Tokyo: Yamato Shuppan.

Kawanari, Mika (1993). Irai-hyoogen (Expressions of request). *Nihongo-gaku* 12(6): 121–134.

Keenan, Elinor (1974). Norm-makers, norm-breakers: uses of speech by men and women in a Malagasy community. In R. Bauman and J. Sherzer (eds.), *Explorations in the ethnography of speaking*, 125–143. Cambridge: Cambridge University Press.

Komori, Yoichi (2000). *Nihongo no kindai (The Japanese language in modern times)*. Tokyo: Iwanami Shoten.

Lakoff, Robin (1975). *Language and woman's place*. New York: Harper and Row.

Lee, Yeounsuk (1996). *"Kokugo" to yuu shisoo (The ideology of "the national language")*. Tokyo: Iwanami Shoten.

Leech, Geoffrey (1983). *Principles of pragmatics*. London: Longman.

Miller, Laura (1996). Subversive subordinates or situated language use? A consideration of *keigo* ideology and sociolinguistic description. Paper presented at the 48th annual meeting of the Association for Asian Studies, Honolulu.

Minami, Fujio (1987). *Keego (Honorifics)*. Tokyo: Iwanami Shoten.

Miyake, Yoshimi (1995). A dialect in the face of the standard: A Japanese case study. In J. Ahlers, L. Bilmes, J. S. Guenter, B. A. Kaiser, and J. Namkung (eds.), *Proceedings of the 21st Annual Meeting of the Berkeley Linguistics Society*, 217–225. Berkeley: Berkeley Linguistics Society.

Nakamura, Momoko (1995). *Kotoba to feminizumu (Language and feminism)*. Tokyo: Keiso Shobo.

Niyekawa, Agnes (1991). *Minimum essential politeness: A guide to the Japanese honorific language*. Tokyo: Kodansha International.

Ochs, Elinor (1993). Indexing gender. In B. D. Miller (ed.), *Sex and gender hierarchies,* 146–169. Cambridge, MA: Cambridge University Press.

Ogino, Tsunao, Yasuko Misono, and Chitsuko Fukushima (1985). Diversity of honorific usage in Tokyo: A sociolinguistic approach based on a field survey. *International Journal of the Sociology of Language* 55: 23–39.

Ohashi, Haruo (1994a). *Josee kara okuru tegami no kaki-kata (How to write women's letters)*. Tokyo: Fujin-seikatsu-sha.

———— (1994b). *Dansee kara okuru tegami no kaki-kata (How to write men's letters)*. Tokyo: Fujin-seikatsu-sha.

Okamoto, Shigeko (1996). Indexical meaning, linguistic ideology, and Japanese women's speech. In *The Proceedings of the 22nd Annual Meeting of the Berkeley Linguistics Society*, 290–301. Berkeley: Berkeley Linguistics Society.

———— (1997). Social context, linguistic ideology, and indexical expressions in Japanese. *Journal of Pragmatics* 28(6): 795–817.

56   HISTORICAL AND THEORETICAL FOUNDATIONS

———— (1999). Situated politeness: Manipulating honorific and non-honorific expressions in Japanese conversations. *Pragmatics* 8(2): 51–74.

Reynolds, Katsue Akiba (1985). Female speakers of Japanese. *Feminist Issues* 5: 13–46.

———— (1990). Female speakers of Japanese in transition. In S. Ide and N. H. McGloin (eds.), *Aspects of Japanese women's language*, 129–146. Tokyo: Kuroshio Shuppan.

Shibamoto, Janet S. (1987). Japanese sociolinguistics. *Annual Review of Anthropology* 16: 261–278.

[Shibamoto] Smith, Janet S. (1992). Linguistic privilege: "Just stating the facts" in Japanese. In K. Hall, M. Bucholtz, and B. Moonwomon (eds.), *Locating power: Proceedings of the Second Berkeley Women and Language Conference*, 40–48. Berkeley: Berkeley Women and Language Group.

Shibatani, Masayoshi (1990). *The languages of Japan*. Cambridge, MA: Cambridge University Press.

Shigemitsu, Yuka (1993). Kaiwa no pataan (Conversational patterns). *Nihongogaku* 12(6): 135–140.

Silverstein, Michael (1979). Language structure and linguistic ideology. In P. R. Clyne, W. Hanks, and C. L. Hofbauer (eds.), *The elements: A parasession on linguistic units and levels*, 193–247. Chicago: Chicago Linguistic Society.

Sugimoto, Tsutomu (1997). *Onna to kotoba ima-mukashi* (*Women and language, now and then*). Tokyo: Yuzankaku.

Suzuki, Kenji (1989). *Suteki na anata o tsukuru: Josee no utsukushii hanashi-kata* (To make youself nice: Women's beautiful ways of speaking). Tokyo: Goto Shoin.

Suzuki, Mutsumi (1993). Joseego no honshitsu: Teeneesa, hatsuwa kooi no shiten kara (The nature of women's language: Viewing from politeness and speech acts). *Nihongogaku* 12(6): 148–155.

Takahashi, Yoshiko (1996). What's cooking? An examination of Japanese male language within media domains. Paper presented at the 5th International Pragmatics Conference, Mexico City.

Takasaki, Midori (1993). Josee no kotoba to kaisoo (Women's language and social class). *Nihongogaku* 12(6): 169–180.

Tanaka, Sumie (1986). *Kashikoi hito ni narinasai:Utsukushiku ikitai anata ni* (Be a wise woman: To you who want to live beautifully). Tokyo: PHP Research Institute.

Trudgill, Peter (1972). Sex, covert prestige and linguistic change in the urban British English of Norwich. *Language in Society* 1: 179–195.

Washi, Rumi (2000). *Nyooboo kotoba* no imisayoo: Tennoosee, kaisoosee, sekushuaritii (In political function of *nyooboo kotoba*: Symbolizing the imperial system, class consciousness, and sexuality). *Joseegaku Nenpoo* 21: 18–35.

Wetzel, Patrica J. (1994). Contemporary Japanese attitudes toward honorifics (keigo). *Language Variation and Change* 6: 113–147.

Woolard, Kathryn A., and Bambi B. Schieffelin (1994). Language ideology. *Annual Review of Anthropology* 23: 55–82.

3

MIYAKO INOUE

Gender, Language, and Modernity

Toward an Effective History of
"Japanese Women's Language"

Japanese women's language" is a socially powerful truth. I mean by this not that the phrase refers to the empirical speech patterns of women. Rather, I mean that "Japanese women's language" is a critical cultural category and an unavoidable part of practical social knowledge in contemporary Japan. The phrase names a space of discourse in which the Japanese woman is objectified, evaluated, studied, staged, and normalized through her imputed language use and is thus rendered into a knowable and unified object. Doxic statements, such as "Women speak more politely than men" and "Women are not capable of speaking logically," are commonly heard in daily conversation. Scholars, too, have produced a highly reflexive and abstract—therefore privileged—knowledge of how women speak (differently from men); they have systematically located female-male differentiation at all levels of the language: phonology, semantics, morphology, syntax, speech acts, discourse (in the technical linguistic sense), as well as prosodic features such as pitch, and they have explained how female-specific values, attributes, and social roles are registered in speech forms and in the management of conversation.

Women's language is also a national issue, a reflexive parameter of civil order and of social change. Nationwide opinion polls are regularly conducted on whether "women's language" is becoming corrupted and how much so; national sentiments over its perceived disappearance are thereby crystallized and circulated in the form of numbers and statistics.[1] This linguistic consciousness of "how women speak" is closely connected with notions of culture and tradition in the assumption that women's language is uniquely Japanese, with unbroken historical roots in an archetypical Japanese past, and inescapably linked with an equally traditional and archetypical Japanese womanhood. For example, Kindaichi Kyosuke, one of the founders of modern Japanese linguistics, noted in his discussion of women's language: "Japanese womanhood is now being recognized as beautiful and excellent beyond compare with the other womanhoods of the world. Likewise, Japanese women's language is so good that it seems to me that it is, along with Japanese womanhood, unique in the world" (1942:293). Kikuzawa Sueo, who is noted as one of the first modern linguists to bring attention to women's language, observed: "Women's speech is characterized by elegance, that is, gentleness and beauty. Moreover, such characteristics correspond with our unique national language" (1929:75). Women's language is also viewed as "cultural heritage," on the brink of vanishing and in urgent need of preservation.[2] As Mashimo Saburo, another scholar of Japanese women's language, puts it, "We can not hope for contemporary Japanese women to be as witty and tactful as were those in the past, but, at least, I would like them to have a sincere and humble attitude and to preserve the cultural heritage passed down from the ancestors without destroying it" (1969:81). Talk of women's language, thus, necessarily always implicates the perceived continuing contradiction between Japanese tradition and modernity.

But how and why did some speech forms and functions come to be identified as "women's language"? How and why have they become promoted from unselfconscious sound to a universalized, national symbol that is a both socioculturally and linguistically discrete index? Most important, how did such an indexical practice—a linkage of speech with social structure and cultural meaning—come to be possible to begin with? Scholars of *kokugogaku* 'national language studies'[3] often date the origin of women's language as early as the fourth century, and they commonly construct a seamless narrative of "Japanese women's language" passed down to the present. Evidence of women's language is traced in premodern literary works and in records of terminology used by sequestered groups of feudal women such as court ladies, Buddhist nuns, and women in the pleasure quarters.[4]

This primordialist discourse, however, provides an adequate historical-linguistic account neither of the development of contemporary women's language nor of a continuous descent from ancient origins. Rather, this discourse merely assumes an essence of "Japanese women's language" that teleologically originates at some ancient time and descends without interruption or transformation down to the present. The isolated and discontinuous examples are meant to illustrate the continuous essence assumed to lie behind them. For our purposes, the point is that because it denies historical contingency and ignores emergent phenomena this discourse paradoxically erases the material traces of women's diverse linguistic experience and ends up simply affirming the transcendental national narrative of culture and tradition. It hides histories by articulating (teleological) History—with a capital *H*.

Bringing this historical threshold into theoretical focus requires a critical method that allows us to recognize discontinuity in history, a goal Foucault (1977:153–155) calls "effective history," whose method is genealogy. This would permit us to locate not the origin of a transhistorical essence but the emergence of a complex ensemble. The concept of emergence presupposes neither teleological continuity nor recalcitrant relativism and requires us to seek the history of the present not in the ideal but in the material and embodied context that entails multiple social forces in conjunction—in this case, Japan's unprecedented capitalist takeoff. In this chapter, I will, thus, examine the genealogy of "Japanese women's language" by locating its one critical moment of ascendancy at the threshold of Japan's modernity during the late nineteenth and the early twentieth century, when state formation, nationalism, capitalist accumulation, industrialization, radical class reconfiguration, colonialism, and foreign military adventurism were in full efflorescence. It was in this context that both language and women came to be problematized as "national issues" and thus to be political and cultural targets of the state authorities and of intellectuals and entrepreneurs who represented the progressive classes. I will show how particular speech forms were carved out, selected, and (re)constructed as "Japanese women's language" and how that process was critically linked to a network of diverse institutional and individual practices bent on modernization—and the particular form Japanese women's language took in its complex mimicry of, and resistance to, the West.

The significance of this history lies not so much in the emergence of specific speech forms associated with "women's language" as in the conditions of modernization and modernity that, to begin with, made possible and thinkable the practice of the indexical signaling of "women" as a nationally regimented category. In other words, history here involved the opening of a new cultural space where women became objectified through their language use and thus became the productive site of knowledge of Japanese women that was overdetermined by the production of knowledge of nation, race, and class. Using Hanks's (1996:278) insightful terminology, it is the historical construction of a "metalinguistic gaze" upon women that is my subject.

In order to zero in on the emergence of women's language, I will focus on the linguistic modernization movements variously pursued for different goals by the government agencies, the literary community, the print media, and linguists and educators from the late nineteenth century to the early twentieth century. These independent initiatives eventually converged and were led by a literary movement called *gembun'itchi* 'speech and writing unification' to create a colloquial written Japanese and to develop modern narrative prose (the novel form, or *shoosetsu*). The novel is a distinctively modern representational institution, shaping and shaped by the advent of industrial capitalism, the rise of the middle class, and the development of mass print capitalism (Anderson 1983). Most important, however, the critical linkage between the novel and modernity lies in the latter's epistemological commitment to realism and referentiality or a modernist certitude that language is a transparent medium that can faithfully and truthfully represent reality. The *gembun'itchi* movement thus engendered a new "language ideology" (Silverstein 1979, Woolard & Schieffelin 1994, Schieffelin, Woolard, & Kroskrity 1998) as to what language is and how language works. This chapter will argue that such a newly developed linguistic consciousness was both the instrument and the critical location of the birth of "Japanese women's language" as the subjects "modern Japanese women" variously emerged in the state, civil society, and the market.

3.1. "Nationalizing" women, modernizing women

The late Meiji period, the two decades from 1888 to 1910, was critical for Japan's modern nation-state formation. This period saw the development of heavy and textile industries, mass communication and transportation systems, and a legal apparatus organized through the promulgation of the Meiji Constitution and Civil Code, the establishment of representative democracy with the opening of the Diet, and the creation of a direct administrative channel between local and central government. The development of print capitalism (in the form of mass-circulation newspapers and magazines) and the instituting of compulsory education further molded a sense of the population not only as an administrative/political body but also as a nation-state, where people came to identify themselves as "Japanese" and to imagine "Japan" as more than an administrative unit. Individuals also came to be directly—but unevenly—connected to the state through education, censuses, taxation, and new (bourgeois) legal rights. At the same time, citizens were differentially positioned, in terms of class, power, and culture, in the newly emerging mosaic of a capitalist society. Modern power, as Foucault tells us, is both totalizing and individuating (1982:208–226). These channels of power converged in the reorganization of the person as the modern (and imperial) subject in the late Meiji period. It was in this context of modern social power in the form of capitalist development and state centralization that "women" as a social category became radically renewed and "modern Japanese women" emerged as an articulable social category burdened with new cultural meanings pertinent to its relationship with the nation-state.

One concrete terrain on which "women" became consolidated as a social category in conjunction with the historical and cultural complexity of Japan's modernity was women's public education. With women's secondary education incorporated for the first time with the state-regulated public education system in 1899, the government actively launched a project to "nationalize" women and shape their roles vis-à-vis the state. Central to this endeavor was the idea of "a good wife and wise mother" (*ryoosai kembo*). The project putatively advocated the "traditional" virtues and values of ideal womanhood, such as obedience to father, husband, and, later, eldest male child. Far from primordial, however, this ideology derived both from the Confucianism espoused by the ex-samurai class and from the imported Western cult of domesticity. Eclectic yet decisively "Japanese modern," the teaching of "good wife and wise mother" prepared women to take on a critical gendered role in an anticipated modern capitalist society, which included an emphasis on motherhood,[5] rational and scientific house management (including hygiene and efficient home economy), and saving.[6]

Woman, here as elsewhere, came to embody the shifting boundary between tradition and modernity, and her body and sexuality became concrete sites where this irrevocable binary was negotiated and policed (Mani 1987, Chatterjee 1990, Stoler 1991). "Women's language" was one powerful effect of cultural work in the realms of politics, the market, civil society, and personal life—cultural work that sought to give the nascent signifier, the "modern Japanese woman," her "voice."

3.2. "Write as you speak": *Gembun'itchi* and the discursive space of the nation-state

For the Meiji elite, "language"[7] was the foremost critical institution to be modernized because it was recognized as an instrument to build a nation-state—to import and simulate Western science and technology and to achieve national integration. In this section, I trace the historical process and various practices of language modernization in the late nineteenth and the early twentieth century, which resulted in a linguistic consciousness intimately connected with the exercise of modern forms of power. The emergence of the metapragmatic category of "women's language" is predicated upon such modern linguistic consciousness, both as a technique with which new knowledge about (modern Japanese) women was produced and as an epistemological ground upon which such new knowledge was made intelligible.

The major language modernization movement was in the literary community, which was called *gembun'itchi*. *Gembun'itchi* 'unifying speech and writing' developed out of the progressive Meiji writers' concern with the lack of an adequate literary style satisfactory for modern narrative prose as found in the Western realist novel they saw as a model. They developed the new style of colloquial written Japanese called *gembun'itchi-tai* '*gembun'itchi* style'. It is not a coincidence that *gembun'itchi* took the lead in language modernization. The novel—with its distinct origin in the late eighteenth- and early nineteenth-century Europe—was a technology that was as constitutive of the modern nation-state as were legislatures, laws, citizenship, policed borders, and standing armies. Its generic framing demands truth telling about the realities of ordinary people and their daily lives. The novel, thus, attempted to put on public exhibition the Japanese citizenry—composed of individual, "ordinary" people. This realist metanarrative condition was inseparably mediated by and inescapably linked with forces emerging with capitalism in Europe, which involved the rise of a middle class, the articulation of possessive individualism, the precipitation of nationalism, and the birth of print capitalism. Through culturally contingent reworking of the Western realist novel, the Meiji progressive writers encountered a new idea of language that enabled and was enabled by such elements of western modernity.

The core of *gembun'itchi* as an effort to create a new colloquial style boiled down to the stylistic question of how to entextualize[8] linguistic excess, the sheer physicality and materiality of the human voice. In an actual face-to-face interaction, we not only exchange the semantic or referential meaning of what we utter, but also, at the same time, we also communicate pragmatic meaning, by how we speak, with respect to elements of the immediate context of the interaction, including the social setting of the interaction and the social attributes of the participants, such as their gender, social rank and roles, age, and so on. The *gembun'ichi* writers sought to include this linguistic excess in the text with verb-ending forms. For the writers, verb-ending forms were the site to deal with such linguistic excess because these function indexically to mark the author's social and psychological position vis-à-vis the characters in the text and the reader in the context. In other words, verb-ending forms are regimented into an indexical order of "different ways of saying the same thing" (Silverstein 1996:280). Depending on the verb-ending form one chooses, different pragmatic effects, with the same referential value, are produced as to how the narrator (speaker) narrates (talks) to the reader (listener) about the characters and events.

During the time between the Sino-Japanese War (1894–1895) and the Russo-Japanese War (1904–1905), the literary *gembun'itchi* movement was appropriated by the state's nationalist effort to create a "national language" (*kokugo*)—and, more precisely, a standard national language. For the state intellectuals in the early Meiji, *gembun'itchi* was not a primary concern in language reform. They were concerned mainly with writing or script reforms for example, whether or not Chinese characters should be used, for modernization meant Westernization and a break with China. When the idea of a national language was introduced, however, the terms of the debate on national-language policy shifted from questions of writing to speech matters.

The *gembun'itchi* movement itself underwent significant transformation as it became mobilized for the technology of the modern nation-state: Against the original advocacy of a "spirit of vernacularism," by the 1910s plain verb-ending forms such as the *da*-copula had won out as the established literary style. Polite and honorific verb-ending forms, which formally indexed context-bound relationships between the author and the reader and between the author and the characters, eventually lost their status in the serious literary style. Concurrent with the predominance of the plain style, the first-person narrative was superseded by that of the third person. In it, the narrator's presence vanishes from the narrated event and the text ceases to acknowledge the context. Instead, standing outside the narrated event and commanding a God's-eye view, the narrator now rationally, objectively, and truthfully represents the scene. This is the linguistic version of Bentham's panopticon (Foucault 1977:195–228). The dictum "Write as you speak," then, presented a contradictory task: it demanded the speechlike effect of immediacy, transparency, and physicality obtained with the plain style, but this very plain style evacuated the pragmatic meaning that would have given the speech polysemy and undecidability. For this new narrative style, context and audience were no longer time-space bound but became the abstracted and imagined "Japan" and "the Japanese." Thus did a linguistic technology help to make an imagined community necessary, even if it did not really exist. The speaking subject of the *gembun'itchi* style literally necessitates and embodies the modern Japanese citizen—it makes him imaginable.

I say "him" because this narrator, this citizen, is presumed to be (the middle-class) male[9] and he alone had full and legitimate access to the newly emerging bourgeois public sphere (Harbermas 1989, Fraser 1990, Warner 1990, Calhoun 1992). In fact, the state language policy designated the speech of "the educated Tokyo middle-class males" as the basis of standard language (Okano 1902). The phrase "educated Tokyo middle-class males" alluded to the newly emerging petite bourgeoisie of salaried workers in Yamanote, the plateau section of the city of Tokyo.

In short, the *gembun'itchi* style came to narrate the nation (Bhabha 1990). This new narrating voice as developed in the *gembun'itchi* movement introduced a new linguistic consciousness: language is a transparent medium, purely and exclusively referential in its function, according to which nothing comes between language and the world and there is an exclusive and context-free, one-to-one correspondence between sound and word, word and meaning, and language and the world. Language is then simply to reflect what is already out there, always one step behind the world, docilely ratifying and confirming it. Such a realist conception is inherently ideological because it effaces the semiotic work of language in actively mediating and producing what is seemingly merely given, reversing the order of things as if the world existed as it is without the mediation of language. Linked up with the regime of modern power, it serves to turn things, categories, events, and ideas into a fait accompli.

In more concrete terms, the new narrating voice functioned at the metalinguistic level to signal that whatever it narrates, reports, describes, represents, and states is true, real, serious, and credible and that it "speaks" not from a particular individual's point of view but from that of the modern rational and national (male) citizen—an omniscient point of view that masquerades as not being a point of view at all. This metalinguistic function was facilitated by formal and diacritic devices that separate the narrating voice and the narrated (Komori 1988). Translating and appropriating the Western realist novel required *gembun'itchi* writers, for the first time, to develop subordinated linguistic space in the form of dialogue and reported speech. It is a formal space where alterity is constructed, highlighted, and neatly kept apart from the self. The novel thus formally created a hierarchical relationship in which the narrated— whether people, events, or things—is always already objectified by, represented through, and subjected to the male gaze of the narrating subject, or of the modern Japanese citizen. And it is precisely this metalinguistic effect that various Japanese institutions and projects intent on their own modernization ultimately adopted from the literary *gembun'itchi* movement. In textbooks, newspapers, magazines, fiction, scholarly essays, public speeches, legal statements, military orders, advertisements, and colonial education, the new narrating voice not only provides semantico-referential information but also functions simultaneously as performative (Silverstein 1979, Lee 1997), to authenticate and factualize that which is enunciated.[10] It is in this linguistic space, a quoted space, objectified, reified, and re-presented by the imbricated gaze of the male, the national, and the modern, that "women's language" was pieced together from heterogeneous origins.

3.3. Quoting "women's language"/producing "the Japanese woman"

Dialogues and reported speech were new linguistic space where the maximum degree of verisimilitude was logically implied. And this is the space where people "heard," for the first time, modern Japanese women "speak." Women's voice was, as mentioned earlier, to center on the use of final particles. Table 3.1 compares a particular form of final particle employed in the popular fiction work titled *Ukiyoburo 'The bathhouse of the floating world'*, which was written in 1813 by Shikitei Sanba, and the narrative prose work titled *Sanshiro*, which was written in 1909 by Natsume Soseki.

Sanba was one of the traditional popular fiction (*gesaku*) writers of the late Edo period, before the Meiji Restoration. *Ukiyoburo* is about the frivolous interactions of people coming to the bathhouse. It consists of dialogues in which they tease, argue, compliment, gossip about, and comment on one another. The characters in *Ukiyoburo* are diverse in age, gender, social stratification, region, and occupation, according to which Sanba carefully differentiates and characterizes individual speech styles. What is glaringly absent in table 3.1 is anything that looks remotely like what contemporary women's language is believed to be.

Soseki was one of the best-known Meiji writers, and *Sanshiro* was published at the culmination of the literary *gembun'itchi* movement. By then, whether Soseki intended to or not, he and other early twentieth-century Japanese writers had

TABLE 3.1 The comparison of
final particles attached to verb-
ending form *da* in two
Japanese novels

Ukiyoburo (1813)		Sanshiro (1909)	
da-naa	M		
da-te	M		
da-te-na	M		
da-te-ne	M		
da-wa-i	M		
da-wa-su	M		
da-yoo	M		
da-ze-e	M		
da-e	F		
da-ne-nee	F		
da-no-ya	F		
da-yo-nee	F		
da-yo-noo	F		
da-mono-o	B		
da-na	B	da-na	M
da-ne	B	da-ne	M
da-nee	B		
da-no	B		
da-noo	B		
da-su	B		
da-wa	B	da-wa	F
da-wa-e	B		
da-wa-na	B		
da-wa-sa	B		
da-yo	B	da-yo	M
da-ze	B	da-ze	M
da-zo	B	da-zo	M
		da	M
		da-koto	F

M: used by male characters only. F: used
by female characters. B: used by both
male and female characters.

The data is drawn from Komatsu (1988).
The reader should note that I have rearranged Komatsu's data to draw my own
conclusions and that I am using his data
for purposes other than those he intended.

inescapably become deeply involved with narrating the nation and its modern subject. *Sanshiro* depicts the lives of modern women and men, new characters that did
not exist prior to Meiji. The significance of *Sanshiro* is that the voices assigned to
these women and men contain both the female-exclusive and male-exclusive final
particles, identical with those of contemporary Japanese. Table 3.1 compares the final
particles attached to the verb-ending form *da* in *Ukiyoburo* and in *Sanshiro*. It is

noteworthy, first of all, that the gender-neutral final particles in *Ukiyoburo* have become gendered into either female-exclusive or male-exclusive in *Sanshiro*. Second, the final particles in *Ukiyoburo*, on the one hand, are not gendered but rather are idiosyncratic: there is a plurality of individual voices in the use of final particles, and final particles are, thus, not in a position to index anything, perhaps because they index *everybody*. In *Sanshiro*, on the other hand, final particles have become systematized and standardized so as to index gender in the modern nation. By this time, female and male Japanese subjects are imaginable components within the nation, and the modern Japanese novel significantly flattens out the individual "grain of the voice," so that one Japanese woman (or man) is interchangeable with another.

Table 3.2 compares another set of final particles in *Ukiyoburo* and in *Sanshiro*. The left-hand column lists the female-exclusive and male-exclusive final particles that appear in *Sanshiro*, and the right-hand column is drawn from *Ukiyoburo*. The

TABLE 3.2 The comparison of final particles between *Ukiyoburo* and *Sanshiro*

Sanshiro (1909)		Ukiyoburo (1813)	
da-koto	F	B	
no	F	B	
NOM. + yo	F	B	
*wa	F	B	
da(COP.)	M	B	
da-ne	M	B	
da-yo	M	B	
na	M	B	
sa	M	B	
zo	M	B	
*na-no	F	/	No example
*no-ne	F	/	No example
*NOM. + nee	F	/	No example
*wa-ne	F	/	No example
*wa-yo	F	/	No example
*da-wa	F	B	Not used by samurai-class females
*no-yo	F	B	Not used by samurai-class females
da-na	M	B	Not used by samurai-class females
da-ze	M	B	Not used by samurai-class females
da-zo	M	B	Not used by samurai-class females
ze	M	B	Not used by samurai-class females
zee	M	B	Not used by samurai-class females
NOM. + ne	F	B	Only few examples seen
ya	M	B	Various usages

M: used by male characters only. F: used by female characters only. B: used by both male and female characters.
COP.Bcopula
NOM.Bnominal

The data is drawn from Komatsu (1988). The reader should note that I have rearranged Komatsu's data to draw my own conclusions and that I am using his data for purposes other than those he intended.

final particles marked with an asterisk are identified today as quintessentially female-exclusive final particles. While the final particle *wa* appeared in *Ukiyoburo*, the other female-exclusive final particles of contemporary Japanese women's language—*na-no*, *no-ne*, nominal plus *ne*, *wa-ne*, and *wa-yo*—did not appear at all in the pre-Meiji work. The next two asterisked final particles, *da-wa* and *no-yo*, which are particularly salient feminine particles in the present, are not assigned to the female characters in the elite (samurai) class. *Da-wa* and *no-yo* were in fact considered to be "vulgar" and "low-class" as late as the end of the nineteenth century, and educators and others strongly advised parents and teachers not to let their daughters use them. We hardly have here a seamless history of a traditional Japanese woman's voice.

My point is not that *Sanshiro* represented women's language because that is how, in actual fact, "Japanese women" had come to speak in 1909.[11] The modern narrating voice may tell us metalinguistically that what is being reported is merely that which is actually spoken "out there," but we should not be deceived by this metalinguistic whispering. Reported speech (Voloshinov 1973, Bakhtin 1981) entails the authorial (and social) act of (re)creating women's voice within a socially produced—and self-reproducing—knowledge of "how women speak." As Voloshinov (1973:82) argues, reported speech "is a social phenomenon," a historical product that wells up from a complex social field in ideological and political flux.

The degree to which the speech of female characters in the modern novel was not, in fact, naturalistically represented during the early stage of the *gembun'itchi* movement is evidenced by the recollections of the *gembun'itchi* writers themselves. For example, writer Sato Haruo notes: "In those days, women's speech in daily conversation was invented by certain writer(s) (though I do not remember who he or she was) and came to be of general use" (1941:18). Tsubouchi Shoyo also recalled late in his life the difficulties of writing the speech of female characters, observing: "In those days, the language used by women in the middle class and beyond was filled with so many honorifics that one could not possibly manage to use it for translation" (1930:7). Many *gembun'itchi* writers developed their modern narrative prose by using Japanese that had been translated from (and thus filtered through) Western languages. Futabatei Shimei, for example, wrote his first novel, *Ukigumo*, while translating Turgenev's A *Sportsman's Notebook* into Japanese. Tsubouchi also translated into Japanese a large body of Shakespeare's work. The irony is that these writers needed the authentic speaking voice of modern Japanese women in order to represent that of white women.

What these writers hit upon to solve the problem of women's reported speech was the speech of *jogakusee* 'schoolgirls' that they claimed that they overheard on the street. Tsubouchi thus exclaimed, "There were unimaginable obstacles and difficulties that writers who were used to hearing *jogakusee-kotoba* 'the speech of schoolgirls' from the end of Meiji—today's *onna-kotoba* 'female speech style'—could not have even dreamed of. Oh, how blessed contemporary writers are!" (1930:7). The modern education policy made it possible for daughters of the elite family to go to girls' high schools. *Jogakusee*[12] thus represented a new social category of female: they were neither producers (workers) nor reproducers (mothers). As *jogakusee* as a cultural construct became increasingly recognized, objectified, and imagined as a metonymy for Japan's modernization, so did their speech. Schoolgirls were reported to use a set of distinctive final particles, including *te-yo*, *da-wa*, *no-yo*, and others, many of which are the essential linguistic features identified today as "women's language."

The final particle *te-yo* first appeared in a novel in 1888 (used by a young woman to a man and to her female friend), *no-yo* in 1885 (used by a young woman to a man), and *da-wa* in 1886 (used by a young woman to her maid and in her monologue; Ishikawa 1972). In female characters' speech, final particles such as *te-yo*, *da-wa*, and *no-yo* were thus initially restricted to the speech of young women or schoolgirl characters. Later, however, they came to be used in a wider variety of dialogues, for example, those between wife and husband, or between daughter and father (Ishikawa 1972). By the early twentieth century, these particles, claimed by writers to have derived from schoolgirls' speech, had become elevated in writing to "women's language," through the work of writers actively to indexicalize the speech of female characters as generic—yet increasingly "feminized"—female speech. The elevation of schoolgirls' speech to generic women's language, the voice of the modern gendered subject, was thus far from being a natural history in any way. Schoolgirls' speech originally raised intellectuals' and educators' eyebrows as "vulgar" and "low-class." For example, writer Ozaki Koyo (1994 [1888]: 4–5) warned in 1888 that, eight or nine years previously, a certain speech style with strange sorts of verb endings such as *te-yo*, *no-yo*, and *da-wa* had first occurred among elementary schoolgirls between close friends and seemed to be spreading among high school girls and even grown women. He insisted that sensible ladies would never use these verb endings because they were originally part of the vulgar speech used by daughters of low-rank samurai families. Intellectuals and educators further developed this origin narrative by locating the original speakers of these verb-ending forms in the pleasure quarters and teahouses. These intellectuals and educators claimed that the speech of these women was adopted by daughters from the low-rank samurai families and, later, by the middle class and elites.

Indexicalization here involved not just the active linking of a sign to a referent but also the active construction of the referent itself. In other words, the speech of schoolgirls—as a constructed voice—could not be (re)signified to become women's language unless the discursive and disciplinary space of "the modern Japanese woman" existed. This critical move took place in the discursive space where the state's intended surveillance of women, print capitalism's interest in women as a market, and women themselves as new consumers intersected at a particular conjunction in Japanese history. This discursive space was also largely without a "head." While it could be argued that the state "had power" because of its power to censor or that consumers "had power" because they could vote with their feet, this discursive space was, as Foucault said of disciplinary power, "multiple, automatic and anonymous power" that functioned from "top to bottom, but also to a certain extent from bottom to top and laterally" (1977:176). In fact, it is the very lack of an actor clearly "in control" within this discursive space that helps to erase the extent to which "the Japanese woman" was socially produced.

This process is most visible in *kateeshoosetsu* 'the domestic novel', a particular form of the Japanese novel that appeared in the early twentieth century. The domestic novel was originally serialized in newspapers, as a technique to expand readership among nonelite readers in order to create a mass market for newspapers. Particularly new among the readers was an increasing number of literate women. With this readership in mind, what would become the female final particles were extensively employed in the domestic novel (Morino 1991:247–248), to the extent that the literary genre of *kateeshoosetsu* became associated with the excessive use of female final particles such as *teyo* and *dawa*. Writer Uchida Roan (1984[1894]), for example, scornfully refers to *kateeshoosetsu* as "*teyo-dawa* novels." Many of these novels had schoolgirls or young women as main characters and exhibited both explicit and implicit allusion to the virtue of "a good wife and wise mother." The goal of the domestic novel is perhaps best explained by Kikuchi Yuho, one of the most successful male domestic novel writers.

> I wanted to write a story which would be a little more secular than the regular novel, not pretentious, but sophisticated, with good taste. I wanted to write it in such a way that it could be read in the family circle, that anyone could understand it, and that no one would blush. I intended to write a novel which would contribute to the joy of home and help to develop good taste. (Kikuchi 1971[1903]:89)

Kikuchi further emphasized that a good female character in his novel represented the ideal Japanese woman expected by society (Kikuchi 1971[1903]:90). As the contemporary literary critic Komori Yoichi (1992) has rightly argued, the domestic novel was in a way complicit with the state apparatus to nationalize women and to enable readers to imagine the modern Japanese womanhood.

But at the same time, the stories of the domestic novel were interesting enough for women to consume. Many featured upper-class women—an unknown yet seductive imaginary for ordinary people. The stories covered a wide variety of dramatic plots that involved, for example, romantic love, bearing illegitimate children, extra- and premarital affairs, elopement, suicide, murder, money and power, deception and betrayal, mother-daughter relationships, and so on. They provided the detail of the imagined urban middle-class sociality, dispositions, and material goods. By the early twentieth century, final particles such as *te-yo*, *da-wa*, *no-yo*, and others, which were once viewed as "vulgar," had come to be increasingly ascribed in the novels to middle-to-upper-class women. In combination with elaborate honorifics, these final particles were thus instituted as the voice of those who were depicted as *haikara* 'high-collar', that is, "modern," well educated and sophisticated, urban, and of good upbringing.

The fact that the novels were consumed and not simply imposed as some kind of elite or state-articulated ideology is critical because of the normalizing power of consumption. This was critical in dissemination. It was not long before the female final particles were not just reproduced in the novels but also circulated in some young women's magazines in the form of letters from "real" Japanese women. These magazines embodied a gender-specific counter public sphere; they constituted a virtual speech community where virtual friends communicated with one another through letter writing. Girls wrote to the editors and their "magazine" friends that they had never met, using female final particles as if they were "speaking" to each other, thus practicing their own "write as you speak." "Women's language" thus came to be no longer a mere quoted voice—a process in which the active voice lies with the one who quotes—but a quoting voice, as young women claimed their new modern Japanese identity and constructed their virtual speech community. Letters came from all over Japan (and its colonies) where the actual dialectal difference might have fatally fractured any sense of common (gendered) Japanese modernity. But in this virtual speech community, everyone "spoke" the speech style of "modern Japanese women" and thus claimed—and was allowed to perform—the subjectivity of "modern Japanese woman." In the emerging young women's counter public sphere made possible by print capitalism (and thus disciplined by both the market and the state), young women staked claim to a new identity.

We do not know for certain who read these magazines, much less who wrote the readers' letters. Various surveys on reading and readership (Nagamine 1997) show, however, that the magazines were read not only by daughters of the urban middle-class family but also later by factory girls (Tsurumi 1990) and young women in peasant families (Smith & Wiswell 1982, Tamanoi 1998). These readers were not, in fact "speakers" of the magazines' *haikara* speech style. The critical point is that the only place that those readers in Japan's periphery "heard" or perhaps "spoke" women's language was in print media—serialized novels and letters in girls' and young women's magazines. In other words, for them the copy was the original. And the way they experienced women's language was by consuming it as a metonymy of the modern, the urban, the national—everything that they were not. It was the consumption of "women's language" that enabled participation in the imagined national (speech) community. The dissemination of "women's language," for these women, had a lot to do with class and region as these became punctuated within the nationalist and capitalist project.

3.4.   Conclusion: Toward an effective history of language, gender, and modernity

I have sought to account for the genealogy of Japanese women's language and to examine the historical process by which the practice of representing gender meanings through speech was brought into being in the early twentieth century in Japan—during its collective yet uneven experience of modernity. I have also argued that the social genesis of the metapragmatic category of "women's language" is not a natural or evolutionary outcome of indexing gender through women's repeated and spontaneous use of certain speech forms. Instead, it is a hazardous effect of modernity in which, far from being relics of feudal Japan, both gender and language became problematized as targets of national and capitalist interest and social reform, and both were significantly reconfigured as various domains of society responded to the project of modernity and as its attendant social formations—capitalism, nationalism, and colonialism—profoundly transformed the contour of social relations. Historical beginnings are "derisive and ironic," to use Foucault's (1984:79) words. Precisely the same new "modern" conception of language that enabled and was enabled by the development of rational bureaucracy, the universal education system, nationalism, the military, the print media, colonial education, science and technology, and mimetic apparatuses such as stenography, the photograph, and the phonograph made possible the emergence of women's language, the sign of Japanese culture and tradition. The representational technique of "write as you speak," which was instrumental in creating the speech forms of women's language, was made necessary by nothing less than the engagement with the Western realist novel.

The experience of women's language was and has been intensely modern and national. Indexing gender in early twentieth-century Japan involved imagining the voice of (the yet to be imagined) modern Japanese women. Indeed, it was in the speech of schoolgirls that the Meiji writers discovered the linguistic forms with which to represent the voice of modern women. These forms became elevated to the rank of "Japanese women's language" only after they were displaced, grafted, quoted, recycled, and circulated in the network of newly available representational genres and media. In this sense there is no original or authentic speaking body that utters "women's language." It is no one's language; indeed, it is disembodied language. What we find is a series of entextualization processes (Bauman & Briggs 1990) in which the empty signifier of "the modern Japanese woman" became (imaginatively) fleshed out and she was given "her voice." The rise of women's language is thus inescapably connected with the development of consumer culture. In short, the majority of women experienced "women's language" not so much as its producer but as its (gendered) consumer. They "heard" modern women "speaking" in the novels and the magazines and "saw" them in the cover pictures of beautiful girls, the advertisements for cosmetics and perfumes, the letters from the readers, and the recipes for exotic Western dishes.

More important, however, the process of constructing "women's language," in its critical articulation with the emergent discourses of nation, race, and class, as well as with those of culture and tradition, opened up a new discursive space where the cultural meanings of women are produced and processed and turned into a concrete object that is knowable and transparent and is readily available for social, not to mention self-, control. This is precisely the condition under which indexing gender itself is possible and thinkable and under which statements such as "Women speak more politely than men" or ontological questions such as "Why do men and women speak differently?" make sense. Paradoxically, however, this new space simultaneously allows for strategic appropriation and subversion. The utopian speech community constructed in the readers' column in young women's magazines attests to this point.

The genealogy of Japanese women's language that I have outlined aims at a historical narrative that problematizes what is claimed to be natural and obvious in the present. The stability of Japanese women's language as a discourse derives precisely from the claim of its ancient origin and of its continuity and linearity up to the present. A genealogy historicizes the past, and by doing so the present is problematized (Scott 1996) in a way that makes visible the potential existence of heterogeneous temporalities, spaces, and experiences. By locating the emergence of what has been essentialized as "women's language" in its historical context and by treating it as one of the historically contingent (yet powerful) events of objectifying the relationship between femaleness and language, we can recognize diverse linguistic experiences as they are situated in and refracted by class and other parameters of social force. The point is not, however, simply to celebrate subaltern voices and resistance but rather to recognize the way in which women's linguistic experiences are shaped by the larger social system of the real world, in which access to women's language is just as unevenly distributed as other forms of capital—of both the cultural and the more familiar kind (Bourdieu 1977, 1991). A focus on indexing forces us to think historically. It is in this sense that historicizing the practice of indexing as I have outlined here echoes a larger and growing concern in linguistic anthropology to bring political economy (social power and its orchestrating and organizing potentialities) into linguistic analysis (Gal 1989, Irvine 1989). A metapragmatic category such as "women's language" is never pregiven but is contingent upon historically specific social arrangements, in which linguistic forms are motivated and regimented to become an "index" by being mediated through broader political and economic processes.

My aim in this chapter has also been to demonstrate the social power of the indexicality of language. Very often, language does not wait until the category it refers to or indexes is "out there." The case of the development of "women's language" shows that indexical practice was involved with the construction of modern Japanese women right from its inception. Indexicality constitutes reality not by naming and pointing to a preexisting object but by inverting the order of the indexed and indexing to make it appear as if the indexed preceded the indexing. Finally, a focus on indexing forces us to think critically and counterfactually, because the process by which a particular speech form is selected or negotiated, out of multiple competing voices and interpretations, to become an institutionally discrete index of femaleness is an inescapably political process. The index is inherently unstable and more a process than a thing, and its reproduction is a perennially political matter of self-naturalization. It is, however, precisely this processual and productive nature of indexicality that allows us to see how much any established "structure" of linguistic rules in a very rule-governed context is in fact saturated with individual strategizing, cultural remaking, politics, and historicity.

Notes

This chapter is a shortened and slightly revised version of Inoue (2002). Reproduced by permission of the American Anthropological Association from *American Ethnologist* 29(2). Not for sale or further reproduction. I would like to thank Shigeko Okamoto and Janet S. Shibamoto Smith for encouraging me to participate in this edited volume.

1. NHK (Japan Broadcasting Corporation) and The Agency for Cultural Affairs (Bunkachoo) in the Ministry of Education, for example, regularly conduct surveys on language consciousness.

2. See Ivy's (1995) important analysis of the reflexive projection of an unsullied essence into the past. In the case of "women's language," contradictorily enough, any statement about perceived corruption then functions to affirm the ontology of the essence by implying that there was once a pure women's language.

3. *National-language studies* (*kokugogaku*) refers to a domestic scholarly circle for the study of the Japanese language. It is aligned institutionally and conceptually more or less with the government's national language policies.

4. See Ide (1994) and Ide and Terada (1998) for a concise introduction to the study of women's language in National Language Studies.

5. See Koyama's (1991, 1999) excellent discussion on the historical transformation of the idea of "a good wife and wise mother" particularly in its linkage with modernity and modernization. Koyama (1991) shows, for example, that the emphasis on motherhood is

relatively absent in premodern primers. From a similar critical standpoint, Muta (1996) compellingly argues that the notion of the family (*ie*) and women's role within it became qualitatively discontinuous from that of premodern Japan. Both authors represent the increasing body of recent critical historical studies that challenge the idea that such institutions as the family and gender continuously and linearly evolve.

6. On the importance of saving as part of women's domestic duties, see Nolte and Hastings (1991). For a rich ethnographic account of the ways in which women in isolated villages in the mid-1930s became "nationalized," see Smith and Wiswell (1982).

7. I put quotation marks around the term *language* to indicate that what I am dealing with here under the name of "language" is neither a system nor an object. "Language" here can be best understood as an assemblage of various statements, practices, and activities to produce a variety of knowledge about what counts as language and what does not. In discussing language modernization, therefore, it does not mean that some kind of structured object, "premodern language," underwent a structural or systematic transformation into a "modern" one. Here I follow Sakai's approach: "Rather I look for various differentiations and oppositions and their interactions, which, when put together, circumscribe an area in human activities called language" (1992:8). I will dispense with the quotation marks around *language* for the remainder of the chapter, but the reader should assume that unless otherwise indicated, the term *language* as used in this chapter carries the implication specified here.

8. See Hanks (1989), Bauman and Briggs (1990), Briggs and Bauman (1992), and Silverstein and Urban (1996) for further theoretical discussions on the concept of entextualization.

9. This, of course, is the gender of the genre, not that of the author, insofar as "the modern Japanese language" interpolates its subject as male. Warner's (1990) studies of the development of the public sphere in eighteenth-century America presents a similar situation, in which "writing" was integrated into a mode of being as white male bourgeois. Exclusion of women, then, is not simply a matter of access but one of cognitive split; as Warner notes, "women could only write with a certain cognitive dissonance" (1990:15).

10. For an insightful discussion on the metalinguistic construction of publicity, as well as the semiotic explication of Habermas's and Anderson's notions of community (public sphere and imagined community, respectively), see Lee (1997).

11. My point here is that it was possible for the author and the reader at that time to socially imagine that women "spoke," "ordinarily spoke," or "should have spoken" in a particular gendered way. My view of the emergence of "women's language" is similar to Foucault's conception of the emergence of disciplinary power: "The [actual] automatic functioning of power, mechanical operation, is absolutely not the thesis of *Discipline and Punish*. Rather it is the idea, in the eighteenth century, that such a form of power is possible and desirable" (Foucault 1980:20)—that it could be socially imagined.

12. See Honda (1990) and Kawamura (1993) for recent social and cultural studies of *jogakusee*.

References

Anderson, Benedict (1983). *Imagined communities: Reflections on the origin and spread of nationalism*. London: Verso.

Bakhtin, Mikhail (1981). *The dialogic imagination*. Austin: University of Texas Press.

Bauman, Richard, and Charles L. Briggs (1990). Poetics and performance as critical perspectives on language and social life. *Annual Review of Anthropology* 19: 59–88.

Bhabha, Homi K. (1990). *Nation and narration*. New York: Routledge.

Bourdieu, Pierre (1977). The economy of linguistic exchanges. *Social Science Information* 16(6): 645–668.

——— (1991). *Language and symbolic power*. Cambridge, MA: Harvard University Press.

Briggs, Charles L., and Richard Bauman (1992). Genre, intertextuality, and social power. *Journal of Linguistic Anthropology* 2(2): 131–172.

Calhoun, Craig (1992). *Jurgen Habermas and the public sphere*. Cambridge, MA: MIT Press.

Chatterjee, Partha (1990). The nationalist resolution of the women's question. In K. Sangari and S. Vaid (eds.), *Recasting women in India: Essays in colonial history*, 233–253. New Brunswick, NJ: Rutgers University Press.

Foucault, Michel (1977). *Discipline and punish: The birth of the prison*. New York: Vintage Books.

——— (1980). *Power/knowledge*. New York: Pantheon Books.

——— (1982). The subject and power. In H. L. Dreyfus and P. Rabinow (eds.), *Michael Foucault, beyond structuralism and hermeneutics*, 208–226. Chicago: University of Chicago Press.

——— (1984). Nietzsche, genealogy, history. In P. Rabinow (ed.), *The Foucault reader*, 76–100. New York: Pantheon Books.

Fraser, Nancy (1990). Rethinking the public sphere: A contribution to the critique of actually existing democracy. *Social Test* 8-9(3-1): 56–80.

Gal, Susan (1989). Language and political economy. *Annual Review of Anthropology* 18: 345–367.

Habermas, Jurgen (1989). *The structural transformation of the public sphere: An inquiry into a category of bourgeois society*. Cambridge, MA: MIT Press.

Hanks, William F. (1989). Text and textuality. *Annual Review of Anthropology* 18: 95–127.

——— (1996). *Language & communicative practices*. Boulder, CO: Westview Press.

Honda, Masuko (1990). *Jogakusee no keefu (The geneology of jogakusee)*. Tokyo: Seidosha.

Ide, Risako, and Tomomi, Terada (1998). The historical origins of Japanese women's speech: From the secluded worlds of "court ladies" and "play ladies." *International Journal of Sociology of Language* 129: 139–156.

Ide, Sachiko (1994). Women's language in women's world. Paper presented at the Third Berkeley Women and Language Conference, University of California, Berkeley.

Inoue, Miyako (2002). Gender, language, and modernity: Toward an effective history of "Japanese women's language." *American Ethnologist* 29(2): 392–422.

Irvine, Judith T. (1989). When talk isn't cheap: Language and political economy. *American Ethnologist* 16(2): 248–267.

Ishikawa, Sadayuki (1972). Kindaigo no "teyo, dawa, noyo" ("Teyo, dawa, noyo" in modern Japanese). *Kaishaku* 18(10): 22–27.

Ivy, Marilyn (1995). *Discourses of the vanishing: Modernity, phantasm, Japan*. Chicago: University of Chicago Press.

Kawamura, Kunimitsu (1993). *Otome no inori: Kindai josee imeeji no tanjoo (The maiden's prayer: The birth of the image of modern women)*. Tokyo: Kinokuniya Shoten.

Kikuchi, Yuho (1971[1903]). *Chikyodai*. In S. Senuma (ed.), *Meiji katei shoosetsu shuu (Meiji family novel collection)*, vol. 93, 89–240. Tokyo: Chikuma Shobo.

Kikuzawa, Sueo (1929). Fujin no kotobano tokuchoo ni tsuite (On the characteristics of women's language). *Kokugo Kyooiku* 14(3): 66–75.

Kindaichi, Kyosuke (1942). *Zooho kokugo kenkyuu (A study of the national language, additional supplement)*. Tokyo: Yakumoshorin.

Komatsu, Hisao (1988). Tokyogo ni okeru danjosa no keesee: Shuujoshi o chuushin to shite (The form of gender differences in Tokyo dialect: Centering on the sentence-final particles). *Kokugo to Kokubungaku* 65: 94–106.

Komori, Yoichi (1988). *Kozoo to shiteno katari (Narrative as a structure)*. Tokyo: Shinyosha.
——— (1992). Buntai to aidentitii (Style and identity). *Gekkan Gengo* 21(10): 48–55.
Koyama, Shizuko (1991). *Ryoosai kenbo to yuu kihan (The norm of a good wife and wise mother)*. Tokyo: Keiso Shobo.
——— (1999). *Katee no seesee to josee no kokuminka (The creation of home and the nationalization of women)*. Tokyo: Keiso Shobo.
Lee, Benjamin (1997). *Talking heads*. Durham: Duke University Press.
Mani, Lata (1987). Contentious traditions: The debate on *sati* in colonial India. *Cultural Critique* 119–158.
Mashimo, Saburo (1969). *Fujingo no kenkyuu (The study of women's language)*. Tokyo: Tokyodo Shuppan.
Morino, Muneaki (1991). Joseigo no rekishi (The history of women's language). In H. Miyaji (ed.), *Nihongo no rekishi: Kooza nihongo to nihongo kyooiku (The history of Japanese: Series on the Japanese language and Japanese language education)*, vol. 10, 225–249. Tokyo: Meiji Shoin.
Muta, Kazue (1996). *Senryaku to shite no kazoku: Kindai nihon no kokumin kokka keesee to josee (Family as a strategy: The modern Japanese nation-state and women)*. Tokyo: Shinyosha.
Nagamine, Shigetoshi (1997). *Zasshi to dokusha no kindai (The modernity of magazines and their readers)*. Tokyo: Nihon editaa sukuuru shuppanbu.
Nolte, Sharon H., and Sally Ann Hastings (1991). The Meiji State's policy toward women, 1890–1910. In G. L. Gernstein (ed.), *Recreating Japanese women, 1600–1945*, 151–174. Berkeley: University of California Press.
Okano, Kyuin (1902). Hyoojungo ni tsuite (On standard language). *Gengogaku zasshi* 3(2): 32–40.
Ozaki, Koyo (1994[1888]). Hayarikotoba (Trendy language). In M. Oka (ed.), *Koyo zenshu (The complete collected works of Koyo)*, vol. 10, 4–5. Tokyo: Iwanami Shoten.
Sakai, Naoki (1992). *Voices of the past: The status of language in eighteenth-century Japanese discourse*. Ithaca, NY: Cornell University Press.
Sato, Haruo (1998[1941]). Shoosetsu (The novel). In T. Sakuragi (ed.), *Kokugo bunka kooza*, vol. 4, 71–98. Tokyo: Asahi Shimbunsha.
Schieffelin, Bambi B., Kathryn Ann Woolard, and Paul V. Kroskrity (1998). *Language ideologies: Practice and theory*. New York: Oxford University Press.
Scott, Joan Wallach (1996). After history? *Common Knowledge* 5(3): 9–26.
Silverstein, Michael (1979). Language structure and linguistic ideology. In P. R. Clyne, W. Hanks, and C. L. Hofbauer (eds.), *The elements: A parasession on linguistic units and levels*, 193–247. Chicago: Chicago Linguistic Society.
——— (1996). Indexical order and the dialectics of sociolinguistic life. In R. Ide, R. Parker, and Y. Sunaoshit (eds.), *SALSA: Proceedings of the Third annual Symposium about Language and Society—Austin*, vol. 36, *Texas Linguistic Forum*, 266–295. Austin: University of Texas, Department of Linguistics.
Silverstein, Michael, and Greb Urban (eds.) (1996). *Natural histories of discourse*. Chicago: University of Chicago Press.
Smith, Robert John, and Ella Lury Wiswell (1982). *The women of Suye Mura*. Chicago: University of Chicago Press.
Stoler, Ann Laura (1991). Carnal knowledge and imperial power: Gender, race, and morality in colonial Asia. In M. di Leonardo (ed.), *Gender at the crossroads of knowledge: Feminist anthropology in the postmodern era*, 51–101. Berkeley: University of California Press.
Tamanoi, Mariko (1998). *Under the shadow of nationalism: Politics and poetics of rural Japanese women*. Honolulu: University of Hawaii Press.

Tsubouchi, Shoyo (1930). *Kaki no heta* (*The navel of persimmons*). Tokyo: Chuokoron.

Tsurumi, E. Patricia (1990). *Factory girls: Women in the thread mills of Meiji Japan*. Princeton, NJ: Princeton University Press.

Uchida, Roan (1984[1894]). Bungakusha to naru hoohoo (How to become a literary scholar). In T. Nomura (ed.), *Uchida Roan zenshuu, shohan* (*The complete collected works of Uchida Roan*), vol. 17, 175–299. Tokyo: Yumani Shobo.

Voloshinov, V. N. (1973). *Marxism and the philosophy of language*. New York: Seminar Press.

Warner, Michael (1990). *The letter of the republic: Publication and the public sphere in eighteenth-century America*. Cambridge, MA: Harvard University Press.

Woolard, Kathryn A., and Bambi B. Schieffelin (1994). Language ideology. *Annual Review of Anthropology* 23: 55–82.

4

RUMI WASHI

"Japanese Female Speech" and Language Policy in the World War II Era

Language evolves naturally over the course of human communication. However, certain aspects of language are molded artificially. France and Germany provide classic examples of the artificial modification of language: each, in the course of building a nation-state, established its own national tongue purified through the elimination of dialectal elements and foreign loanwords. A similar process began in Japan at the end of the nineteenth century, when developments in Germany and the rest of Europe were followed with interest. The state, specifically the Ministry of Education, launched a series of surveys to lay the groundwork for the establishment of a standardized national language.

The form of modern "Japanese" employed principally by women is in some respects an artificial construct. One argument is that female education in the pre–World War II years produced and ingrained gender differences. Sugimoto asserts that from the 1890s to 1912 in the Meiji period "every effort went into making women more 'feminine', to a greater extent even than in the Edo Period (1603–1867), although women gained some social rights in the Meiji Period. The acquisition of a single predetermined feminine form of speech was relentlessly pursued as part of schooling"(1997:35).[1] He seems to be alluding to the instructional content of such school subjects as *Shuushin* 'Morals' and *Sahoo* 'Manners'.[2] This argument treats instruction in "female speech" as part and parcel of female education, the goal of which was restricted to providing training to women in their role as wives and mothers on the basis of the *ryoosai kembo shugi* 'ideology of a good wife and wise mother'.[3] Another view holds that the spread of "female speech" was accelerated by the teaching of Standard Japanese. In an interview with Usami Mayumi, Endo Orie remarks that the development of female speech "may be connected with the trend toward standardization of the language in the Showa era (1926–1989)" (1997:70–71). The contention here is that, during the war-racked Showa period, beginning in the 1920s, so-called national-language classes started to provide more direct instruction in Standard Japanese, including female-oriented forms of speech. Both views assert that language policy played a role in the development of "female speech" through education. Or, to change perspective, girls were trained by the state to use "female speech," that is, the norms of the Japanese language for women.

This chapter explores the relationship between the establishment of norms of language for women and language policy by considering how those norms were fostered through education. Specifically, it traces the formulation and propagation of *Reehoo yookoo 'Essentials of etiquette'*, a set of guidelines on instruction in good manners compiled by the Ministry of Education in 1941, and examines the collaborative relationship that emerged between female educators and the Kokugo Kyookai 'National Language Association' (NLA), which campaigned for language policy during the years in question. My investigation covers the period from the 1920s to 1945, years during which "the attempt to standardize" the language for women was especially intense. Furthermore, during this period the Emperor Showa was inaugurated and the Japanese government embarked on a total war for the first time and lost. As we shall see, World War II's character as an all-out conflict was one of the primary factors that motivated the establishment of a new curriculum in etiquette and prompted the emergence of a cooperative relationship between the NLA and female educators.

In this chapter, the terms "Japanese" and "national language" both denote what is now referred to as *kyootsuugo* 'common language', which is based on a Tokyo dialect[4] spoken by middle-class people.[5] I have excluded channels used to educate women whose native tongue was not Japanese, such as women in the Korean peninsula, then a Japanese colony.

4.1. Language policy

4.1.1. Definition

Language planning is defined as an attempt by a group or individual to solve a problem relating to the use of language with a specific objective in mind. The entity doing the planning need not necessarily be the state (Kaplan & Baldauf 1997:3–4). Language planning typically assumes concrete shape in several stages: survey work, a survey report, establishment of policy, formulation of a plan of action, and implementation (Kaplan & Baldauf 1997:106). However, in order for a problem to be regarded as such, some type of ideal model must already exist in the mind of the planners. Therefore, it would be wise to assume that a provisional policy is postulated before the survey work even begins.

In Japan, the state first embarked on language planning at the beginning of the twentieth century. In 1903, the *Kokugo Choosa Iinkai* 'National Language Research Council' was established under the Meiji government. The following definition of language policy appears in the *Kokugogaku jiten 'Dictionary of Japanese language studies'* (Kokugo Gakkai 1955), the first compilation of the cumulative results of research by the Kokugo Gakkai 'Society for the Study of Japanese Language' to be offered to the public after World War II. The writer is Ishiguro Yoshimi, who was also a member of the NLA.

> [Language planning is a] method whereby a government or other public agency attempts to reform, rationalize and improve, or propagate language with a particular intention . . . In formulating language policy, an organization may be established in order to carry out research, engage in deliberations, and oversee implementation. . . . The policies established are implemented in the form of legislation or through education, newspapers, radio, and so forth. (Ishiguro 1955:331–332)

Language planning strategies at the national level were not essentially different from those of today.

4.1.2. Language policy for women

As Ishiguro (1955) observes, the language policy that the state disseminates through education and the media is generally the end result of state-sponsored surveys and policy deliberations. However, in the case of "female speech," no single public institution dedicated itself to the task of establishing and propagating norms. The Ministry of Education was directly involved in the Kokugo Shingi-kai 'Council for National Language', which played a role in language policy and in education. During the period in question, linguistic gender differences and "female speech" fell beyond its purview. However, the 1930s witnessed mounting criticism of the form of language employed by women in such media sources as radio, newspapers, and magazines. The issue of what form of speech women should adopt came up repeatedly in debates among national-language scholars (e.g., Yoshida 1935), linguists (e.g., Shinmura 1938), and commentators (e.g., Hasegawa 1941). A consensus about the ideals and standards of national language for women emerged as the result of their criticisms of the language employed by women.[6] There were, therefore, multiple channels that prescribed ideals and standards for what form "female speech" should take, that selected specific grammar and vocabulary for it to employ, and that provided education about "female speech" usage, and these channels functioned together as a composite. The consensus was reflected in the classroom, and a propaganda campaign was launched to foster the spread of the new norms. The state, for its part, in taking over certain elements of this debate, incorporated standards of "female speech" into documents distributed to members of the public. One of these was *Reehoo yookoo*.

4.2. *Reehoo yookoo* 'Essentials of etiquette'

In April 1941, the Ministry of Education released *Reehoo yookoo*, which was originally a new textbook for secondary schools (boys' middle schools, girls' high schools, and technical schools).[7] This manual defined standards of *reegi-sahoo* 'etiquette and manners' for people of all classes as well as for those who were attending secondary schools. In section 5 on *Kotobazukai* 'language use', it explicitly prescribed gendered forms of standardized speech.

> 2. For the first person, *watakushi* 'I' should normally be used. In addressing a superior one may on occasion use one's surname or given name. Men may use *boku* 'I' when addressing a social equal, but not when addressing a superior.

> 3. For the second person, when addressing a superior one should use an honorific appropriate to rank. When addressing an equal one should normally use *anata* 'you'. Men may also use *kimi* 'you'. (Ministry of Education 1941:6)

Since this text was written not only for boys' middle schools or girls' high schools but also for the education of the nation, the exhortation that *watakushi* 'I' should normally be used applies to both women and men. These stipulations on first- and second-person usage came in the wake of criticisms in the media and by the Kokumin Seeshin Soodooin Chuuoo Renmee 'Central Federation for the General Mobilization of the National Spirit' that female students in Tokyo were using the terms *kimi* 'you' and *boku* 'I', which were considered proper only for men. (See the article "Onna wa onna-rashiku—keego o wasureru na 'Ladies should be ladylike—don't forget your honorifics'" in the Tokyo *Asahi Shimbun* August 8, 1938.)[8] The next month saw publication of *Reehoo yookoo kaisetsu 'Commentary on the essentials of etiquette'* (Reehoo Kenkyuu-kai 1941). This commentary prescribed in detail the speech style appropriate for women. As a matter of principle, it stated, "men should generally use masculine language, while women should use feminine language" (Reehoo Kenkyuu-kai 1941:65). In other words, both this commentary and Kokumin Seeshin Soodooin Chuuoo Renmee claimed that women should use more polite and humbler expressions than men. The state was not attempting merely to control language usage. The government's aim, it is clear, was to reinforce hierarchical social relations and gender roles by regulating language. That is plain from a proposal—to be discussed later—made at the Kyooiku Shingikai 'Education Council' by Tokugawa Yoshichika, who oversaw the compilation of *Reehoo yookoo*, and from the state's overall policy of strengthening hierarchical social relations under the emperor in preparation for total war.

The concept of *Reehoo yookoo* became embodied when a proposal for the spread of etiquette was made in the Education Council by Tokugawa, a marquess and a member of the House of Peers, who had also chaired the Etiquette Research Association. The Education Council was formed in 1937 by the cabinet of Prime Minister Konoe Fumimaro for the purpose of reorganization of educational policy, as he was trying to establish a general national mobilization in order to win the war. Tokugawa's speech to the third general meeting of the Education Council held in January 1938 asserted that reform in education had to be reform in the inculcation of the national spirit. However, only the general mobilization of the nation's spirit was appealed to, and no concrete plan was made. One concrete way of putting this appeal into practice was to propagate etiquette throughout Japan. In order to correct the spirit, it was held to be important to propagate certain aspects of etiquette, such as being dutiful to parents or being faithful to masters, that can be learned in the family (Ishikawa

1957:545–549). Tokugawa considered etiquette the expression of spirit, made it a goal to have the nation behave as instructed, and proposed control over the Japanese nation by establishing a comprehensive social hierarchy and clear sex role distinctions. The Ministry of Education carried out this plan.

Propaganda for the spread of *Reehoo* was widely disseminated. According to *Shoseki nenkan Shoowa 17 nen ban 'Books almanac, 1942 edition'*, during a single year—1941—six publishers produced *Reehoo yookoo* as well as 13 types of explanatory commentaries (Kyodo 1942). Women's magazines gave extra space to special feature articles on this manual, and interpretive articles appeared serially in the newspapers. Tokugawa and other members of the committee spoke on nationwide radio broadcasts.

Nonetheless, it should be noted that in reality a small percentage of the female population of Japanese were directly taught "female speech" on the basis of *Reehoo yookoo*, because in the 1940s people who could speak Standard Japanese were in the minority (Kokuritsu Kokugo Kenkyuujo 1951). Also, the instruction in "female speech" that was offered at educational institutions at the secondary level and above on the basis of this textbook was directed exclusively at girls of elite background, because in 1941 the number of students enrolled in secondary educational institutions, both young women and young men, was equivalent only to about 20% of the number of pupils who were attending primary school.[9]

Reehoo yookoo, however, appears to have exercised considerable influence on the teenagers of the day—the generation that formed the backbone of postwar Japanese society. This is a fact that previous research (e.g., Sugimoto 1997) has almost completely overlooked.

I now turn to a detailed investigation of one official (or semiofficial) body and its role in mediating between state policy and women and in gaining the support of prominent women, including educators who taught *Reehoo yookoo*, for the implementation of a state language policy.

4.3. The NLA and female educators

4.3.1. The Kokugo Kyookai 'National Language Association'

The NLA was founded in 1930 with the goal of supporting the language policies of the Ministry of Education. According to article 2 of the "Regulations of the National Language Association," the NLA's objective was to "strive for the rationalization and improvement of the national language and lovingly preserve it" (Kokugo Kyookai 1937:back cover). The NLA's activities are described thus in article 3: "In pursuit of this objective, [the NLA] will conduct research, organize various types of meetings, publish magazines and books, and undertake other suitable endeavors" (Kokugo Kyookai 1937:back cover). The NLA was thus devoted expressly to implementing language policy. Articles 4 and 17 stipulated that the association's expenses were to be defrayed from membership fees, donations, business revenue, and so forth. Superficially, then, it had the trappings of an economically independent private body. However, in a Ministry of Education directive dated November 7, 1945, immediately after the war, the NLA is described as an external organ of the Ministry of Education (Ministry of Education 1980). Its president was Konoe Fumimaro, who became prime minister in the year of its establishment. The vice president was Minami Hiroshi, then head of the Council for National Language. One of the members of the board, Hoshina Koichi, likewise belonged to the Council for National Language. In reality, therefore, the NLA would more accurately be described as an extension of government that lay halfway between the Ministry of Education and the public and put language policy into practice while assimilating the sentiments of both the Ministry of Education and the public.

What vantage point did the NLA membership adopt in carrying out its programs? One leading figure in the association, Shimose Kentaro, an army physician with the rank of major general, wrote on the necessity of "improving the national language" in the NLA's monthly bulletin. Noting the abstruseness of the diction used in announcements by the military authorities and in speeches for the "general mobilization of the national spirit," Shimose declared the need for language that anybody could understand. As grounds for this contention, he cited "the fact that the vast majority of the [Japanese] people—85%—barely have a primary-school education, and so their reading abilities are quite rudimentary" (1937:1). The NLA's members believed that they, as intellectuals, had a mission to guide the semi-illiterate, poorly educated masses in what they themselves regarded as the right direction.

4.3.2. Establishment of the women's wing

In March 1939, the NLA commenced preparations for establishing a women's wing. Table 4.1 summarizes developments between the NLA's foundation and the inaugural ceremony of the women's wing, including changes in the course of the women's movement and government approaches to female educators and the movement's leaders.

The women's wing was established not in response to the wishes of female members but rather at the encouragement of the NLA's leaders. During the March meeting at which the preliminary arrangements were made, Minami, the association's vice president, remarked that he had extended the invitation "in order to request the understanding and obtain the cooperation of women in preserving and honoring the national language and with regard to the NLA's work" (Kokugo Kyookai 1939:49). Hoshina, who was on the board, spoke on the subject of women and language and emphasized the important role that women had to play in this area.

The launch of a women's wing by the NLA was of considerable significance. It suggests that the association had fallen into step with other ministries such as Finance and Welfare, which were increasingly encouraging women to participate in the nation's policies as the whole country mobilized for war. The fact that the organization of the wing and the recruitment of leading female members occurred in parallel leads to the same conclusion. The women who joined the association or were appointed coordinators were prominent figures who held official positions at the national level as committee members with the Central Federation for the General Mobilization of the National Spirit, for example, or as Ministry of Finance instructors. Ichikawa was the leader of the movement for women's suffrage. Ishimoto admired Margaret Sanger

TABLE 4.1 Evolution of the NLA

1937

June	The NLA is founded. General meeting.
July 7	War breaks out between Japan and China.
Sept. 28	The League of Japanese Women's Organizations is established through an amalgamation of leading women's groups, including Gauntlett Tsune's Japan Woman's Christian Temperance Union and Ichikawa Fusae's Fusen Kakutoku Doomee 'Alliance for Women's Suffrage'.
Oct.	The Kokumin Seeshin Soodooin Chuuoo Renmee 'Central Federation for the General Mobilization of the National Spirit' is launched. (Yoshioka Yayoi is appointed to the Central Federation council.)

1938

Aug. 5	Minister of Education Araki attends a roundtable discussion with the Central Federation for the General Mobilization of the National Spirit, during which he criticizes the speech of female students in Tokyo for "not being ladylike." He arouses a considerable response.

1939

March 2	Ichikawa Fusae, Gauntlett Tsune, Muraoka Hanako, and others are appointed "Ministry of Finance Women Instructors for the Encouragement of Savings."
March 14	A meeting is held to make arrangements for establishing the women's wing of the NLA. (In attendance: eleven women, including Yoshioka Yayoi, Inoue Hide, and Kiuchi Kyo, and seven men, including Minami, the vice president; Hoshina Koichi; and Ishiguro Yoshimi.)
March	Dan Michiko, Ishimoto Shizue, Ichikawa Fusae, and several other women join the association.
July 14	Inaugural ceremony of the women's wing of the NLA. Five coordinators are appointed for the women's wing, among them Inoue Hide and Otsuma Kotaka.
July	Inoue Hide, Kiuchi Kyo, and other elite female leaders join the association.

---

and promoted the movement for birth control. The NLA recruited an especially large number of female educators. Yoshioka was the founder of Tokyo Women's Medical University. Inoue was headmistress of Japan's Women's University, Kiuchi of an elementary school. Otsuma established Otsuma Women's University. Authors such as Muraoka also joined up, as did the singer Dan. As Kiuchi endeavored to improve the status of female teachers, many of the women who joined in the women's division of NLA were also involved in the movement for women's liberation and the equality of women and men. However, the NLA did not simply follow the lead of the government ministries. Aware of the role that mothers played in language education, it chose as members educators and authors capable of both teaching other women and serving as models for them. Female campaigners for the rights of working women like Yamakawa Kikue and Oku Mumeo did not join the organization even though they, too, advocated improving the status of women. The association, it can be conjectured, was not primarily concerned about members of the working class content to work outside the home; rather, through exemplars of the same sex it sought to drive home language policy among middle- and upper-class women who were dedicated to becoming mothers and aspired to the ideals both of *onnarashisa* 'femininity' and *ryoosai kembo* 'good wife and wise mother'.

The women's wing did not prove very active, perhaps because of the escalation of the war. It did, however, carry out studies of "household language." For example, at a meeting that was attended by the national-language expert Yoshida Sumio, author of *Fujin no kotoba 'Ladies' language'* (Yoshida 1935), Miyake Takuro, and Yoshioka Yayoi (Kokugo Kyookai 1941: 27), the discussants debated what term was appropriate for a husband to use when addressing his wife.

4.3.3. The ideal of "female speech"

The NLA, which was not overly enthusiastic about the question of "female speech," nevertheless increased its exposure in the mass media after establishing the women's wing, targeting educated middle-class women and propagating the ideal of "female speech." Before moving on to the question of the NLA's propagatoin of "female speech," however, let us examine the ideal of "female speech" itself.

The studies of "female speech" that started to appear in the late 1920s directed their attention primarily to the *yuujogo* 'courtesans' speech' of the Edo period (1603–1867) and the *nyooboo kotoba* 'court ladies' language' of the Muromachi period (fourteenth to sixteenth centuries). *Yuujogo* 'courtesans' speech' is the unique language spoken by *yuujo* in red-light districts where the houses kept young women who entertained men with singing, dancing, serving drinks, and providing sex. *Yuujogo* was adopted in Shimabara, the red-light district in Kyoto, and then spread to the Yoshiwara, its Edo (Tokyo) counterpart. Many *yuujo* were from poor families in towns or villages other than Kyoto or Edo. The distinctive characteristics of *yuujogo* were its unique first- and third-person pronouns and verb endings. In example (1), a represents Standard Japanese and b *yuujogo*.

(1) a. <u>*Watashi*</u> no   kimono wa   soko ni <u>*arimasu*</u>.
    b. <u>*Watchi*</u>   no   kimono wa   soko ni <u>*arinsu*</u>.
      I   GEN kimono TOP there LOC is

     'My kimono is there'.

Both of the preceding examples mean "my kimono is there," but in *yuujogo* the first-person pronoun is *watchi* instead of the more usual *watashi*. The end of the verb *arimasu* 'is' is changed to *n* from *ma*. The form *arinsu* 'is' is considered typical of *yuujogo*.

Nyooboo kotoba first appeared in fourteenth-century records.[10] It began to be used by court ladies, the daughters of noblemen who attended the emperor. The duties of court ladies included looking after the emperor and sometimes doing clerical work for court events. Some court ladies even gave birth to babies of emperors to provide successors. The main characteristics of *nyooboo kotoba* were the frequent use of honorific prefix *o-* with nouns and various neologistic formations that replaced nouns for many domestic items. In examples (2–4), b represents *nyooboo kotoba*.

(2)   Abbreviation
    a. *matsutake* 'matsutake mushroom'
    b. *matsu*

(3)   Adding *-moji* to the end of an abbreviation
    a. *tako* 'octopus or kite'
    b. *ta-moji*

(4)   Adding *-mono* 'thing' to descriptive words for things.
    a. *tofu* 'bean curd'
    b. *shiro-mono* 'white thing' (i.e., bean curd)

Some *nyooboo kotoba* such as *oishii* 'delicious' and *oden* 'Japanese stew' have become common words in modern Japanese.

Kikuzawa Sueo (1929) was the first scholar to consider "female speech" an object of national language research. He regarded *nyooboo kotoba* as the ideal of "female speech," describing it as courteous and "feminine." This was an ideology (i.e., a body of knowledge turned to a particular political purpose) of "female speech" rooted in language policy. In subsequent research, he went on to compare *nyooboo kotoba* with *yuujogo*, not only analyzing their grammar and vocabulary but also passing judgment on them. The former, he declared, exuded genuine feminine grace, while the latter possessed a "vulgar beauty" (Kikuzawa 1933:39). For example, *tamoji*, the *nyooboo kotoba* equivalent of *tako* 'octopus,' and *arinsu*, the *yuujogo* version of *arimasu* 'to be', elicited quite contrary appraisals, the grounds of which cannot be traced to the words themselves. His assessment merely reflects the stereotypes attached to the court ladies and courtesans who used the terms. Yet Kikuzawa's analysis was to be reiterated later by other national-language scholars, such as Yoshida (1935), who advanced the theory that the original characteristic of "female speech" was its elegance and that elegant "female speech" had originated in the language of court ladies. He emphasized that the language peculiar to women was created in the court and spread to the lower classes. His argument was that "female speech" was a symbol of both femininity and upper-class status, so that women in the lower classes should learn "female speech," too. In the context of Japan's emperor system, a discourse that held the language of court ladies to be the origin of "female speech" had the potential to serve as a tool in integrating women into the national culture and thus making them more likely to submit to the ultranationalistic program in wartime (Washi 2000).

4.3.4.   Propaganda for the ideal of "female speech" by the NLA members in mass media

The subject of "female speech" was taken up by various commentators in newspapers and magazines in the wake of the 1938 roundtable discussion between Education Minister Araki and the Central Federation for the General Mobilization of the National Spirit (see table 4.1). The majority of national-language scholars who dealt with the issue were the NLA members. As shown in table 4.2, many of their views

TABLE 4.2 Publications and commentaries on "female speech" by NLA members

1929

Jan.   Kikuzawa Sueo: Radio broadcast "Fujin kooza: Fujin no kotoba no tokuchoo ni tsuite" 'Course for ladies: On the characteristics of ladies' speech'.

March   Kikuzawa Sueo. "Fujin no kotoba no tokuchoo ni tsuite" 'On the characteristics of ladies' speech'. *Kokugo kyooiku 'National-language education'*.

1935

March   *Yoshida Sumio: Radio broadcast "Kotoba no kooza: Fujin no kotoba" 'Language course: Ladies' speech'.

May   *Yoshida Sumio. "Fujin no kotoba" 'Ladies' speech'. *Kotoba no kooza 2 'Course in language 2'*. Japan Broadcast Publishing.

Dec.   *Hoshina Koichi: Radio broadcast "Gendaigo kooza: Fujin no kotoba to kodomo no kotoba" 'Modern language course: Ladies' speech and children's speech'.

1936   *Hoshina Koichi. "Fujin no kotoba to kodomo no kotoba" 'Ladies' speech and children's speech'. In *Kokugo to nihon seeshin 'The national language and the Japanese spirit'*. Jitsugyoo no Nihon Sha.

1938

Nov.   "Kokugo kokuji mondai no kenkyuu" 'Studies on the question of the national language and national script', a series of occasional articles in *Fujo shimbun 'Ladies' news'*.

1939

Jan.   *Takakura Teru. "Josee to kokugo no mondai" 'Women and the national-language question'. *Fujo shimbun*.

July   The NLA launches its women's wing.

1940

Oct.   *Ishiguro Yoshimi begins a fifty-installment series titled "Kokugo no wadai" 'Topics in national language' in *Fujo shimbun*.

Dec.   *Ishiguro Yoshimi. "Kokugo no wadai 8: Josee no kotoba/10: Nyooboo kotoba" 'Topics in national language 8: Women's speech/10: Court ladies' language'. *Fujo shimbun*.

1941

Jan.   *Ishiguro Yoshimi. "Kokugo no wadai 13: Fujin to kotoba" 'Topics in national language 13: Women and language'. *Fujo shimbun*.

April   Ministry of Education. *Reehoo yookoo*.

Dec.   *Yanagi Yae. "Fujin no kotoba" 'Ladies' speech'. In *Kokugo bunka kooza 5: Kokugo seekatsu hen 'Course in national language culture 5: National language in life'*. Asahi Shimbun-sha.

1943

July   *Ishiguro Yoshimi. *Utukushii nihongo 'Beautiful Japanese'*. Kofukan. "Jogakusee no kotoba-zukai" 'Language use of female students'. *Shoojo no tomo 'Girls' companion'*.

Aug.   *Ishiguro Yoshimi. "Jogakusee no kotoba-zukai." *Shoojo no tomo*.

Sept.   *Ishiguro Yoshimi. "Jogakusee no kotoba-zukai". *Shoojo no tomo*. *Dan Michiko. *Josee to kotoba 'Women and language'*. Sakuragi Shobo.

Nov.   *Inoue Kiyoshi. *Josee no kotoba: Keego no tsukaikata 'Women's language: How to use honorifics'*. Bokutaku-sha.

Asterisks indicate NLA members.

appeared in the weekly *Fujo Shimbun 'Ladies' News'*, a publication for educated middle-class female readers. *Fujo Shimbun* for its part spotlighted the so-called question of national language and national script in the belief that this issue was of deep concern to women.

While Ishiguro was especially prolific, Hoshina, the announcer Yanagi, and Yoshida likewise produced discourses that enshrined *nyooboo kotoba* as the ideal of "female speech." Ishiguro's serialized column in *Fujo Shimbun* makes no mention of *yuujogo*, nor does Yoshida. Repeatedly the point was driven home that the origins of Japanese "female speech" lay in *nyooboo kotoba*. Although from about 1943 on, as paper shortages grew more serious, the publication of books required governmental approval (Kyodo Shuppan 1942), Dan and K. Inoue were still able to bring to press their work that promoted "female speech." This favorable treatment can be ascribed to the fact that, being NLA insiders, they wrote in accord with the state's policy of controlling women, as members of the Japanese nation, through language.

4.3.5.   Female educators and "female speech"

Finally, I consider the implications of the establishment of a collaborative relationship between women's leaders and the NLA's women's wing, a vehicle of official language policy. Why were female educators so prompt to respond to the rallying cry of this organization dedicated to honoring and improving the national language? Why did they adopt a cooperative stance by conducting studies of "household language" and recruiting new members? One reason is that their membership in the association was another instance of *yokusanka* 'collaboration with and absorption into the regime' (see Suzuki 1997), just like their decision to help the national war effort by merging the various existing women's movements into one or the assumption of official posts by female educators.

Another reason is that the higher educational institutions for girls run by NLA members pursued the same policy of instructing women to use feminine language. It was natural, then, that women's leaders cooperated with the vehicle of language policy. If anything, they appear to have regarded language as their own proper sphere of competence. "Female speech" was sometimes discussed in terms of the Edo period (1603–1867) concept of *fugen* 'ladies' speech', the ideal language to which women were supposed to aspire. The following are the words of Shimoda Jiro (1872–1938), who was active in female education in the Meiji period. "Women should display femininity in their speech and demeanor. They should be gentle and modest, not blunt like men. These constitute the qualities of *fugen* 'feminine speech' and *fuyoo*, [two] of the *shigyoo* 'four ways'" (Shimoda 1977[1904]:359). *Shigyoo* refers to the four doctrines of Confucianism. *Fuyoo* means the courteous behavior proper to women. Both *fuyoo* and *fugen* were used by Kaibara Ekken, a Confucian scholar of the seventeenth century. Kaibara employed *fugen* in the sense of 'words of obedience to men'. However, as the meaning of words changes with their context, the *fugen* that Shimoda used in the passage quoted earlier has a different significance from the *fugen* that Kaibara employed. Shimoda explains as follows: The duties of a woman are, first, to observe the code of morals incumbent on her sex; second, to be a good wife; and third, to be a wise mother. Fourth, she should undertake suitably feminine

employment: "People today, whether male or female, should not practice blind obedience" (Shimoda 1977[1904]: 358–359). *Ryoosai kembo shugi* 'the ideology of a
good wife and wise mother' was more than a mere vestige of feudalism (Koyama
1991; see note 3). It was a concept that aimed to achieve what might be termed "separate but equal" status for women—a concept that assimilated Western ideas of family (see Muta 1992). Female educators such as Yoshioka, Otsuma, and H. Inoue, the
founders of today's women's universities, emerged from educated middle-class circles
brought up in this tradition of *ryoosai kembo shugi*. Most of them collaborated with
the war effort, and most were readers of and contributors to *Fujo Shimbun*, which
molded educated middle-class female opinion.

But the ideal of "female speech" that these female educators upheld differed
slightly from that propounded by national language scholars, the viewpoints of *Reehoo
yookoo* and of the Central Federation for the General Mobilization of the National
Spirit. Otsuma, for whom use of language was a prime concern, wrote as follows.
(The term *beranmee kotoba* that appears in the quotation refers to the lower-class
speech of the Tokyo dialect, which Otsuma viewed as lacking in refinement.)

> Say there is a lady. Say she possesses the beauty of a flower, looking as one imag-
> ines Yang Guifei or Cleopatra to have been in days of yore. . . . What would it be
> like if that lady then opened her mouth and spoke in *beranmee kotoba*? Alas! her
> lovely countenance and arching brow would lose their luster; her very garb would
> appear a sham. Thus decorous language is more beautiful still than fair looks.
> (Otsuma 1929:1–2)

These words express pride in femininity as a human quality different from those possessed by men. In other words, Otsuma insisted here that "female speech" is an important tool for sexual charm in the same way as beautiful looks. However, as we have
seen in section 4.2, both the commentary of *Reehoo yookoo* and the Central Federation
for the General Mobilization of the National Spirit claimed that women should employ
more polite and humbler expressions than men. They did not instruct women to use
"female speech" to express their sexual charm. Nonetheless, both the female educators and upper- and middle-class women agreed that "female speech" expressed achievement of a higher status in society. National-language scholar Hoshina analyzed the
attitude of the educated middle-class women of the day as follows.

> In middle-class and higher society, a lady of breeding will generally use honorifics,
> that is, reverential language . . . While there may be no obstacle to her employing
> rough speech when addressing an inferior, that would be demeaning to her, and so
> she will naturally use refined, courteous language. (1936: 227–228)

The following instance supports Hoshina's analysis. Otsuma, principal of a girls' high
school, liked the farewell phrase *gokigenyoo* 'good-bye', which was employed by
members of the imperial families and the nobility, and made her students use it. For
them and their upper-class counterparts, "female speech" was a representation of
femininity, that is, sexual charm and social status.

Already highly regarded by women themselves, "female speech" was then af-
firmed as an element of the state's national language policy with scholarly backing

from national language research. Therein lies the significance: the establishment of a cooperative relationship between the state's language policy and women's leaders. As far as female students and educated middle-class women in Tokyo were concerned, we may surmise, the idea was implanted that their own speech was the standard to be followed (see chapter 5 of Washi 2003).

4.4. Conclusion

The objective of this chapter has been to demonstrate the existence of channels for educating women as an element of Japanese language policy. I have recounted the history of *Reehoo yookoo* in order to demonstrate that the Ministry of Education propagated gendered speech for women. This manual, released by the Ministry of Education in 1941, officially prescribed gendered forms of standardized speech for the first time. *Reehoo yookoo* was originally a new textbook of etiquette for second-ary schools, but the state propagated it as appropriate for all citizens regardless of class and especially directed it toward women through various forms of mass media. Girls were thereby instructed by the state to use "female speech." Second, I traced the activities of the NLA, which served as the organization of language policy, to demonstrate the fact that some educated women even cooperated actively with the NLA to promote "female speech." As we have seen, the NLA took advantage of women's media and female leaders to foster the idea of "preserving" the national language and to encourage the use of "female speech" among women. The estab-lishment of a cooperative relationship with language policy-making bodies was, for female leaders, part of a broader pattern of collaboration with the war effort. It also meant that education in language use pursued at higher institutions of learning for women was now officially recognized by the state as an element of language policy backed up by national language research.

As I pointed out earlier, in reality only a small percentage of the female popula-tion of Japanese was directly taught "female speech," which was simply Standard Japanese for women, because in the 1940s people who could speak Standard Japa-nese were in the minority. It was not until after the war that "female speech" gained widespread currency. Yet it is crucial to recognize that "female speech" is an artifi-cial construct serving state interests in an ideology of femininity, a construct that was developed largely as a state project during the war years but which was also strongly supported by elite women educated during this period.

Notes

I thank Professor Oso Mieko for her invaluable suggestions and help with my English. I also thank Suzui Junko and Naito Kikue for their kind help in its preparation.

1. All the translations from Japanese into English are mine.
2. *Shuushin* as a school subject is equivalent to religion in schools of some European countries. *Shuushin* was based on National Shintoism, one of the Japanese religions. *Sahoo* 'Manners' is equivalent to comportment, which was taught, for example, in convents in some

European countries. The Meiji government studied European manners and introduced some European elements into its nationalist project of *Sahoo* modernization.

3. Koyama (1991) examines the ideal of *ryoosai kembo* in detail. Here I restrict myself to a summary based on Koyama (1991) to assist in understanding the ideas of the female educators discussed later. The *ryoosai kembo* ideal of womanhood emerged at the end of the nineteenth century. It is neither peculiar to Japan nor a relic of Edo-period Confucianism. Rather, it is a modern concept designed to justify gender roles, one that evolved continuously right up to the period in question. *Ryoosai* means a "good wife" capable of doing housework and managing household affairs. Unlike in the Edo period, more was expected than mere obedience to one's husband. *Kembo* 'wise mother' refers to the qualities of mind needed to bring up children properly, child rearing being thought to be the woman's instinctive role. In the Edo period women were seen as stupid and inferior to men, and mothers in samurai households were not entrusted with the education of their children.

As Koyama (1991) points out, this view of womanhood was underpinned by the belief that women and men were polar opposites both physically and mentally. Given their different makeup, it was thought only natural that men should work outside the home while women took care of the housework and children. Furthermore, although in reality women were by no means equal to men, they were regarded as being so due to the complementary roles of the two sexes, and over the course of time educators came to extol the ideal of *onna rashisa* 'femininity' as the badge of womanhood. Shimoda Jiro, who came under the influence of Havelock Ellis during his studies abroad (see section 4.3.5, "Female educators and 'female speech'"), was among the first to advocate this view of gender differences. The ideal is thus a modern one that, if anything, resembles Victorian thinking on the issue.

During the years under examination this ideal of *ryoosai kembo* lay at the core of middle-school education for girls, which the Ministry of Education tailored very much to the middle class.

4. The Japanese government chose the dialect spoken in the capital to make a national language that would serve as a tool to integrate the nation. But the Japanese case was not a special one. For example, it is well known that Standard French is based on the dialect that upper-class people spoke in Ile-de-France, with Paris at its center (e.g., Jespersen 1925).

5. Both the denotation and connotation of the term *middle-class* before World War II are different from those at present in Japan. Before the war, people termed middle-class were not a majority of the population, as they are today, but were rather considered by the Japanese government to be leaders of society; therefore, before World War II, the term *middle-class* referred to wealthy upper-class people below the nobility and imperial families. (For a discussion of the nobility in Japan, see Lebra 1993.)

6. While a host of conflicting views arose on points of detail, it was agreed that standard spoken Japanese for women should be based on the language of cultured women of the middle and higher classes in Tokyo. Therefore, debate on "female speech" from the outset excluded distinctive female locutions in the regional dialects, except in special cases. It was restricted in scope—geographically, socially, and with respect to age and level of schooling—to the language of cultured adult women with at least a secondary education who dwelled in Tokyo and belonged to the middle class. See chapter 1 of Washi 2003.

7. Boys went to middle school for five years, while girls went to girls' high school for four years. The content of education in girls' high schools was different for some subjects from that in boys' middle schools and was easier.

8. The cabinet of Prime Minister Konoe launched Kokumin Seeshin Soodooin Undoo 'The General Mobilization of the National Spirit Movement' to prepare to prosecute total war in 1937. *Kokumin Seeshin* referred to the spirit of the nation, whose citizens would sacrifice themselves for the state regardless of class, sex, or age.

9. Secondary educational institutions for girls were girls' high schools, technical schools, and the like. In 1941, 5,119,638 girls and 5,248,241 boys attended elementary school, representing an enrollment rate of 99.73% and 99.70%, respectively (Nihon Tookee Kyookai 1988:213). In the same year, 454,423 girls were enrolled at girls' high schools and 364,486 boys were enrolled in middle school (Nihon Tookee Kyookai 1988:243).

10. *Nyooboo kotoba* was used not only by court ladies but also by the nobility, including men. *Nyooboo kotoba* is also known as *kuge kotoba* 'the nobility's language'. It seems reasonable to suppose that the name *kuge kotoba* represents the actual status of the jargon more properly than the name *nyooboo kotoba*.

References

Dan, Michiko (1943). *Josee to kotoba* (*Women and language*). Tokyo: Sakuragi Shobo.

Hasegawa, Nyozekan (1941). Kokugo to shakai seekatsu (National language and social life). In T. Sakuragi (ed.), *Kokugo bunka kooza 5: Kokugo seekatsu hen* (*Course in national language culture 5: National language in life*), 17–34. Tokyo: Asahi Shimbun-sha.

Hoshina, Koichi (1936). Fujin no kotoba to kodomo no kotoba (Ladies' speech and children's speech). In K. Hoshina (ed.), *Kokugo to nihon seeshin* (*National language and the Japanese spirit*), 227–228. Tokyo: Jitsugyoo no Nihon-sha.

Inoue, Kiyoshi (1943). *Josee no kotoba: Keego no tsukaikata* (*Women's language: How to use honorifics*). Tokyo: Bokutaku-sha.

Ishiguro, Yoshimi (1940–1941). Kokugo no wadai (Topics in national language). *Fujo shimbun* 2112: 13, 2114: 15, 2117: 25.

——— (1943a). *Utsukushii nihongo* (*Beautiful Japanese*). Tokyo: Kofukan.

——— (1943b). Jogakusee no kotoba-zukai (Language use of female students). *Shoojo no tomo* 36(7): 104–107, 36(8): 96–98, 36(9): 92–95.

——— (1955). Gengo seesaku (Language policy). In Kokugo Gakkai (The Society for the Study of Japanese Language) (ed.), *Kokugogaku jiten* (*Dictionary of the Japanese language studies*), 331–332. Tokyo: Tokyodo Shuppan.

Ishikawa, Ken (1957). *Kindai Nihon kyooiku seedoshi dai 14 kan* (*History of the educational system in modern Japan*), vol. 14. Tokyo: Dainippon Yuben-kai Kodansha.

Jespersen, Otto (1925). *Mankind, nation and individual from linguistic point of view*. London: Williams and Norgate.

Kaplan, Robert B., and Richard B. Baldauf Jr. (1997). *Language planning from practice to theory*. Clevedon, UK: Multilingual Matters.

Kikuzawa, Sueo (1929). Fujin no kotoba no tokuchoo ni tsuite (On the characteristics of women's language). *Kokugo Kyooiku* 14(3): 66–75.

——— (1933). *Kokugo kagaku kooza 3. Kokugogaku Kokugo isoo ron* (*Course in national language science 3: National-language studies: The phasic theory of national language*). Tokyo: Meiji Shoin.

Kokugo Kyookai (1937). Kokugo kyookai no kisoku (Regulations of the National Language Association). *Kokugo undoo* 1(1): back cover.

——— (1939). Kokugo kyookai ni fujinbu ga dekita (Women's wing established in the National Language Association). *Kokugo undoo* 3(9): 49.

——— (1941). Dai 5 kai kokugo kyookai sookai (Fifth general meeting of the National Language Association). *Kokugo undoo* 5(7): 27.

Kokuritsu Kokugo Kenkyuujo (National Language Research Institute) (1951). *Gengoseekatsu no jittai* (*Language survey in Shirakawa City and its neighboring rural district*). Tokyo: Shuei Shuppan.

Koyama, Shizuko (1991). *Ryoosai kenbo to yuu kihan* (*The norm of a good wife and wise mother*). Tokyo: Keiso Shobo.

Kyodo, Shuppan (1942). *Shoseki nenkan Showa 17 nen ban* (*Books almanac, edition of the 17th year of Showa*). Tokyo: Kyodo Shuppan.

Lebra, Takie Sugiyama (1993). *Above the clouds: Status culture of the modern Japanese nobility*. Berkeley: University of California Press.

Ministry of Education (1941). *Reehoo yookoo* (*Essentials of etiquette*). Tokyo: Noogyoo Tosho Kankoo-kai.

——— (ed.) (1980). *Shuusen kyooiku jimu shori teeyoo dai 1 shuu* (*Summary of educational administrative procedures at the end of the war*), vol. 1. Tokyo: Bunsendo Shuppan.

Muta, Kazue (1992). Senryaku to shite no onna: Meiji, Taisho no "onna no gensetsu" o megutte (Woman as strategy: On women's discourses in the Meiji and Taisho periods). *Shisoo* 812: 211–230.

Nihon Tookee Kyookai (Japan Statistical Association) (1988). *Nihon chooki tookee sooran dai 5 kan* (*Compendium of long-term statistics on Japan*), vol. 5. Tokyo: Japan Statistical Association.

Otsuma, Kotaka (1929). *Nichijoo jooshiki giree sahoo* (*Etiquette and manners as daily knowledge*). Tokyo: Okamura Shoten.

Reehoo Kenkyuu-kai (Etiquette Research Association) (1941). *Reehoo yookoo kaisetsu* (*Commentary on the essentials of etiquette*). Tokyo: Kokoku seenen kyooiku kyokai.

Shimoda, Jiro (1977[1904]). Joshi no kyooiku (Female education). In M. Tametomo (ed.), *Nihon fujin mondai shiryoo shuusee 4 kan. Kyooiku* (*Anthology of materials on women's issues in Japan*), vol. 4: *Education*, 359. Tokyo:Domesu Shuppan. [=1904, *Joshi no kyooiku* (*Female education*). Tokyo: Kinkodo.]

Shimose, Kentaro (1937). Atarashii kokugo ishiki e (Toward a new sense of national language). *Kokugo undoo* 1(5): 1.

Shinmura, Izuru (1938). Josee no kotoba (Women's speech). *Fujin no tomo* 32(9): 96–98.

Sugimoto, Tsutomu (1997). *Onna kotoba ima-mukashi* (*Women and language, now and then*). Tokyo: Yuzankaku.

Suzuki, Yuko (1997). *Shinban Feminizumu to sensoo: Fujin undooka no sensoo kyooryoku* (*New version feminism and war: The cooperation of women activists in the war effort*). Tokyo: Maruju-sha.

Takakura, Teru (1939). Josee to kokugo no mondai (Women and the national-language question). *Fujo shimbun* 20: 12.

Usami, Mayumi (1997). *Kotoba wa shakai o kaerareru* (*Language can change society*). Tokyo: Akashi Shoten.

Washi, Rumi (2000). *Nyooboo kotoba* no imisayoo: Tennoosee kaisoosee sekushuaritii (The political function of *nyooboo kotoba*: Symbolizing the imperial system, class consciousness, and sexuality). *Joseegaku Nenpoo* 21:18–35.

——— (2003). Jendaaka shita Nihongo: Keeseekatei oyobi shoochooteki imi to seejiteki kinoo (Gendered language in Japan: Its development, symbolic meaning, and political function). Unpublished Ph.D. dissertation, Graduate School of Nagoya University.

Yanagi, Yae (1941). Fujin no kotoba (Ladies' speech). In *Kokugo bunka kooza 5: Kokugo seekatsu hen* (*Course in national-language culture 5: National language in life*), 248–268. Tokyo: Asahi Shimbun-sha.

Yoshida, Sumio (1935). Fujin no kotoba (Ladies' speech). In *Kotoba no kooza 2* (*Course in language 2*), 145–156. Tokyo: Japan Broadcast Publishing.

5

WIM LUNSING
CLAIRE MAREE

Shifting Speakers

*Negotiating Reference in Relation
to Sexuality and Gender*

In what ways, if any, does a speaker's personal sense of gendered and sexualized self influence language use? What gender and sexuality norms police the borders of Japanese language use? How do speakers negotiate these borders? How can we attend to the particularities of Japanese language, gender, and sexuality paradigms while at the same time problematizing prejudices within the sociocultural realm? These issues form the entry points of our inquiry into the intertwining of language, gender, and sexuality in spoken Japanese.

Due to the widespread conflation of gender with sexuality, notions of gender-appropriate language simultaneously invoke notions of gender-appropriate sexuality. Consequently, socially conceptualized and shared norms of gender-appropriate language remain overwhelmingly heterosexist. These norms are, however, both shared and contested, overarching and contradictory. Research on gender and language thus far has produced an eclectic discourse, which both problematizes and solidifies notions of gendered language performance. Since the 1990s, research that contests the supposed intrinsic social link between gender and sexuality has increased. Collected volumes include Leap (1995), Harvey and Shalom (1997), and Livia and Hall (1997). Work on gender, sexuality, and language in Japanese includes Ogawa and [Shibamoto] Smith (1997), Maree (1997, 1998), and Vanbaelen (1998). Issues of linguistic gender performances in Japanese, however, remain to be unraveled from dominant discourses of compulsory heterosexuality intertwined with overt and covert cultural misogyny.

In order to build on the body of current literature, it is imperative to show how issues of gender and sexuality are entwined in the language use of Japanese speakers. At the same time, it is necessary to untangle gender norms from dominant heterosexist discourses of gender. In this chapter, which constitutes an exchange between two researchers of differing academic backgrounds and methodological approaches, we address these issues in our discussions of real Japanese spoken by lesbian and gay people. In section 5.1, we discuss the conflation of gender and sexuality and what strategies people may employ to confront this. Section 5.2 discusses uses and abuses of terminology for male homosexuality and issues of self referencing in relation to sexual activity, based on Lunsing's work with gay men, lesbians, and others in Japan. Discrepancies between various experiences of terminology and reference provide grounds for contesting heterosexist discourse as well as possibilities for self-assertion. Section 5.3 discusses the linguistic negotiation of self-reference by a lesbian, based on Maree's work with lesbians and gay men in Tokyo. Personal metadiscursive accounts of language use provide insights into the multiplicity of meanings indexed by everyday self-reference terms and into the negotiating strategies individual speakers employ in everyday interactions. Section 5.4 offers conclusions illustrating the extent to which prescription is never fully reflected in actual language use, where speakers' negotiation of gender and sexuality norms intersects with their individual sense of self and contextual/situational pressures.

5.1.   Disentangling the entwined

Sedgwick (1990) and Rubin (1993) have clearly demonstrated the need to disentangle theories of sexuality from those of gender. While this demarcation is necessary, it is simultaneously essential to emphasize the ways in which gender and sexuality inter-relate as social phenomena in the popular mind. The complex connection between sexuality and gender has been articulated both in Japanese gay and lesbian studies and in popular lesbian and gay writings. For example, Sunagawa (1999:145) argues against the idea of heterosexuality as an identity, claiming that few Japanese overtly or explicitly identify themselves as heterosexual. Instead, Japanese hetero-society pivots on strict gender norms and roles whereby women have romantic relationships and sex with men and vice versa. Thus, from a heterosexist viewpoint, men who love men and women who love women are in effect transgendered (Lunsing 2001b).

Although, as Butler (1993:238) suggests, "a non-causal and non-reductive connection between sexuality and gender is . . . crucial to maintain," gender is not the direct cause of sexuality and it cannot merely be reduced to sexuality. In fact, there is no natural relation between gender and sexuality other than the conflation in many people's minds, similar to the manner in which sex and gender are commonly conflated (Lunsing 2001a). Under compulsory heterosexism (to borrow Rich's 1980 term), both sex and gender are constructed as natural. This belief effectively obstructs understanding sex/gender as a naturalized social custom (Butler 1990). In the contemporary Japanese social context, with its widespread conflation of heterosexual desire with gender and its idealization of heterosexual romantic love, homosexuality is implicated as trivial and abnormal and is often greeted with the phrase *kimochiwarui* 'sickening'. Furthermore, *jooshiki* 'common sense'—a term Lunsing's lesbian, gay, straight, and other consultants used very often in dismay at what they were up against—deems heterosexual marriage the natural (*shizen na*) way to live and by implication denaturalizes relational possibilities other than heterosexuality (Lunsing 2001b). Homosexuality, thus, is regarded as *hentai*, alternately translated as 'perverse' (Frühstück 1997), 'obscene' (Pflugfelder 1999), and 'queer' (Lunsing 1997).

These issues have implications for the question of gendered language. Current research has documented wide-ranging synchronic and diachronic variation within women's speech styles in Japan, thereby contesting the notion of a monolithic women's language (*joseego/onna-kotoba*), and consequently the notion of a monolithic men's language (*danseego/otoko-kotoba*). For example, Abe (1993, chapter 11, this volume), Matsumoto (chapter 13, this volume), Miyazaki (chapter 14, this volume), Okamoto (1994), and Sunaoshi (chapter 10, this volume) document women's language use that diverges from normative usage. Similarly, Inoue (1994, chapter 3, this volume), Endo (1997), and Washi (chapter 4, this volume) discuss the historical construction of (normative) women's language. As Okamoto (1994:578) writes, "Japanese women's choice of speech styles is a complex process involving the simultaneous consideration of multiple social attributes associated with identity and relationships. Based on their understanding of themselves in specific relationships and contexts (Kondo 1990), Japanese women strategically choose particular speech styles to communicate desired pragmatic meanings and images of self."

As will be demonstrated in this chapter, the language use of lesbians and gay men is highly strategic. Since there are prevalent gendered and sexualized stereotypes of language use and other behavioral aspects that speakers must negotiate, lesbians and gay men may alternately choose to comply with the existing stereotypes of "masculine lesbians" and "effeminate gay men" or remain invisible as lesbian or gay to those who do not see past these stereotypes by adhering to more normatively feminine or masculine speaking patterns (Valentine 1997). It is necessary to have some understanding of this complicated process and its interrelationship with heterosexist gender norms when discussing issues of gender, sexuality, and language use in Japanese.

5.2. Gay male speech, sexual activity, and homophobia

This section investigates various aspects of gay male speech that are often the source of controversy within gay circles: meanings of words identifying gay men, effeminate speech, and self-reference terms. These aspects are discussed in relation to sexual activity and homophobia, based on data acquired by extended participant observation; in-depth interviews, most of which were audiotaped; group discussions; surveys; and vernacular written sources. Methodologies are discussed in detail in Lunsing (1999b, 2001a, 2001b).

5.2.1. Between *okama* and *gei*

In the Edo period (1603–1868), male homosexuality in Japan was characterized either by transgenderism, in which case the penetrated person possessed characteristics associated with the female gender, or by transgenerationality, in which case the penetrated person possessed youthful characteristics (Furukawa 1994, Pflugfelder

1999). The penetrated person yielded to the penetrating person, analogous to the structure of heterosexual relations, in which the woman was supposed to yield to the man's wishes. During this period, the term *okama*, a type of pot, came into use to refer to homosexual men and, more specifically, the penetrated person. The adult man was understood to have the option to penetrate either women or feminine or youthful men and hence stayed outside of the category of *okama*. The penetrated man was not expected to enjoy anal penetration per se, as it was supposed to be painful (Pflugfelder 1999:41–42). Therefore, ways of enticing the *okama* were necessary. The *okama* was, for instance, supposed to love the inserter enough to endure the pain. Power imbalance was another means to make the *okama* agree to insertion. Most important, however, was the *okama*'s financial reward for engaging in sex work.

The term *okama* is still one of the most popular terms to refer to a homosexual man, usually in a derogatory manner. The term is used to refer to an effeminate man who makes use of a language close to stereotyped women's speech. In 1971, one of the most vocal Japanese gay men of the twentieth century, Togo Ken, ran for the first time as a candidate for Parliament. Dressed in traditional *kimono* and wearing make up, as he usually does on festive occasions, he introduced himself to the media with the words: *Watashi wa okama no Togo Ken desu* 'I am Togo Ken, the *okama*'. By using the derogatory term *okama*[1] in self reference, Togo confronted his prejudiced audience, who view gay men as effeminate and interpret his clothing choice as transvestism—and him as thus somehow less worthy than other men. Most Japanese gay organizations, which originated in the 1980s, distanced themselves from Togo's strategy and instead started using borrowed English terms like *homo* (from 'homosexual') and the now most popular *gei* 'gay'. Instead of Togo's *watashi wa okama*, they say *boku wa gei*, whereby the use of the normatively masculine pronoun *boku* instead of the normatively feminine *watashi* also stresses masculinity. The explanation the gay activist group Occur gave for this trend is that *okama* and, to a lesser extent, *homo* are derogatory terms (Lunsing 1999a). It seems that the use of *gei* is propagated due to its relation and homophony with the English *gay* and the relatively positive implications it has in Anglo-American contexts. However, activists' choice of the term *gei* has its own flaws. *Gei* was, in the past, used by straight people interchangeably with the term *gei booi* 'gay boy', which was typically understood to refer to transvestite gay men whose transvestism was part of their occupational activities, be it as sex workers, as theatrical performers, or as singers, such as Miwa Akihiro.[2] *Nyuuhaafu* 'new half' is a newer term to refer to a similar transgendered category, and it is equally commonly confused with *gei* by straight people and others who have not sufficiently acquainted themselves with gay and new-half scenes in Japan. Male homosexuality is generally confused with transgenderism, as reflected in popular interpretations of reference terms.

Similarly, *gei baa* 'gay bar(s)' is a term that, to the general public, refers to bars where transvestites perform a type of transgender act to entertain a predominantly straight patronage. In gay circles, such bars are referred to as *kankoo baa* 'tourist bars', bars for straight people being tourists in the gay world; gay men refer to their own bars as *gei baa*. Gay patrons of *gei baa* overwhelmingly choose styles and clothes commonly regarded as masculine. For straight people *gei* is a male performance of femininity, which confirms their misperception of male homosexuality as transgendered.

At a performance in 1993 with the classically trained female singer Haruka Mari, the drag queen singer Shimoonu Fukayuki (Simone Deepsnow) explained to the mixed gay and straight audience that he was not a woman but a gay man. In this context, Fukayuki used the term *gei*. Only later in life did he come to use the term *okama*, which he had come to avoid after negative experiences in his youth. He wrote in a short essay on queer culture that by using the term *okama* he felt that he finally had overcome the self-oppressive feelings so common among gay men in Japan (Fukayuki 1996)—and elsewhere.

5.2.2.   *Onee kotoba* 'older sister speech'

Togo's self-introduction to the media *watashi wa okama* is an example of *onee kotoba* 'older sister speech', effeminate camp language used by gay men (and some lesbians; see section 5.3.1). In Japan (as elsewhere), young gay men making first contacts with other gay men tend to feel awkward about those who use *onee kotoba*, who are perceived as more queer than supposedly normal gay men. Projects aimed at a broader gay audience hardly use *onee kotoba* at all. An example is the Kamigata DJ Club tape project, in which a group of mostly gay men made, without resort to *onee kotoba*, cassette tapes that resembled radio programs on gay issues and sent them to gay men throughout Japan. In order to appeal to isolated gay men, common masculine speech is used in such contexts, as it is in most gay contexts. In many gay circles in Japan, *onee*-type men are scorned. Gay men often profess to prefer "real" men over effeminate ones, and speech style is a focus of contention. This concerns more than just words. Users of *onee kotoba* typically accompany their words with intonational contours and gestures that are also seen as effeminate. In addition, their clothing may be relatively flamboyant or they may wear women's clothes.

While some gay activists in Japan demand that gay men be depicted as just as masculine as any other men in order to counteract the effeminate stereotype, many gay men do not behave accordingly. This repeatedly leads to controversy, such as the one that followed the 1991 documentary film *Rasen no sobyoo* '*Rough sketch of a spiral*', used by Ogawa and [Shibamoto] Smith (1997) as the basis for their analysis of gay language. In the film, one of the gay partners assumes the woman's role, including the use of effeminate language, or *onee kotoba*. The other partner assumes the man's role and uses masculine language. Schoolteacher Hirano Hiroaki, who also appeared in the film, later wrote that he was very unhappy with yet another depiction of a gay relationship that mimics a stereotypical heterosexual one, wondering who had "murdered" the film (Hirano 1994). The depiction in the film was, however, an accurate rendering of the actual relationship of the two men.

Onee kotoba is not, moreover, simply effeminate speech. It often distinguishes itself from conventional female speech by its crudity, as in the following example: *Atashi ima karee kuttara geri da wa* 'If I ate curry now, I'd get diarrhea'. Here the topic itself is uncouth as is the verb *kuu* for eating, while the pronoun *atashi* and the ending *da wa* suggest femininity. The cruder-sounding term *okama*, instead of *gei*, is more likely to be used by those who employ *onee kotoba* than by those who do not.

Such crudity, often combined with sarcasm, can easily be misunderstood. Miwa Akihiro, as well as the gay twin television personalities Osugi and Piiko, who are not transvestites, use *onee kotoba*. Miwa once remarked that he had never experienced sex with women, followed by the remark: *"Watashi wa kiree"* 'I am clean' (quoted in Ueno 1991[1986]). This is a typical example of *onee kotoba*. Consultants say things like *Atashi wa kitanai* 'I am dirty' when they have had sexual intercourse with men and *Saikin no atashi wa kiree* 'Lately I have been clean' when they have had a period without sex. Within the Japanese feminist framework, Miwa's comment can be interpreted as misogynous, as Ueno Chizuko (1991[1986]) once did. However, it may also be seen as a typical example of *onee kotoba*. Making jokes about women, like Osugi and Piiko often do, is an integral part of *onee kotoba*, as is making jokes about almost anyone or anything available. Two lesbian consultants, who were also ardent feminists, said that they appreciated Osugi and Piiko's performance, even if it could be interpreted as misogynous. To them, it was of more importance that Osugi and Piiko ridiculed heterosexism.

Usage of *onee kotoba* is largely determined by environmental circumstances. One has to learn to employ it. Those who have learned it usually feel the need to employ it only in the right situations, which may not be easy, as noted by a consultant, who was horrified to find himself employing it at his office.

5.2.3. Self-referencing—between masculine and feminine

Self-referencing is an area of contest not only when people employ *onee kotoba*. As Miyazaki (chapter 14, this volume) observes, in popular understanding *watashi* 'I' is regarded as a feminine or perhaps neutral term for self-reference, but definitely not as masculine. In the earliest mainstream publication by a gay man in Japan's so-called gay boom of the early 1990s (Lunsing 1997), Fushimi Noriaki wrote that in his youth he had been ridiculed for using *watashi* (Fushimi 1991). It was not that he wanted to appear feminine but rather that he could not bring himself to use the masculine informal equivalent *boku*, a more common term for boys. Likewise, Hirano Hiroaki had the same problem with his inability to use the even more masculine *ore* (Hirano 1994). As first-person pronouns are normatively gendered in Japanese, uneasiness about self-reference is a common phenomenon, in particular among young gay men. This may be why, instead of *watashi*, *boku* became the most commonly used self-reference term in most gay activist circles in the 1980s (Lunsing 1999a), though many other gay men feel uncomfortable using *boku* and persist in calling themselves *watashi* or *atashi*, which is even more explicitly feminine. Fushimi reports that he eventually came to use *boku* but more recently has reverted to *watashi* or *atashi* in many cases and even uses the female name Noriko to refer to himself as part of a performance of femininity. While in his youth he felt compelled to overcome his emotional resistance to *boku*, later in life he adopted *watashi* again as part of a performance he deemed useful for his purposes. It appears that he came full circle and ended up reappraising his youthful emotions.

In 1999, one of us interviewed Shimoonu Fukayuki and we discussed, among other issues, his self-reference choices as a gay man who performs in drag. On stage,

Fukayuki refers to herself as *watashi*. During the interview, however, the interviewer spoke with her nonperforming male alter ego. In this situation, Fukayuki also used *watashi* and the more formal *watakushi* for self-reference. When asked whether he ever used *boku*, he replied that he often did in his daily life but that in the interview situation he felt that *watashi* was the correct term, being more deferential and polite than *boku*. Indeed, in many contexts both straight and gay men feel obliged to make use of *watashi* rather than *boku* for simple reasons of politeness or other contextual factors.

In the same period, the coauthor interviewed D. K. Uraji, who also performs as a drag queen. Uraji consistently referred to himself by the term *watashi*. He told me that he always does and that he has never seen himself as a boy or a man. In fact, he said that it was not until he reached the age of 18 that he was first confronted with the idea that he was a man. His mind wrapped up in fairy tales like "Snow White," Uraji had come to identify with the heroine and declared his love to a male classmate he saw as fitting the role of the hero. Uraji's classmate wrote a letter that said such a relationship could not be, because Uraji was a man. Totally shocked by this confrontation, Uraji entered a period of major depression, which lasted for about 10 years. He felt that his very existence was denied. It was not until he made contact with a group of drag queens that he found a way to live with himself.

In performing as a woman onstage in front of an audience, Uraji found a way to express his being. However, he said that when doing drag performances onstage he feels more masculine than at any other time. He maintains that in drag performance masculinity has to show through in order to make the performance interesting. It is the imperfection in his impersonation of a woman that makes it enjoyable to watch. In his daily life, however, he is less masculine. As he sees it, he performs various roles, that of a son to his parents and that of a hardly gendered illustrator in his occupational capacity. In public contexts, he usually passes for a woman. He has found love and lovers, most of whom are heterosexual men, thus fitting the type of hero he needs to complete his love fantasy. He prefers to avoid calling himself *gei*, because that does not fit Uraji. When talking of homosexuality in general, however, he uses the terms *okama* and *gei* interchangeably. When people are young, self-reference terms are usually chosen because of their feelings. Once confronted with reactions from their environments, they may develop strategies of employing varying terms for varying occasions.[3]

5.2.4. Speech and sexuality

The language use of gay men is often considered indicative of their preferred sexual activities, but this is not necessarily the case. Japanese gay men distinguish one another based on a number of qualities, of which age is a major one. When a gay man is discussing what type he feels attracted to, *toshishita* 'younger' and *toshiue* 'older' are often the first determinant. Another important dichotomy is that of *tachi* 'top' and *neko* 'bottom'. Though commonly used among gay men—and lesbians— these terms are not reliable as references to what sexual activities actually take place. A *neko* is supposedly sexually passive in the sense that he is the one who is penetrated by the *tachi*. In the Japanese heterosexist power structure this would mean that the *neko* is also the more feminine. The case of a younger man would be similar. In actual practice, however, individual sexual attraction precedes the question of whether someone is younger rather than older or bottom rather than top. In the words of a consultant: "If there is love (in this case, *koi*), then [these categories] matter little."

Indeed, while the general image of homosexual activity is that of anal penetration, in Japan this activity is only engaged in by a minority of gay men (e.g., Za Gei Henshuubu 1992, Lunsing 2001b: 284–285). Uraji does not like sex characterized by what he calls *pisuton undoo* 'piston motion', a common Japanese term for the up-and-down movement that characterizes anal (and vaginal) intercourse. He does not like penetrative sex at all. Many *okama* or *gei* who behave in a relatively more feminine manner do not. At the same time, Lunsing found quite a number of instances in which, contrary to the expectation based on heterosexist patterns, the one who employed *onee kotoba* actually became the penetrator, be it oral or anal, during sex. There is no simple direct link between a gay man's use of language and his sexual activities. A *watashi* can be just as sexually aggressive as a *boku* or an *ore*, and the term *okama*, when used for self-reference, is no indication of the type of sex the speaker desires other than that it is with a man. Mainstream depictions of homosexuality may influence the language use of gay men, but such depictions have much less influence on their actual sexual activities.

Although the heterosexist language system leads toward a binary system within which one would expect gay men to divide into active/masculine and passive/feminine categories, in fact such a division is not related in a direct manner to the use of language. How people perform in bars or other social contexts does not predict what they do in bed. Furthermore, the historical discourses introduced earlier (section 5.2.1) must be approached cautiously. They appear to be largely informed by heterosexist discourses in which power relations are supposed to be evident. Much of these discourses can simply be regarded as prejudice, prejudice that remains largely intact today.

It seems that those who have changed their language use and come to refer to themselves by the term *okama* feel a self-confidence that helps them find their place in Japanese society and that homophobia is found more in those who avoid the use of *okama*, which does not mean that those who use *gei* or *homo* are necessarily always more homophobic or ill at ease with their sexuality. Similarly, gay men who use *watashi* in peer or gay contexts without feeling awkward may in some cases be more likely to have come to grips with their sexuality than those who use *boku* or *ore*. By using *okama*, *(w)atashi*, or *onee kotoba*, gay men may identify with a culturally deeply entrenched construction of homosexuality and thereby confront its inherent prejudices, rather than avoid them. Among the many people Lunsing has spoken with, those who used *ore* in gay or peer contexts tended to be young and often did not regard themselves as gay. Typically, they also had a strong dislike of people who employed *onee kotoba*. Nevertheless, the words people use cannot be taken as simple indications of their feelings toward their sexuality. Much depends on the individual case.

5.3. Negotiating compulsory heterosexist gender and language: A lesbian's personal history of discourse

The preceding discussion points to the diversity of gay men's relationships to language and to the fact that language use in itself is not indicative of individual sexual activity or vice versa. This section focuses on the speech of women who identify as lesbian and who, in a continuous process of shifting identification with same-sex sexuality, negotiate the terrain of heterosexist gendered language norms. Derived from a study of linguistic negotiative strategies employed by Japanese speakers (Maree 2002a), the data (in which Maree occupies the position of both researcher and participant) comprise two hours of conversation among seven speakers in a roundtable discussion about "language and sexuality" convened by the researcher, an informal dinner conversation that followed the roundtable discussion, and follow-up interviews.[4] In focusing on lesbian-identified language users, the aim is not to demonstrate their supposed uniqueness, or deviation from the norm, but to indicate how all speakers of Japanese negotiate spoken communication and to trace the ways in which negotiation processes are remembered and repeated in the speech acts of all speakers.

The key to the following discussion is this very notion of negotiation (Maree 2002a,b). Japanese speakers, like all speakers, repeatedly and reflexively negotiate complex contexts in which they position and perform multiple identities. Speakers position their multiple identifications within interactive acts via an ongoing process of negotiation (see Bucholtz, Liang, and Sutton 1999 for further discussions of gendered self in discourse). The *term multiple identities* invokes the notion of a totality of multiplicity, which the speaker negotiates at every point of the speech act and in all speech situations. A speaker's negotiation of complex contexts is aided by her or his creative use of language. This creativity is founded in individual experiences of language and personal histories in which discourse can uncover speakers' conscious negotiation of coercive language norms. In particular, metadiscursive narrative, a speaker's talk of personal language experiences, offers insights into negotiation processes. Like other narratives, metadiscursive narratives both are born of and shape experiences, for, as speakers, "we come to know ourselves as we use narrative to apprehend experiences and navigate relationships with others" (Ochs & Capps 1996:21). In these narratives, speakers elaborate on and explain incidents and personal feelings that are pertinent to their understanding of language norms and attitudes toward them.

Narratives featured frequently in the aforementioned roundtable discussion, and the topic of self- reference was extensively discussed. The Japanese self-reference system is generally explained according to factors such as gender, age, region, the vertical social relationships and in-group/out-group relationships between interlocutors, the level of formality of the exchange, and so on.[5] These factors are said to influence choice of first-person pronouns and other self-reference terms. (In casual conversation it is common to refer to oneself not only using pronouns, e.g., *atashi*, *boku*, but also using kinship terms, e.g., *okaasan*, lit. 'mother'; occupational titles, e.g., *sensee*, lit. 'teacher'; or one's own name or nickname, e.g., Junko or Junchan.)

In short, self-reference terms in Japanese not only directly index the person who currently speaks but also simultaneously constitute elements of the social. (For a general overview of social deixis see, for example, Foley 1997.) It is no surprise that, when we focus on the entwining of gender and sexuality in Japanese, self-reference is highlighted as a linguistic strategy subject to continued (re)negotiation.

5.3.1.   The coercive force of *watashi*

Participants in the roundtable discussion each spoke of their individual language experiences. Of the participants, Sayuri, Oka, and Marina spoke in detail of their experiences with self-reference terms. Sayuri, a young woman who uses *onee kotoba* in her personal interactions with friends and with her partner, recounted shifts in her use of self-reference terms. In her teens, Sayuri accommodated her straight-identified girlfriend by making use of the normative masculine pronoun *boku* and avoiding normative feminine forms. However, when Sayuri formed a relationship with a lesbian-identified woman, she avoided using *boku* and switched to using the more stereotypically feminine form *watashi*. Oka, Sayuri's partner at the time of this research, also spoke extensively of her use of *onee kotoba*. Oka, who describes herself as not being overtly feminine,[6] prefers to use the more informal *atashi* because in doing so she can let people know that she is a "woman/female" (*atashi o tsukau to yatto mina-san ni atashi wa onna da to yuu koto o wakatte moraeru no ka na to ka omou* 'by using *atashi* I think I can probably kind of finally let everyone know that I am a woman/female'). For both Oka and Sayuri *onee kotoba* is not a reproduction of conventional feminine speech but a parody of stereotypical femininity that counteracts the stereotype of the butch lesbian and at the same time constitutes affinity with gay male friends (Maree 2002b). In this context, Oka's and Sayuri's metadiscursive explanations of their self-reference choices illustrate the complex relationship between the speaker's image of self, the gendered norms of the self-reference system, and cultural expectations. In what follows, we focus on the self-referencing strategies of Marina, who spoke in considerable detail of her memories of childhood language use, and investigate her negotiation of heterosexist language norms. Marina's metadiscursive narratives clearly show the layers of meanings speakers traverse in real-life interactions. Self-reference choice is not the result of a speaker's gender identification but a reflexive negotiative strategy.

As she explains in the roundtable discussion, Marina refers to herself as *Marina* and does not use first-person pronouns. Although she says she does use the so-called masculine pronouns *ore*, *boku*, and *washi* when she is joking with intimates, she is particularly careful to avoid using the so-called feminine pronouns *watashi* and *atashi*. She explains that she constantly struggled to overcome the gender expectations held by her parents and recounts unpleasant experiences with first-person pronouns from early childhood. In the narrative in example (1), she recalls her experiences of being reprimanded for using the boyish pronoun *boku*.

(1)   Marina's experiences of *boku*[7]
    1 M: ... *ue ni futari no, ani ga iru desho? soosu to mazu, see nanka*
    2   *wakaranai toshi kara, mazu kotoba o oboeru ja nai? sosu to anikitachi*

3   *ga sa, boku da no boku da no ttsu tte itte, de issho ni natte asonderu wake*
4   *dakara, sore ga kotoba ga chan to hanaseru yoo ni natta toki ni (a daijoobu*
5   *yo), boku mo- to ka tte mazu yuu ja nai? boku mo boku mo to ka,boku mo-*
6   *to ka itta toki ni (bashitto kita) (3) sono-, boku ja arimasen yo, watashi tte*
7   *iinasai tte iwareta toki ni, pokkaan to suru to ka ne,*

> . . . above me, two, I have two brothers right, so first of all, I mean you learn
> language before you have any understanding of sex/gender right, so my brothers
> would, OK, say *boku* this and *boku* that, and because I'm playing together with
> them [and] the thing was, when I could speak properly (oh, it's OK), I would say
> first *boku mo boku mo* [me too, me too] and like that, when I said *boku*, too, (it
> floored me) (3) when I was told like it isn't *boku*, say *watashi*, I was left stunned,
> with my mouth hanging wide open,

As Marina indicates here, she was required to modify her speech before she became
aware (or was made aware) of sex/gender itself (lines 1–2). She expresses her lack
of understanding and her surprise as a child by describing her reaction with the onomatopoeic *pokkaan to suru* 'to be left mouth wide open, to be shocked speechless'
(line 7). Later, when Marina is questioned on whether she has specific memories of
being reprimanded for using *boku*, she recounts an incident when she echoed her
brothers' use of it. Her reaction to this reprimand was one of total surprise: *moo
mawari no otonatachi to• ano anikitachi mo issho ni natte, dame tto ka iwarete,
pokkaan to shite* 'well, the surrounding adults and my brothers joined together, telling me no, I was shocked speechless'. In both instances in which she uses the phrase
pokkaan to suru, the extended vowel [a] and the geminated [k], which shape the mouth
into an expression of astonishment, emphasize Marina's expressions of inability to
understand demands to modify her speech. She estimates that she was still a young
child at the time: *yoochien e iku mae ka yoochien kurai* 'probably just before or after
I started kindergarten'.

A little further into the roundtable discussion, Marina recounts that she continued to refer to herself by her pet name Maachan upon entering preschool. While use
of a pet name (generally comprising the child's first name or part thereof and the
suffix *-chan*) is not unusual among young children, it is generally maintained that as
children enter school and experience group socialization their use of self-reference
terms alters from pet names to first-person pronouns (Ide 1990). Marina, however,
reports that she resisted the pressure adults placed on her to use particular pronouns.

Marina relates that her continued use of the pet name Maachan was met with
frequent warnings from other speakers. In fact, through laughter and repetition she
stresses that as she grew from a preschool to a primary-school-aged child, when she
continued to call for inclusion using the phrase *Maachan mo*, literally, 'Maachan,
too', she received warnings such as *moo iikagen ni shiro* and *iikagen ni shinasai*
'enough is enough, already'. The difference in style between the verb forms *shiro*
(stereotypically masculine) and *shinasai* (stereotypically feminine) in these phrases
indicates that multiple speakers warned Marina about her language use on multiple
occasions. The phrase *iikagen ni shiro/shinasai* and the adverb *moo* 'already' both
indicate that the act in question, in this instance childish talk and, by extension, the
refusal to speak in gender-appropriate ways, has persisted beyond the dictates of

common sense. Marina forges ahead (*gooin ni* 'stubbornly') with her use of *Maachan* even though she is aware of, or indeed in spite of, the response it provokes. The strength of confrontation Marina reports that she encountered is implied in the reiteration of warnings cited in her narrative and alerts us to the difficult terrains negotiated in language.

In situations of great contextual pressure to use *watashi*, Marina concedes, she used the form, however, gritting her teeth all the while. In example (2) she recalls one such ocasion when she was summoned to the teachers' room and punished. In a comparatively formal situation, in which an imbalance of power exists between reprimanding teacher and punished student, she reports that she temporarily ceased using *Maachan*.

(2) Relenting to *watashi*

   8 M: *gakkoo wa sasuga ni ne, moo shokuinshitsu ni itte shikarareru yoo na toki wa*
   9   *ne? watashi tte dooshite mo tsukawanakya ikenai toki ya, ha kuishibatte*
  10   *itteta n dakedo,*
  11 S: *(sonna ni iya datta no?)*
  12 M: *hontoo ni iya datta no,*
  13 S: *a soo?*
  14 M: *de ima wa ne, hontoo ni ne, heeki de, kore wa moo, ima wa ne, anoo, tsukaeru*
  15   *yoo ni natta no, [sore*
  16 S: *[moo itsu mo wa* Marina *da yo ne? ima wa,*
  17 M: *soo*

   8 M: well at school it was like you know, when I was called into the teachers' room
   9   and told off and stuff, at times when I just had to use *watashi*, I gritted my teeth
  10   and said it but,
  11 S: (you hated it that much?)
  12 M: I really hated it,
  13 S: really?
  14 M: well now you know, really, without hesitation, this is like, now you know,
  15   well, I've become able to use it, [it,
  16 S: [now you always use *Marina*, don't you? now
  17 M: right

Although she no longer uses the nickname Maachan, Marina repeatedly used the expression *Marina wa* 'as for Marina' in the roundtable discussion, the subsequent dinner, and the follow-up interview. In fact, the only time she used *watashi* was in her highly formulaic introduction at the beginning of the discussion session. Sayuri's interrupting comment (line 16) indicates that Marina's use of *Marina* is well known and accepted.

In this interaction, Marina at first says that she is now able to use the first-person pronoun *watashi* (lines 14–15). It is over 40 years since she first experienced discomfort with *watashi*. However, even though she can now articulate the word, she concedes she cannot collocate it with her real or honest opinions. In another utterance spotted with hesitancy, truncated phrases, rephrasing, and intrautterance verification seeking, Marina stresses that she definitely cannot use *watashi* when expressing her true self: *de mo sore de mo ne? yappari, anoo, jibun no chan to shita iken to yuu ka kan• ano nani? zenbu jibun dashitai toki ni wa watashi nante kotoba wa (zettai ni*) *dasenai* 'but you know even so? all the same, for my own real opinions and stuff, feel• what? when I want to express the real me I (definitely can't) use a word like *watashi*'. It is, therefore, impossible to dismiss Marina's refusal to use *watashi* as merely an aspect of a child's process of language socialization.

As example (3) indicates, to Marina, *watashi* is not merely a first-person pronoun; it is an expression of heterosexist femininity (line 20) and patriarchal space (line 22–24). Marina understands from experience that *watashi* produces and reproduces social relations anchored in heteropatriarchal norms. Rejecting these coercive norms entails rejecting the use of *watashi*. For Marina, to use *watashi* is to impose on herself, and to create through her personal discourse, a social self she can neither embrace nor control. Consequently, she selects alternative expressions of self.

(3)   Multiple meanings of *watashi*
   18 M: *tada,* [*Marina no ano jidai ni wa watashi to yuu kotoba ni wa,*
   19 C: [<@*hahahaha*@>
   20 M: [<*F hetero noF*>, *on• onna no,aa, soshite* (*prefecture name* [*where Marina grew up*])=
   21 C: [*un, un*
   23 M: =*to yuu* <*F hijoo ni kafuchoosee no tsuyoi F*> <@<*Hx*>@>,
   24 C: *un,*
   25 M: [*basho no,* [*imi ga subete komerarete te,*
   26 C: [*un,*   [*un, un,*
   27 M: *sono* <*F dono ichi F*> *ni mo zoku• zoku suru ki wa arimasen deshita to yuu*
   28   *koto de sa-,*

   18 M: but [still, in Marina's time the word *watashi,*
   19 C: [<@*hahahaha*@>
   20 M: [<F hetero F>, wo• women, um, and, <F the extremely patriarchal (prefecture name [where Marina grew up])
   21 C: [yeah, yeah
   20 M:
   21   grew up] F>=
   22 C: yeah,
   23 M: =<@<Hx>@>, [place, [contained all of those meanings
   24 C: [yeah, [ah-ha, ah-ha
   25 M: and I didn't want to be a pa• part of any of those categories,

In the preceding passage, Marina articulates her strong desire to pull away from outside pressure to conform to heteropatriarchal femininity. Her continued reiteration of nonpronominal self-reference is a relatively simple linguistic strategy. She does not want to be inadvertently implicated in heteropatriarchal femininity via use of *watashi*, so she negotiates her way around it. This is less a function of desire than of ability. In the follow-up interview, when asked how she responded to societal pressures to "speak more like a woman," Marina replies, "*Yarenai to yuu koto* <@*de norikoeta hahaha*@>" 'I surmounted it by not being able to do it'. By ridiculing it, the laughter that accompanied this utterance underscores her powerful denial of heterosexual femininity. It is not simply that Marina does not conform to society's expectations of feminine speech but that she cannot, and subsequently will not, implicate herself in traditional femininity.

Marina's negotiative stance is molded by situational context and interpersonal relationships. In the past, her negotiation of situational pressures such as teacher-student power relations resulted in her use of *watashi*. In such a situation, contextual pressure invokes dominant gender norms. This invocation does not signal Marina's subjugation to those norms and the temporary suspension of her agency but, as her account of gritting her teeth illustrates, manifests intentional linguistic negotiation. As contexts develop, speakers respond to complex interactions of self, interlocutor, formality, situation, and so on. Similarly, Marina's current usage of *watashi* in conversations with intimates indicates that, perhaps where there is no threat of being implicated in heterosexist femininity, she is able to negotiate parts of her speech to incorporate *watashi*. However, as her contradictory utterances imply, even though Marina now allows herself to use *watashi*, it seems clear that when discussing her true opinions she will avoid the term as much as possible.

Marina's metadiscursive narratives make it clear that the distaste she feels toward *watashi* is anchored in the coercive heteropatriarchal femininity posited by Japanese socioculture. At the same time, her narratives offer examples of situations where the nonthreat of heteropatriarchal femininity enables her to use *watashi*. Marina's current speech demonstrates the struggle between wider society's expectations of the feminine (= heterosexist femininity) and her desire to express herself as Marina. She negotiates the language terrain in front of her, her creative language use enabling her not to become bogged down in the restrictive norms that lie there.

As briefly discussed in the beginning of this section, Marina's negotiative self-referencing strategies are not shared by all the speakers who participated in the roundtable discussion, dinner conversation, and follow-up interviews. Although there is no space to examine them here, all the speakers employ self-referencing strategies that are reflexive choices anchored in their current image of self and continuing linguistic performance of gender and sexuality.

5.4.   Conclusion

Heterosexism in the Japanese language poses a problem for people who feel that they do not fit into this binary structure, lesbian and gay people foremost among them. They are confronted with surroundings that ask them to be either heterosexual women or heterosexual men. Given that homosexuality is understood effectively as an act of transgenderism within this heteronormative system, this means that they are continually forced, or at least pressured, to hide their sexual preference.[8] A way of subverting this pressure linguistically is to employ types of what is generally seen as transgendered language, for instance using *onee kotoba* in the case of gay men or using transgressive language, as in the case of Marina's persistent avoidance of *watashi* in self-reference.

People can master highly individuated language practices. Both Marina and Uraji as children used the self-reference term attributed to the other sex and both were shocked to be confronted with the fact that others did not see them as they saw themselves (in Uraji's case) or that adults prescribed self-reference use according to gender (in Marina's case). Marina employs various negotiative strategies to avoid using *watashi* unless in situations of great contextual normative pressure, while Uraji uses *watashi* and establishes himself as feminine in those contexts in which he wants to be seen as such. It appears that Uraji met with less resistance than Marina, which may be partly attributed to the fact that *watashi* is not exclusively feminine, whereas *boku* is perceived as clearly masculine (but see chapter 14, this volume). Furthermore, Marina's avoidance of pronouns clashes with sociocultural expectations for adult speakers to use pronouns rather than other reference terms (e.g., kinship terms or nicknames) in nonintimate situations. It may also be that transgressive males are perceived as less threatening than transgressive females.

Gender restrictions seek to normalize sexual relations between female and male and, as part of that project, to prescribe differences in language use for women and men. However, when we view the speech of real Japanese speakers, we witness the extent to which prescription is never fully reflected in actual language use. Speakers' negotiations of language prescription and gender/sexuality norms intersect with their sense of multiple selfhood and with contextual/situational pressures. This process results in creative uses of language that may exploit available sociolinguistic and cultural rules. In our discussion, we have focused on the intersections of gender and sexuality within a social environment that conflates the two. In conclusion, we emphasize how important it is to incorporate notions of negotiation and speakers' relationships with gender and sexuality norms, in future research.

Notes

We are sincerely thankful to all who collaborated in data collection and who have allowed their words to be used here. Their comments, observations, and support were invaluable.

1. Togo maintains, based solely on his own imagination, that the term *okama* stems from the Sanskrit *karma* and therefore is a beautiful term, which, again according to him, means "love."

2. Miwa Akihiro (born in 1935) made his debut as a singer in 1952 and had his first megahit, "Mekemeke," in 1957. Since then, he has remained active as a television personality (Miwa 1992).

3. The development of varying strategies for self- and other-reference is a dynamic process. For example, Uraji is referred to in the masculine here, because in the network of friends in which he is known to one of the authors, he does not pass for female nor make any effort to do so and is regarded as male, though obviously not a particularly masculine one. Here he is foremostly known as Uraji, the person, and neither his gender nor sex is the object of special scrutiny.

4. Although it is standard in sociolinguistic studies to provide detailed information about the interlocutors, this study problematizes the simplistic mapping of language to social identity, and therefore no such supporting data is offered. See Maree 2002a for a full discussion of this issue.

5. For scholarship that discusses self-reference and gender in Japanese see, for example, Ide (1990) and Kanamaru (1993).

6. In this section, Oka refers to herself as being frank (*atashi kekkoo sabasaba shitete* 'I'm quite frank'), as not having feminine characteristics (*joseeteki to iwareru yoo na yooso wa nai* 'don't have so-called feminine characteristics'), and as not being feminine internally/

mentally (*naimen* • *naimen ga sugoi joseeteki ja nai kara* 'because I'm internal-internally very not feminine').

7. Transcription conventions are: •: truncated word; [: simultaneous speech; =: latching; ?: rising intonation; .: falling intonation; ,: brief pause; -: extended sound or syllable; <@ @>: laughter; <Hx>: exhalation; <F F>: loudness; (): unintelligible or uncertain speech; (1): pause in seconds.

8. The term *preference* here keeps open the question of whether people choose their sexuality or not, as the word itself does not stipulate how the preference came about.

References

Abe, Hideko (1993). The speech of urban professional women. Unpublished Ph.D. dissertation, Arizona State University, Tempe.

Bucholtz, Mary, A. C. Liang, and Laurel A. Sutton (1999). *Reinventing identities: The gendered self in discourse*. Oxford: Oxford University Press.

Butler, Judith (1990). *Gender trouble: Feminism and the subversion of identity*. New York: Routledge.

——— (1993). *Bodies that matter: On the discursive limits of "sex."* New York: Routledge.

Endo, Orie (1997). *Onna no kotoba no bunkashi (A cultural history of Japanese women's language)*. Tokyo: Gakuyo Shobo.

Foley, William A. (1997). *Anthropological linguistics*. Oxford: Blackwell.

Frühstück, Sabine (1997). *Die Politik der Sexualwissenschaft: Zur Produktion des sexologischen Wissens in Japan 1908–1941 (The politics of sexology: On the production of sexological knowledge in Japan 1908–1941)*. Vienna: Universität Wien, Institut für Japanologie.

Fukayuki, Shimoonu (1996). [Untitled]. In Kuia Sutadiizu Henshuu Iinkai (ed.), *Kuia sutadiizu '96 (Queer studies 1996)*, 108–109. Tokyo: Nanatsumori Shokan.

Furukawa, Makoto (1994). Sekushuariti no henyoo: Kindai nihon ni okeru dooseeai o meguru mittsu no koodo (The changing nature of sexuality: The three codes framing homosexuality in modern Japan). *Nichibei Josei Jaanaru* 17: 29–55.

Fushimi, Noriaki (1991). *Puraibeeto gei raifu: Posuto renairon (Private gay life: Post love theory)*. Tokyo: Gakuyo Shobo.

Harvey, Keith, and Celia Shalom (eds.). (1997). *Language and desire: Encoding sex, romance and intimacy*. London: Routledge.

Hirano, Hiroaki (1994). *Anchi-heterosekushizumu (Anti-heterosexism)*. Tokyo: Pandora Books.

Ide, Sachiko (1990). Person references of Japanese and American children. In S. Ide and N. H. McGloin (eds.), *Aspects of Japanese women's language*, 43–62. Tokyo: Kuroshio.

Kanamaru, Fumi (1993). Ninshoo-daimeeshi, koshoo (Personal pronouns and address terms). In S. Ide (ed.), *Joseego no sekai (The world of women's language)*, 15–32. Tokyo: Meiji Shoin.

Kondo, Dorinne (1990). *Crafting selves: Power, gender, and discourse of identity in a Japanese workplace*. Chicago: University of Chicago Press.

Leap, William (ed.) (1995). Beyond the lavender lexicon: Authenticity, imagination, and appropriation in gay and lesbian languages. Buffalo: Gordon and Breach.

Livia, Anna, and Kira Hall (eds.) (1997). *Queerly phrased: Language, gender, and sexuality*. New York: Oxford University Press.

Lunsing, Wim (1997). "Gay boom" in Japan: Changing views of homosexuality? *Thamyris: Mythmaking from Past to Present* 4(2): 267–293.

——— (1999a). Japan: Finding its way? In B. Adam, J. W. Duyvendak, and A. Krouwel (eds.), *The global emergence of gay and lesbian politics: National imprints of a world-wide movement*, 293–325. Philadelphia: Temple University Press.

——— (1999b). Life on Mars: Love and sex in fieldwork on sexuality and gender in urban Japan. In F. Markowitz and M. Ashkenazi (eds.), *Sex, sexuality, and the anthropologist*, 175–195. Urbana: University of Illinois Press.

——— (2001a). Between margin and centre: Researching "non-standard" Japanese. *Copenhagen Journal of Asian Studies* 15: 81–113.

——— (2001b). *Beyond common sense: Sexuality and gender in contemporary Japan*. London: Kegan Paul.

Maree, Claire (1997). Jendaa shihyoo to jendaa no imisee no henka: Eega *Shinjuku Boys* ni okeru onabe no baai (Gender indexicality and semantic shifts in gendered meanings: The case of an *onabe* in the documentary film *Shinjuku Boys*). *Gendai Shisoo* 25(13): 263–278.

——— (1998). See no aru kotoba (Sexual words). *Gendai Shisoo* 26(10): 122–135.

——— (2002a). See(sa) no gengotai: Kotoba no kojinshi kara yomitoru "jendaa," "sekushuariti," "fukugoo-identiti" (The language ecology of gender: Personal narratives of "gender," "sexuality," "multiple identities"). In H. Ishida and Y. Komori (eds.), *Gengogaku to gengotai*, vol. 5: *Shakai no gengotai 'Linguistics and language style*, vol. 5, 117–135. Tokyo: Tokyo University Press.

——— (2002b). Nihongo to jendaa oyobi sekushuariti—negoshieshon—jibun ga jibun [atashi, boku, ore] de iru tame ni (Negotiation of Japanese language, sexuality, gender—maintaining "(my)self"). Unpublished Ph.D. dissertation, University of Tokyo.

Miwa, Akihiro (1992). *Murasaki no rirekisho (A purple curriculum vitae)*. Tokyo: Sui Shoboo.

Ochs, Elinor, and Lisa Capps (1996). Narrating the self. *Annual Review of Anthropology* 25: 19–43.

Ogawa, Naoko, and Janet S. Shibamoto Smith (1997). The gendering of the gay male sex class in Japan: A preliminary case study based on *Rasen no Sobyoo*. In A. Livia and K. Hall (eds.), *Queerly phrased: Language, gender, and sexuality*, 402–415. New York: Oxford University Press.

Okamoto, Shigeko (1994). "Gendered" speech styles and social identity among young Japanese women. In M. Bucholtz, A. C. Liang, L. A. Sutton, and C. Hines (eds.), *Cultural performances: Proceedings of the Third Berkeley Women and Language Conference*, 569–581. Berkeley: Berkeley Women and Language Group.

Pflugfelder, Gregory M. (1999). *Cartographies of desire: Male-male sexuality in Japanese discourse 1600–1950*. Berkeley: University of California Press.

Rich, Adrienne (1980). Compulsory heterosexuality and lesbian existence. *Signs: Journal of Women in Culture and Society* 5(4): 631–660.

Rubin, Gayle S. (1993). Thinking sex: Notes for a radical theory of the politics of sexuality. In H. Abelove, M. A. Barale, and D. M. Halperin (eds.), *The lesbian and gay studies reader*, 3–44. New York: Routledge.

Sedgwick, Eve Kosovsky (1990). *Epistemology of the closet*. Berkeley: University of California Press.

Sunagawa, Hideki (1999). Nihon no gei/rezubian sutadiizu (Japanese gay/lesbian studies). *Queer Japan* 1: 135–153.

Ueno, Chizuko (1991 [1986]). *Onna to yuu kairaku (The pleasure of womanhood)*. Tokyo: Gakuyo Shobo.

Valentine, James (1997). Skirting and suiting stereotypes: Representations of marginalised sexualities in Japan. *Theory, Culture and Society* 14(3): 57–85.

Vanbaelen, Ruth (1998). Dansee dooseeaisha no kotobazukai: Intabyuu no bunseki o chuushin ni (Language use of male homosexuals: From interviews). *Shakaigengokagaku Gakkai Dai 2kai Kenkyuukai Yookooshuu (Synopsis of Papers from the 2nd Meeting of The Japanese Association of Sociolinguistic Sciences, Kyoto University)*, 17–22. Tokyo: The Japanese Association of Sociolinguistic Sciences.

Za Gei Henshubu (1992). Daigokai Za Gei ankeeto (Fifth survey of The Gay). *Za Gei*, July: 42–52.

PART II

LINGUISTIC IDEOLOGIES
AND CULTURAL MODELS

6

JANET S. SHIBAMOTO SMITH

Language and Gender in
the (Hetero)Romance

"Reading" the Ideal Hero/ine through Lovers'
Dialogue in Japanese Romance Fiction

Romantic category fiction (love stories) provides a rich source of data about women's and men's romantic expressivity. Such texts offer cultural models of how heterosexual couples falling in love are represented as thinking and speaking about their feelings. This chapter centers around a linguistic analysis of the dialogue between female and male protagonists in a set of nine romances drawn from the three major subgenres of Japanese romance fiction.[1] The goal of this chapter is not to describe how real Japanese women and men act as they embark on the projects of courtship and seduction but to begin to understand what cultural models are available to at least some of them—that is, the largely female readership of romance novels—as they set about falling in love. This chapter, then, brings issues of emotionality and sexuality, specifically heterosexuality, into Japanese language and gender studies. Or, more properly, since it is not my intention to conflate either a particular "feminine" or "masculine" emotional condition or sexuality with gender, it brings these issues into juxtaposition with Japanese language and gender studies in ways that facilitate shifting the focus of our research from fixed gender identities to the role of language in producing gendered subject positions in particular activities through appeal to culturally grounded semiotic practice (as called for in a somewhat different context in Kulick 2000:272–273). The particular activity I address here is "falling in (true) love."

Examining how heterosexual desire and romantic love are communicated—or, to be more precise, how such feelings are *represented* as being communicated—is the goal of this chapter. In particular, I argue that Japanese readers of romance fiction respond to the "sounds" of true love as represented in the lovers' dialogue

([Shibamoto]Smith 1999, Shibamoto Smith & Occhi n.d.). I argue that the dialogue between the women and men encountered in the texts of my corpus constitutes a primary site for the expression of one aspect of gendered language politics. I further argue that the very gendered patterns in the spoken words of love in these novels can tell us a great deal about prospective lovers as they are depicted as attractive and attracted and about how they use language in dialogue with each other to convey their femininity or masculinity. One of the messages Japanese romances convey is where (in language) and how (by being maximally "feminine" or "masculine") to locate and enact attractiveness. This study, then, not only sheds a new light on how language ideologies play out in the cultural construction of "ideal" women and men engaged in an activity central to "doing" womanhood or manhood—heterosexual pair-bonding—but also contributes significantly to issues of Japanese language and gender through the investigation of the complex relationship of sex/gender/sexuality to language ideologies and representations of language practices in a heretofore unstudied context.

Along with other aspects of identity, "the formalisms of love and desire," that is, the frameworks for romance, are "instances of socially-mediated, institutionally regimented and regimenting, metapragmatic discourses . . . Whether implicitly or explicitly these discursive frames indicate how persons should calculate and calibrate the stakes, pleasures and risks" of being in the particular type of "formed space" called the heteroromance (Povinelli 1999:3). In examining Japanese category romance fiction for evidence of how women and men are held properly to engage in projects of courtship and seduction, I begin to uncover some of the normative standards being represented to which real women and men may make reference when they are in a true love relationship. To borrow further from Kulick, who writes rather more directly about desire, "being in love" is "signaled in culturally codified ways"; and the range of semiotic codes used to convey being in love are "recognizable as conveying desire"—or in the case of the present study, "being in love"—"because they are iterable signs that continually get recirculated in social life" (Kulick 2000:273).

6.1.   The data

I report here the results of a linguistic analysis of the dialogue between female and male protagonists in nine representative novels, three from each subcategory, from a corpus of novels that spans the three major subgenres of Japanese romance fiction published in the period 1980–1999. All novels in the corpus center around stories of heterosexual romance. The domestic romance field of Japanese mass literature is not as clearly divided from other popular genres as it is in North America (Mulhern 1989), and although a number of Harlequin-like romance series have been initiated since the 1979 introduction of Harlequin romance translations to Japan, none has succeeded in becoming a permanent part of the mass literature scene. Thus, the criteria for inclusion of novels in this category are adjusted slightly from those used by Radway (1984) in her study of American romance texts and readers. The status of the genre notwithstanding, writers of romance fiction are well known and very prolific; and *ren'ai shoosetsu* 'romance novels' have a history that stretches back to the early years of the Meiji period (1868–

1912; Noguchi 1987, Atsumi, Arimitsu, & Kobayashi 1991). Contemporary *ren'ai shoosetsu* fall into one of three subgenres: tales of blighted love (*hiren*), domestically produced romances with happy endings (*happii-endo*), and Western, Harlequin-style romances in Japanese translation. In previous research, I have looked primarily at the metaphoric models of "true love" and found some differences between domestically produced romances and translated Harlequin-type romances from the United States and England (Shibamoto Smith 1997, 1999, forthcoming).

In this chapter I instead begin to elucidate the verbal process of identifying an attractive prospective romantic partner and of presenting oneself as attractive. To this end, dialogue between the romancing pair is extracted from each text and analyzed for the presence of gendered language forms. Verbal interactions between the heroines and heroes of the novels in my study are traced from first meeting through the happy (or unhappy) end to their romance in order to examine gendered patterns in spoken words of love as they are inscribed in fictional form. I suggest, in fact, that one salient way Japanese heroines and heroes signal heterosexual attractiveness is through their verbal behaviors and that this stands in marked contrast to the Harlequin-style translations, where attractiveness is depicted in other ways. In particular, I submit that it is through the intensified use of privileged forms of verbal femininity, termed *joseego* 'women's language' by many linguists and disseminated as part of twentieth-century nationalist discourse (see chapter 3, this volume, chapter 4, this volume), and its much less fixed—but fairly well known—counterpart, "men's language," or *danseego* (Sturtz 2001, chapter 15, this volume), that this attractiveness is most clearly portrayed. *Joseego* establishes a complex of features stereotypically associated with women that stands in opposition to a complex of forms associated with men. That this normative understanding of Japanese female and male personhood excludes much of the citizenry of Japan is a point that many of the chapters in this volume make abundantly clear; that the terms *joseego* and *danseego* themselves may be part of that exclusionary project may be less clear, but to avoid the potential "taint" of these labels, I here refer to these complexes of features as "normative women's language" and "normative men's language," respectively. The elements of these gendered language norms/stereotypes examined in the romance text dialogues are outlined in subsequent sections. The following analysis links dialogue found in romance texts to gendered language use as indexical of normative femininity and masculinity and, hence, of heterosexual attractiveness.

6.1.1. Looking like a lover, Harlequin style

How, then, do the fictional women and men in my corpus of romances know that they are "the ones" for each other? In particular, how are their sexualities, their attractiveness, and their emotional appeal represented to the reader?

Radway (1984) describes ideal heroes and heroines for Western romances. The Harlequin-style hero is spectacularly masculine, sexually (hyper)experienced, reserved (or bad-tempered), and seemingly indifferent, but with some small feature that prefigures tenderness or softness, such as a love of animals or small children. A great deal is made of his masculine good looks, both on the book covers and in textual descriptions. In example (1), one hero of a Japanese Harlequin translation, Mitcheru

'Mitchell', is first encountered by Guen 'Gwen' as she sits dazed in her automobile after the two have collided on a narrow, winding mountain road.

(1)   *Dorodarake no kawa no buutsu ga me ni hairu. Hidoku ooki na ashi da. Sore wa kaaki-iro no zubon ni tsuzuite, hosoi kawa no beruto no ue ni wa buruu no furanneru no hiroi mune ga atta. Soshite sono ue ni wa, hiyake shita nodo no hifu to, chikarazuyoi ago. Teire no ii kuroi hige wa, hageshiku musubareta kuchibiru no sen o kakushite inai. . . . Tankisoo na hanasuji no ue de, tsuyoi hikari o tataeta me ga, Guen no shisen o toraeta. Sono mabuta no iro wa . . . soo, yuugure no hikari no naka de kirameku sekitan no katamari no yoo da. Sore mo, kyoo yama de mitsuketa yawarakai rekiseetan de wa naku, motto kooshitsu no muentan*

Muddy leather boots enter her line of vision. [On] very big feet. Following upon khaki pants, [and] above a narrow leather belt, appeared a broad blue-flannel [shirted] chest. Then, above that, a sunburned throat and a strong chin. A well-kept black beard [fails] to hide the line of tightly compressed lips. . . . Above a sharp nose, bespeaking a quick temper, flashing eyes captured Gwen's gaze. The color of the eyes . . . yes, [they] were like [the color of] lumps of coal glittering in the twilight. Not the soft bituminous coal that [she] had found today in the mountains, but the harder anthracite. (Browning/Nakagawa 1985/1987:8)

All heroes may be tall, but not all are dark; 31-year-old Chaaruzu 'Charles', the new CEO of a major urban department store, is blond and something of a tease. He is rich and powerful (*ooganemochi de kenryoku mo aru*), he dresses well (e.g., he wears expensive-looking [*kookasoo na*] suits and tasteful [*shumi (no) ii*] silk neck-ties), and his resolve to push forward (*tsukisusumu*) toward the achievement of his goals is a commanding aspect of his personality (*rippa na mono da*). Harlequin-style heroes have *munage* 'chest hair', which peeks out from unbuttoned shirts and the like, hard muscles (*hikishimatta kinniku*), narrow waists, nice hips, and, when the occasion arises, impressive [evidence(s) of] arousal (*takaburi* [*no shooko*]).

Radway also provides a characterization of the ideal Western heroine: she is unusually intelligent or unusually honest/moral/true or both; she may or may not have a fiery disposition but is generally given to impulsive but well-intentioned actions; she invariably has a childlike innocence and inexperience when it comes to love no matter how professional or sophisticated she is otherwise. Although she need not be virginal—she can, in fact, be a mother, like *Kasandora* 'Cassandra' in (2b)—she just cannot truly have enjoyed sex before encounters with her "true love." Above all, she is possessed of an extraordinary but unselfconscious beauty (see ex. 2). Although she may not start out this way, she will, by the end of each novel, dress pretty well, too, maybe even somewhat provocatively, although this is usually contrived to be accomplished without her agency.

(2a)   *Ooki na masshuruumu no yoo na booshi o kaburu to, Joojiina no haato-gata no kao wa odoroku hodo hikitatte mieta. Nagai kuri-iro no kami o booshi no naka ni takushikonde ita toki, genkan no beru ga natta. Nagai matsuge ni fuchidorareta Joojiina no tankasshoku no mabuta ni fuan no iro ga yogitta.*

'When she put on the large, mushroom-shaped hat, it brought out [the beauty of] Georgina's heart-shaped face to a surprising degree. As she tucked her long chestnut hair up into the hat, the doorbell rang. An uneasy look filled Georgina's light brown eyes framed by long lashes'. (Lawrence/Yamanouchi 1997/1998:5)

(2b) *Kinkasshoku no mabuta to ii, shikkoku no nagai kami to ii, masa ni uri futatsu da. Tada kaodachi wa to yuu to, Besanii no hoo wa kodomorashiku fukkura to shite i[ru] . . . Ippoo, Kasandora no hossori to shita kao ni tadayou no wa yuubi na otona no utsukushisa datta.*

'Whether it was their chestnut gold eyes or their long jet black hair, they were truly two peas in a pod. Only their faces [differed, with] Bethany (Cassandra's daughter) having the full face of a child. . . . For her part, Cassandra's delicate face had an elegant, adult beauty'. (Mortimer/Hirae 1993/1994:6)

True heroines, then, are marked by the unselfconscious, unaware possession of such attributes as heart-shaped faces (*haato-gata no kao*), long chestnut hair (*nagai kuri-iro no kami*) that flows down their backs like rivers of flame (*honoo no kawa no yoo ni*), and elegant (*yuubi na*) rather than showy (*hanayaka na*) beauty (*utsukushisa*), the latter being characteristic of "false loves." They also, it is generally revealed somewhat later in the texts, have long, slender legs, tiny waists, and perfectly shaped breasts, fleetingly visible through inadvertently opened blouse buttons or V-necked evening gowns.

6.1.2. Doesn't s/he sound loverly?

Japanese ideal heroines and heroes are a bit different from their Western counterparts; Japanese romances rarely have covers that depict the principal characters, and the text descriptions are by no means as detailed as in the Harlequin-style texts. Clothing is not, in my corpus, ever used as a tool of seduction, and no lovers' furtive glances at escaping chest hair or heaving breasts or quick but intoxicating looks at glimpses of beautiful long legs through the slits of skirts help our Japanese lovers know that they have found Ms. or Mr. Right.

Japanese heroes, when they are described, are generally depicted as more average than the Harlequin heroes; and, in fact, are often depicted as vulnerable in a variety of ways, making mistakes, errors of judgment—even, according to Mulhern (1989), more mistakes than the heroines. Certainly Japanese heroes sometimes are "special"; they are often rich, they may be tall or robust (e.g., possessing *supootsu de kitaeta ii taikaku* 'a good physique built up by sports'), and they may even seem arrogant or sardonic. But virtually all heroes, even the tall, rich ones, have a sense of humor; and most of them are just ordinary, nice men (ex. 3a), acting in relatively ordinary or even awkward ways (ex. 3b).

(3a) *Kushoo shita kao ga asaguroku, doko ka hitonatsukkoi kanji no suru seenen de aru.*

'His wryly smiling face was swarthy; he was a youth with an amiable look about him'. (Hiraiwa 1982:9)

(3b)   *Kare wa shashinka no donarigoe ni, tekipaki to ugoite iru. Totemo adaruto bideo o*
       otoshite atafuta shite ita otoko to dooitsu jinbutsu to wa omoenai.

       'He was moving briskly [in obedience to] the photographer's barked orders. It was
       totally hard to believe that this was the same man who got flustered over dropping an
       adult video'. (Yuikawa 1997:54–55)

Heroes are often characterized as *seenen* 'youth(s)', as in example (3a); they are
employees, as in (3b), as well as employers or independently wealthy men. Flattering
physical descriptions, while not absent from the domestic texts,[2] are generally much
abbreviated. And descriptions are often less than flattering. In example (3a), for example, the hero is described as "swarthy" as distinguished from "tanned"; this is not a
compliment (Ashikari 2000). Wealth, power, and social position are also not guaran-
teed our heroes, although there is a systematic glossing over of socioeconomic status.
Tooru, the young man in example (3b), who is described simply as *otoko* '[the] man'
for the first several chapters of his story, is a photographer's apprentice, photogra-
phy being an interest he turned to when his parents cut off support after he was "dismissed" from college after eight years. Other heroes range from company employees
(*sarariiman*) to company owners, with a fair sprinkling of artists and men from the
katakana shokugyoo kai 'world of Western/contemporary/"foreign" occupations'.[3]
None, however, match the Harlequin-style imports in their glorious physical specimens
of overtly sexual masculinity with money, position, and power to spare.

The Japanese heroine, too, as noted by Mulhern (1989) is neither socially isolated, as Western heroines often are, nor sexually repressed. She is generally self-
confident, as in example (4), often enjoys a career, and frequently has had (or takes
during the course of the romance) lovers other than her "true" love. And, most important to my argument here, she is not necessarily a great, sexually compelling
beauty, as in example (5). Japanese heroines' looks are no more often described than
are those of the heroes, and often in sketchy fashion. When heroines are described in
some detail (as in ex. 4b), they are as often described in terms of relatively realistic
self-evaluation, which suggests a more down-to-earth self-awareness on the part of
the Japanese heroine than is the norm for the Harlequin-style woman, with her shin-
ing beauty cloaked in a veritable fog of unselfconsciousness.

(4a)   *Yoofuku erabi wa, Chikako nari ni jishin o motte iru.*

       'When it came to choosing clothes, Chikako had her own self-confidence'. (Yuikawa
       1997:8)

(4b)   *Kagami no mae ni tatta. Ookiku wa nai ga, warenagara ii kakkoo da to omoeru chibusa,*
       uesuto wa shimatte iru shi, koshi mo maamaa marukute onnappoi. Jiipan ga niau kara
       to itte, soo suteta mon de mo nai to Sayaka wa moderu no yoo na poozu o totte mita.

       'She stood in front of the mirror. Not large, but nicely shaped breasts, even if she
       says so herself; a small waist, and her hips are passably round and womanly. Think-
       ing "Just because jeans suit me, I'm not so bad," Sayaka struck a model's pose'.
       (Hiraiwa 1982:43)

(5a) *Sore ni shite mo irokebusoku de aru koto wa inamenai.*

'Even so, [she/Sayaka] could not deny that she lacked sex appeal'. (Hiraiwa 1982:43)

(5b) *. . . bijin taipu de mo nai. . . . Dare mo ga kookan o motsu, atama no yosa o hikerakasanai, shitashimiyasui hodohodo no bijo. . . . Yuri wa, korera no jooken ni pittari atehamatte ita . . .*

'[She] wasn't a beauty. . . . [She was someone whom] everyone liked, a so-so beauty who didn't show off her intelligence and whom everyone found easy to be friends with. . . . Yuri fit these criteria perfectly'. (Hanai 1989:9)

But no matter that the ideal Japanese heroine is competent and socially fulfilled, she won't be a romance heroine unless she falls in love and is fallen in love with. She need not, readers may be relieved to know, be a great beauty; but to attract her man, she will have to participate in the heterosexual marketplace in ways that will signal her qualifications and her willingness to be partnered if she is, in the end, to be happily partnered—or, since one subgenre is the tragic love story, unhappily but "truly" partnered. In Harlequin-style translations, this signaling is accomplished for both women and men via a particular sexually compelling kind of physical beauty. Women are completely unaware of it, as described earlier. For men, such signaling involves rugged handsomeness, great wealth, and a superficial coldness that covers raging sexual desires. The domestic romance texts in my corpus do not contain signals of this sort. Heroines are much more likely to be characterized by *sunaosa*, that cheerful enthusiasm and unresisting participation in work or social activities described by Peak (1989) as sought after in preschool children in Japan, than they are by great beauty, and—truth be known—so are the heroes.

If the Japanese heroines and heroes of category romances are not glorious physical specimens of overtly sexual femininity and masculinity, if they are not lush, albeit unselfconscious and innocent, beauties and gorgeous men whose demeanor situates them just this side of the sexual predator, where *is* their femininity or masculinity being encoded? My preliminary survey of a small number of texts suggested that the signaling of a prospectively successful heterosexual attractiveness/attraction came less in the descriptions of the lovers than in the dialogue between them. One way Japanese heroines and heroes signal heterosexual attractiveness may be through their verbal behaviors—in particular, in their use of normative women's language (see Shibamoto Smith 2003 for discussion of normative women's language) and normative men's language (chapter 15, this volume).

6.1.3. Normative women's language/normative men's language

I examined several elements of normative women's language and normative men's language in the romance text dialogues. I report on two here: (1) first- and second-person pronominal and other self- or other-referring forms and (2) sentence-final particles.

Reference and address.   First- and second-person referring forms have been one of the centerpieces of the literature on language and gender in Japanese. Pronouns are the most often cited gendered forms. As is widely reported in the literature, normative usage in standard Japanese would have it that women and men share the formal first-person pronouns *watakushi* and *watashi*, although the contexts in which they are used by speakers of either sex differ (Ide 1979, Shibamoto 1985, Shibatani 1990, Shibamoto Smith 2003). In less formal contexts, male-speaker-associated first-person pronouns are *boku, ore, jibun*, and *washi*, the latter two of which are somewhat specialized (but see chapter 11, this volume); female-speaker-associated first-person pronouns are *atakushi, atashi*,[4] and *atai*, which last form we also will not encounter in my data. Table 6.1 summarizes these forms. It is crucial to the goal of this volume—intended as a demonstration that ideology plays an important shaping but also significantly constraining and exclusionary role in understanding the relationship of sex/gender to language practice—to stress that the following tables outline *normative* usage; data in chapters 5, 10, 11, and 14 all shows quite different usages.

Second-person pronouns are shown in table 6.2; women and men share the formal *anata* and the less formal, less "classy" *anta*. Men have two forms, *kimi* and *omae*, that are relatively to very informal or intimate, as well as two very aggressive or vulgar forms, *kisama* and *temee*. We should not expect to see any of these latter, since our guys are busy loving women, not fighting with other men.

There are also conventions for the ways wives and husbands address each other. Today most young couples call each other by their first names, without -*san*, or by nicknames until they have children; however, older conventions still seem to obtain to a reasonable degree in these novels, and these are shown in example (6). Since our lovers are not parents, we should not expect to see forms for 'mother' and 'father' in our corpus.

(6)   Husband → Wife   Wife → Husband
       first name   first name + *san*
       kimi   *otoosan* 'father'
       omae   *anata*
       okaasan 'mother'

                                                          (from Lee 1976)

In sum, then, Japanese first- and second-person reference is significantly marked for gender and for formality.

TABLE 6.1. First-person pronominal forms

		Context	
	Formal—————	——————————	————Informal
Women	*watakushi*	*watashi*	*atashi*
	(*atakushi*)		(*atai*)
Men	*watakushi* *watashi*	*boku*	*ore*
	(*jibun*) (*washi*)		

TABLE 6.2 Second-person pronominal forms

		Context			
	Formal——————————————————————Informal				
Women	anata			anta	
Men	anata		kimi	omae	kisama
					temee
		(anta)			

Pronoun use is also, unlike English, characterized by the use of a zero form wherever possible. Speakers also refer to others by titles, names, or other devices in preference to second-person pronominal forms. We may conclude, then, that the appearance of these forms is quite marked. And so it was of some interest to me to note, in a small sample of romantic text material, relatively high frequencies of first- and second-person reference compared to natural conversations. It seems reasonable to suggest, then, that, among other gendered forms, terms of self-reference and address may be serving to signal or represent heteronormative attractiveness or mutual attraction in these texts. The results of my quantitative analysis may be seen in tables 6.3 and 6.4, where overt first- and second-person reference frequency is measured.

Relatively high frequencies of overt first- and second-person reference are observed in the texts. This is hardly surprising for the Harlequin novels, which we might expect to follow a pattern that accommodates the grammatical requirements of English. But, especially in the case of first-person reference, we see pronouns and a handful of other forms used at similarly high levels in the Japanese texts as well. And they are used in unusual ways, as in example (7), where instead of the expected zero first-person reference there is a repetition of *watashi*.

(7)   *Watashi, jihyoo dashita no yo. Watashi, Makoto-chan ni warui koto o shite shimatta n da mono. Watashi wa . . . kono mama Makoto-chan to kao o awasete iku wake ni wa ikanai no yo.*

'I submitted my resignation. I did a bad thing to Makoto, you know. I . . . [just] can't go on facing him as before'. (Kamata 1991:159–160)

Comparisons of first-person reference frequency across genres and sex of speaker[5] (table 6.3) show that *hiren* 'blighted romance' lovers produce slightly fewer first-person references than other lovers. This result is entirely due to the fact that men in blighted-love stories produce fewer first-person pronouns than men either in *happii-endo* romances or Harlequin translations.

More interesting than the absence of *boku*s and *ore*s in the blighted-love stories, however, is the fact that the Japanese men in *happii-endo* novels produce as many such forms as Harlequin men do, as in example (8).

(8)   *Tonari no onna to wa, heya ni yotta dake dakara, ore wa nani mo shinai. Ore wa ano onna to wa, nani mo shinai. Ore, kokoro o irekaeru kara. Hoka no onna to wa, moo zettai ni tsukiawanai. Ore, kore kara NHK dake ni suru.*

TABLE 6.3 First-person reference by women and
men, by text type

Text Type	Women		Men	
Hiren	42.9%	67/156	35.3%	79/224
'blighted	atashi	6	ore	38
romance'	FN	3	boku	36
	watashi	53	jibun	4
	other	5	kotchi	1
Happii-	43.8%	110/251	45.9%	144/314
endo	atashi	1	ore	89
'happy	uchi	1	boku	46
ending'	FN	3	jibun	6
	watashi	97	kotchi	1
	other	8	LN	2
Harlequin	43.1%	88/204	42.9%	102/238
translations	watashi	88	boku	100
			jibun	2
All genres	43.4%	265/611	41.9%	325/776

FN = first name; LN = last name.

'[I] just stopped by the apartment of the girl next door; I didn't do anything. I didn't do anything with her [lit., with that woman]. I'll become a new man. [I] absolutely won't go out with other women. I'll stick with just NHK [the Japan Broadcasting Corporation] from now on'. (Kamata 1991:15)

There could be a number of reasons for this, and more qualitative analysis is required.

Heroines, unlike their partners, exhibit a similar pattern of first-person reference across the three subgenres; although women in *hiren* novels produce very slightly fewer first-person referents than those in *happii-endo* or Harlequin novels, the difference by no means reaches significance. There is, it should be noted, more variability across the texts in the *hiren* category, which suggests that more attention is required to variability in what constitutes "tragedy." And it is important to keep in mind the close similarities of the *happii-endo* novels to the Harlequin translation, our benchmark for "high" first-person pronoun use.[6]

Further, I suggest that the particular first-person referent forms chosen signal something along the lines of "heterosexual attractiveness" or, at least, "heterosexual attentiveness." In the Harlequin translations, women refer to themselves as *watashi*, men as *boku*; use is so close to categorical that one might speculate that corporate guidelines as to appropriate pronoun choice were provided to translators, a speculation that I was unable to verify through Harlequin Tokyo. In the other two subgenres, women use *watashi* most of the time, with a sprinkling of the somewhat more feminine *atashi*, *uchi*—a "new" pronoun used by girls (see chapter 14, this volume)—and first name, another self-reference practice associated with young girls (see chapter 5, this volume). This "sprinkling" is a bit thicker in the *hiren* than in the *happii-endo* novels (13.4% vs. 4.5%),[7] which suggests that *atashi*, *uchi*, and first name, if used too often, are bad news. Women in love should stick to *watashi* rather than turning to more "feminine" forms of self-reference. Certain kinds of hyperfemininity are, it seems, not desirable (see chapter 6, this volume).

Men, however, never use *watashi*; even on a first and occasionally rather formal meeting, men use a mixture of *boku* and *ore*, except for the Harlequin heroes, who never use anything but *boku*. Choice between *boku* and *ore* seems to be somewhat context sensitive; except in the case of one *happii-endo* text from the 1990s, the more masculine *ore* appears to be used more often in scenes of heightened emotion or after a sexual relationship has been established. More *ore* use occurs in *happii-endo* texts than in *hiren* texts (61.8% vs. 48.1%).[8] Successful male lovers, apparently, say it with *ore*.

A similar, though not identical, situation obtains for the second-person forms (table 6.4). First, it seems most plausible to assume that, due to translation effects, Harlequin heroines and heroes produce significantly more second-person forms— all pronouns—than do any other lovers.[9] Second, women in the domestic genres make significantly fewer overt second-person references than men. This tendency is highly significant ($\chi^2 = 8.94$, $p \leq 0.01$). One might expect this, since second-person pronouns are avoided by subordinate members of status-asymmetric dyads. It is hardly surprising that the cultural model of male superiority over women is evidenced in these texts, leading women to be represented in both blighted love and happy ending texts as avoiding second-person pronouns, in just the way subordinate members of dyads properly should. And throughout, the actual forms used, when they are used, are consistent with the status-asymmetric forms held to be used by husband-wife couples, as seen in (6). Since these are pre-husband-wife couples (except in the *hiren*

TABLE 6.4 Second-person reference by women and men, by text type

Text Type	Women		Men	
Hiren	35.7%	51/143	46.3%	93/201
'blighted	*anata*	22	*omae*	23
romance'	pet name	1	*kimi*	24
	FN	4	FN	38
	LN-*san*	24	FN-*san*	2
			Anata	4
			LN-*san*	1
			other	1
Happii-	28.0%	53/189	42.7%	112/262
endo	*anata*	26	*omae*	15
'happy	FN-*san*	1	*kimi*	41
ending'	FN	1	FN	17
	LN-*san*	16	FN-*chan*	1
	LN-*kun*	1	*an(a)ta*	2
	pet name	8	LN-*san*	35
			other	1
Harlequin	58.1%	86/148	57.0%	135/237
translations	*anata*	72	*kimi*	118
	FN	12	FN	14
	pet name	2	pet name	3
All genres	39.6%	190/480	48.6%	340/700

subgenre), the data suggest that first- and second-person reference prescriptions of normative women's and men's language, at least, form a moderately productive site for the encoding of attraction.

One form that deserves special mention is the male-speaker-associated pronoun *omae*. This form is not used by Harlequin heroes and is used somewhat sparingly in the *hiren* and *happii-endo* texts (24.7% vs. 13.4%, respectively). This difference turns out to be highly significant ($\chi^2 = 18.25$, $p \leq 0.001$). *Omae* is an old-fashioned second-person pronoun and one with more condescending connotations than the competitor *kimi*; heroes who hope for a happy ending are advised to minimize its use.

Sentence-final particles.   Like pronouns, sentence-final particles (SFPs) are central to ideologies of gendered Japanese, despite the existence of diverse use in real speech (Okamoto 1995; see also chapters 10, 13, and 15, this volume). They belong to a larger category of sentence extenders. Japanese is a verb-final language, and sentence extenders are elements that occur postverbally. As a group, sentence extenders serve to index a speaker's stance or attitude toward the propositional information conveyed in the preverbal to verbal portion of an utterance. One type of sentence extender is the sentence-final particle. Figure 6.1 provides a continuum of normatively masculine to normatively feminine SFPs.[10]

The following examples illustrate some of the normatively "gendered" SFPs drawn from my data; normatively feminine SFPS used by heroines are given in example (9) and normatively masculine SFPs used by heroes in example (10).

(9a) *Anata no   kokoro no   naka de utsu **no**.*
      you   GEN heart   GEN in   at hit

      'You'll hit [me] in your heart'.
      (Mori 1986:170)

(9b) *Masaka, hitori   nan desu **mono**.*
      really   one person NOM COP

      'Really [of course not, you silly], I live alone'.
      (Setouchi 1996:40)

(9c) *Shun-chan, mata kita **wa**.*
      Shun   again came

      'Shun, I came [back] again'.
      (Tachihara 1970:49)

zo	ze	da yo	neg	IMP	na	sa	V + yo	ne	kashira	no	NP~AN	mon(o)	wa
				na								Ø + yo	

masculine		"relatively" masculine	neutral		"relatively" feminine		feminine

FIGURE 6.1. Sentence-particle continuum

(10a) *Ato   ikkagetsu da   **zo**.*
       later one month COP

       'It's just one more month'.
       (Kamata 1991:35)

(10b) *Totemo omoe-   nai **na**.*
       utterly can think [that] NEG

       'I just don't think so'.
       (Setouchi 1996:194)

(10c) *Dotchi ga katte   nan   da **yo**.*
       which SU selfish NOM   is

       'Who's the one who's being selfish?!'
       (Hanai 1989:104)

Given the centrality of these SFPs in gendered language ideologies, coupled with their salience—derived from their utterance-final position—and their availability for inclusion in a much broader range of utterances than personal pronouns, I argue that we should expect to find in the representations of the speech produced by "proper" romantic heroines and heroes a high frequency of sentence particles, which, *so long as they are stereotypically gender-differentiated*, will tell the reader as well as the romantic heroine or hero's prospective romantic partner that the speaker is an appropriately feminine or masculine potential "true" lover. Thus, we may expect to find that romances' fictional pairs would display their attractiveness/attraction to each other through both a very high use of interactional particles and a very feminine or masculine selection from among particle options. Results of the first aspect of this analysis are presented in table 6.5.

The immediate conclusion to be drawn is that our novels' true lovers do, indeed, produce a very high frequency of SFPs when in dialogue with each other. Women use interactional particles more than men (χ^2 for women vs. men across all texts = 44.19, $p \leq 0.001$), especially if they are foreign (that is, a Harlequin heroine, χ^2 = 47.16, $p \leq 0.001$) or if their love is doomed (χ^2 = 18.80, $p \leq 0.001$). Neither the at-

TABLE 6.5 Sentence-final particles, by text type

Text Type	Year	Women		Men	
		% SFP/All Utterances		% SFP/All Utterances	
Hiren	1980s	46.1%	106/203	33.6%	111/330
'blighted	1990s	56.9%	83/146	38.9%	81/208
romance'	All	50.3%	189/376	35.7%	192/538
Happii-endo	1980s	32.1%	63/196	47.6%	109/229
'happy	1990s	53.8%	177/329	42.1%	188/447
ending'	All	45.7%	240/525	43.9%	297/676
Harlequin	1980s	75.4%	144/191	53.8%	113/210
translations	1990s	66.8%	139/208	43.5%	123/283
	All	70.9%	283/399	47.9%	236/493

tractiveness of the heroine nor her attraction to the hero is signaled by elevated frequencies of SFP use relative to her hero in love affairs with happy endings ($\chi^2 = 0.32$, not significant). The profile of lesser overall SFP use for men seems to derive in part from the relatively infrequent use of SFPs by *hiren* heroes (χ^2 for *hiren* vs. *happii-endo* men and Harlequin men are 8.13, $p < 0.01$, and 15.19, $p \leq 0.001$, respectively). We recall that these heroes do not make much use of the most masculine first-person pronoun, *ore*, either.

What has been reported up to this point is simply the frequency of SFP use. However, claims of SFP use in the construction of womanly women and manly men will not hold if the actual SFPs used do not conform to the ideological alignments of certain particles with womanly women or manly men. It is, therefore, necessary to look at the SFPs selected by our heroines and heroes. I examined a selected subset of heroines' use of strongly feminine SFPs (*wa*, noninterrogative *no*, *mono*, and ø *yo*, along with the single occurrence in a 1996 *hiren* text of *-te↑*) measured against heroes' use of a similar subset of masculine SFPs (*zo*, *ze*, *da yo*, *dai*, negative imperative *na*, and certain other *na*-type SFPs). Results are presented in table 6.6.

The production rates of strongly feminine or masculine SFPs by our heroines and heroes is most striking when compared to real speaking data. Okamoto (1995, 1996) reports only 4.5% strongly feminine SFP use by the 10 students in her study—the women who most closely resemble our heroines—and 18.1% for 10 older women. And young men may use strongly masculine SFPs even less than this; Sturtz Sreetharan (chapter 15, this volume) reports 0% strongly masculine SFP use in her Kansai data and only 5% in the Tokyo data. Of course, the contexts of speaking in these studies are quite different from the contexts in which fictional lovers encode their mutual attraction. Nonetheless, the differences are striking; these SFPs are clearly used much more to construct gendered images in fiction than they appear to be in real life.

Table 6.6 also shows that our heroines are, across the board, constructing femininity with feminine SFPs much more than their heroes are constructing masculinity with masculine SFPs ($\chi^2 = 126.23$, $p \leq 0.0001$). This may simply have to do with the analytic choice to examine only SFPs rather than including a larger set of sentence-final forms. But these results are also in line with Eckert and McConnell-Ginet's argument that women have to work harder at inhabiting social categories than do men (Eckert & McConnell-Ginet 1995).

Another point with respect to feminine SFP use is that *happii-endo* women use significantly fewer than do *hiren* and Harlequin women ($\chi^2 = 13.19$ and 20.58, respectively, $p \leq 0.001$). This, in a more detailed comparison across the two decades of this

TABLE 6.6 "Feminine" and "masculine" sentence-final particles, by text type

Text type	Women's Use of "Strongly Feminine" % SFPs/All Utterances		Men's Use of "Strongly Masculine" % SFPs/All Utterances	
Hiren	69.8%	132/189	29.2%	56/192
Happii-endo	52.1%	125/240	30.0%	89/297
Harlequin	71.7%	203/283	38.6%	91/236
All	64.6%	460/712	32.6%	236/725

study, turns out to be due to very low use of feminine SFPs in the novels from the 1980s (22.2%); *happii* heroines in the texts from the 1990s produced feminine SFPs at rates very similar to heroines in the other subgenres (62.7%). And, although it did not create a significant difference in the production of masculine SFPs by genre overall, this increase in the femininity encoding via SFPs seen in the *happii* women is echoed by a large increase in the masculinity encoding work via SFP done by their men (from 10.1% in the 1980s to 41.5% in the 1990s). What accounts for this major shift is as yet unclear.

It seems, then, that SFPs are less a part of the verbal package of masculinity in romance novels than of femininity.[11] Whether the larger group of sentence extenders such as evidentials and the like play such a role for heroes as well as heroines, however, must still be investigated further. And it is also possible that bare sentences, particularly those that end in plain verbal forms, which were not included in table 6.6, may be precisely where masculinity is located. When utterances that end in *da* 'is', the plain nonpast form of the copula *to be* that is strongly associated with masculinity, are added to the preceding numbers, men may be seen to be constructed as manly at sentence's end in ways more similar to women's construction as feminine than they appear when SFP forms are singled out as the only possible resource for so doing. Adding *da*, bald imperatives, and other forms strongly associated with masculine speech to the mix—although beyond the scope of this work—should demonstrate that heroes, too, use the ends of sentences to hint at their masculinity and their attraction to the heroine.

The use of interactional particles does, nonetheless, add significantly—and saliently—to the hypergendered nature of the dialogue between each of the romancing pairs and, coupled with their pronoun use, indexes the interactions between the pairs in each novel as *love talk*. Love talk, I suggest, plays a role in both Japanese and translated category romances similar to that of *looking love(r)ly* (that is, having an appropriately sexually appealing physical appearance) in the Western trash romance.

6.2. Conclusions

Japanese women who read romance fiction read romantic narratives built around women and men who are suitable candidates for being "true" lovers. In a penetrating analysis of Japanese women's magazines, Rosenberger (1995:143–144) argues that print consumed by women has "some power over the way women categorize themselves and their sexual desires" for particular Others. Readers "establish a discourse of ideas and practices that, while not always coherent within itself, presents an alternative to the discourse of ideas and practices" available to them through dominant institutions and, in doing so, construct imaginary communities to which they may "belong" (see chapter 7, this volume). This is equally true of romance novels. It is important, therefore, to understand how the heroines and heroes of these novels are presented for reader consumption. One of the messages romances convey is where to locate and enact attractiveness. In the Japanese category romance, beauty is in the ears, not the eyes, of the about-to-be-significant romantic Other.

Being in love is "signalled in culturally codified ways," and the range of semiotic codes used to convey "being in love" are recognizable as "being in love" because they are "iterable signs that continually get recirculated in social life" (Kulick 1999:10). Japanese category romance fiction provides evidence of how women and men are held properly to engage—verbally, at least—in being in love. My analysis uncovers some of the normative standards to which real women and men may make reference when they judge whether they are or are not in a true love relationship and provides us with a glimpse of how ideologies of gender and ideologies of heterosexuality relate to each other as they are simultaneously manifested in language.

Notes

This research was supported through a 1999–2000 University of California Faculty Development Award and a 2000–2001 University of California Faculty Research Grant. I would like to thank Debra Occhi, Cindi Sturtz Sreetharan, and, most of all, my coeditor, Shigeko Okamoto, for their many helpful comments on this work.

1. See [Shibamoto] Smith and Schmidt (1996) and Shibamoto Smith (1999) for a description of the major subgenres and the metaphoric models of true love found therein.

2. See, for example, Noriko's first glimpse of Goo: "*Kochira e yatte kuru futari no otoko o mitsuketa. Hitori wa se ga takaku wanryoku ga tsuyosoo de, ugoki no hayai ashi to, arakezuri na kokkaku o motta seenen [de aru]*." '[I] caught sight of two men coming this way. One [was] tall and muscular-looking, a fast-walking young man with a rough-hewn physique' (Tanabe 1978:114).

3. The term comes from the fact that words for such occupations are written in *katakana*, the Japanese syllabary used to encode foreign words.

4. Uchida (1997:89) notes a change since the 1970s; *atashi* is apparently now gaining ground on or even superseding *watashi* for use in all but the most formal contexts in standard Japanese (cf. chapter 14, this volume).

5. Comparisons were made using $2 \times 2 \chi$-tests for homogeneity, each with a single degree of freedom, with Yates's correction.

6. It is worthwhile to inquire whether this is the only result of translation effect in the case of the Harlequin texts or these forms function even further to heighten the (hyper-) sexual attractiveness of the Harlequin lovers, but this question must remain for future investigation.

7. $\chi^2 = 3.38$; thus, this finding is "significant" at the .07 level or, perhaps more properly, suggestive of a real but not fully characterizable textual meaning.

8. Oddly, here, too, $\chi^2 = 3.38$; the similarity between this result—a "tendency" toward hypermasculine self-reference in happy romances for men, one might say—and the "tendency" for hyperfemininity to associate with bad outcomes is interesting but, for the moment, inexplicable.

9. $\chi^2 = 7.98$, 14.6 for the women and men of Harlequin vs. *hiren* texts and 22.45, 19.18 for the women and men of Harlequin vs. *happii-endo* texts across all utterances. In the first case, $p \leq 0.01$; in all the rest, $p \leq 0.001$.

10. Abbreviations are as follows: IMP = imperative, neg = negative, NP = noun phrase, AN = adjectival noun, NOM = nominalizaer, COP = copula, and SU = subject.

11. This is, perhaps, to be expected, as the problems of the hypermasculine SFPs' simultaneous association with masculinity and with an undesirable working-class identity make them less available for use in a linguistic construction of male attractiveness than their counterpart hyperfeminine SFPs.

Source Texts

Browning, Dixie/Nakagawa, Reiko, tr. (1985/1987) *Something for herself/Tomadoi no kisetsu (The lost season)*. Tokyo: Harlequin.

Hanai, Aiko (1989). *Futari jikan (Time for the two of us)*. Tokyo: Shueisha.

Herter, Lori/Minami, Rutsu, tr. (1996/1998) *How much is that couple in the window?/Shoo uindoo no hanayome (The show window bride)*. Tokyo: Harlequin.

Hiraiwa, Yumie (1982). *Kekkon no toki (Time for marriage)*. Tokyo: Kodansha.

Kamata, Toshio (1991). *Koishite mo (May I love you?)*. Tokyo: Kadokawa.

Lawrence, Kim/Yamanouchi, Fumie, tr. (1997/1998). *Wedding-night baby/Kekkonshiki no yoru ni (On our wedding night)*. Tokyo: Harlequin.

Mori, Yoko (1986). *Onnazakari (In the prime of her life)*. Tokyo: Kadokawa.

Mortimer, Carole/Hirae, Mayumi, tr. (1993/1994). *Hunter's moon/Kiseki no uedingu (Miracle wedding)*. Tokyo: Harlequin.

Setouchi, Jakucho (1996). *Kawaku (Thirst)*. Tokyo: Kodansha.

Tachihara, Masaaki (1970). *Takiginoo (Torchlight Noh)*. Tokyo: Kadokawa.

Tanabe, Seiko (1978). *Iiyoru (Approach)*. Tokyo: Bungei Shunju.

Yuikawa,, Kei (1997). *Kisu yori mo setsunaku (Crueler than a kiss)*. Tokyo: Shueisha.

References

Ashikari, Mikiko (2000). Urban middle-class Japanese women and the white faces: Gender, ideology and representation. Unpublished Ph.D. dissertation, University of Cambridge.

Atsumi, Takako, Takashi Arimitsu, and Sachio Kobayashi, (eds.) (1991). *Ren'ai no kindai bungaku (The modern literature of love)*. Tokyo: Sobunsha Shuppan.

Eckert, Penelope, and Sally McConnell-Ginet (1995). Constructing meaning, constructing selves: Snapshots of language, gender and class from Belten High. In K. Hall and M. Bucholtz (eds.), *Gender articulated: Language and the socially constructed self,* 469–507. New York: Routledge.

Ide, Sachiko (1979). *Onna no kotoba, otoko no kotoba (Women's language, men's language)*. Tokyo: Nihon Keizai Tsushinsha.

Kulick, Don (1999). Language & gender/sexuality. *Language and Culture: Review Language and Culture Symposium #6*. Online: http://www.language-culture.org/colloquia/symposia/kulick-don/.

——— (2000). Gay and lesbian language. *Annual Review of Anthropology* 29: 243–285.

Lee, Motoko Y. (1976). The married woman's status and role as reflected in Japanese: An exploratory sociolinguistic study. *Signs: Journal of Women in Culture and Society* 1(4): 991–999.

Mulhern, Chieko Irie (1989). Japanese Harlequin romances and transcultural woman's fiction. *Journal of Asian Studies* 48(1): 50–70.

Noguchi, Takehiko (1987). *Kindai nihon no ren'ai shoosetsu (Romance fiction in modern Japan)*. Osaka: Osaka Shoseki.

Okamoto, Shigeko (1995). "Tasteless" Japanese: Less "feminine" speech among young Japanese women. In K. Hall and M. Bucholtz (eds.), *Gender articulated: Language and the socially constructed self,* 297–325. New York: Routledge.

——— (1996). Indexical meaning, linguistic ideology, and Japanese women's speech. *The Proceedings of the 22nd Annual Meeting of the Berkeley Linguistics Society,* 290–301. Berkeley: Berkeley Linguistics Society.

Peak, Lois (1989). Learning to become part of the group: The Japanese child's transition to preschool life. *Journal of Japanese Studies* 15(1): 93–123.

Povinelli, Elizabeth (1999). Subject of desire. *Language and Culture Review: Language and Culture Symposium #6*. Online: http://www.language-culture.org/archives/mailing-lists/l-c/199911/msg00005.html.

Radway, Janice A. (1984). *Reading the romance: Women, patriarchy, and popular literature*. Chapel Hill: University of North Carolina Press.

Rosenberger, Nancy (1995). Antiphonal performances? Japanese women's magazines and women's voices. In L. Skov and B. Moeran (eds.), *Women, media and consumption in Japan*, 143–169. Honolulu: University of Hawaii Press.

Shibamoto, Janet S. (1985). *Japanese women's language*. New York: Academic Press.

Shibamoto Smith, Janet S. (1997). *Koishi, Aisuru*: Competing images of Japanese men in love. Paper presented at the American Anthropological Association 96th Annual Meeting, Chicago.

—— (1999). From *hiren* to *happii-endo*: Romantic expression in the Japanese love story. In G. B. Palmer and D. J. Occhi (eds.), *Languages of sentiment: Pragmatic and conceptual approaches to cultural constructions of emotional substrates*, 147–166. Amsterdam: John Benjamins.

[Shibamoto] Smith, Janet S. (1999). The speaking patterns of Japanese "true love": Love's dialogue as seen in the romance novel. Paper presented at the Talkin' Gender and Sexuality Symposium, Aalborg, Denmark.

Shibamoto Smith, Janet S. (2003). Gendered structures in Japanese. In M. Hellinger and H. Bussmann (eds.), *Gender across languages*, vol. 3, 201–225. Amsterdam: John Benjamins.

—— (forthcoming). Translating true love: Japanese romance fiction, Harlequin-style. In J. Santaemilia (ed), *Gender, sex and translation: The manipulation of identities*. Manchester: St. Jerome Publishing.

[Shibamoto] Smith, Janet S., and David L. Schmidt (1996). Variability in written Japanese: Towards a sociolinguistics of script choice. *Visible Language* 30(1): 46–71.

Shibamoto Smith, Janet S., and Debra J. Occhi (n.d.). It sounds like love to me: The speaking patterns and mimetics of Japanese "true love" in romance fiction and *manga*. Unpublished manuscript.

Shibatani, Masayoshi (1990). *The languages of Japan*. Cambridge, MA: Cambridge University Press.

Sturtz, Cindi L. (2001). *Danseego da zo!* Japanese men's language: Stereotypes, realities, and ideologies. Unpublished Ph.D. dissertation, University of California, Davis.

Uchida, Nobuko (1997). Kaiwa koodoo ni mirareru seesa (Sex differences seen in conversational interaction). In S. Ide (ed.), *Joseego no sekai (The world of women's language)*, 74–93. Tokyo: Meiji Shoin.

7

MOMOKO NAKAMURA

"Let's Dress a Little Girlishly!" or "Conquer Short Pants!"

Constructing Gendered Communities in Fashion Magazines for Young People

Like all forms of mass communication, fashion magazines for young people use language to construct the identity of their readership. This identity is both imaginary and specific. Texts for mass audiences such as magazines often assume target readers and use language so as to communicate to them. In the process, the imaginary reader is constructed as having particular interests, values, and experiences—that is, as having a particular identity. Actual readers have choices to make about whether they will use the identity of an imaginary reader as a resource to construct their own identities. In order to compete with other fashion magazines, furthermore, each magazine needs to make very specific the identity of its imaginary reader. This chapter focuses on questions of how magazine producers construct specific feminine and masculine identities of imaginary readers and how magazine discourse makes these imaginary identities meaningful to actual readers. Focusing on the notion of a magazine community, I demonstrate that magazine discourse constructs gendered communities by incorporating stereotypical gender organizations and conceptual frameworks.

The data is drawn from two fashion magazines for young women, *Junon* and *Non-no*, and two fashion magazines for young men, *Popeye* and *Men's Non-no*. *Junon* started in 1973 and had a circulation of 380,000 in 1999. *Popeye* started in 1976 and had a circulation of 220,000 in 1999 (Media Research Center 2000). *Non-no* started in 1971 and had a circulation of 1,040,000 in 1999. Its men's counterpart, *Men's Non-no*, started in 1986 and had a circulation of 370,000 in 1999 (Media Research Center 2000). They were selected because fashion is one of the few topics shared by both women's and men's magazines. The data comes from issues of these magazines published in 1999 and 2000. I first analyze one article on hairstyles in *Junon* (March

1999; fig. 7.1) and one article on hair removal in *Popeye* (February 1999; fig. 7.2), both on the topic of "hair." By focusing on similarities between women's and men's magazines, I will present three strategies magazine writers employ in constructing magazine communities. I then compare the captions that appeared on the fashion pages in *Non-no* (May 2000) and *Men's Non-no* (June 2000). The comparative analysis will reveal how gender ideologies are used, and reproduced, to engender magazine communities.

7.1.   A dynamic model of language and gender studies

Language and gender studies have developed dramatically by integrating the recent feminist conception of gender not as predetermined by "essential" features but as a dynamic process we actively perform in our interactions with others. The objectives of the field have turned from how women and men use language differently to how subjects construct gender identities in discourses. Women are redefined as active language users, who "reinvent" identities as well as reproduce given ones (Bucholtz, Liang, & Sutton 1999). The focus of analysis, too, has shifted from normative inter-actions to subversive and resisting performances (Butler 1990), which transform existing gender relations.

Along with the benefits of a conception of gender as constructed in discourses, however, some problems emerge (Nakamura 2001:123–124). The first problem is related to the diversity of gender identities. The constructive view of gender denies the dichotomous female/male distinction and emphasizes the diversity of female identities. But if the differences among women are so wide, we are forced to ask whether we should dispense with the single category of "woman," which has united the various forms of the feminist movement (Weedon 1997[1887]:177). The second problem is how we can characterize the difficulties speakers face in their attempts to subvert existing gender relations. To redefine women as active language users em-phasizes the agency of each individual woman and assumes that the choice of whether to reproduce or subvert gender relations is available to her. In order to explore the difficulties of performing subversive practices, we need to consider what Gal (1991:177) has called "symbolic domination," ideological control on the macrosocietal level. Finally, the third problem is how to integrate studies that focus on different aspects of language and gender, such as sexist lexical structures (e.g., Miller & Swift 1979[1976]), the stereotypes and norms of women's language use (e.g., Lakoff 1975), and sociohistorical dimension of gender construction (e.g., Fou-cault 1976). Thus, a dynamic and integrative model of language and gender studies is required, which will incorporate (1) a poststructural view of gender as constructed in discourses and a process of subversive identity construction, (2) both the single category of "woman" and a variety of female identities, (3) a model of ideological control through discourse practices, and (4) both sociohistorical constructions of gender representations and discursive constructions of gender identities.

In my previous work (Nakamura 1995:236), I reformulated Fairclough's model of the dialectic relationship between social structures and discourse (1989:38) and

FIGURE 7.1. *Junon*, March 1999 p. 88. Courtesty of Shufu to Seikatsu Sha

claimed that those dialectic relationships are mediated by ideologies. If we are to account for the language use of Japanese women, which, like the language use of all speakers, constantly changes and varies, it is crucial to distinguish the stereotypes and norms of women's language use from women's actual language use (Nakamura 1990:77). "Women's language" is then conceptualized as "a set of abstract norms to which actual usage may conform to a greater or lesser extent" (Milroy & Milroy 1985:23), that is, the ideology of "women's language" (Silverstein 1979:1193). The

FIGURE 7.2. *Popeye*, February 1999 p. 114. Courtesy of Magazine House

ideology of "women's language" mediates between male dominance in social structures and Japanese women's discourse practices. It redefines the diversity in women's language use as the result of individual women's active choices, that is, their varied responses to the norms of "women's language," as well as to many other norms related to the speaker's age, occupation, sexuality, and ethnicity.

Thus, a model for language and gender studies that focuses on the gender aspect of these dialectic relationships can be outlined (see fig. 7.3). Figure 7.3 indicates that the dialectic relationships between gender relations and gender identities constructed in discourse practices are mediated by gender ideologies. *Gender identities* refers to a variety of gender-related identities that subjects actively (re)construct in discourse practices. *Gender ideologies* include gender-related categories, social subjects, social relationships, and conceptual frameworks, which have been historically constituted and ordered by previous discourse practices. *Gender relations* refers to the gender-related power structures in society.

The dialectic relationships between gender ideologies and gender identities constructed in discourse practices are represented by the two arrows ↓ and ↑. In the direction indicated by the downward arrow ↓, gender ideologies both restrict and provide resources to discourse practices. Gender ideologies restrict the ways individual discourse practices are performed. At the same time, gender ideologies offer categories, subject positions, social relations, and conceptual frameworks, which can be used as resources in discourses (e.g., a Japanese speaker can perform a variety of identities by using or not using feminine language precisely because the notion of "women's language" exists in Japanese gender ideologies). In the direction indicated by the upward arrow ↑, discourse practices produce, reproduce, and subvert existing gender ideologies, which, in turn, construct, maintain, and transform existing gender relations. Gender ideologies in a particular society have been historically con-

Gender Relations (Social Structures)

↓↑

Gender Ideologies   (Discourse Orders)

↓↑

[restrict and provide resources to]   [produce, reproduce and subvert]

↓↑

Gender Identities (Discourse Practices)

FIGURE 7.3. Dynamic model of language and gender studies (Nakamura 2002:29)

structed by discourse practices. We reproduce gender ideologies, for instance, by taking subject positions provided in dominant ideologies (e.g., a woman may perform a feminine identity by following the norms of "women's language"). At the same time, discourses subvert gender ideologies in the sense that no discourse practice is a perfect reproduction of ideologies (e.g., even if a woman intends to follow the norms of "women's language," her practice more or less deviates from the norms). The transformation of gender ideologies ultimately subverts gender relations in social structures. Reflecting the dynamic relation between ideologies and practices, I call my model *the dynamic model of language and gender studies*.

The model resolves the three problems brought out by the new conception of gender discussed earlier. First, the diversity of female identities is captured on the level of discourse practices, while the norms, stereotypes, and categorizations applied to the category of "woman" are captured on the level of gender ideologies. For example, the norms of "women's language" in gender ideologies are applied to all women's language use—that is, to all members of the category of "woman"—since, on this level, women are believed to form a homogeneous group whose behavior is determined by their female sex (Nakamura 1990:109). But on the level of discourse practices, an individual woman responds to the norms differently depending on the kind of identity she intends to construct.

Second, the difficulties concomitant with performing subversive discourse practices can be captured on the level of gender ideologies. We can examine the difficulties by studying the contradictions among gender ideologies. For instance, the category of "women's language" creates the twin standards of standard (male) language / deviant (female) language and, for women only, good (feminine) language / bad (unfeminine) language, which put women in the situation of a double bind (Lakoff 1975:61). The difficulties can also become evident through analyzing the relations between gender ideologies and other ideologies (e.g., "women's language" is reinforced by other ideologies such as "the beautiful Japanese tradition" and "the unique character of Japanese language"; Nakamura 1995:263).

Third, and finally, in the dynamic model the contributions of previous studies on sexist lexical structures are incorporated into the analysis of gender ideologies. I consider sexist lexicons the extreme case of dominant gender ideologies, ideologies that have been naturalized enough to be represented in lexical structures. Sexist lexicons provide resources for sexist discourse practices. Furthermore, by defining gender ideologies as constituted by discourse practices the model productively connects sociohistorical studies of the construction of gender ideologies to linguistic analyses of discourse practices.

This chapter investigates how the model accounts for the process of inventing a specific gender identity by analyzing magazine discourse. Identity construction often has been conceptualized as the process by which a person constructs a variety of gender identities by taking subject positions within gender ideologies (Gough & Talbot 1996).[1] A person constructs herself (or himself) as a feminine woman, for instance, by speaking women's language, that is, by taking the subject position of a feminine woman based on the distinction feminine woman / unfeminine woman and the connection between "feminine woman" and "women's language" in gender ideologies. Similarly, the process of creating a new identity is conceptualized as the process either of resistance to taking a subject position or of combining subject positions (Fairclough 1989:39). A girl who speaks boys' language, for example, is constructing a new identity by resisting the subject position of a traditional girl associated with "women's language." In any case, subject positions are presupposed before discourse practices are performed. In producing a youth fashion magazine discourse, however, writers need to construct the specific identity of "a *Junon* girl" or "a *Popeye* boy." Instead of simply taking subject positions in gender ideologies, they have to invent new identities not preestablished in gender ideologies. This chapter analyzes how magazine discourse constructs a specific gender identity for the reader and how the dynamic model accounts for the process.

7.2. Constructing magazine communities

Since magazine discourse communicates to mass audiences, its meaning varies depending on the variety of ways audiences receive magazine texts. Thus, magazine producers first make informed guesses about the targeted audience, that is, the implied reader, and then set out to formulate their messages in the form most appealing to this imaginary reader. The distinctive ways language is used in magazine discourse create the identity of the imaginary reader. Furthermore, analyses of a British teen magazine (Talbot 1992) and the U.S. Shopping Channel (Bucholtz 2000) have demonstrated that media discourse often constructs an imaginary community, which offers potential consumers membership in the community. In this section, I demonstrate that both women's and men's magazines construct imaginary communities for their implied readers.

7.2.1. Constructing interactions between the writer
and the readers

The texts in youth fashion magazines for both women and men are full of linguistic features that construct interactions between the writer and the readers. For example, the use of informal style of speech, along with the frequent use of exclamation marks, increases the sense of interaction.

Another way this effect is achieved is through the use of linguistic features that presuppose imagined responses from the receivers. Typical examples are sentence-final particles such as *ne* and *yo ne*, which have functions similar to tag questions. Example (1) demonstrates how the addition of *yo ne* to the simple statement *togechatta* implies responses such as "yes" or "that's right" from readers.[2]

(1) *"Kamisama, Moo Sukoshi Dake" de wa   odoroku hodo*
     God   more a little   only   in TOP surprise extent
     no   henshin   o   togechatta   yo ne (Junon, March 1999)
     GEN   transformation OBJ accomplished

     'In [the television show] *God, Just a Little More*, [actress Fukada Kyoko] has accomplished a surprising transformation of herself, *hasn't she?*'

Interaction is also implied by the use of the imperative (ex. 2) and hortative (ex. 3) forms, which directly address the readers.

(2)   Imperatives
      hitsudoku! (*Popeye*, February 1999)
      must-read-IMP

      'Required Reading!'

(3)   Hortatives
      chokkotto suiito de ikoo! (*Non-no*, May 2000)
      a little   sweet by let's-go

      'Let's dress a little girlishly!' [lit., 'in a sweet little way'].

In addition to constructing interaction between the reader and writer, magazine discourse involves the reader in the process of production by deleting whole clauses for the reader to fill in.

(4)   *daisuki*   *wanpiisu de odekake shitara . . .* (*Non-no*, May 2000)
      like-very-much dress   in go-out   DO-if

      'If [I] go out in my favorite dress, . . .'

In example (4), the reader is expected to be able to supply the whole main clause, as in: "If I go out in my favorite dress, something wonderful will happen." Through the act of completing the text, the reader transforms herself from a mere recipient of the message into a co-participant in the production of the message.

7.2.2.   Constructing the reader's voice

Along with constructing interactions, magazine discourse actively constructs the reader's utterances. The reader's voice is directly presented within double quotations, as in example (5).

(5)   *dokusha minna*   *kara no "mane shitai" to yuu*
      readers everybody from GEN imitate want-to QT say
      atsuui rabu kooru (*Junon*, March 1999)
      hot   love call

      '[There have been] many phone calls [lit., hot love calls] from all the readers saying, "[I] want to imitate [her]."'

The reader's voice is also indirectly implied as in example (6), where the term *watashi* 'I' indicates that the statement is represented as voiced by the reader.

(6)   *motto 'kyooun na'   watashi ni   naru* (*Non-no*, May 2000)
      more 'good fortune' I   GOAL become

      '[I] become a more "lucky" person' [lit., 'a more "lucky" myself'].

Another indirect way to present the reader's voice is to use the conversational structure of adjacency pairs (Talbot 1992:182). Example (7), for instance, can be interpreted as the writer's answer to an unstated question from the reader, as shown in example (8).

(7) *kami o   agetari, maku dake de*
     hair OBJ do-up   curl only
     soku   otona no kao ni!   (*Junon*, March 1999)
     instantly adult of face to [become]

     'Simply by pinning up or curling your hair, you instantly look more mature!'

(8) [Reader: 'How can I become more mature-looking?']
     Writer: 'Simply by pinning up or curling your hair, you instantly look more mature!'

By presenting only the response element of the adjacency pair question-response, the text makes the reader infer the question and, thus, constructs an active role for the reader as the utterer of the question.

The use of the desiderative morpheme *–tai* 'want to' and the verb *hoshii* 'want' in subject-deleted structures also produces readers' voices. Hayashi (1997:368) points out that *–tai* is used only for the first person, since it expresses the speaker's own desire. In order to make coherent interpretations of examples (9) and (10), therefore, the reader needs to interpret the deleted subject as the first-person "I" or "we."

(9) Desiderative morpheme *–tai* 'want to' + subject deletion
     de motte,   onna no ko   ni mote   -tai! (*Popeye*, February 1999)
     and   girls   by be-liked   want-to

     'And [I, we] *want to* be liked by girls'.

(10) Verb *hoshii* + subject deletion
      iro   T-shatsu ga   hoshii (*Non-no*, May 2000)
      color T-shirt SUBJ   want

      '[I, we] *want* a colored T-shirt'.

The writer sometimes even speaks out on behalf of the readers. Example (11) asks Dr. Izawa, a doctor in an aesthetic orthopedic clinic, how to remove hair.

(11) *oshiete, Izawa-sensei* (*Popeye*, February 1999)
      teach   Izawa doctor

      'Please teach [me, us], Dr. Izawa'.

This has two possible readings depending on who utters it. One interpretation is that example (11) is uttered in the reader's voice ("Teach me"). But of whom may the reader ask the question? Possibly the writer, because the writer, not the reader, is assumed to know the expert. So the other interpretation of example (11) is that it is uttered in the writer's voice (i.e., "Teach us"). The two readings position the writer as "a representative of the readers" (Hayashi 1997:369). In order to make the writer a representative of the readers, moreover, example (11) must presuppose a community of men who find value in hair removal.

The same effect is achieved by interrogative forms with unstated subjects. Most interrogative forms in magazine discourse are not used to elicit answers from readers. Rather, they are used to introduce the topic as a problem and to ask for the solution of the problem, which will be given by the magazine. Example (12) can be uttered both in the writer's voice as a representative of the readers ("we") or in the reader's voice ("I").

(12)　*sate kono taimoo,   doo ni ka shori*
　　　now this   body hair somehow get-rid-of
　　　dekinai mono ka !? (Popeye, February 1999)
　　　DO   Q

　　　'Now, how can [we, I] get rid of this body hair?'

The strongest evidence for the construction of the magazine community, however, is the voice(s) of other readers.

(13)　*sore dare? tte   kikareru hayamimi kyara   o*
　　　this who   QT ask PASS rapid-ear character OBJ
　　　sagase! (Non-no, May 2000)
　　　look for-IMP

　　　'Find a new animation character, [so that you will] be asked, "Who is it?"'

Example (13) encourages the reader to find a T-shirt printed with a new animation character and to wear it, so that people will be impressed and ask the reader who the character is. Thus, "Who is it?" in this case is not a mere request for information but conveys approbation for finding a new character so quickly. This question and the attendant implied approval would only be voiced by someone who shares with the reader the value in finding a new character, that is, the other members of the *Non-no* community.

7.2.3.　Constructing shared practices, knowledge, and values

These strategies of constructing interaction and the readers' voice function to create specific practices, knowledge, and values as shared by the writer and the readers. In addition to these, magazine discourse has other strategies to accomplish a sense of shared community. One is reference to other popular media. In example (1), the television program *God, Just a Little More* is simply mentioned as if the readers of *Junon* shared not only the practice of watching the series but also the knowledge and the value of the television star's transformation.

In the same article, *minna* 'everybody' (i.e., all the readers of *Junon*) is used to create the same effect. It presupposes that the readers share an interest in Kyoko's hairstyle and a desire to imitate it, as in *ima, minna ga daichuumoku na no ga Fukada*

Kyoko-chan no kamigata 'Now, what everybody pays attention to is the hairstyle of Fukada Kyoko'; *minna ga mane shitai Kyoko sutairu* '[the] Kyoko style everybody wants to imitate'. The readers even share the act of making a phone call to the writer shouting, *Mane shitai!* '[I] want to imitate [her]'! as in example (5).

Another way knowledge is constructed as shared in magazine discourse is through the mention of technical terms and the names of commodities without any explanation. In the *Junon* article on hairstyle, technical terms such as *beesu hea* 'base hair', *shagii* 'shaggy', *reiyaa katto* 'layered cut', and *suraido katto* 'slide cut' are simply mentioned as if all the readers already know what each term means. Names of commodities necessary to create hairstyles, such as *haabu uootaa* 'herb water', *sutoreeto airon* 'straight iron', and *wakkusu* 'wax', also appear abruptly, as if all the readers already possess them, know how to use them, and actually use them daily.

New expressions and novel uses of existing words also increase the sense of shared knowledge. For instance, the ideas expressed by the compound nouns *iro T-shatsu* 'a colored T-shirt' in example (10) and *hayamimi kyara* 'rapid-ear character' in example (13) are usually expressed by relative clause + noun constructions, such as *iro no tuita T-shatsu* 'a T-shirt that has color' or *dare mo mitsukete inai kyara* 'an animation character nobody has found'. By being expressed in compound nouns without explanation, the ideas are presented as presupposed categories. *Iro T-shatsu* establishes colored T-shirts as one category in the semantic field of T-shirts. *Hayamimi kyara* establishes new animation characters as a category distinctive from other characters already printed on T-shirts. These categories are not known to those who do not read the magazine. Accordingly, they serve as secret codes that unite members of the magazine community. The process of interpreting these new expressions is a process of learning and aligning oneself with these secret meanings of the magazine community.

It is worth noting here that magazine discourse positions the members of the community in different ways. In the fashion magazine communities I analyzed, television-stars, fashion models, and celebrities are positioned as core members. They represent community membership in its idealized form. Readers are positioned as more or less peripheral members who are oriented toward the community and are in the process of learning its practices (Wenger 1998:167). The writer is positioned as the mentor who mediates between the core members and the readers. An actual reader who reads a magazine for the first time may position herself or himself as a peripheral member, while others, who have read the magazine before, may position themselves closer to the core members. The simulation of heterogeneity gives a sense of progress toward increased membership in the community and personal improvement on the part of the actual readers.

Therefore, the community constructed in the discourse of fashion magazines for young people is an imaginary interactive community. Constructing magazine communities creates a set of membership identities, a process that transforms the information in the magazines into resources for constructing those identities. In this way, a T-shirt is transformed from just a piece of clothing into a symbol of membership in a particular magazine community. A magazine community provides identity resources to the actual readers in the form of membership.

7.3. Gendering magazine communities

Thus far, I have shown the similar strategies of both young women's and men's fash-ion magazines in creating a community. This section examines the differences be-tween women's and men's magazine discourses and analyzes how stereotypical gender ideologies are incorporated into them. I use as data the captions on the cover pages, the content pages, and the first 57 pages (except advertisement pages) of *Non-no* and *Men's Non-no*. The total number of caption sentences analyzed is 318 from *Non-no* and 264 from *Men's Non-no*.

The analysis shows that magazine communities are gender-differentiated in the ways that community members are organized and participate in the community and in the ways that magazine communities conceptualize the topic of fashion and posi-tion their members.

7.3.1. Gendered organization of community members

Non-no and *Men's Non-no* differ from each other in several respects. Some of the differences are absolute (some styles are restricted to either *Non-no* or *Men's Non-no*), but many of the differences are a matter of frequency (one uses a particular style more often than the other). These relative differences combined together, however, make the magazines very different.

The discursive styles that I have observed much more often in women's maga-zines than in men's magazines are (1) exclamation marks; (2) the use of the sentence-final particles *da ne*, *da yo ne*, and *da yo* rather than *da*, and (3) more frequent use of hortatives and interrogatives and less frequent use of imperatives. These differences contribute to constructing different kinds of relationships between the writer and the readers, namely, egalitarian relationships in the women's magazines and hierarchi-cal relationships in the men's magazines.

The differences found in the use of exclamation marks and sentence-final par-ticles show that there is less interaction between the writer and the readers in men's magazine communities. First of all, the number of exclamation marks is 123 (38.6%) in *Non-no* but only 60 (22.7%) in *Men's Non-no*. As noted earlier, exclamation points simulate the effect of informal interaction.

Sentence-final particles are also used differently, as shown in table 7.1, which shows that the use of the simple declarative *da* form in *Men's Non-no* is more fre-quent than in *Non-no* (4.1%, 1.8%), in part because *Non-no* prefers to add sentence-final particles *ne*, *yo ne* (1.8%), and *yo* (2.8%). *Men's Non-no* does not add these sentence-final particles at all (0%).[3] Both *ne* and *yo* "strongly require responses from the interpreters" (Maynard 1993:111). The addition of *ne*, *yo ne*, and *yo* after *da* in women's magazines, therefore, creates a sense of interaction.

Similar differences are observed in the relationship between the readers and the core members of the respective magazine communities. In *Junon*, the television star Fukada Kyoko confesses that "because my hair is curly, coarse, and full, I take the greatest caution not to make my head look too big." Here even an ideal member of the community suffers from the same mundane problems as the readers. The equal relationship is established by emphasizing similarities. *Men's Non-no*, however,

TABLE 7.1. The occurrence of sentence-final particles in *Non-no* and *Men's Non-no*

	Non-no (*n = 318*)	*Men's Non-no* (*n = 264*)
da	6 (1.8%)	11 (4.1%)
da ne, da yo ne	6 (1.8%)	0 (0%)
da yo	9 (2.8%)	0 (0%)

describes a television star, Kimura Takuya, as the man who "outshines everybody in his love of T-shirts" and "wears T-shirts stylishly." Here his perfection and confidence are emphasized, which foreground the distance and difference between him and the readers.

The occurrences of hortatives, interrogatives, and imperatives are also different between *Non-no* and *Men's Non-no*. Table 7.2 shows that *Non-no* uses more hortatives and interrogatives, while *Men's Non-no* uses more imperatives. These differences construct different interactions between the writer and the readers. The interactions constructed by hortatives and interrogatives in *Non-no*, on the one hand, are mutual and equal. They present the writer as a friendly sister of the readers (Talbot 1995). The interactions invoked by imperatives in *Men's Non-no*, on the other hand, are unilateral and hierarchical.[4] Thus, the stereotypes of women's egalitarian relationships and men's hierarchical relationships are incorporated into magazine discourses in the different ways magazine communities are organized.

The different organizational relationships seen in women's and men's magazine communities imply different forms of reader participation in these communities. The reader of the women's magazines enters into the community, expecting friendly help from an "older sister." The reader learns the shared practices of the community in which intimacy and similarity are fostered. The reader of the men's magazine, in contrast, enters a community led by a confident superior. The reader will be ordered to acquire the shared practices of the hierarchically structured community. Thus, stereotypical gender ideologies are drawn into magazine discourses in the gendered structures of participation in the women's versus the men's magazine communities.

7.3.2. Gendered frameworks for conceptualizing topics

Comparison of the women's and men's magazine discourses reveals that they adopt distinctive conceptual frameworks of their primary topic: fashion. One of the major sets of contrastive frameworks is that of FASHION AS TASK in women's magazines

TABLE 7.2. The occurrence of hortatives, interrogatives, and imperatives in *Non-no* and *Men's Non-no*

	Non-no (*n = 318*)	*Men's Non-no* (*n = 264*)
Hortatives	10 (3.1%)	1 (0.3%)
Interrogatives	17 (5.3%)	2 (0.7%)
Imperatives	2 (0.6%)	11 (4.1%)

versus FASHION AS BATTLE in men's magazines. These different frameworks position the writer and the readers in different relationships.

Women's magazine discourse defines fashion as a difficult task of dressing well imposed on the reader. *Non-no* frequently uses *kokufuku* 'get over' (ex. 14), *tsuyoi mikata* 'strong supporter', and *kowai mono nashi* 'nothing to fear'. For the reader who struggles to "get over" the task of dressing well, the magazine gives information about what clothing can be her "strong supporter" (ex. 15) and what clothing can make her feel there is "nothing to fear" (ex. 16).

(14) *'mitame nenrei' kokufuku meiku   juku (Non-no*, May 2000)
       look   age   get over make-up seminar

       'The Make-up Seminar to Look Appropriate to Your Age' [lit., 'The Make-up
       Seminar to Get Over Your Age (Which People Determine) Based on How You Look']

(15) *sappari shatsu ga   tsuyoi mikata (Non-no*, May 2000)
       tidy   shirt SUBJ strong supporter

       'A tidy shirt is [your] strong supporter'.

(16) *kore sae   areba kowai   mono nashi (Non-no*, May 2000)
       this only BE-if frightening thing BE-NEG

       '[If I/you have] this, there is nothing to fear'.

Here fashion is conceptualized as a set of tasks to fulfill and a burden or problem to solve. The reader is positioned as a frightened, nervous learner who needs the magazine's help. The writer is positioned as an intimate, helpful sister who tells the reader *maruhi aitem* 'top secret items' and *anshin aitemu* 'relief items'.

The framework of FASHION AS TASK and the positioning of the reader as a nervous learner in the women's magazine function to feminize the topic of fashion. Women are born with female bodies, but they need to work and rework their bodies in order to remain women, since ideologically "women's bodies are always imperfect" (Smith 1988:47). For the reader of the youth fashion magazine who is beginning to enter the world of femininity, the conception of FASHION AS TASK places fashion magazines in a helpful, counseling genre. The egalitarian relationships found in the women's magazine community reinforce this conception of women's magazine as the genre of advice.

Men's magazine discourse, in contrast, conceptualizes fashion as something to conquer and dominate as in examples 17, 18, and 19.

(17) *shooto pantsu o   kooryaku suru! (Men's Non-no*, June 2000)
       short pants OBJ conquer   DO

       'Conquer short pants!'

(18) *shuchoo no aru T-shatsu de kokoroshite*
       assertion of BE T-shirt by carefully
       mukaeutsu (Men's Non-no, June 2000)
       shoot-to-repulse

'Fight back by wearing a T-shirt that expresses the real you' [lit., (We/You/I) shoot the (attacking enemy) in the T-shirt with an assertion'.]

(19) *natsu   no 3dai aitemu kanzen seiha* (*Men's Non-no*, June 2000)
      summer of 3-big items   perfect conquer

      'The Perfect Conquest of Summer's Big 3'

These examples draw upon the framework of FASHION AS BATTLE to conceptualize fashion. The reader is positioned as a fighter or a soldier who is expected to conquer fashion. The writer is a commander who gives the orders and leads the troops (readers) into battle. By applying the FASHION AS BATTLE framework, men's magazine discourse masculinizes fashion. The hierarchical relationships among the members of the men's magazine community reinforce this conception of fashion, because armies are the organizations most characterized by strict hierarchy.

7.4. Conclusion

My analysis demonstrates that (1) youth fashion magazine discourse constructs an imaginary, interactive, and gendered magazine community and (2) the specific identity of magazine readers such as "*Junon* girls" or "*Popeye* boys" is invented as membership in the community. The notion of magazine community plays an important role in two respects. First, it enables the writers to construct the specific identity of the implied reader as a community member. Second, it encourages actual readers to refer to community membership when they construct their own identities, by providing a variety of membership positionings in the community and a sense of progress from the margin to the center of the community. One of the ways to invent a specific gender identity, therefore, is to construct a gendered community.

My analysis demonstrates that magazine discourse attempts to construct specific reader identities, such as "*Junon* girls" and "*Popeye* boys," which are defined by consumption of specific styles of fashion as well as gender. These specific identities, however, cannot be constructed simply by taking the subject positions of "young women" and "young men" predetermined by gender ideologies. In order to construct identities specific to each magazine, magazine producers create a gendered magazine community by drawing upon other resources contained within gender ideologies, that is, gendered social relationships and conceptual frameworks. In other words, instead of directly taking preestablished subject positions for young people in gender ideologies, magazine discourse invents a magazine community membership identity by using other stereotypical gender ideologies.

The result of my analysis supports the dynamic model discussed in the introduction to this chapter in demonstrating that, even in inventing a new identity, some aspects of gender ideologies are reproduced. My analysis shows that magazine discourse contributes to both reproducing and altering gender ideologies. It reproduces stereotypical gendered organizations and conceptual frameworks in gender ideologies. At the same time, it transforms the subject positions of young women and men preestablished in gender ideologies in the sense that it invents identities defined by consumption of specific fashions. The dynamic model accounts for the mechanism by which the invention of new identities often accompanies the reproduction of stereotypical gender ideologies, rather than simply replacing them.

Notes

I am most grateful to Shigeko Okamoto, Janet Shibamoto Smith, and Mary Bucholtz for helpful comments and to Janet Shibamoto Smith and James Placzek for assistance with English.

1. I distinguish identity constructed in discourse practices from subject position in gender ideologies. The notion of *gender identity*, on the one hand, refers to an infinite array of gender identities, constantly constructed in discourse practices. The notion of *subject position*, on the other hand, refers to the gender identities that have been produced over a considerable range of discourse practices and are ordered in gender ideologies. One can invent, create, and improvise a variety of gender identities in discourse practices. But in order to be included in gender ideologies as subject positions the identities need to be performed iteratively over a variety of discourses.

2. Abbreviations for grammatical items are: BE (various forms of the verb *be*), DO (various forms of the verb *do*), GEN (genitive marker), GOAL (goal marker), IMP (imperative marker), NEG (negative marker), OBJ (object marker), PASS (passive marker), Q (question marker), QT (quotative marker), SUBJ (subject marker), and TOP (topic marker).

3. This does not mean that these sentence-final particles never occur in men's magazines. In fact, the clinic doctor in the hair removal article in *Popeye* used *ne* seven times. The use of *ne* functions to shorten the distance between the middle-aged doctor and young readers.

4. Construction of the less interactive and more hierarchical relationships in men's magazines may be considered to contradict the notion of community. Tannen (1993:170) correctly points out, however, that hierarchy does not necessarily preclude closeness and that the Japanese relationship is characterized by a hierarchical interdependency; i.e., the members lower in rank are protected by the members higher in rank and they unite to cope with odds (Hayashi 1997:362).

References

Bucholtz, Mary (2000). "Thanks for stopping by": Gender and virtual intimacy in American shop-by-television discourse. In M. Andrew and M. M.Talbot (eds.), *All the world and her husband*, 192–209. London: Cassell.

Bucholtz, Mary, A. C. Liang, and Laurel A. Sutton (eds.) (1999). *Reinventing identities: The gendered self in discourse*. New York: Oxford University Press.

Butler, Judith (1990). *Gender trouble: Feminism and the subversion of identity*. New York: Routledge.

Fairclough, Norman (1989). *Language and power*. London: Longman.

Foucault, Michel (1976). *The history of sexuality*. New York: Random House.

Gal, Susan (1991). Between speech and silence: The problematics of research on language and gender. In M. di Leonardo (ed.), *Gender at the crossroads of knowledge: Feminist anthropology in the postmodern era*, 175–203. Berkeley: University of California Press.

Gough, Val, and Mary Talbot (1996). "Guilt over games boys play": Coherence as a focus for examining the constitution of heterosexual subjectivity on a problem page. In

C. Caldas-Coulthard and M. Coulthard (eds.), *Texts and practice: Readings in critical discourse analysis*, 214–230. London: Routledge.

Hayashi, Reiko (1997). Hierarchical interdependence expressed through conversational styles in Japanese women's magazines. *Discourse & Society* 8(3):359–389.

Lakoff, Robin (1975). *Language and woman's place*. New York: Harper and Row.

Maynard, Senko K. (1993). *Kaiwa bunseki (Conversation analysis)*. Tokyo: Kuroshio Shuppan.

Media Research Center (2000). *Zasshi shimbun soo katarogu (Japan's periodicals in print)*. Tokyo: Media Research Center.

Miller, Casey, and Kate Swift (1979[1976]). *Words and women: New language in new times*. Harmondsworth: Penguin.

Milroy, James, and Lesley Milroy (1985). *Authority in language: Investigating language prescription and standardization*, 2nd ed. New York: Routledge.

Nakamura, Momoko (1990). Onna no gengo shiyoo kaitai: Shakai gengogaku ni okeru seisa kenkyu kara (The deconstruction of women's language use: Critical review of socio-linguistic studies on sex differences). *Shizen, Ningen, Shakai* 11:45–123.

———(1995). *Kotoba to feminizumu (Language and feminism)*. Tokyo: Keiso Shobo.

———(2001). *Kotoba to jendaa (Language and gender)*. Tokyo: Keiso Shobo.

———(2002) The dynamic model of language and gender studies. *Shizen, Ningen, Shakai* 32:1–26.

Silverstein, Michael (1979). Language structure and linguistic ideology. In P. R. Clyne, W. Hanks, and C. L. Hofbauer (eds.), *The elements: A parasession on linguistic units and levels*, 193–247. Chicago: Chicago Linguistic Society.

Smith, Dorothy (1988). Femininity as discourse. In L. G. Roman and L. K. Christian-Smith (eds.), *Becoming feminine: The politics of popular culture*, 37–58. New York: Falmer Press.

Talbot, Mary (1992). The construction of gender in a teenage magazine. In N. Fairclough (ed.), *Critical language awareness,* 174–199. London: Longman.

——— (1995). A synthetic sisterhood. In K. Hall and M. Bucholtz (eds.), *Gender Articulated*, 143–165. New York: Routledge.

Tannen, Deborah (1993). The relativity of linguistic strategies: Rethinking power and solidarity in gender and dominance. In D. Tannen (ed.), *Gender and conversational interactions*, 165–188. New York: Oxford University Press.

Weedon, Chris (1997[1887]). *Feminist practice and poststructuralist theory*. Oxford: Blackwell.

Wenger, Etienne (1998). *Communities of practice: Learning, meaning, and identity*. Cambridge: Cambridge University Press.

8

LAURA MILLER

You Are Doing *Burikko*!

Censoring/Scrutinizing Artificers of Cute Femininity in Japanese

A journalist writing for the *New York Times* (Kristof 1995) offered the following description of a female elevator operator at the Mitsukoshi department store in Ginza: "The Voice is as fawning as her demeanor, as sweet as syrup, and as high as a dog whistle. Any higher and it would shatter the crystal on the seventh floor." The author is reporting on the high-pitched voice frequently considered a stereotypical feature of the *burikko,* a derogatory Japanese label used to describe women who exhibit feigned naïveté. The word is derived from the term *buru* 'to pose, pretend, or act' and the suffix *-ko*, used for "child" or "girl," to mean something like "fake child" or "phony girl." This chapter will argue that the *burikko* designation does not simply reflect the uniform affectation of a childlike persona but rather is primarily established through situated social judgment elicited by a combination of speaker, recipient, and setting. A variety of linguistic and nonverbal phenomena are assessed as constituting the makeup of a *burikko* performance. I will look at some folk perceptions and media representations of the *burikko* and will also provide examples of socially contextualized occasions of talk in which *burikko* features in its evaluation. One outcome of a *burikko* performance is that it downplays or masks the adult sexuality of the woman doing it. An exploration of *burikko* supports a growing scholarly interest in the interconnections between linguistic ideology and gender performativity and also contributes to the literature on labeling practices.

According to Cherry (1987), the term *burikko* was invented by female singer Yamada Kuniko on a television program in 1980. Whether or not this is true, by at least 1981 *burikko* was commonly used in colloquial conversation, and the editors of an encyclopedia of postwar culture provided it on their list of trendy new words that were popular that year (Sasaki et al. 1991:1049). It certainly reached mainstream status by 1982, as evidenced by the song title for the debut single by the pop music group Grease, "*Burikko* Rock 'n' Roll." Although use of the word these days has decreased, Inoue (1986) found that during the years 1983–1984 *burikko* was one of the most popular new coinages used among young people.

Burikko was one of several neologisms formed during the first half of the 1980s through the suffixing of *-ko*. Yonekawa (1996:150) mentions *gameko*, coined in 1980 and clipped from *gametsui ko* 'a chintzy, money-grubbing girl' (Kansai dialect). There was also *kidoko,* from *kidotte iru ko* 'a girl who puts on airs', and *yumeko*, from *yume miru ko* a 'girl who dreams', for a romantic girl or woman. Once *burikko* was established, there was a gradual semantic broadening of the concept that allowed new coinages, including *majime burikko* 'child who pretends to be serious' and *burikko joshidaisee* 'cutesy-coeds', clipped from *joshi daigakusee* 'female college students'. Most recently we find *burikko kogyaru* 'phony KoGal'. *Kogyaru* originated as a media term used for young women who have bleached hair, loose socks (knee-length socks worn hanging around the ankles), and big shoes (Miller 2000). The term *kogyaru* is most likely a clipped version of *kookoosee gyaru* 'high school girl', and is not derived from the morpheme *ko*, which means "small," as many folk etymologies claim. *Kogyaru* has overtones of rebellious insolence and unchecked sexuality. The *burikko kogyaru* is therefore not a real KoGal at all but only someone pretending to be naughty and cool.

One problem connected to the *burikko* tag is that it has become synonymous, in some writing, with *young woman*. When the subject of women's language arises, the *burikko* label may worm its way into the discourse, especially among male writers. In Inoue's (1989) report on linguistic changes in the speech of women, he discusses the shift in pronunciation of the syllable *shi* to "si" as a phenomenon named *burikko hatsuon* '*burikko* pronunciation'. This label is used because only young women employ the new pronunciation, but it has the effect of classifying all young women as *burikko*.

Despite its use in numerous other contexts, the core meaning of *burikko* remains that of a woman who displays bogus innocence. Now the frequent object of ridicule, only a few decades ago the *burikko* was the natural product of the cult of cuteness so deliciously described by Kinsella (1995) and McVeigh (2000). The reified cute aesthetic that Treat (1996:283) once termed a "celebration of vapidness" was perfectly expressed by women who acted the part of the contriving maid. The master and prototype for exemplary *burikko* style was 1980s singer Matsuda Seiko. Wearing the hair of Gidget and the petticoats of Marie Antoinette, Matsuda with her pigeon-toed impersonation of a 14-year-old is still remembered as the epitome of the type more than 20 years later, even though she has since reinvented herself as a more mature celebrity. In my interviews, young people only a few years old when Matsuda first appeared still offer her first when asked to name *burikko*. Matsuda was part of the stream of childlike performers, called *aidoru* 'idols', who populated the 1980s pop music scene. Although these days *aidoru* tend to be much more womanly, a modified style of ultrafeminine cuteness is still a fashion option. For example, a women's magazine categorizes *burikko* as a trendy style obtainable through wearing pastels and lace (Tokyo go dai GAL sutairu zukan 2002).

Scholars have historically had an interest in how women are labeled and how these labels may reflect sexist, stereotypical viewpoints. A critique of such words is important because they often serve as vehicles for assumptions that are uncritically accepted as normal and therefore go unchallenged. As Cameron (1990:12) asserted, "Like other representations, linguistic representations both give a clue to the place of women in culture and constitute one means whereby we are kept in our place." A feminist perspective assumes that use of denigrating labels for women is not simply the reflection of an individual's nasty opinion or attitude but is also the manifestation of patriarchal social structure (Flax 1979). One goal of a feminist analysis is to explore the ways in which labeling and naming fortify a patriarchal system.

Although negative labels for women have been a focus of research in many languages, discussions of terms rarely incorporate an analysis of the contexts of their use and their evaluation. Researchers of language and gender note the scholarly history of ignoring women's experience in studies of language in society (Eckert & McConnell-Ginet 1992, Ochs 1992, Bucholtz 1999). While this erasure has been addressed in current research on Japanese, the speech of women characterized as *burikko* is still avoided as silly, inconsequential, and embarrassingly unworthy of academic attention. Stimulated and aided by the work of [Shibamoto] Smith (1992), Okamoto (1995), and others, I have been thinking about the nature of the *burikko* designation, what it means, and how it relates to a Japanese cultural ideology about proper female behavior. My interest in this topic was also aroused when I observed Japanese women I admired for their intelligence, good sense, and capability occasionally performing behaviors judged as *burikko*-ish. In the same manner in which Okamoto (1995) questions the category "Japanese women's language," I want to view the *burikko* not as a fixed personality or character type but as an evaluative interpretation of the behavior exhibited through linguistic, paralinguistic, prosodic, and nonverbal means in specific social settings. In other words, although some people are dismissed for "being" *burikko*, they are in fact simply "doing" *burikko*. Indeed, one often hears the expression *burikko suru* 'to do *burikko*'. This phrase indicates that there is a certain level of awareness on the part of scrutinizers and observers that *burikko* is a gender performance.

This approach to social identity means that individuals are not viewed as linguistic versions of the "social dope" (Giddens 1976) or as unthinking "types" who unthinkingly carry and broadcast their social identities at all times. Rather, we should see speakers as consciously and unconsciously drawing on linguistic and nonverbal repertoires that reflect idealized norms. In this case, some women who select too generously or inappropriately according to cultural norms from a menu of "feminine" and "childish" indexical forms will be negatively sanctioned through labeling as *burikko*. This is not to say that there is some absolute threshold level of linguistic forms that will trigger the evaluation or that there is a set amount of frilly femininity that will automatically doom the behavior as *burikko*. Because they draw from the same gendered cultural system, many of the features that typify a *burikko* performance are also part of acceptable female gender presentation or innocent girls' talk. When a woman is regarded as doing *burikko* because she is displaying overly feminine, innocent, or cute childishness in a specific situation, it is because these otherwise valued traits are thought to be inappropriate for her or for the situation at hand.

What is considered too much or inappropriate femininity or cuteness will also depend on the evaluator's stance. Young men might view this through jaded postmodern acerbity as impishly fake, while an older man thinks it sweetly girlish. In short, the same display of cuteness, childishness, or femininity can be seen as real or fake, depending on who is the actor and who is doing the evaluation.

Before offering examples of folk representations, I will begin with a description of some features that are thought to mark feminine or childish speech and commonly accompany the manifestation of *burikko* behavior.

8.1. Vocal drag and other features considered part of a *burikko* performance

In addition to the grammatical features of talk considered part of the female register (Shibamoto 1985, Ide & McGloin 1990), the performance characterized as that of a *burikko* may include specific vocal attributes. A combination of linguistic, prosodic, paralinguistic, and nonverbal features contributes to an interpretation of speech as *burikko*-like. Although representations and interpretations of *burikko* do not always distinguish these as separate indices, the most readily associated traits are the falsetto voice and a glissando movement through a pitch range. Additional features include a nasalized delivery, use of a baby-talk register, a sprinkling of amusing coinages, and mannerisms such as covering the mouth when smiling or laughing.

Vocal pitch is only partially the product of anatomical differences between women and men (Mattingly 1966). Pitch also reflects a pattern of cultural training that funnels speakers' voices into expected grooves. Differences in adult voices are due to unconscious pitch selection that approximates a vocal image that reflects culturally expected attributes. Although the manipulation of the vocal tract in order to correspond to gender expectations is usually learned early, transgender and transsexual media often includes books and tapes on voice passing. In a sense, the *burikko* voice is a similar form of vocal drag. For decades foreign observers of Japan have commented on the noticeably high voices of some female train station announcers, department store clerks, elevator girls, and television commercial narrators. The heightened pitch combined with formulaic politeness phrases used by these women is sometimes called the "service voice." Ohara (chapter 12, this volume) discusses the change of pitch heights in the service voice according to interlocutor. Moreover, despite superficial impressions, Japanese women's public voices show a range of variation and are not uniformly high-pitched. Morita Miyuki, an evening news anchor for Japan's public broadcasting corporation, was first rejected when she entered the broadcasting business because it was thought that her voice was too low, and an esteemed member of the Japanese Diet, Doi Takako, is often characterized as having a voice on the extreme low end of the scale.

The seemingly marked nature of women's vocal pitch in Japan led many researchers to embark on more empirical analyses, with the aim of examining actual pitch variation. Yamazawa and Hollien (1992) review three different studies that reported a higher average pitch for Japanese women than for Euroamerican women. Loveday (1981) measured pitch in two Japanese women's speech while uttering formulaic expressions. While the average pitch range for American and English women is

214 hertz (van Bezooijen 1995:253), Loveday found soaring pitch peaks between 310 and 450 hertz for the Japanese women. We should note that most often these studies are carried out in foreign laboratory settings, where subjects are usually from elite social backgrounds and are speakers for whom a particular version of femininity impression management is important. In another study, Ohara (1992) found that Japanese women modify their pitch when reading English sentences, producing speech in a slightly lower pitch range. The average pitch frequency for her subjects was 19 hertz greater when speaking Japanese. The outcome was explained as unconscious, learned behavior: "Displaying femininity is an automatic process in most cases. Controlling the larynx to produce higher-pitched sound may be a part of the automatic process" (Ohara 1992:474). Van Bezooijen (1995), working in Japan, asked 8 Japanese women to read a narrative text and used a recording of their voices as the stimulus for ratings by 30 other Japanese subjects. She did not find the expected high pitches in the speakers she used in her study. However, she did find that listeners associated women's higher pitch with the values of femininity, weakness, meekness, and dependency. She also found that listeners considered a medium and a high pitch more attractive in women than a low pitch.

When a woman is performing *burikko*, her pitch will often rise to a level above that she normally uses in casual speech. This *burikko* voice, with its air of ineffectuality, is thought to most often be elicited in the presence of powerful males. It announces that the speaker is unsure, weak, or less powerful. In my interviews and in my reading of women's magazines, I frequently encounter the belief that it is *otoko no mae* 'in front of men' that the *burikko* voice is most frequently manifested. In order to stay within the bounds of gender expectations, Japanese women have been described as using a variety of techniques when faced with conflicting role responsibilities, such as managerial positions in corporate life. They may, for instance, use a combination of listening behaviors, repetition, sentence particles, intonation patterns, and prefacing to buffer managerial directives. [Shibamoto] Smith (1992) has suggested that use of a mother register, or "Motherese," is one strategy women in positions of authority employ when dealing with male subordinates. *Burikko* talk may be exploited as another type of linguistic strategy, this one used on the part of subordinate women for dealing with male authority. A wheedling pitch is used for the same reason we find it in other language communities, because speakers "calculate that it is most likely to bring the ends they desire" (McConnell-Ginet 1983:83). A woman who takes on the social role of a *burikko* is asking to be given the same lenience and indulgence accorded to an unschooled child. Of course, the speaker herself must be aware of her fake performance for it to be considered intentional. She is consciously placing herself in the role of the innocent, reflecting cultural expectations that women not be knowledgeable about certain cultural domains.

It is not just a high pitch that leads to an interpretation of the speaker as simulating innocence but also a melodic swoop over the vocal cords (physiologically, the speed of the vibration of the vocal folds varies from low to high). The importance of this element became clear to me when I watched a Japanese television series named *Hotel* with a Japanese female friend.[1] In one scene a prostitute mistakes one of the main male characters for a customer. When he explains the misunderstanding, the woman riffs through a protestation of surprise, exclaiming, with a particularly sweet and sugary voice, "*Nan da. Anata mita toki rakkii to omota no ni*" 'Oh, gee. When I saw you I thought I got lucky'. As she watched, my friend sneered, "*Burikko!*" at the screen. Here, despite the fact that the character's interlocutor demonstrated knowledge of her activities as a sex worker, the actress presented her character as a pristine pixie expressing disappointment at a failed date. She did this through the manipulation of the features of pitch range often attributed to the *burikko* character.

The doing of *burikko* may also be accomplished through use of a nasalized delivery that accompanies the high-pitched voice. I located an example in a television program titled *Tokyo erebeetaa gaaru* 'Tokyo Elevator Girls', a soap opera series about the young women who greet and assist customers in posh department stores.[2] Interspersed throughout the narrative are scenes of the elevator girls being trained in how to properly address customers with just the right words and cheery intonation, the so-called service voice. In one scene, an elevator girl (played by actress Miyazawa Rie, considered something of a *burikko* herself by some critics) is out visiting a shrine on an illicit date with a married coworker. Although they have been standing next to it for some time, she "suddenly" notices a box that sells fortunes and exclaims in a high-pitched voice, "*Ahh . . . ne, omikuji ikoo, omikuji ne*" 'Hey! Let's go for a fortune—a fortune, OK?' After paying her fee, she reaches into the box to grab a fortune paper while imploring the gods to be kind, chanting, "*Ii no ga demasu yoo ni*" 'Let a good thing come of it', a formulaic way of requesting a happy wish, yet here uttered with emphasized nasality. The viewer of this performance knows that the character has seen the fortune box prior to the exclamation of noticing it, that she is not in a happy situation (she sneaks around to see her married lover), and that her childlike expressions and innocent vocal qualities are not at all reflective of her actual status.

When *manga* 'comic book' artists want to illustrate *burikko* behavior, they often use drawn out syllables in speech bubbles to represent the high-pitched, nasalized voice. For example, figure 8.1 (Moritsugu 1998:458) features a 21-year-old OL character (*OL* or *Office Lady* is used to mean a female clerical worker), who responds to a question about how her lover is doing with, "*Iya~~ne, himitsu yo*" 'Oh, dear . . . it's a secret'. Elongation of the syllable *ya* is indicated with a wavy line. The hand-to-cheek gesture also suggests that she is overacting the role of an unsophisticated girl.

Another important feature attending the *burikko* display is a baby-talk register that casts the speaker in the role of a credulous innocent who ought to be the recipient of the listeners' indulgence. Features characteristic of baby talk are avoidance of Chinese loans, use of the honorific prefix *o-*, phonological modifications, use of onomatopoeic words, and reduplication. Avoidance of Chinese loans entails rejection of erudite *kango*, words of Sinitic origin that suggest complex concepts beyond the *burikko*'s hazy scope. An example would be using *uso* 'lie' but never *kyogi* 'falsehood'. The use of the honorific prefix *o-*, often considered polite and refined and hence a feature of the female register (Shibamoto 1987), is extended to everyday words such as *otete* in place of *te* for "hand" and *omeme* for "eye" rather than *me*. There are often phonological modifications, such as *katchoi*, from *kakkoii* 'cool', and *yappashi*, from *yappari* 'after all'. Similar forms are *kawayuui* for *kawaii* 'cute' (Inoue 1986) and *utchoo* in place of *uso* 'lie' (Horiuchi & Omori 1994). Onomatopoeic words and mimetic nouns are used liberally, such as *wanwan* 'bowwow' for "dog" (the unmarked form is *inu*) and *chu chu* for "small bird" (rather than *kotori*). In her research

FIGURE 8.1. Comic book representation of *burikko* behavior

on Japan's cultural aesthetic of cuteness, Kinsella (1995) suggests that some favorite *burikko* words derive from the deliberately contrived speech of pop idol Sakai Noriko. During 1987, Noriko's coinages, uttered with an endearing lisp and called *Norippi-go* 'Noriko language', were widely emulated by others. These cute labialized forms included *ureppi*, from *ureshii*, meaning "happy," and *kanappi* from *kanashii* for "sad." Yonekawa (1996:83) also includes *okabii* from *okashi* 'funny' and *batchishi* from *batchiri* 'right on' or 'no sweat' on his list of Noriko words. Reduplication is often used for animals, body parts, or indelicate concepts, as in *nenne* in place of *neru* 'to sleep', which has a euphemistic connection to sex, and *babatchi* from *baba* 'poo-poo' for "icky poo" or "yucky."

Other features that imbue speech with *burikko*-ness involve special lexical and stylistic forms, such as extended use of diminutive or familiar title suffixes with names, novel lexical clipping, and display of hesitation or uncertainty. For example, address terms are used for inanimate objects, animals, or parts of the body. One example is *taku-chan* 'Little Mr. Taxi' for "taxi." This is derived from a clipped form of *takushii* 'taxi' combined with the diminutive address term *-chan* (Yoshioka 1993). Indeed, both the elfin *-chan* and the familiar *-kun* have proven to be very productive for the creation of "cute" lexical items. Other combinations I have heard used by adult women include *wanchan* 'Mr. Bowwow' to refer to a dog and the appellation *tsuru tsuru-kun* 'Mr. Smooth' used in reference to young men who use hair removal products on their chests in order to be more attractive (in accordance with new beauty norms; see Miller 2003). Talk may be heard as girlishly cute when it contains an abundance of amusing coinages or charming constructions of the *wasee eego* 'Japan-made English' type, which frequently involve novel lexical clipping (Miller 1998b). For example, there is *pii suru* for *PHS o kakeru* or "use a cell phone," *PHS* is an acronym for "personal handyphone system." Another amusing coinage is *kenta-kun* 'Mr. Kentucky Fried Chicken', used to refer to relatively young men who have beards and are sort of fuddy-duddyish (Yonekawa 1991). This is created through a clipped form of *Kentucky* combined with the intimate address term *–kun* and is presumably derived from the Kentucky Fried Chicken logo, which features the company's goateed founder, Colonel Sanders. Although use of new or trendy lexical items in and of itself does not transform the speaker into a *burikko*, their use in otherwise formal situations may have that result. A type of syntactic clipping, in which sentences are left incomplete or drift off into inaudibleness, will also mark speech as timorously artificial.

Nonverbal correlates of the *burikko* performance include a head tilt to the side and clasping the hands in front of the body when one hand is not demurely covering the mouth. The use of the hand to shield the mouth when smiling or laughing is a custom traced to at least the Edo period (Casal 1966), and most likely is related to an underlying interpretation of teeth display as an aggressive signal. Covering the teeth is therefore seen as a form of submissiveness. These days many young women are expressing opposition to the enduring custom of enshrouding the female mouth by emphasizing their white teeth and by refusing to cover their mouths when laughing or giggling. The result is that when they are "doing *burikko*" this aspect of the performance is highlighted.

An assemblage of vocal features, linguistic usage, and nonverbal behaviors as described earlier contributes to a gendered performance that may therefore become the object of criticism or commentary. These reactions to the *burikko* display frequently surface in books, magazines, and other media.

8.2. Media and folk assessments
of *burikko* performances

An etiquette book titled *Anthology of OL Taboos* (Zennikku Eigyohonbu Kyoiku-kunrenbu 1991:181) admonishes female clerks to avoid loading their office desks with "character goods," such as Mickey Mouse pencils or Hello Kitty staplers (fig. 8.2). A woman who surrounds herself with such items is said to be *yoochi* 'in-fantile' and incompetent. Advice like this tells us that while cuteness is thought to be an approved aspect of femininity display, it is nevertheless sanctioned within certain age/status limits or locales.

In an interview with *Harvard Magazine*, an anthropologist in the United States classified *burikko* as a cultural style of consumption and self-expression. According to him, the quintessential *burikko* collects toys, wears girlish clothing, and is heard "giggling and squealing in a high-pitched voice" (Hodder 1997). But his description suggests that *burikko* is an all-or-nothing identity, rather than a social evaluation that arises from situated behavior. His characterization, in fact, is more properly that of the *shoojo* 'young miss' rather than the *burikko*. Treat (1996:281) describes the *shoojo* as one whose sexual energy is directed toward stuffed animals and cute artifacts. The concept of the *shoojo* implies an adolescent postpubescent space that revels in all that is cute, pink, fluffy, and adorable, with an absence of heterosexual experience (but not necessarily of homosexual experience; see Robertson 1989:59). In some cases then, women too obviously beyond the *shoojo* age-group who perform childlike behaviors will be termed *burikko*. The display meant to neutralize adult sexuality, when performed by those clearly beyond an age of innocence, unmasks the artifice of the maneuver. A disjuncture between the speaker's age and her display of cute-ness is a critical aspect of many cases of *burikko* ascription. This fact is illustrated by reactions to women's use of an orthographic fashion popular among schoolgirls, the use of writing called *maru moji* 'round characters' (Yamane 1986; see also Kataoka 1997). Some women retain this innovation from girls' culture as they enter the

FIGURE 8.2. Cute goods in the office. Published with permission of Goma Shobo

workforce, where it may become an object of commentary and ridicule or mark them as doing *burikko*. In conduct literature such as *Anthology of OL Taboos* (Zennikku Eigyohonbu Kyoikukunrenbu 1991:100), female clerks are advised not to use round script in memos to coworkers, even when they do so because they think it will make the information easier to understand. In figure 8.3, a male colleague expresses exasperation at the use of round characters he finds in a memo from an OL, which says: "*Nakamura-san kara Tel arimashita. Keeko*" 'There's a telephone message from Mr. Nakamura. Keiko'.

Complaints about *burikko* can be found in Japanese women's magazines, which have become a forum where expressions of anger or dissatisfaction with others may be safely vented. In one feature article that discusses disliked behaviors of coworkers, people complained about women they termed *burikko* (Uchi no kaisha no kanchigai OL 1996). One writer deplores a woman who uses nicknames on the telephone, saying things like *Waa . . . Kin-chan* 'Ohh! . . . Kinnie!' In this case, it is felt that use of a diminutive nickname and the diminutive address term *-chan* is evidence of babyishness and immaturity. Another reader provided the example of a 30-year-old woman in her office who uses a kittenish, obsequious voice to say things like *Gomen nachyaa* 'Ooohh, I'm sorryy!' The hearer's reaction is *Kimochi warui* 'It gives me the creeps'.

In popular media and in interviews, *burikko* are characterized as both shallow airheads and crafty flatterers. People often say a distinctive feature of *burikko* talk is that they always utter *hazukashii* 'I'm embarrassed' even though it's clear they aren't the least bit mortified. And as noted earlier, most commentators suggest that it is *otoko no mae* 'in front of men' that the *burikko* is most likely to make her appearance. Former pornographic film star Ikuma Ai once performed a classic *burikko* drill on TV when

FIGURE 8.3. Cute 'round characters'. Published with permission of Goma Shobo

she covered her mouth while giggling and saying, "*Hazukashii!*" 'How embarrassing!' in response to a talk show host's impertinent questions. When young men were asked to name the top five celebrities they would not want to be married to, they included actress Miyazawa Rie (Otoko hyakunin ga yuu onna no fushigi rankingu 1996). Miyazawa represents a *burikko* type because early in her career she publicly presented the image of a sheltered upper-class daughter of the suburbs but in fact has done some racy things behind the scenes, such as posing nude and having a love affair with a Sumo wrestler (Schilling 1992).

Readers of a women's magazine asked to provide examples of "really nauseating *burikko* OLs" (*choo mukatsuku burikko OL*) offer examples that illustrate how the switch to counterfeit behavior is often triggered by the presence of men (Uchi no kaisha no kanchigai OL 1996). One clerk writes to complain that a coworker uses *amaeta koe* 'bootlicking voice', a sweet, smarmy tone used to wheedle things out of silly male section heads and managers. A 27-year-old man writes in to gripe about a woman who aggressively chastises juniors and coworkers, yet "her voice goes up one octave in front of male seniors" (*jooshi no mae de wa ichi okutabu koe ga takaku naru*). Another woman reports on a coworker who graphically talks about anything and everything imaginable among girlfriends when they are in private areas such as the ladies' room, but if there's naughty talk in front of men she modestly exclaims, "*Ya daa! Hazukashii*" 'That's disgusting! I'm so embarrassed'. Describing a woman who does *burikko* in her office, someone else writes: "She uses a saccharine voice to butter up male superiors. I can't tell you how disgusting it is when I see her stroking his arm while saying things like, 'Section head, the shirt you have on today is really fab'" ("*Chokuzoku no otoko no jooshi ni amattarui koe de obekka o tsukau 'Kachoo kyoo no Y-shatsu suteki desu ne' to ude no atari o surisuri shite iru tokoro o mita toki ni wa, akirete mono ga ienakatta*").

That some women will use a *burikko* performance to manipulate an older male coworker points up another dimension to interpretation. Not all observers will agree on whether or not a given performance is *burikko*-like. It is clear that there will be different attitudes on the part of those from different age and social backgrounds and that interpretation also hinges on the social situation in which *burikko* behavior occurs. In other words, one person's *burikko* is another's proper well-bred miss. Contemporary young people, both female and male, react negatively to extreme forms of docility and cuteness, but older Japanese men may still admire and endorse the subservient pose of those who do *burikko*. Even if an older man discerns the fakeness of a *burikko* stance, he may still like what the pose represents. As feminist writers remind us, the cute infantilization of women places them in a weaker social position. According to a male critic, while seeing *burikko* behavior as somewhat silly, some men will still consider it "ear massage" (Hosokawa Shuhei, personal communication). Since the 1990s, there has been a change in younger men's attitudes and women who are coy, overly docile, and indecisive have been disparaged (Miller 1998a). When asked which type of women they least like, young men polled by a men's magazine ranked *burikko* number 9 on their list of top 10 peeves (Kore dake wa yurusen! 1999).

The concept of the *burikko*, then, has much to do with the perceiver and her or his ideas about gendered talk. Conflicting evaluations of speech marked as "feminine" illustrates the way in which norms have been changing. During her first official public interview after her marriage to the Crown Prince, Princess Masako, an articulate woman who attended Harvard University, sat demurely and meekly, saying very little. On the one hand, I heard older observers exclaim, "She's marvelous," approving of her display of modesty and reserve. On the other hand, young women who now have revised ideas about female propriety suggested that Masako was a *burikko* sellout.

When one of the university students I interviewed teasingly urged his female classmate to "*burikko yatte mite*" 'try doing *burikko*', she stonily refused, not finding it an amusing request at all. The *New York Times*' Japan correspondent Kristof (1995) interviewed a 15-year-old girl who said, "When girls speak in really high voices, I just want to kick them in the head. It's totally fake and really annoying. It gives me a headache." McVeigh interviewed a female university student who expressed a similar view.

> I hate this word [*burikko*]. Girls in Japan tend to be different when they are with girls or with boys. Their voice changes. I have seen my sister, so I know. When the telephone rings, they clear their throats, and I don't know where this voice comes from, but a cute little voice comes out from somewhere. I hate this moment. They are lying to the people they are talking to . . . *Burikko* women are hated by most women and liked by only a few men. I just want them to stop pretending. (2000:147)

Despite these negative assessments, such *burikko* behaviors as high pitch are connected to prescribed cultural norms of femininity. Conduct literature, ethnographic research (Lebra 1984, McVeigh 1996), and other sources have provided a clear picture of the relationship between Japanese gender ideology and canons for appropriate female behavior and language for middle-class women. One of the traits valued as an aspect of femininity is cheerfulness. For example, in a "how-to" book titled *Fundamental Checklist of OL Manners* (Nakamura 1993:137), readers are cautioned about proper vocal attributes: "Pay attention to the volume, tone and speed of your voice. For the person with a low-pitched voice, rather than using your ordinary voice, it's probably better to speak in a slightly higher pitch. That way you will impart a cheery, bright image." Although the behavior and mannerisms advocated by Nakamura may "work" for young women in some contexts, these rules for good speech behavior may also fall flat, depending on the speaker and the degree to which her sincerity is seamlessly accepted. When speech is delivered in such a manner by a woman of the wrong age, status, or class, it could be negatively evaluated.

We also find that conduct literature advocates behaviors that in other instances are denigrated as insincere meekness. Conflicting messages directed at women are not at all uncommon in popular writing (Miller 1998a). These discrepancies are sometimes the result of media targeting readerships from different age or class backgrounds, but in some instances the contradictory information is presented in the same book or article. For example, while handing out advice on how to display proper deference to male superiors and to raise one's vocal pitch in order to be more "cheery," Nakamura (1993) also admonishes readers not to be too self-effacing or unsure of themselves. Likewise, in a women's magazine article on dating behaviors that aggravate men, women who only utter platitudes along the lines of "Oh, that was interesting" or who keep saying, "Anywhere is fine," while on a date are severely chastised as graceless ticklebrains: "Don't you know any other words?" ask commentators (Hajimete no deai de, kirawarechau hito, daisuki ni sasechau hito 1994). While they may be reading this type of advice in one place, women will be told the opposite in etiquette manuals such as *Manners for Age Twenty and Over* (Tanaka 1993), where they are cautioned not to express their ideas or opinions and to play it safe by falling back on bland generalities.

8.3. Evaluations of situated *burikko* performances

Performing ultrafeminine behaviors reveals a desire to showcase a decorous *ojoosama* 'proper young miss' upbringing, but it could have unfortunate consequences for those who misjudge the recipients of their act or the setting in which it is performed. Even in cases in which a display of modesty is expected, the speaker may nevertheless fall victim to *burikko* labeling. A look at a few instances of situated talk in which the woman was described as "doing *burikko*" illustrates how, while aspects of their performance accord with acceptable feminine conduct, other attributes confound or disturb this meaning.

On one occasion I witnessed a *burikko* performance at the building where I was housed with other foreigners associated with a Japanese engineering university. Students frequently came by to hang out upstairs on a balcony. One day I went there to talk to a small group about men's *esute* 'body aesthetics', or male beauty work. This school had once been an all-male university, and there are still very few female students. The women who are there have entered by virtue of superior math and science skills that enabled them to beat out male competitors. All the women I met were highly intelligent, straightforward, serious, and unpretentious. As I talked with them on the balcony, an American male student came up and, not understanding what we were discussing, asked for a translation. When I explained that many Japanese women find body hair on men unattractive, which has led to the development of new products and services for male body hair removal, he was incredulous. He refused to believe me, claiming that chest hair in particular indicates that one is a "real man," and that women universally "dig it." I suggested that different aesthetic sensibilities are in operation, but he continued to protest against such an idea. Just then Naoko, a female student as bright as any I met, came up to join our group. The American chap, deciding to simply test my theory empirically, lifted his shirt to display his hairy chest, asking her what she thought. Naoko screamed, "*Iya da!*" 'How hateful!' in a shrill voice and ran to hide behind a door while periodically peeking out to whimper at the unspeakable sight. One of the Japanese men who witnessed this muttered in puzzlement, "*Dooshite burikko shiteru no?*" 'Why is she doing *burikko*?' It took me by surprise to see someone I never expected had an ounce of artifice in her instantly portray the precious imp. Yet it served to illustrate the degree to which *burikko* behavior may be elicited by situations that demand a public display of modesty (or legitimate revulsion) and is therefore not a persona a woman adopts or continually performs. Indeed, had Naoko openly stared at the naked male chest, she would have been the recipient of other denigrating labels. Some days later I asked Naoko her opinion of *burikko*. "They're disgusting," she told me.

This instance reveals that there are settings or topics of conversation that are likely to create a *burikko*-like response. According to a discourse of heightened femininity, there are aspects of the world a proper woman ought not to possess knowledge of, just like a young and unsophisticated child. Hence, when sex and sexuality are introduced into talk, squeak-toy disclaimers are to be expected. The former porn star who claims a sense of disgust at sexual innuendo and the college-aged woman who acts as if she's never seen a bare male chest are both expected to show modesty yet both are accused of doing *burikko* because there is good reason to suspect that these are not truthful responses.[3]

I offer a final example of a *burikko* performance, although not a real one, that was negatively sanctioned. One evening I went with my coworkers, two other female professors, to a local restaurant for something to eat after work. Two of us went ahead in one car to be joined later by the other, the director of the program. We arrived before her and were talking when I mentioned that I was wondering about the nature of *burikko*. As a joke, my colleague Hiromi went into a *burikko* imitation. Raising her pitch level a few octaves, she began uttering inanities. In the midst of her act the director walked in and, hearing her subordinate, yelled at her, "*Nan de burikko shiteru no?!*" 'Why are you acting like a *burikko*?!' Of course, we explained the situation and laughed about it, and Hiromi resumed her normal speaking manner.

However, on other occasions I witnessed this same chastising director, a woman in her thirties, perform self-acknowledged *burikko* behavior. While discussing the problems that women still face in the workplace, especially in academic settings, she told me of how they must be careful to display deferential behavior to their male colleagues to avoid threatening them. Contemplating her own career trajectory, she said (in English), "I have to learn to do *burikko* better to get ahead." It is interesting that she would view *burikko* behavior done to manipulate men as necessary yet see *burikko* behavior performed in a women-only group as totally unacceptable. A few occasions on which her female colleagues reported that she affected *burikko* mannerisms included while she was speaking to male principals during a trip to a local school and greeting male dignitaries at a formal reception. At these times she reportedly assumed a lacy vocal singsong uplift (distinguished by a thin, light voice quality, giving an impression of immaturity) and spoke with numerous self-corrections and hesitation markers. She also covered her mouth while smiling or giggling.

In searching for the *burikko*, I found that tenets for proper female behavior place some women in a behavioral paradox. While a woman is taught that docility, innocence, femininity, childishness, and cuteness are desired commodities, if such a display doesn't suit her age or status or the situation, her behavior will be judged as phony *burikko* pretense. Like Naoko's dilemma when faced with the foreigner's bare torso, this could be a frank instance of damned if she does and damned if she doesn't. As we have seen from magazines, television, and other representations, as well as from situated instances, a disjuncture between what we know about someone and the sort of "feminine" behavior she is pressured to exhibit can sometimes result in fleeting *burikko* scenes.

As Ochs (1992) has pointed out, indexing of gender is not a simple process of hooking up linguistic forms to speaker sex. Instead, speakers draw from a menu of stereotypical forms to enact social identities. Could it also be that, like a bad actor, the woman evaluated as a *burikko* is really just caught "doing gender" red-handed?

Is it the case that she deploys indexical forms unbefitting her situation and is disliked because the manipulation of expected gender traits becomes just too transparent, too camp? Perhaps a *burikko* performance makes us uncomfortable because it asserts a hard truth about gender roles in general, which is, as American drag queen RuPaul put it, that we're all born the same and the rest is drag.

From the study of *burikko* we may detect a rising consciousness that the way one speaks is intimately tied to social position. There is increasing evidence that a change in gender roles and expectations is changing speech behavior. Many younger women are eschewing features of language considered markers of the "feminine" and are incorporating aspects of the male register into their own speech (Okamoto & Sato 1992, Okamoto 1995). There have been enough of these latter types that a negative label was coined to categorize them. This is the *oremeshi onna* 'me-food woman', a term that parodies an autocratic husband's command. *Oremeshi onna* are said to totally reject features of talk characteristic of the *burikko* in favor of hypermasculine forms. In the worldview of younger, contemporary Japanese, the type of sugary child exhibitionism displayed in *burikko* performances is viewed as deceitful and creepy, and they would rather risk being called *oremeshi onna* than *burikko*. Although this change suggests that ideas about women's speech are opening up a space for variation, it also tells us that women continue to be objects of intense social surveillance. Whether they are conforming to gender norms, challenging them, or overdoing them, Japanese women continue to be the recipients of derogatory labeling.

Notes

A version of this chapter was first presented at the 1997 meeting of the American Anthropological Association, in Washington, D.C. I would like to thank Jan Bardsley, Mary Bucholtz, Yuka Fukunaga, Yuko Hoshino, Shuhei Hosokawa, Shigeko Okamoto, and Janet S. Shibamoto Smith for their comments and suggestions. All translations and mistakes are my own.

1. *Hotel* was a five-part Tokyo Broadcasting System television drama that first began airing in 1990, about workers and guests at a luxury hotel.

2. *Tokyo erebeetaa gaaru*, written by Komatsu Eriko, aired on the Tokyo Broadcasting System during Winter 1992. The English loan *girl* has two forms in Japanese, *gaaru* and *gyaru*. This TV program used the former.

3. The line between acceptable feminine behavior and *burikko* categorization may also relate to other factors besides age or innocence, particularly class status. A display of pro forma sweetness might be tolerated when done by debutante girls from elite family backgrounds, yet the woman or girl who lacks cultural capital and displays her class origins will have her failed efforts described as *burikko*-ish.

References

Bucholtz, Mary (1999). "Why be normal"? Language and identity practices in a community of nerd girls. *Language in Society* 28(2): 203–223.

Cameron, Deborah (1990). Introduction: Why is language a feminist issue? In D. Cameron (ed.), *The feminist critique of language*, 1–28. London: Routledge.

Casal, U. A. (1966). Japanese cosmetics and teeth blackening. *Transactions of the Asiatic Society of Japan* 9: 5–27.

Cherry, Kittredge (1987). *Womansword: What Japanese words say about women.* Tokyo: Kodansha International.

Eckert, Penelope, and Sally McConnell-Ginet (1992). Think practically and look locally: Language and gender as community-based practice. *Annual Review of Anthropology* 21: 461–490.

Flax, Jane (1979). Women do theory. *Quest* 5(1): 20–26.

Giddens, Anthony (1976). *New rules of sociological method.* New York: Basic Books.

Hajimete no deai de, kirawarechau hito, daisuki ni sasechau hito (Detestable people and people who are really likable in first encounters) (1994). *Say* 137: 196–200.

Hodder, Harbour Fraser (1997). Right now: Tokyo Disney. *Harvard Magazine*, July–August. Online: http://www.harvard_magazine.com/issues/ja97/right.disney.html.

Horiuchi, Katsuaki, and Yoshiko Ômori (1994). Wakai josee no kotoba no gokee, gogi no tokushoku (Characteristics of word form and word meaning in young women's speech). *Nihongogaku* 13: 72–80.

Ide, Sachiko, and Naomi Hanaoka McGloin (eds.) (1990). *Aspects of Japanese women's language.* Tokyo: Kuroshio.

Inoue, Fumio (1986). Sociolinguistic aspects of new dialect forms. *International Journal of the Sociology of Language* 58: 73–89.

——— (1989). Shiin no hatsuon no henka (Changes in the pronunciation of consonants). In S. Miyoko (ed.), *Nihongo no onsee, on'in (The voice and vocal sounds of Japanese)*, 109–134. Tokyo: Meiji Shoin.

Kataoka, Kuniyoshi (1997). Affect and letter writing: Unconventional conventions in casual writing by young Japanese women. *Language in Society* 26: 103–136.

Kinsella, Sharon (1995). Cuties in Japan. In L. Skov and Brian Moeran (eds.), *Women, media and consumption in Japan*, 220–254. Honolulu: University of Hawaii Press.

Kore dake wa yurusen! '99 Saisho no rankingu (Just this is not permitted! Our first ranking of 1999) (1999). *Rankingu Daisuki,* March, 88.

Kristof, Nicholas (1995). Japan's feminine falsetto falls right out of favor. *New York Times*, December 13.

Lebra, Takie Sugiyama (1984) *Japanese women: Constraint and fulfillment.* Honolulu: University of Hawaii Press.

Loveday, Leo (1981). Pitch, politeness, and sexual role: An exploratory investigation into the pitch correlates of English and Japanese politeness formulae. *Language and Speech* 24: 97–107.

Mattingly, Ignatius (1966). Speaker variation and vocal tract size. *Journal of the Acoustical Society of America* 39: 1219.

McConnell-Ginet, Sally (1983). Intonation in a man's world. In B. Thorne, C. Kramarae, and N. Henley (eds.), *Language, gender and society*, 69–88. Boston: Heinle and Heinle. (= 1978 *Signs* 3: 541–559).

McVeigh, Brian (1996). *Life in a Japanese women's college: Learning to be ladylike.* London: Routledge.

——— (2000). *Wearing ideology: State, schooling and self-presentation in Japan.* Oxford: Berg.

Miller, Laura (1998a). Bad girls: Representations of unsuitable, unfit, and unsatisfactory women in magazines. *U.S.-Japan Women's Journal* 15: 31–51.

——— (1998b). *Wasei eigo*: English "loanwords" coined in Japan. In J. Hill, P. J. Mistry, and L. Campbell (eds.), *The life of language: Papers in linguistics in honor of William Bright,* 123–139. The Hague: Mouton/De Gruyter.

———— (2000). Media typifications and hip *bijin*. *U.S.-Japan Women's Journal* 19: 176–205.

———— (2003). Male beauty work in Japan. In J. Roberson and N. Suzuki (eds.), *Men and masculinities in contemporary Japan: Dislocating the salaryman doxa*, 37–58. New York: Routledge.

Moritsugu, Yahiro (1998). *Kaihoo no shirushi: Hana to yume (The scars of liberation: Flowers and dreams)*, 456–501. Tokyo: Hakusensha.

Nakamura, Yoichirô (1993). *OL manaa kihon chiekku (Fundamental checklist of OL manners)*. Tokyo: Isetan.

Ochs, Elinor (1992). Indexing gender. In A. Duranti and C. Goodwin (eds.), *Rethinking context: Language as an interactive phenomenon*, 335–358. Cambridge: Cambridge University Press.

Ohara, Yumiko (1992). Gender-dependent pitch levels: A comparative study in Japanese and English. In K. Hall, M. Bucholtz, and B. Moonwoman (eds.), *Locating power: Proceedings of the Second Berkeley Women and Language Conference*, 469–477. Berkeley: Berkeley Women and Language Group.

Okamoto, Shigeko, (1995). "Tasteless" Japanese: Less "feminine" speech among young Japanese women. In K. Hall and M. Bucholtz (eds.), *Gender articulated: Language and the socially constructed self*, 297–325. New York: Routledge.

Okamoto, Shigeko, and Shie Sato (1992). Less feminine speech among young Japanese females. In K. Hall, M. Bucholtz, and B. Moonwomon (eds.), *Locating power: Proceedings of the Second Berkeley Women and Language Conference*, 478–488. Berkeley: Berkeley Women and Language Group.

Otoko hyakunin ga yuu onna no fushigi rankingu (Strange ranking of women according to 100 men) (1996). *Say* 153: 7.

Robertson, Jennifer (1989). Gender-bending in paradise: Doing "female" and "male" in Japan. *Genders* 5: 50–69.

Sasaki, Takeshi, Tsurumi Shunsuke, Tominaka Ken'ichi, Nakamura Masanori, Masamura Kimihiro, and Murakami Yôichirô (eds.) (1991). *Sengoshi daijiten 1945–1990 (Encyclopedia of postwar Japan 1945–1990)*. Tokyo: Sanseido.

Schilling, Mark (1992). Worshiping the naked Goddess: The media, mores, and Miyazawa Rie. *Japan Quarterly* 105(23): 218–224.

Shibamoto, Janet S. (1985). *Japanese women's language*. New York: Academic Press.

———— (1987). The womanly woman. In S. Philips, C. Tanz, and S. Steele (eds.), *Language, gender and sex in comparative perspective*, 26–49. Cambridge, MA: Cambridge University Press.

[Shibamoto] Smith, Janet S. (1992). Women in charge: Politeness and directives in the speech of Japanese women. *Language in Society* 21(1): 59–82.

Tanaka, Toshiyuki (1993). *Hatachi kara no manaa (Manners for age twenty and over)*. Tokyo: Shobunsha Shuppan.

Tokyo go dai GAL sutairu zukan (Picture book of five big Tokyo Gal styles) (2002). *Popteen*, July, 76–82.

Treat, John (1996).Yoshimoto Banana writes home: The *shôjo* in Japanese popular culture. In J. Treat (ed.), *Contemporary Japan and popular culture*, 275–308. Honolulu: University of Hawaii Press.

Uchi no kaisha no kanchigai OL (The clueless OLs in my company) (1996). *Can Cam* 174: 419–423.

Yamane Kazuma (1986). *Hentai shoojo moji no kenkyuu (Research on abnormal girls' characters)*. Tokyo: Kodansha.

Yamazawa, H., and H. Hollien (1992). Speaking fundamental frequency of Japanese women. *Phonetica* 49: 128–140.

Yonekawa, Akihiro (1991). *Wakamono-go jiten* 4 (Dictionary of young people's speech 4). *Gengo* 20(8): 19.

——— (1996). *Gendai wakamono kotobakoo* (*Analysis of current youth language*). Tokyo: Maruzen.

Yoshioka, Yasuo (1993). Wakamono-go inobêshon (Innovations in young people's speech). *Gengo* 22(1): 110.

van Bezooijen, Renee (1995). Sociocultural aspects of pitch differences between Japanese and Dutch women. *Language and Speech* 38(3): 253–265.

Zennikku Eigyohonbu Kyoikukunrenbu (ed.) (1991). *OL tabuushuu* (*Anthology of OL taboos*). Tokyo: Goma Shobô.

9

ORIE ENDO
JANET S. SHIBAMOTO SMITH, TRANSLATOR

Women and Words

*The Status of Sexist Language in Japan
as Seen through Contemporary Dictionary
Definitions and Media Discourse*

One often hears the argument that in order to eliminate sexist language, it is first necessary to eliminate sexism; as long as there is sexism, it is useless to problematize sexist language alone. However, I argue that the existence of sexist language supports and reproduces sexist attitudes and it is, thus, *essential* to problematize sexist language itself. In this chapter, I focus on three of the many derogatory words used to describe women in Japanese. I examine their treatment both in a sample of Japanese language dictionaries and, more briefly, in the media. While the use of sexist expressions in the media has decreased considerably over time, in dictionaries the treatment of many sexist words remains largely unchanged. Although media have their own shaping effects on the public understanding of gender (see chapters 6 and 7, this volume), they must, ultimately, attract and retain their audience; not surprisingly, then, popular media are found to be more responsive than dictionaries to social change. Lexicographers, however, are experts who authenticate the words and word meanings we use (Gal 1989). As authenticators of symbolic capital (Bourdieu 1977), they have a different relation of symbolic power vis-à-vis the public and tend toward a conservative vision of word meaning and usage. One thinks, in this vein, of dictionaries as offering such authoritative information about lexical items as "correct" pronunciation, meaning, orthography, etymology, usage, and the like. However, if lexical items are defined without regard for the discriminatory nature of sexist terms, they do not provide appropriate information to dictionary users. Vigilant scrutiny of these authoritative texts is, therefore, imperative.

This chapter is organized as follows: Section 9.1 discusses the discriminatory nature of the three sexist terms chosen for this study; section 9.2 examines the changes in the use of these three terms in postwar media; section 9.3 then assesses how dictionaries do or do not reflect these changes. Finally, section 9.4 reviews the social context in which the changes in usage have occurred in popular media but not in most dictionaries.

9.1. Sexist terms in Japanese: *Onnadatera (ni)*, *rooba*, and *oorudo misu*

Sexist language exists at two levels in Japanese. First, at the lexical level, there are terms such as *busu* 'ugly [woman]' and *urenokori* 'old(er), unmarried woman' (lit., 'unsold merchandise')', the semantic representations of which contain discriminatory elements. Then, at the level of the utterance, there are terms that are sexist when used in particular social contexts or in particular fixed phrases. Examples of these include *uchi no onna no ko ni ikasemasu* 'I'll have my girl go', uttered by an employer about one of his female employees, and *onna no kuse ni namaiki da* 'you're pretty uppity for a woman'. The discriminatory content of these forms includes evaluations of the looks or age of a woman, criticism or ridicule for women's delay or failure to marry, presupposition of women's inferiority to men, and denial of women's human rights, which derives from the old *ie seedo* 'household system'.[1]

In this chapter, I examine three terms as representatives of sexist words, selected from each of the three tiers of the Japanese lexicon, *wago* '[native] Japanese words', *kango* 'Sino-Japanese words', and *gairaigo* 'loanwords', the last most commonly from Indo-European languages. These terms are: (1) *onnadatera (ni)* 'despite [being] a woman', (2) *rooba* 'hag/crone', literally, 'old woman', and (3) *oorudo misu* 'old maid', literally, 'old miss'. An understanding of how these terms do or do not appear in contemporary texts and dictionaries will give us a basis for assessing the status of sexist language in Japanese more generally. I first discuss the three terms in question, drawing on examples both of dictionary definitions and uses in newspapers and novels.

9.1.1. *Onnadatera (ni)* 'despite [being] a woman'

The term *onnadatera ni*, a *wago* 'native word', appears in two forms in dictionary entries: *onnadatera* and *onnadatera ni*; there is no difference in meaning and I treat them together here. This term comprises two morphemes, with the suffix *-datera* attaching to the word *onna* 'woman'. The suffix *-datera* is defined as follows.

> *Definition 1*: Following a word that expresses sex, status, or position (*tachiba*), [*datera*] expresses the sense that [something is] inappropriate or unbecoming to that sex, status, or position. *Onna____ni* 'despite [being] a woman], *hooshi____* 'despite [being] a Buddhist priest'. (DJS 1995:1656)[2]

Onnadatera thus is a form used to rebuke or criticize a woman when her behavior falls outside the framework of what men think is appropriate for women.

In the 1980s, examples such as (1) appeared in newspapers, showing that women had not, up to that time, been considered fit to be politicians.

(1)   *Josee seejika o "<u>onnadatera ni</u>" to hyoosuru no wa hansee suru*
      hitsuyoo ga aru.

> 'We need to stop thinking of women politicians as being so <u>despite being women</u>'. (*Asahi Shimbun*, July 12, 1987)

Even very recently, a student reported to me that when as a high school student she aspired to college, her grandmother's reaction was "Onnadatera ni daigaku nanzo itte doo suru" 'what will you—(despite being) a woman—do going to college?'" (personal communication, June 27, 2000). Such statements are clear expressions of bias against women.

9.1.2.   *Rooba* 'old woman' ('old crone')

Rooba 'old woman/hag' is a *kango* "Sino-Japanese word" used to disparage or reject a woman on the basis of her age. The basic meaning of *rooba* is found in definition 2: other definitions (definition 3) offer a slightly different, more negative interpretation.

> *Definition 2*:   An old woman, lit., a woman who has aged (SGS 1998: 1351)

> *Definition 3*:   A woman who clearly shows her age (SMKJ:5 1997: 1498)

The morpheme *ba* of *rooba* is also an element in such polymorphemic words as *onibaba* 'witch, ogress' and *yaritebabaa* 'procuress/Madam Go-getter', which are negative or derogatory; *ba* is also repeated in the derogatory word *babaa* 'old woman/bitch'. The morpheme *ba* carries negative connotations, present in the word *rooba* as well.

A search of *CD-ROM-ban shinchoo bunko no hyakusatsu 'A hundred volumes of Shincho-paperback editions on CD-ROM'* (hereafter, *Shincho CD*) yielded examples such as ex (2).

(2)   *Shige wa mukashi no "oku" zutome no jochuu no hitori de atta ga, ima wa chiisaku*
      shinabita, kanari kenkai na <u>rooba</u> to natte ita.

> 'Formerly, Shige was one of the "inner house" maids, but now she had become a withered, petty, narrow-minded <u>old woman</u>'. (*Nireke no Hitobito 'The House of Nire'*, 1964 [1568]; Shincho CD)

Examples where *rooba* is used to create negative images of people support the claim that it is an offensive word.

9.1.3.   *Oorudo misu* 'old maid'

The term *oorudo misu* 'old maid' is a Japanese-made construction based on English loanwords that conveys disdain for women who remain single after a certain age. It has a long history, having been used since the Meiji period (1868–1912). It was an entry in *Meekai kokugo jiten* (MKJ) (1997 [1943]), the first dictionary to focus on contemporary Japanese (Muto 1997).

Definition 4: (fr. Eng. old + miss) (made in Japan) A woman past marriageable age. An old maid. High miss. [Translator's note: "High miss" is another term derived from English but made in Japan, also meaning "old maid"]. (KSK 1981: 136)

Hongo notes that "when [a woman] remains single past a certain age, society suddenly turns against her, and starts calling her *oorudo misu*, *urenokori*, and the like" (1985: 80).

9.2.   *Onnadatera* (*ni*), *rooba*, and *oorudo misu* in the media

9.2.1.   *Onnadatera* (*ni*)

A search of the novels in the *Shincho CD* yields examples such as ex (3) and (4).

(3)   *Ginko ga ichiban kurushinda no wa yahari <u>onnadatera ni</u>, tanshin, otoko dake no gakkoo ni norikonda koto ni atta.*

'What Ginko was most troubled by was that, <u>despite being a woman</u>, she had pushed her way into an all-male school'. (*Hanauzumi 'Buried in Flowers'*, 1970: 348; Shincho CD)

(4)   *<u>Onnadatera ni</u> kenjutsu no hoo wa sootoo na mono da ga . . .*
'<u>Despite being a woman</u>, [she] was pretty good at fencing and *kendo* . . .' (*Kenkaku Shoobai 'The Swordsman Business'* 1973: 235; Shincho CD)

All such examples were produced nearly 30 years ago, and the novels were set in the earlier Edo (1600–1868) and Meiji (1868–1912) periods.

   In today's newspapers, *onnadatera ni* . . . is not used to criticize women's activities. A search of the 1993–1998 *Mainichi Shimbun 'Mainichi Newspaper'* based on *CD-Mainichi Shimbun 'CD-Mainichi Newspaper'* (*Nichigai Asoshieetsu* 1993, 1994, 1995, 1995, 1996, 1997, and 1998) yielded examples such as ex (5).

(5)   *Tora-san wa "<u>onnadatera ni</u> e nan ka kaite ru yatsu ni, roku na no wa nai n da" to kankan.*
'Tora-san was furious, [ranting,] "Women who paint [lit., women who paint despite being women] are just scribblers".' (*Mainichi Shimbun*, September 8, 1996)

This, however, is a quotation from Tora-san (the main male character in a popular film series) and not something a journalist wrote on her or his own. There are no direct examples of a journalist using this word to characterize a woman in the entire *Mainichi* corpus. Journalists and newspaper publishers, it appears, recognize the sexism of this word.

   Newspaper publishers issue usage handbooks, and in the eighth edition of one such handbook, Kyodo Tsushinsha's *Kisha handobukku 'Journalists' handbook'* (2000), discriminatory or offensive terms to avoid are specified in various categories, such as "disability" and "race." Under the heading *seesabetsu* 'Sex Discrimination,' two words, *joryuu* 'female, woman' and *joshi* 'Madame', are listed as forms to avoid, with the additional comment that *joketsu* 'heroine, outstanding woman', *jojoofu* 'tough and dependable woman', *onnadatera ni*, and the like—which stress that the person being referred to is female—should be avoided to the extent possible" (Kyodo Tsushinsha 2000:85). However, the category of sexist language did not appear until the seventh edition, which appeared in 1997. Avoidance of sexist terms in newspaper writing is a very recent phenomenon.

9.2.2. *Rooba*

Unlike *onnadatera (ni)*, *rooba* is used even in contemporary newspapers when characters in serialized novels are described (ex. 6), but such uses do not seem to have negative connotations.

(6)   *Kinoshita Keesuke Kantoku "Narayama Bushikoo" (58–nen) wa Tanaka Kinuyo ga sashiba o 4-hon nuite <u>rooba</u> o enjita.*
      'In Director Kinoshita Keisuke's *Ballad of Narayama* (1958), Kinuyo Tanaka took out four dental implants and played an <u>old woman</u>'. (*Mainichi Shimbun*, March 5, 1996)

However, the use of *rooba* to describe older women, focusing attention on their age, in actual news reports has changed greatly from 1945 to the present. Endo (1988) examines the terms used to describe elderly women in the headlines from *Mainichi* and *Asahi* newspaper metropolitan pages and regional editions over the postwar years. In the late 1940s, *rooba* was used as in examples (7) and (8). But from the late 1960s, usage shifted to terms such as *roojo* 'old woman' or *roofujin* 'old lady', as in examples (9) and (10).

(7)   *<u>Rooba</u> o koroshi, umeru*
      'An <u>old woman</u> killed and buried' (*Asahi Shimbun*, March 15, 1948)

(8)   *<u>Rooba</u>goroshi torawaru*
      'The killer of an <u>old woman</u> captured' (*Mainichi Shimbun*, September 16, 1948)

(9)   *<u>Roojo</u> futari hanerare shinu*
      'Two <u>old women</u> struck by a car and died' (*Asahi Shimbun*, evening edition, March 13, 1978)

(10) *<u>Roofujin</u> no ie, tochi nottori*
      '<u>Old lady</u> swindled of home, property' (*Mainichi Shimbun*, June 4, 1978)

And today such persons are denoted by age, as in example (11).

(11) *<u>Nanajuuni-sai josee</u> no itai suukagetsu hoochi*
      'Body of a <u>seventy-two-year-old woman</u> undiscovered for several months' (*Mainichi Shimbun*, evening edition, June 7, 2000)

And, as in example (12), news articles appear in which only the term *josee* 'woman' is used in the headline and the age of the woman is noted only in the text.

(12) *Sakeobi jiko josee shinaseru*
      ... oodanchuu no mushoku Uta Tami-san (78) ga ... no kuruma ni
      hanerare sokushi shita.

      'Alcohol-related accident kills <u>woman</u>'
      '... Uta Tami-san (78, unemployed) was hit by a car driven by ... and killed instantly'.
      (*Asahi Shimbun*, June 1, 2000)

In *NET Iikaeshuu*, an unpublished collection of alternatives to discriminatory words circulated in 1974, *rooba* was described as discriminatory under section 1, "Words That Violate Human Rights," article c, "Derogatory Words"; replacement of *rooba* with *roojo* or *roofujin* was recommended. And even in the 1975 edition of *Torikimeshuu 'Usage agreement'*, issued by *Asahi Shimbun*, one of Japan's major national newspapers, replacement of *rooba* with *roojo* or *roofujin* is specified. In the face of these various cautions and guidelines, journalists no longer use *rooba* to denote elderly women.

9.2.3. *Oorudo misu*

Two examples of this word were found in the *Mainichi CD* database. In both examples, *oorudo misu* appears as a quotation and not as the words of the writer her- or himself, as in example (13).

(13) *Chuugokujin no kankaku de wa, kekkon tekireeki o mukaeta danjo no uchi, mikonsha*
      wa josee ni ooi to miraregachi de, yoron no doojoo mo "oorudo misu" ni atsumatte
      ita ga, genjitsu wa igai ni mo gyaku datta to yuu wake.

      'The Chinese perception was that more women remained unmarried after a "marriageable" age (*kekkon tekireeki*) and there was considerable public sympathy for these "<u>old maids</u>," but the reality, surprisingly, was the opposite'. (*Mainichi Shimbun*, October 23, 1993)

In the *Shinchoo CD* database, there are examples such as (14). This example is drawn from the background description in a novel written in the 1950s but set in premodern times.

(14) *Korera no imeeji wa sono mama sakuhin no mochiifu to nari, sono mama hitori no*
      ningen no sugata o shoochoo shi, sorezore, shuui no hakugan ni taeru oita mekake,
      rinshoku de kenkai na oorudo misu no sugata to kasanariau.

      'These images, just as they were, became the motif of the work, and, thus, came to symbolize the figure [*sugata*] of a single being; the old mistress bearing up against society's disdain and the picture of a miserly, narrow-minded <u>old maid</u>, respectively, merged'. (*Asunaro Monogatari* 1954: 378)

Gendai yoogo no kiso chishiki 'A basic encyclopedia of current terms' (henceforth *Gendai kiso*), an annual collection of neologisms published by Jiyukokuminsha provides another measure of a word's popular currency. Appearance in *Gendai kiso* represents a public acknowledgment of new terms' currency and stability in contemporary discourse. Until the 1960s, *oorudo misu* did not appear there. In the 1970s, there was a change of editor and a new chapter, "Neologisms and Loanwords in the Mass Media," was added. *Oorudo misu* was found among these "loanwords and neologisms" and was defined as follows.

> *Definition 5*:   Old miss (Japanese-produced form). Spinster (a woman who remains unmarried beyond marriageable age); correctly, old maid (*Gendai Yoogo no kiso 1972* 1972: 1346)

The entry remains unchanging through the 1990 edition, but in the 1991 edition *oorudo misu* is defined differently, as follows.

> *Definition 6*:   * Old miss. Old failure; a colloquialism meaning old wound. (*Gendai Yooga no kiso 1991* 1991: 1389)

We see, then, the following shift. *Gendai kiso* began publication in 1948 as a collection of "current terms, practical (common) terms, popular words, slang, loan words, and abbreviations" (from the preface to the first edition; Hasegawa 1948:1). *Oorudo misu* was neither a new nor a "current" term and did not appear. After a change of editors, it was included in the 1972 and subsequent editions until 1991. In that edition, the definition was changed to the obscure "old wound." After 1994, this entry again disappeared.

9.3.   Dictionary treatments

There is very little research on the relation between Japanese dictionaries and sexist language (Endo 2000), but the role of dictionaries in combating sexist language should not be overlooked. Decisions not to include sexist words in dictionaries may help reduce these words' vitality. Failing to find a word in the dictionary can send the message that it is used so seldom as not even to merit an entry. Alternatively, an entry that explicitly details the sexist nature of the word and explicates its connotations in usage can send the message that the word should be used only cautiously or not at all. Unfortunately, few of today's Japanese language dictionaries grapple seriously with biased language.

How unfortunate the consequences of this failure can be became clear in April 2000, on the occasion of the *sabetsu hatsugen* 'racist remarks' of Tokyo governor Ishihara Shintaro in an address to the Nerima Corps of the Ground Self-Defense Forces. Ishihara intentionally used the obsolete discriminatory word from Japan's colonialist past *sangokujin* 'third country people' to refer to Chinese and Koreans. When challenged by newspaper reporters, Ishihara declared that since the respected dictionary *Daijirin* does not define the term as discriminatory or derogatory, it is not a discriminatory term (*Mainichi Shimbun*, April 4, 2000). The dictionary served, thus, as an authoritative text, reference to which invokes the speaker's mastery of the dominant system of legitimate language (Bourdieu 1991) and puts him beyond the reach of reporters' criticisms.

I next analyze Japanese dictionaries' treatment of sexist lexical items, using the three sexist terms *onnadatera ni, rooba*, and *oorudo misu*. My corpus includes dictionaries of modern Japanese published over nearly a 60-year-period, from *Meekai kokugo jiten* (MKJ 1943) to *Sanseedoo kokugo jiten dai5han* (SKJ:5). It comprises 66 dictionaries, which range in size from the large (NKDJ:2, with 500,000 entries) to the very small (CKJ, with about 40,000). Categorized by size, the corpus includes 2 large (more than 300,000 entries), 16 medium-sized (100,000–300,000 entries), and 48 small (fewer than 100,000 entries) dictionaries. See the appendix at the end of this chapter for details.

My survey focuses on the following three questions: (1) is the word included (Q1), (2) if included, are there examples of usage (Q2), and (3) does the entry include supplementary explanations or guidelines with respect to meaning or usage (Q3)?

9.3.1. *Onnadatera (ni)*

This term is composed of *onna* 'woman' + the suffix *-datera (ni)*, so I consider the treatment both of the word itself and of the suffix. The majority of the dictionaries include an entry for each.

9.3.1.a. *Onnadatera (ni)*

Q1. Fifty-four of the 66 dictionaries in my corpus had an entry for *onnadatera (ni)*. Twelve, all small dictionaries, did not (IKJ:4, IKJ:5, KHK, GSK, SKJ:5, SGS, CKJ, RSK:1–4). *Reekai shinkokugo jiten* (the RSK series, 1984–1994) has never included *onnadatera (ni)*. Perhaps the editors in 1984 found it obsolete already, or perhaps they judged it of little use to their primary target users, middle school students. *Charenji kokugo jiten* (CKJ), which similarly targets middle school students, also does not include it. Then, too, these dictionaries are small, so the reason for non-inclusion may be size.

The fifth editions of *Iwanami kokugo jiten* (IKJ:5 1994) and *Sanseedoo kokugo jiten* (SKJ:5 2001) dropped *onnadatera (ni)*, exhibiting a change of policy from previous editions. IKJ:5 changed the example provided in the entry for *-datera* from *onna* 'woman'_____*ni* to *kodomo* 'child'_____*ni*, and the subsequent IKJ:6 continued with this substitution. In fact, the term *onnadatera (ni)* disappeared completely from this dictionary series. *Sanseedoo gendai shinkokugo jiten* (SGS 1998) also decided to drop this entry, a change from the dictionary's previous policy (SGK:2 1992). *Gakken shinkokugo jiten* (GSK) first appeared in 1994 and *Kadokawa hikkee kokugo jiten* (KHK) in 1995; neither of these included the term, suggesting recognition of its sexist and obsolete character. One early dictionary, *Meekai kokugo jiten* (MKJ 1943), also did not include this word, but in such an early publication one might speculate that the reason was its vulgarity rather than its sexist nature.

In IKJ:5, SKJ:5, and SGS (dictionaries of the more-than-60,000-entry size), *onnadatera ni* was omitted. When one contrasts this with the other dictionaries of similar size that continue to include the same entries from previous editions, these three dictionaries can be commended for their thoughtful treatment of discriminatory words.

Q2. Recently dictionaries have given more weight to examples of usage than formerly and have been marketed with promises of abundant examples of usage. Examples of *onnadatera* (*ni*) in use, however, are extremely rare. Of the 54 dictionaries in my corpus that had an entry for *onnadatera* (*ni*), only 15 had examples of its use: 2 large dictionaries (NKDJ, NKDJ:2), 8 medium-sized dictionaries (KKD, GKD:1, GKD:2, GSN, KJE:4, KJE:5, DJR:1, DJR:2), and 5 small dictionaries (IKJ:3, IKJ:4, OKJ:r, SCGK, RKJ).

And, looking at the examples given, with the exceptions of *Nihon kokugo daijiten* (NKDJ) , *Gakken kokugo daijiten* (GKD:1 and 2), and *Shinchoo gendai kokugo jiten* (SCGK), which offer concrete examples drawn from literary works, we find that only constructed examples are provided. Further, these constructed examples center around only three situations: [*onnadatera ni*] ". . . *oozake o nomu*" '[Despite being a woman, she] drinks heavily', ". . . *agura o kaku*" '[. . . she] sits cross-legged', and ". . . *tanka o kiru*" '[. . . she] swears'. In other words, only these three situations come to lexicographers' minds when constructing examples. The replication of these examples in dictionaries produced separately and independently suggests just how very limited and biased this word is in contemporary Japanese.

Judgments on whether drinking heavily, swearing, and sitting cross-legged are actions appropriate for a woman or not are formed in particular sociohistorical contexts. Today these actions are not uncommon among Japanese women and cannot simply be regarded as unbecoming. Accordingly, such examples of usage can no longer be considered apposite.

Q3. One might think that the more recent the dictionary, the more meticulous usage labels and supplemental notes would be. However, in this study, we see that *Reekai kokugo jiten* (RKJ 1955), one of the older dictionaries in the corpus, had usage labels, while the newest, *Shuueesha kokugo jiten: 2* (SEK:2 2000), had none. The presence of usage labels or supplemental notes seems linked neither to the dictionary's publication date nor to its size. Rather, these decisions are related to the attitudes of the dictionary's producers. Of those dictionaries with long publication histories, *Shinsen kokugo jiten: 7* (SSKJ:7), *Shinmeekai kokugo jiten: 4* (SMKJ:4), and a few others may be commended for adding notes on the discriminatory nature of sexist words.

When a dictionary includes a discriminatory word as an entry, it needs to specify the history and circumstances of the word's use. Some dictionaries have provided such information in supplemental notes. *Meeji shoin seesen kokugo jiten* (MSS), for example, incorporated a notes column and included the following supplemental information in its entry for *onnadatera* (*ni*),

> *Onnadatera ni* Note: A term used to express the feeling that something is not appropriate for a woman to do. Used to confine women within a narrow framework [of "suitable" activities] and to ridicule or deride those women who attempt to move beyond that framework. (1994: 170)

This is one of the most detailed and appropriate of descriptions of sexist language in Japanese dictionaries currently being published. The Notes column expends three lines to point out the word's meaning, the speaker's intentions when it is used, and the fact that it was used in the past but not today—that it is, in fact, an archaic word. MSS's Notes demonstrate that even a small dictionary can provide supplemental guidelines, when seen as necessary, about the meaning or usage of sexist words. Other dictionaries have supplemented their *onnadatera ni* entries with the following information: (1) that previously one could say "*otoko* 'man' *-datera*" 'despite being a man' as well (GKR:1 [first edition only]); (2) that *onnadatera* can be used critically (SSKJ:7, GSN, DJS, DJR:1 [but not 2], RKJ, NKDJ, NKDJ:2); (3) that it can be used in censuring (OHK, OHK:r, SGK:1, SGK:2); (4) that it can be used in ridicule or contempt (MSS); and (5) that it can be mixed with criticism or amazement (SMKJ:4, SMKJ:5).

Relatively recent dictionaries such as *Sanseedoo gendai kokugo jiten* (first published in 1988), *Daijirin* (1988), and *Daijisen* (1995) have included usage labels and supplemental notes from their first editions. However, time has not improved the picture in all cases. *Gendai kokugo reekai jiten 1* (GKR:1 1985), for example, included information about the counterpart word *otokodatera* 'despite being a man' and provided appropriate supplemental notes concerning the historical facts surrounding the word, but these were deleted in the revised edition (GKR:2 1993). *Daijirin*'s notes concerning usage were also eliminated from its second edition, demonstrating that some revisions represent changes for the worse. And, of course, it is regrettable that few dictionaries followed *Reekai kokugo jiten*'s very early (1955) example of including such guidelines.

9.3.1.b. Datera

Q1. All but three dictionaries (GKR:1, GKR:2, RSK:1) have entries for the suffix *-datera*. Commendably, neither *Gendai kokugo reekai jiten*'s first nor second editions (GKR:1, 2) carry an entry for this morpheme, reflecting its decline. However, although *Reekai shinkokugo jiten*'s first edition (RSK:1) has entries neither for *onnadatera* (*ni*) nor for *-datera*, in the second edition (RSK:2), an entry for *-datera* is added and *onnadatera ni* is given as an example, resurrecting this discriminatory form.

Q2. Derivations that use the suffix *-datera* are extremely limited today. Examples drawn from classical texts include *hooshidatera* 'despite being a priest/ monk', *oyadatera* 'despite being a parent', *keeseedatera* 'despite being a beauty', and *choonindatera* 'despite being a merchant'; but examples given as contemporary are restricted to two: *kodomodatera* 'despite being a child' and *onnadatera*. Dictionaries that include an entry for *-datera* must, nonetheless, present examples of derivative terms that use it, and of the 58 dictionaries that gave examples, 54 gave *onnadatera ni*. Behind this frozen collocation of *onna* and the *-datera* suffix lurks a discriminatory social stereotype, a stereotype that continues to be authorized by the appearance of this form in dictionaries. Dictionaries' failure to incorporate changes in the word usage and their uncritical replication of material from earlier editions contribute to reproducing past, discriminatory practices using the authority of lexicographical expertise. While large and medium-sized dictionaries should include an entry for this suffix, in order to acknowledge its historical existence they should also provide adequate supplemental notes about the historical background of its use.

Q3. There were 23 small and 3 medium-sized dictionaries with some sort of usage label or supplemental note for the suffix *-datera*. Small dictionaries such as *Charenji kokugo jiten* (CKJ; see also RSK:1–4) are targeted at middle school users who are likely to need some guidelines for these terms. These dictionaries do not have entries for *onnadatera* (*ni*) and, thus, usage notes occur only with -*datera*. Examples of the usage labels and supplementary notes for -*datera* include: (1) vulgar parlance/slang (CKJ); (2) a lowbrow way of saying something (RSK:2, 3, 4); (3) a word used in criticism, scorn (IKJ: 4, 5, 6; FKJ; OHK:r; GSK; SMKJ:1, 3, 3-3, 4, 5; GKD:1, 2; KJE:5); (4) used in a critical sense (OKJ:9); (5) not used in a positive sense (SKJ:2–5); and (6) not used in a very positive sense (SGK 1, 2; SGS). The supplemental notes for -*datera* differ from those for *onnadatera* (*ni*), which are restricted to women as the object. For -*datera*, guidelines that focus on its generally pejorative nature (e.g., *ii imi de wa tsukawanai* 'not used in a positive sense') are more numerous.

We see, then, that both *onnadatera* (*ni*) and -*datera* are terms that have lost vitality as contemporary forms to such an extent that no original examples can readily be provided. Despite this, many dictionaries have entries for both. This may not be necessary; in small dictionaries, an entry for one or, in fact, for neither would suffice. If entries are to be included, however, it is imperative that dictionaries follow the example of *Meeji shoin seesen kokugo jiten* (MSS 1994) and allocate space for usage labels and supplemental notes that inform young users in particular about the discriminatory nature of the words and draw attention to the problems attendant upon their use.

9.3.2. *Rooba*

Q1. Since this word is hardly used today, one might consider an entry unnecessary, at least in small dictionaries. However, entries for *rooba* were found in all 66 dictionaries examined.

Q2. Dictionary makers apparently find examples of the use of this word unnecessary. Only two large (NKDJ, NKDJ:2) and one medium-sized (SCKJ) dictionary provide examples of its use—and those are examples from classical texts. There were absolutely no examples of its use as a contemporary lexical item. This could be because: (1) the meaning of the word is so self-evident as to require no exemplification; (2) the word is not actually in current use, so no appropriate examples exist; or (3) the word is obsolete, so exemplification is pointless.

Q3. I found no supplemental notes that indicated this word was critical or derogatory. Some dictionaries did provide notes concerning register: *bun* 'literary' (SKJ:2–4), *bunshoogo* 'written language' (SGK:1, 2; SGS), and *zokugo* 'slang' (KKJ:1). Characterizing *rooba* as "literary" seems to be based on the fact that although it is not used in everyday conversation, it is—or, at least, has been—used in writing. The label *zokugo* 'slang', however, can be interpreted as a claim that it is a vulgar usage in spoken language and not used—or at least, no longer used—in ordinary written language. Each of these characterizations undoubtedly reflects a partial truth.

An additional and interesting aspect of the definitions of *rooba* is that when they include something like *toshi o totta onna* 'an old woman' (lit., 'a woman who has aged'), one sees a shift over time from . . . *onna* 'woman' , which has connotations of woman-as-sexual, to other expressions, such as . . . *josee* 'woman' or . . . *onna no hito* 'woman', which convey much more positive images than *onna*, as Jugaku (1979) also notes. Unmodified by such forms as *toshi o totta* 'old' or by *no hito* 'person', *onna* stresses the sexual aspects of womanhood; the relatively unrefined connotation of *onna* is mitigated by the addition of *no hito* in one common contemporary term for "woman," *onna no hito.*[3] The term *fujin* has slightly formal overtones, is used to denote women in public discourse, and de-emphasizes women's sexuality. *Josee* is currently the most unmarked term for women (Urushida 1993). Changes in dictionaries' choices of words for "woman" in definitions of *rooba* over time are displayed in table 9.1.

From *Meekai kokugo jiten* (MKJ 1943) through *Koojien-2han* (KJE:2 1969) only *onna* was used, but in *Shinmeekai kokugo jiten* (SMKJ:1 1971) *fujin* was used and in *Reekai shinkokugo jiten* (RSK:1 1984) *onna no hito* was used. *Josee* appears for the first time in the first edition of *Daijirin* (DJR 1988) and in *Sanseedoo gendai kokugo jiten* (SGK:1 1988). Most dictionaries in my corpus with first editions in 1990 or later (e.g., KHK, SGS, SEK:1 and 2, SPK, CKJ, MSS, JR, DJS) used *josee*. Of newer editions, only *Gakken shinkokugo jiten* (GSJ), with a first edition published in 1994, has *toshi o totta onna*. The other six cases of *onna* occurring in definitions of *rooba* in dictionaries published after 1990 are all in second or subsequent editions of a dictionary and simply reproduce a first edition definition using *onna*. In the case of the *Iwanami kokugo jiten* (IKJ) series, we see that IKJ:4, 5, and 6, all published after 1985, eliminated the entry *onnadatera* and changed the examples given in the entry for *-datera*; despite this, for the definition for *rooba*, *toshi o totta onna* remains unchanged from the first edition on. *Koojien* (KJE:1–5), too, uses *onna* from the first through the fifth edition. However, usage has generally changed from . . . . *no onna*, a form offensive to women, to . . . *no josee* or . . . *no onna no hito*, suggesting that dictionary makers recognize the social changes in the attitudes toward and treatment of women that have taken place in the latter part of the twentieth century.

9.3.3.   *Oorudo misu*

Q1. Fifty-four of the dictionaries in my sample have entries for *oorudo misu*; 10 (IKJ: 5–6, OHK:r, KHK, CKJ, MSS, RSK: 1–4), all published after 1983, did not. Of these latter 10, this represents a change from previous editions for 2 (IKJ:5, OHK:r). One can speculate that publishers judged this word obsolete or sexist. Alternatively, changes in Japanese views of marriage—i.e., the growing number of women and men who do not marry, the rise in average age of marriage, etc.—may have had some influence on publishers.

Q2. Only three dictionaries (RKJ, NKDJ, NKDJ:2) included examples of usage. This is hardly surprising, since *oorudo misu* is widely recognized to be a sexist term.

Q3. This word is a collocation of English *old* and *miss* that was produced in Japan. Where present, supplemental notes centered exclusively around that fact. There

TABLE 9.1 Words used for "woman" in
definitions of *rooba*

Word	Through 1989	1990–
onna	25	8
josee	3	18
onna no hito	2	2
fujin	6	1
None	1	0
Total	37	29

was no mention whatsoever of its sexist nature. One does see, however, a shift in the use of *onna* versus *josee* similar to that in the definitions of *rooba* in the definitions of *oorudo misu* (as, for example, *konki o sugite mo kekkon shinai de iru onna (josee)* 'a woman who remains unmarried even after the normal time for marriage') (see table 9.2). Among those dictionaries first published in 1990 or later, only *Gakken shinkokugo jiten* (GSK) used *onna* in the definition—as they did for *rooba*—ignoring the tides of change. In the other dictionaries, *josee* was recognized as more appropriate than *onna*.

9.3.4. Summary

In this chapter, I have examined the treatment of three words in terms of Japanese dictionaries. These terms, which have almost completely fallen out of use in the media, continue—with the exception of one group of "improved" dictionaries—to appear just as before even in small dictionaries. However, if dictionaries are to boast that they are "a 'mirror' accurately reflecting the meaning of words" (from the preface to *Sanseedoo kokugo jiten 3* [SKJ:3 1982:1]), many changes are needed before they adequately reflect the changes in society's view of gender relations and the words that encode them.

Medium-sized and large dictionaries can afford the space to record sexist and other discriminatory words, but if they do, they have an obligation to describe the history and discriminatory nature of the words and to make efforts to avoid lending their authority to offensive language, as happened in the Ishihara declaration. The majority of today's dictionaries are not useful mirrors that "reflect" society as it is today. We have also seen, however, that some publishers produce dictionaries that do reflect the changes in society. One strongly hopes that, in the future, the majority of dictionary makers, who continue unreflectingly to reproduce outdated entries, will learn from these latter volumes and make thorough revisions.

9.4. Changes in words for describing women in public discourse and the media

In contrast to the conservative practices of most lexicographers and dictionary editors, Japanese public discourse and the Japanese media have come to avoid sexist

TABLE 9.2 Words used for "woman" in definitions of *oorudo misu*

Word	Through 1989	1990–
onna	23	4
josee	11	15
onna no hito	1	0
None	0	2
No entry	2	8
Total	37	29

language. The 1970s saw the beginning of demands to eliminate the use of discriminatory language in the media—primarily centered around *buraku sabetsu* 'discrimination against *burakumin*'.[4]

Sexist language became another object of protest. The movement against sexist language took on clearer focus in 1975, the International Women's Year. Further, after the 1985 ratification of the United Nations Convention on the Elimination of All Forms of Discrimination against Women, domestic laws had to be brought into compliance, which resulted in the 1986 passage of the Equal Employment Opportunity Law. In order to implement this and other laws, women's liberation and independence had to be promoted, and for that, the deep-rooted notion of *danson johi* 'androcracy' (lit., 'respect for men, contempt for women') had to be reformed. Old attitudes inhere in old, biased words and impede reform. Hence, reevaluation of sexist language was required.

Another stimulus to the reevaluation of sexist words was the changes in their use by the media. Newspaper publishers and broadcasting companies produced handbooks of *iikae* 'alternative wording' for old, discriminatory words and tried to make comprehensive changes. The media's reforms were in part voluntary and in part the result of external forces. Takagi notes that "the use of expressions which reflected traditional views of women as inferior to men was protested by women's liberation organizations, and the mass media came to avoid their use. . . . *Roojo* came to be substituted for *rooba*, the use of which, it was feared, would hurt older women" (1988:605).

One of the women's liberation organizations was the Kokusai Fujinnen o Kikkake ni shite Koodoo o Okosu Onnatachi no Kai 'The Women's Action Group Occasioned by the International Women's Year',[5] which criticized a food company 1975 commercial *Watashi tsukuru hito, boku taberu hito* 'I [feminine first-person pronoun] make it, I [masculine first-person pronoun] eat it'. Then, in 1989, the Japan Women's Studies Association presented a list of demands to each private television station and NHK 'Japan Broadcasting Corporation', Japan's public television station. The association demanded that these media outlets cease using expressions that derogated women or fostered sex discrimination. Among such expressions were those that connoted that women's value depended primarily on their appearance.

It is unclear whether media shifts in terminology were caused by these protests and demands by women's organizations or the media voluntarily added sexist language to their revisions of discriminatory words in general in the wake of the Buraku Liberation League's censure, but the activities of women's organizations were widely publicized and clearly influential in changing media practices (see also chapter 1, this volume). As seen from the newspaper and fictional examples presented earlier, media use of sexist terms has changed to suit the changing social landscape in ways that dictionary treatments of the same terms have not.

9.5. Conclusion

My analysis of media and dictionary materials has shown that, over the course of the late twentieth century, media have progressed much further toward eliminating sexist language than have dictionaries. Feminist representations to the media have been influential in bringing attention to sexist linguistic practice. What has played an even larger role, however, seems to be the government's reevaluation of the biased lexicon. In this regard, a particularly important role was played by the Kanagawa Women's Plan (August 1984), which called for reexamination of all publications produced under prefectural auspices with regard to (1) language that discriminates against or derogates women, (2) passages that implicitly valorize traditional, fixed gender roles, and (3) words and phrases for family, married couples, women, and men that evoke the old patriarchal family system. This movement influenced other regional and local governments, and revision movements flourished.

Then, in 1987, the Headquarters for Women's Issues (headed by the prime minister) agreed upon the New National Action Plan toward the Year 2000, which made clear, from a long-term perspective, the fundamental direction in which policy toward women should be geared. This plan had the integrated goals of eliminating ideas about fixed sexual divisions of labor, enabling women to realize their full potential by creating social conditions within which women can participate fully in society, and working toward the formation of a society where women and men can equally contribute to development and stability.

The government's Headquarters for Promoting Gender Equality (Danjo Kyoodoo Sankaku Suishin Honbu) issued their Plan for Gender Equality 2000 in 1996. Among its 11 major aims were "reconsideration of existing social systems and practices from the perspective of equal participation, and enhancement of public awareness" and "respect for the human rights of women in the media." In terms of concrete measures, this plan included language reform through their "promotion of the use of non-sexist phrases in all informational and other publications produced by public agencies." To that end, the plan encouraged all regional and local administrative offices to produce guidelines. Following this, Hyogo Prefecture produced a *Hyoogen handobukku 'Phrase handbook'* (Hyogo-kenritsu Josei Sentaa, 1996), Tokyo produced *Danjo byoodoo shakai e no michisuji—Gaidorain 'The route to a gender equal society—guidelines'* (Tokyo-to Seikatsu Bunkakyoku, 1995), and Kanagawa Prefecture produced *Media to josee no jinken 'Media and the human rights of women'* (Kanagawa Josei Sentaa, 1997), among others, appealing to the public to rethink their everyday language practices. For example, *Media to josee no jinken* points out that the stereotypical picture of a housewife often portrayed by the media reproduces and reinforces the gendered division of labor, and urges women to become speaking subjects to empower themselves (14–28).

In 1999, the Basic Law for a Gender-equal Society was implemented. It stipulated that the "formation of a gender-equal society shall be promoted based on respect for the human rights of men and women, including: no gender-based discriminatory treatment of men or women; and the securing of opportunities for men and women to exercise their abilities as individuals" (Law No. 78, article 3).

In this way, with the government taking a leadership role, the concrete revision of language has proceeded. This, one may argue, has resulted in mass media reducing their use of sexist language. Women's movements in Japan, however, have been a significant force that causes the government to act. Even though they may not themselves have taken language reform as a direct goal, they worked to push for governmental action. The fruits of these efforts are slowly emerging in media practice. Activism seems not, however, to have influenced the production of dictionaries in the same way. We have seen that changes in Japanese dictionaries are rather roundabout and are too slow to be called reforms. The dictionary provides speakers with a list of authorized meanings for words; it gives them a fixed and timeless meaning—timeless, that is, at least until the dictionary's next edition. Speakers can and do use dictionary entries to make and, at times, to justify their lexical choices; it is incumbent upon lexicographers and dictionary makers, therefore, to take adequate care not to perpetuate past social injustices in the lexical realm. Including sexist terms such as *onnadatera ni*, *rooba*, and *oorudo misu* without indicating their sexist nature—no matter how dictionary makers may claim they are just providing socially neutral semantic descriptions of such words—fails to capture the damaging consequences of their use in real interactional contexts. Further, the very claim that dictionaries should be excused from reform efforts because they simply describe word meanings rather than prescribe their uses ignores the fact of their textual authority. And that textual authority is political rather than linguistic (Cameron 1985). It is regrettable that dictionaries—the ultimate "authoritative source" for words and their uses—are not more help in the process of lexical reform. Still, we must keep firmly in mind that the strength of readers and society is essential to the project of changing the attitudes of editors and lexicographers. We must continue to call problems in the choice, definition, and exemplification of words to their attention.

APPENDIX. List of dictionaries

Name	Code	Publisher	Date	# Words
A. Small Dictionaries				
Iwanami kokugo jiten: 1	IKJ:1	Iwanami Shoten	1963	> 57,000
Iwanami kokugo jiten: 2	IKJ:2	Iwanami Shoten	1971	> 57,000
Iwanami kokugo jiten: 3	IKJ:3	Iwanami Shoten	1979	> 57,000
Iwanami kokugo jiten: 4	IKJ:4	Iwanami Shoten	1986	> 57,000
Iwanami kokugo jiten: 5	IKJ:5	Iwanami Shoten	1994	> 57,000
Iwanami kokugo jiten: 6	IKJ:6	Iwanami Shoten	2000	63,000
Oobunsha kokugo jiten, shinteiban	OKJ:r	Obunsha	1973	~ 76,000
Oobunsha kokugo jiten: 9	OKJ:9	Obunsha	1998	81,500
Oobunsha hyoojun kokugo jiten	OHK	Obunsha	1965	~ 41,000
Oobunsha hyoojun kokugo jiten, shinteeban	OHK:r	Obunsha	1991	43,000
Kadokawa shinkokugo jiten	KSK	Kadokawa Shoten	1981	~ 70,000
Kadokawa hikkee kokugo jiten	KHK	Kadokawa Shoten	1995	52,000
Gakken shinkokugo jiten	GSK	Gakushu Kenkyusha	1994	~ 65,000
Gendai kokugo reekai jiten	GKR:1	Shogakkan	1985	~ 65,000
Gendai kokugo reekai jiten: 2	GKR:2	Shogakkan	1993	~ 65,000
Koodansha kokugo jiten, shinban	KKJ:1	Kodansha	1981	> 73,000
Koodansha kokugo jiten: 2	KKJ:2	Kodansha	1991	> 76,000
Sanseedoo kokugo jiten: 2	SKJ:2	Sanseido	1974	62,000
Sanseedoo kokugo jiten: 3	SKJ:3	Sanseido	1982	62,000
Sanseedoo kokugo jiten: 4	SKJ:4	Sanseido	1992	73,000
Sanseedoo kokugo jiten: 5	SKJ: 5	Sanseido	2001	76,000

continued

APPENDIX. *continued*

Name	Code	Publisher	Date	# Words
Sanseedoo gendai kokugo jiten	SGK:1	Sanseido	1988	~ 60,000
Sanseedoo gendai kokugo jiten: 2	SGK:2	Sanseido	1992	~ 62,000
Sanseedoo gendai shinkokugo jiten	SGS	Sanseido	1998	~ 70,000
Shuueesha kokugo jiten	SEK:1	Shueisha	1993	92,000
Shuueesha kokugo jiten: 2	SEK:2	Shueisha	2000	~ 92,000
Shuueesha poketto kokugo jiten	SPK	Shueisha	1996	72,000
Shinsen kokugo jiten, shinban	SSKJ:1	Shogakkan	1974	~ 73,800
Shinsen kokugo jiten: 6	SSKJ:6	Shogakkan	1987	~ 81,500
Shinsen kokugo jiten: 7	SSKJ:7	Shogakkan	1994	~ 83,000
Shinchoo gendai kokugo jiten	SCGK	Shinchosha	1985	77,000
Shinmeekai kokugo jiten	SMKJ:1	Sanseido	1971	68,385
Shinmeekai kokugo jiten: 2	SMKJ:2	Sanseido	1974	68,386
Shinmeekai kokugo jiten: 3	SMKJ:3	Sanseido	1981	~ 70,000
Shinmeekai kokugo jiten: 3, 3rd printing	SMKJ:3-3	Sanseido	1985	~ 70,000
Shinmeekai kokugo jiten: 4	SMKJ:4	Sanseido	1989	~ 73,000 +
Shinmeekai kokugo jiten: 5	SMKJ:5	Sanseido	1997	~ 73,000
Charenji kokugo jiten	CKJ	Fukutake Shoten	1991	~ 40,000
Deerii konsaisu kokugo jiten: 2	DKK:2	Sanseido	1995	70,000
Fukutake kokugo jiten	FKJ	Fukutake Shoten	1989	60,000
Meekai kokugo jiten (Reproduction edition, 1997)	MKJ	Sanseido	1943	~80,000
Meekai kokugo jiten, Kaiteeban	MKJ:r	Sanseido	1952	unknown
Meeji shoin seesen kokugo jiten	MSS	Meiji Shoin	1994	~ 50,000
Reekai kokugo jiten	RKJ	Chukyo Shuppan	1955	> 40,000
Reekai shinkokugo jiten	RSK:1	Sanseido	1984	> 40,000
Reekai shinkokugo jiten: 2	RSK:2	Sanseido	1987	45,000
Reekai shinkokugo jiten: 3	RSK:3	Sanseido	1990	46,000
Reekai shinkokugo jiten: 4	RSK:4	Sanseido	1994	48,000

B. Medium-size Dictionaries

Name	Code	Publisher	Date	# Words
Kadokawa kokugo daijiten	KKD	Kadokawa Shoten	1982	~ 155,000
Gakken kokugo daijiten	GKD:1	Gakushu Kenkyusha	1953	~ 100,000
Gakken kokugo daijiten: 2	GKD:2	Gakushu Kenkyusha	1988	102,000
Gensen	GSN	Shogakkan	1986	150,000
Koojien	KJE:1	Iwanami Shoten	1955	~ 200,000
Koojien: 2	KJE:2	Iwanami Shoten	1969	~ 200,000
Koojien: 3	KJE:3	Iwanami Shoten	1983	> 200,000
Koojien: 4	KJE:4	Iwanami Shoten	1991	~ 220,000
Koojien: 5	KJE:5	Iwanami Shoten	1998	~ 230,000
Shinchoo Kokugo Jiten—Gendai, Kogo	SCKJ:1	Shinchosha	1965	unknown
Shinchoo Kokugo Jiten -Gendai, Kogo: 2	SCKJ:2	Shinchosha	1995	> 130,000
Jirin	JR	Sanseido	1993	unknown
Daijisen	DJS	Shogakkan	1995	> 220,000
Daijirin	DJR:1	Sanseido	1988	~ 220,000
Daijirin: 2	DJR:2	Sanseido	1989	~ 223,000
Nihongo daijiten	NDJ	Kodansha	1989	175,000

C. Large Dictionaries

Name	Code	Publisher	Date	# Words
Nihon kokugo daijiten	NKDJ	Shogakkan	1973	450,000
Nihon kokugo daijiten 2-han	NKDJ:2	Shogakkan	2000	500,000

Key: r = revised.

Notes

1. The *ie* 'household' system describes a patrilineal stem family/corporate unit, continued through male primogeniture; until World War II, the household head enjoyed considerable power and authority over other members of the unit. The system was abolished upon the enactment of the post–World War II Civil Code, but the *ie* construct continues to have considerable cultural force even today.

2. All definitions and examples are translated from the original Japanese. Each dictionary examined is identified by a code provided in the appendix in this chapter.

3. The relation of the unrefined and sexual connotations of *onna* to connotations of class position is interesting but falls outside the scope of this study.

4. In the Tokugawa period (1603–1868), a system that assigned persons in specific professions to a status lower than the general population was institutionalized; these people were forced to live in certain restricted areas (*buraku*) and were called *burakumin* 'people of the *buraku*'. This system was abolished in the Meiji period (1868–1912), but bias against residents of the areas associated with this status and people who come from those areas remains.

5. This group changed its name to Koodoo suru Onnatachi no Kai 'Women's Action Group' in April 1986, and in 1996, their original goals deemed accomplished, they disbanded.

References

Bourdieu, Pierre (1977). The economics of linguistic exchanges. *Social Science Information* 16(6): 645–668.

——— (1991). *Language and symbolic power*. Cambridge, MA: Harvard University Press.

Cameron, Deborah (1985). *Feminism and linguistic theory*. New York: St. Martin's Press.

CD-Mainichi Shimbun (*CD-Mainichi Newspaper*) (1993–1998). Tokyo: Nichigai Asoshieetsu.

CD-ROM-ban shinchoo bunko no hyakusatsu (*A hundred volumes of Shincho-bunko on CD-ROM*) (1995). Tokyo: Shinchosha.

Endo, Orie (1988). Oi o arawasu kotoba (2)—Shimbun ni miru sengo 40nen no suii (Words describing old age (2)—Transitions in 40 years of postwar newspapers). *Kotoba* 9: 41–61.

——— (2000). Ninki dorama no hanashikotoba ni miru seesa: TV dorama "Byuutifuru raifu" no mojika shiryoo kara (Sex differences in the dialogue of popular dramas: From the script of the TV drama "Beautiful life"). *Kotoba* 21: 13–23.

Gal, Susan (1989). Language and political economy. *Annual Review of Anthropology* 18: 345–367.

Gendai yoogo no kiso chishiki 1972 (*A basic encyclopedia of current terms, 1972*) (1972). Tokyo: Jiyukokuminsha.

Gendai yoogo no kiso chishiki 1991 (*A basic encyclopedia of current terms, 1991*) (1991). Tokyo: Jiyukokuminsha.

Hasegawa, Kunio (ed.) (1948). *Gendai yoogo no kiso chishiki* (*A basic encyclopedia of current terms*). Tokyo: Jiyukokuminsha.

Hongo, Akemi (1985). Shoojo kara musume e no shoo (From little girl to young lady). In Kotoba to Onna o Kangaeru Kai (eds.), *Kokugo jiten ni miru josee sabetsu* (*Sexism in Japanese dictionaries*), 67–88. Tokyo: San-ichi Shobo.

Jugaku, Akiko (1979). *Nihongo to onna* (*The Japanese language and women*). Tokyo: Iwanami Shoten.

Kyodo Tsuushinsha (eds.) (2000). *Kisha handobukku dai8-han* (*Journalists' handbook, 8th edition*). Tokyo: Kyodo Tsushinsha.

Muto, Yasuo (1997). Kaisetsu (Commentary). *Meekai kokugo jiten: Fukkokuban* (*Meikai Japanese dictionary: Reproduction*). Tokyo: Sanseido.

Takagi, Masayuki (1988). Fukaigo (Offensive words). In H. Kindaiichi et al. (eds.), *Nihongo hyakka daijiten* (*The encyclopedia of Japanese*), 605. Tokyo: Taishukan Shoten.

Urushida, Kazuyo (1993). "Fujin," "onna," "josee": Onna no ippan koshookoo ("Matron," "woman," "lady": Thoughts on common terms for women). In K. [Reynolds] Reinoruzu-Akiba (ed.), *Onna to nihongo* (*Women and the Japanese Language*), 123–158. Tokyo: Yushindo.

PART III

REAL LANGUAGE, REAL PEOPLE

10

YUKAKO SUNAOSHI

Farm Women's Professional
Discourse in Ibaraki

Recent studies on language and gender in Japanese (e.g., Okamoto 1995, Inoue 2002, chapter 3, this volume) suggest that "Japanese women's language" as characterized in terms of a set of linguistic features in Standard Japanese (SJ)[1] is in fact a prescribed norm and thus does not represent the way Japanese women actually use language. While this realization is an important step in the study of women's language use in Japanese, it must also be pointed out that we still know relatively little about the real language practice of Japanese women and men, who are socially diverse and heterogeneous, and that its investigation entails a consideration of how gender interacts with other social variables, such as region, class, and occupation.[2] Although the image of the stereotypical Japanese woman is associated with the wife of a businessman (the so-called *saraiiman* 'white-collar worker', lit. 'salaryman') or with an educated urban middle-class woman, the lives of women who do not belong to this category have been increasingly studied by scholars from anthropological and sociohistorical perspectives (e.g., Dore 1978, Kondo 1990, Hunter 1993, Roberts 1994). These studies show that Japanese women's lives are truly diverse. Unfortunately, however, none of these studies has investigated how such diversity manifests itself in women's language use or how it is related to the notion of "Japanese women's language." Whether we say that "Japanese women's language" is an ideological norm or an (at least partial) reality for some Japanese women, Japanese women's language practice is still viewed from the perspective of highly educated women (and men) who are living in or aspiring to be associated with Tokyo. However, for women who are outside this category, and especially for those who reside in regional Japan, "Japanese women's language" most likely plays a different role, if any at all. As Bucholtz

(1999) pointed out, the field of language and gender has traditionally exoticized linguistic "others" who are not part of the dominant group. The case of the Japanese language is no exception. In fact, studies of linguistic "others" have barely started with respect to "Japanese women's language" use. What needs to be done now is to analyze and understand the speech of those linguistic "others" in their own right instead of treating them as deviant examples. For example, women who live in regional Japan and who are in working-class occupations may not use features of "Japanese women's language," not because they are unable to master them but because features of "Japanese women's language" are simply not in their daily language repertoire. Nevertheless, the speech of these women could be regarded by those who closely associate themselves with "Japanese women's language" as marginal, of lower quality, or even not really part of the speech of "real" Japanese women.

This chapter investigates the language use of four women engaged in agriculture in rural Ibaraki Prefecture in Japan. In order to understand the women's dialect-dominant speech, the relationship between regional dialects and SJ is reviewed first from a historical perspective. Then I analyze tape-recorded interactions of three Ibaraki female farmers and an Agricultural Extension adviser. My analysis reveals that these women used few, if any, "Japanese women's language" features to construct their gender; instead, they used dialectal and SJ features to negotiate their relationships and interactional outcomes. The findings of this chapter suggest that "Japanese women's language" is not shared by all women as an ideology and hence not practiced by all women.

10.1.   Historicizing and diversifying the research of language and gender

It is well documented that the process of selecting a standard variety for Japanese speakers was a painstaking and controversial one about which a number of scholars and policy makers had argued various possibilities since the late nineteenth century (Shibata 1980, Sanada 1991, Lee 1996). Among those who discussed the selection of SJ was the influential professor Ueda Kazutoshi. He suggested in 1895 that SJ should be based on the Tokyo elite's language. The very fact that a number of intellectuals had to repeatedly state that SJ should be based on Tokyo speech shows how prevalent regional dialects were in the lives of Japanese (Lee 1996).

While SJ was gradually implemented in elementary education across Japan since the early twentieth century, the strong antidialect attitude called the *hoogen bokumetsu undoo* 'dialect extermination movement' created resentment on the part of dialect speakers (Sanada 1991). In the last few decades SJ has become much more accessible and familiar to Japanese all over the country. At the same time, the overall attitude toward dialects has softened and using one's own regional dialect remains an essential part of a Japanese person's daily speech. In contemporary Japan, people commonly use their own regional dialects and SJ in a diglossic manner (Sanada et al. 1992). However, as Okamoto's (2000) data shows, SJ is not in complementary distribution with a regional dialect in any given person's speech. Rather, the two tend to be mixed in a complex manner in one utterance, depending on the setting and the addressee.[3] It is in this context that the dialect-dominant speech of the four women in this chapter can be better understood.

Currently morphological and lexical features of "Japanese women's language" (as well as those of "Japanese men's language") are commonly treated as if they were part of (spoken) SJ grammar, as can be seen in Japanese language textbooks for foreign learners (Siegal & Okamoto 1996). Extensive use of "Japanese women's language" features may, however, give the impression that the speaker is a traditional housewife from Yamanote. Yamanote is the western part of Tokyo, a middle- and upper-class residential area, whereas the eastern part, Shitamachi, is associated with lower-middle-class and blue-collar workers (Hibiya 1988). However, the Yamanote/Shitamachi designation has now become symbolic of class divisions rather than a strict geographic division (Lebra 1993), and a distinct speech style is associated with each. Miyako Inoue (2002, chapter 3, this volume) regards "Japanese women's language" as a product of Japan's modernization, part of which started to emanate via the *kateeshoosetsu* 'domestic novel' in the late nineteenth century. Although more investigation into this historical process is needed, it seems safe to say that SJ was modeled after Yamanote speech and that the current "Japanese women's language" evokes the image of a stereotypical Yamanote woman. It can also be said that "Japanese women's language" is the feminine version of standard spoken Japanese.[4] Accordingly, it is understandable that women's language use in regional Japan exhibits a completely different pattern from "Japanese women's language."

There are at least two possibilities regarding the relationship between "Japanese women's language" and the language use of women in regional Japan. The first possibility is that such women's use of "Japanese women's language" is proportional to the degree of their use of SJ. The second possibility is that their dialect has its own system of gender marking. The reality may differ from community to community and from individual to individual. M. Inoue (in preparation) mentioned a female consultant who worked in Tokyo but was originally from regional Japan. For her, the use of "Japanese women's language" features demonstrated her urbanization rather than her femininity. Likewise, other women in regional Japan may not consider their use of "Japanese women's language" an essential part of being a 'womanly woman'. As for the two possibilities mentioned earlier, neither was confirmed by the current data. The women whose speech is analyzed here exhibited virtually no morphological or lexical features of "Japanese women's language," though there were features of SJ in their speech. Their speech needs to be compared with that of female aspirers in Ibaraki, who align with Tokyo-based hegemonic 'feminine' identities and use relatively more SJ features. The current data did not conclusively show whether or not their dialect had its own gender-marking system. These results suggest that the role of gender norms for speech should be reconsidered, since they may not be uniformly relevant to all Japanese women.

10.2. Methodology

This chapter analyzes interactions between an Agricultural Extension adviser and three farm women. The data was drawn from conversations that took place in a farming village in Ibaraki Prefecture during the summer of 1994, supplemented by follow-up interviews with Hayashi-san, the Agricultural Extension adviser (the most recent interview took place in late 2002).[5] Ibaraki is my home prefecture, which was helpful in finding study participants and understanding the dialect.[6] I accompanied Hayashi-san as she conducted her routine visits to the family farm of each of the three women. Hayashi-san had mentioned to the three women earlier that someone interested in her work and their language would come with her. Each visit was 30 minutes to one hour in length, and the conversations were tape-recorded. Hayashi-san talked mainly with the women, but their husbands were also present or joined them later in the conversation.

Ibaraki is an agricultural prefecture located approximately two hours north of Tokyo, with its own dialect called Ibaraki-ben 'Ibaraki vernacular' or Ibaraki hoogen 'Ibaraki dialect'. All four women have lived in Ibaraki throughout their lives. Hayashi-san is in her early fifties, and has worked as an adviser for 30 years in different local offices in Ibaraki Prefecture. After high school she attended a specialized school to study agriculture in order to become an adviser. The three women interviewed here, Hada-san, Oki-san, and Nagano-san, are all in their forties, and grew up in or near the community where they currently live. All of their parents are *sengyoo nooka* 'full-time farmers', and these women and their husbands are full-time farmers as well. These women and their husbands all completed high school, and all three couples were married with the help of matchmakers. The main reason that the women married into farm families was, according to Hayashi-san, that they (and their parents) thought they would not suffer from poverty, since a farm family always has land and a house. The Hadas grow rice, tomatoes, and lettuce; the Okis, roses and rice; and the Naganos, *maitake* mushrooms and rice.

Although the three women's profiles are typical of those of traditional 'farmers' wives' (*nooka no yome*), they also hold leading positions in their farming community. Hada-san is president of Seekatsu Kaizen Guruupu, 'Local Life Improvement Group', a women's group, which promotes the community's products locally and fosters communication with other members of the community. Oki-san and Nagano-san are 2 of the 30 *fujin noogyoo shi* 'female agricultural specialists' in the prefecture, who play a role as community leaders. These positions, which show active involvement in the farming community, are some of the recent outcomes of the efforts of the adviser and the farm families to elevate women's status in their community. Before examining these women's interactions, in the next section, I briefly describe attitudes toward and features of Ibaraki dialect (henceforth, ID).

10.3. Language attitudes and dialect features

10.3.1. Attitudes toward ID

Ibaraki is one of the northernmost prefectures of the central Kanto region (to which Tokyo belongs), located at the border with the Tohoku region, an agricultural area located at the northern part of the main island. Linguistically, ID is considered much closer to Tohoku dialects than to other varieties spoken in the Kanto region (Kindaichi

1977[1957]). According to Fumio Inoue's (1989) survey of Japanese attitudes toward regional dialects, ID was rated close to Tohoku dialects, which were given the most negative evaluation of all dialects examined with regard to emotion- and intelligence-related associations, receiving evaluations such as *zonzai* 'rough', *wakai josee ni fusawashiku nai* 'not suitable for young women', and *kikitori nikui* 'difficult to comprehend'.

The use of ID may strike Japanese hearers, whether or not they themselves are speakers of ID, as *tsuchi-kusai* 'earthy' and *inakappoi* 'countrified'. As Labov (1972) said, users of stigmatized features themselves can hold a negative attitude toward the use of those features. Speakers of ID are no exception. At the same time, as the current data shows, this does not necessarily mean that all speakers of ID attempt to speak in SJ. In other words, at one end of the scale are aspirers—those in Ibaraki who are aware of this negative image and aspire to the values and speech of the Center.[7] At the other end of the scale are those who have much more locally centered values and norms, like the participants in this study. While they are capable of comprehending SJ in television news and in newspapers and other print materials, they do not seem to be concerned about talking like the people of Tokyo. That is, in formal settings they use what they consider "standard" features in (at least some parts of their) speech (cf. Sanada 1996). Yet their speech overall, regardless of its level of formality, usually retains more dialectal features than the speech of aspirers. It seems that those who are engaged in agriculture tend to have this latter, locally centered mentality.

10.3.2   Features of ID

Hoogengaku 'dialectology' is an established field in Japanese linguistics, and most major regional dialects, including ID, have been documented and described using data from representative speakers of these dialects. Table 10.1 below lists some representative features of the dialect. Example (1) illustrates these features with excerpts taken from my own data.

(1) (a) Voicing of stops
      [Hayashi-san]   . . . *shigodo yaruttsuttatte igenai wake dakedo* . . .
      [SJ equivalent]   . . . *shigoto yarutte ittatte ikenai wake dakedo* . . .
      [English translation]   . . . (we) can't go to work even if (we) were to work
     (b) Long vowels
      [Nagano-san]   . . . *mi:nna iretchaa* . . .
      [SJ equivalent]   . . . *minna irechau* . . .
      [English translation]   . . . (I'll) go ahead and put everything . . .
     (c) /i/ - /e/Vowel merger
      Shokuin 'workers' and *shokuen* 'salt' as pronounced by ID speakers sound virtually identical.
     (d) Deletion of question/confirmation marker
      [Hayashi-san]   . . . *a soo na no ke* (falling intonation)
      [SJ equivalent]   . . . *a soo na no* (falling intonation)
      [English translation]   . . . is that right?

TABLE 10.1 Representative features of Ibaraki dialect

Features of Ibaraki dialect	Remarks
Phonological characteristics	
(a) Voicing of /k/ and /t/ word-internally and word-finally (Miyajima 1961, Kanesawa 1984)	
(b) Diphthongs such as /au/, /ai/ tend to become long vowels /aa/, /ee/ respectively (Kanesawa 1984)	/ai/→/ee/ is mentioned in Ide (1990) as one of the "vulgar expressions" that women cannot use in Standard Japanese/ "Japanese women's language"
(c) Vowels /i/ and /e/ lose their distinction and both become centralized (Miyajima 1961, Kanesawa 1984)	
(d) Sentences have "final rising intonation" while the pitch-accent pattern of the rest of the sentence is flat (*ikkee akusento* 'flat/single-pattern pitch-accent') (cf. Kanesawa 1984 and Kindaichi 1995 [1948])	
Morphological characteristics	
(e) Question marker -*ke* with a rising intonation Confirmation marker -*ke* with a falling intonation (Kanesawa 1984)	
Stylistic characteristics	
(f) Absence of honorifics, except for a few addressee honorifics (Miyajima 1961, Kanesawa 1984, Yamada 1986, Taguchi 1995 [1944])	Ibaraki is known to be an "honorific-less area" (*mukeego chitai*)

Among the features in table 10.1, (c) and (d) are not indicated in the transcripts in the examples used in this chapter, although both features were constantly present throughout the recording.[8] In particular, as *akusento* 'pitch-accent pattern' is said to be the most difficult area to standardize (Kindaichi 1977), the speakers' *ikkee-akusento* 'flat/single-pattern pitch-accent' speech pattern is evident, making their speech sound more dialect-dominant than may sometimes appear in the transcript. The four women's speech consisted of features of both ID and SJ, and it was sometimes difficult to separate them neatly (see Okamoto 2000 for similar examples). Nevertheless, overall their speech would be considered relatively heavy ID not only by outsiders but also by Ibaraki people themselves, especially those who live in cities.

The absence of honorifics, as described in (f) in table 10.1, needs to be discussed further. In general, the presence or absence of honorifics in a particular dialect depends on how historically complex (that is, class- or caste-stratified) the region has been (Yamada 1986; cf. Miyake 1995). For example, Kyoto dialect, the dialect of the historical capital, is known to have an elaborate system of honorifics. The existence of higher and lower caste speakers in Kyoto contributed to the dialect's development of honorifics. As Ibaraki has mainly been an agricultural prefecture, the simplicity of its system of honorifics makes sense according to this logic.[9] In the grammar of ID, there are no referent honorifics and only a few occasional examples of addressee honorifics (e.g., *nansho* 'please', as in *asobi ni ki-nansho* 'Please come visit'; however, none was observed in the current data).

This near absence of honorifics in the dialect leads one to think that gender differences in honorific use are unlikely to be observed in ID. According to Ide (1990), one characteristic of "Japanese women's language" is women's more frequent use of honorifics than men's as a result of using politer forms to the same addressee. But if honorifics are hardly available to any speaker in the Ibaraki repertoire, then this characteristic of women's honorifics use would not hold in ID. However, nowadays it is difficult to find speakers who use exclusively dialectal features in their speech, due to their exposure to SJ through education and the mass media. Thus, speakers in Ibaraki have access to honorifics in SJ, as seen later in example (4). Consequently, it is possible that the women and men of Ibaraki may employ these honorifics in SJ to varying degrees as a way of gender marking.

There is no mention of gender differences in ID in the literature. This is a curious fact, considering how thoroughly dialectologists have examined other aspects of the dialect. Compared to the abundant literature in the field of Japanese dialectology in general, only a small number of studies have dealt with gender contrasts (some of the few exceptions are Haig 1990 and J. Nakamura 1996 on the retention of phonological features in Nagoya and Ina of Nagano respectively, and Yamada 1986 on gender differentiated honorific use in a community in Aichi).[10] Kindaichi (1977[1957]) asserted that gender contrast in speech is a recent, urban phenomenon and is rarely observed in farming and fishing villages, though he did not elaborate on exactly how it became an urban phenomenon.

When I inquired about this issue to several female and male farmers in Ibaraki (not the speakers in this chapter), they answered that it is difficult to give a clear answer as to how women and men speak differently in ID. The farmers thought that sentence-ending forms such as *dappe* and *dabe* (SJ: *daroo*, expressing conjecture) are uttered more strongly and with more confidence by men than by women. The other tendency the farmers pointed out is that, among the younger generation, men seem to use more dialectal features than women (cf. Labov 1972, Trudgill 1974, Nakamura 1996). Of course these intuitive observations require a careful analysis of actual data in order to be confirmed. Nevertheless, it seems to be the case that gender difference in ID is not nearly as observable or as established as in SJ, and is clearly less salient at the ideological level. At least at the morphological and lexical level, there does not seem to be a marked difference. Moreover, as (b) and (f) in table 10.1 show, there are some features that are considered manly or vulgar (and thus available only to men) in SJ but are used gender-neutrally in ID. Another example of this category is the first-person pronoun *ore*, which is supposed to be available only to male speakers. However, my observations show that a group of farm women frequently used *ore* as a standard first-person pronoun at their product development meeting, as seen in example (2), (cf. chapters 11 and 14, this volume).

(2) [ID]   ***Ore***   *ge sa kita ra . . .*
     [SJ equivalent]   *Watashi no uchi ni kita ra . . .*
     [English Translation] If you come over to my place . . .

In short, such examples illustrate how important it is to observe language use by women and men in regional Japan independently from the "Japanese women's language" ideology.

10.4. The work of the Agricultural Extension adviser in contemporary Japanese agriculture

Due to financial difficulties and insecurity in contemporary Japanese agriculture, it is now common for one or more members of a farm family (most likely the husband) to have another job outside farming. Consequently, in 1992 about 70% of the agricultural laborers between 30 and 59 years of age were women (Soorifu 1993).

Though it is evident from these statistics that women are indispensable in Japanese agriculture, the role of farm women has been underestimated. It is well known that *nooka no yome* 'farmers' wives' have traditionally been treated as *ushi ya uma* 'chattel' (lit., 'cattle and horses'). However, such an attitude has made it difficult for farmers' sons to find wives now that women have started having more options in their lives (cf. Gal 1978).

In addition to the problem of finding wives, competition with domestic and foreign products is getting stiffer; now farms need to change and improve their methods of management so that they can attract the younger generation and expand or even maintain their businesses. This desperate situation, along with the general decline of agriculture in Japan, has led even some of the most conservative Japanese farmers and government officials to reconsider their attitudes toward women and the traditional ways of running family farming businesses.

The *kairyoo-fukyuu-in* 'Agricultural Extension adviser' (hereafter adviser) is a position in the regional offices of *Noogyoo-kairyoo-fukyuu-sentaa* 'The Agricultural Extension Service', which is under the control of the Ministry of Agriculture, Forestry, and Fisheries. Even though many advisers mainly deal with technical improvements such as teaching farmers how to grow products more effectively, another important goal has been to improve the quality of life of farming families. This effort was started to attract the younger generation, especially women, to agriculture in order to stem the decline in this sector (*Japan Agricultural News*, July 6, 1994). Thus, some of the advisers, including Hayashi-san, the one in this study, specialize in dealing with issues relating to the improvement of the lives of farming families.

Advisers work toward small goals and use these as stepping stones to the ultimate goal. The ultimate or macrogoal in this case is to improve women's status in the farms, and smaller or micro goals include dividing jobs clearly within a farm family and providing wives with the knowledge and skills necessary for them to be able to perform their tasks responsibly. The means by which advisers help farm households include changing their management styles to enable women to have regular days off, to employ a monthly payment system, to encourage wives to create personal bank accounts, and to teach wives how to keep accounts using computers and to be actively involved in promoting their products.

The county agent, then, educates, supports, and advises women (and men) in these agricultural family businesses. All parties involved (i.e., adviser, wives and husbands in farming families) are aware that raising women's status is a main goal in the work of the adviser. However, in reality, the degree of acceptance of this idea differs across gender and generation.

10.5. Dialect use, solidarity building, and empowerment of farm women

In the current data, the word *empowerment* most accurately describes the women's interactions, and it seems to be a two-way process. That is, as described earlier, Hayashi-san's very job is to empower farm women, but her effort needs to be reciprocated by their active involvement in the dialogue. In the interactions between Hayashi-san and the three women, two major strategies are found. The first strategy is the use of ID, or the avoidance of SJ, especially honorific features, as a means of building solidarity. The use of this strategy also means that morphological and lexical features of "Japanese women's language" are rarely used in single-sex professional interactions. The second strategy is regarding the women as the representatives of their households who manage family business matters, rather than treating them as "farmers' wives." In this discursive construction of the three women's new position in their family businesses, both Hayashi-san and the farm women were equally eager participants. Before, when visits were made by advisers who only taught technical matters, extensive communication between the wife of a farmer and an adviser was uncommon. Hada-san and Oki-san said that until Hayashi-san started visiting them they had thought it was their husband's job to talk to the advisers from the governmental office (i.e., to people with superior status).[11]

Oki-san's husband was present during the entire conversation, but he remained a listener almost throughout and made comments only occasionally. Hada-san's and Nagano-san's husbands joined their wives and Hayashi-san later in the conversations. Hayashi-san paid attention to the husbands and actively included them in the conversations by, for instance, asking Mr. Hada how his sprained foot was. However, the husbands seemed to be aware of the conversational dynamics; that is, they acted as if Hayashi-san was talking to their wives, not to them, about whatever the wives were in charge of in the agricultural business. This dynamic seemed to be created as a result of Hayashi-san's clear intention to treat the women as professionals who were as competent as their husbands. Her treatment of the women was reciprocated by their articulating business matters and their needs.

In (3), both strategies enumerated earlier are observed. Hayashi-san and Hada-san are talking.

(3)[12] Hayashi-san = H, Hada-san = HW, Mr. Hada = HH, R = Researcher
    (Hayashi-san tells Hada-san that the researcher has been studying in the United States.)
  1   HW: *hnnn **kanshin shitchaa** kanshin **shitchimaa***
  2   (to R, who replies 'no, no') *itteppe yoo honto da yoo naa*

3   H: *nee mukashi wa watashira no koro ni wa*(.)*sonna toko e*
4   *iku nante yuu no wa kangae mo* <u>*tsuka-nee*</u>

(Hada-san agrees and switches her topic to her recent *noogyoo kenshuu* 'agricultural study trip' to Europe sponsored by Hayashi-san's government office.)

5   HW: <u>*dagaa*</u> *ii chansu da naa* <u>*ado*</u> *ni mo* <u>*sagi*</u> *ni mo kore wa* <u>*nee*</u> <u>*naa*</u> <u>*do*</u> *omotta gara*

6   **<u>*toochan nantsuoo-to kantsuoo-to kama-nee yaa*</u>** *to omotte*

(Mr. Hada comes home and enters through the door in front of where we are seated.)

7   H: **konnichi wa**(.)**ojama shitemasu** *doomo*
⌈8 HH: *iya doomo*   *mada:*   *mada*(xxx)
⌊9 H: *mada*(.) *mada:*   *mada*
10 H: <u>*konda kageashi a deginai ne*</u>

English Translation
1   HW: Hmmm, I'm so impressed! I am so impressed!
2   (to R, who replies 'no, no') Really, I'm telling you, I mean it.
3   H: Right, in the old days, in our days, we couldn't even imagine
4   going to such a place [i.e., abroad].

(Hada-san agrees and switches her topic to her recent *noogyoo kenshuu* 'agricultural study trip' to Europe sponsored by Hayashi-san's government office.)

5   HW: So, because I thought it would be a good opportunity, there wouldn't be this [kind of opportunity] later on,
6   I thought I wouldn't care no matter what my husband says [about my going on the trip].

(Mr. Hada comes home and enters through the door in front of where we are seated.)

7   H: Hello, how are you?
⌈8 HH: Hi, how are you?   not yet   not yet (xxx)
⌊9 H: (looking at HH's sprained foot)   not yet not yet   not yet
10 H: you probably can't run with this (foot), can you?

In this excerpt, Hayashi-san and Hada-san use dialect-dominant language. In fact, to those unfamiliar with ID, Hada-san's utterance *kanshin shitchaa, kanshin shitchimaa* (SJ/"Japanese women's language" equivalent: *kanshin shichau, kanshin shichau wa*) in line 1 may sound strong or even coarse (thus unfeminine) due to the long vowel /aa/ instead of /au/, a vulgar feature according to ideologies of SJ / "Japanese women's language."

Likewise, Hada-san's utterance <u>*toochan nantsuoo-to kantsuoo-to kama-nee yaa*</u> (SJ /"Japanese women's language " equivalent: *otoosan ga nante ioo to kamawanai wa*) in line 6 must sound rather masculine and unsophisticated by the standard of SJ /"Japanese women's language." First, the term of reference *toochan*, literally 'father', is a variant that can be used to refer to one's husband. Other variants include *otoosan* and *papa*, where the former sounds most generic and the latter has a "Western" flavor, indexing certain (desired) attributes of the family such as urban, educated, or Westernized. According to the standard of SJ /"Japanese women's language," *toochan*, the form Hada-san used, sounds less sophisticated compared to the other two variants. *Nantsuoo* is a truncated form of *nante ioo*, and again, according to the rules of SJ and "Japanese women's language," it indexes coarseness. Moreover, in *kama-nee,* the long vowel /ee/ instead of the diphthong /ai/ was used, which supposedly indexed coarseness like the other features.

However, these features are all acceptable and normal and do not index coarseness in ID; and the dialectal form of the utterances shows Hada-san's active involvement in the conversation and her open relationship with Hayashi-san. The content is tied both to Hada-san's professional growth and to her personal feelings about it. When Hada-san's husband suddenly comes home and joins the conversation, however, Hayashi-san uses a more formal expression in line 7 *konnichi wa, ojama shitemasu,* greeting him not only in SJ but also with an addressee honorific form, *-masu.* This utterance makes a sharp contrast with the rest of the utterances, which are dialect-dominant and contain virtually no honorifics. Hayashi-san's remark to Mr. Hada in line 10 quickly reverts to the dialect-dominant speech. After line 10, once she showed her concern about his sprained foot and introduced me to him, Hada-san became the main conversational partner once again and Mr. Hada became a bystander. In this interaction, the formal-informal contrast is expressed as the contrast between SJ and ID. Hayashi-san switched her speech in a similar way when Mr. Nagano joined her conversation with Nagano-san.

Hayashi-san was successful in relating to each woman's situation during her visits. Among the three visits recorded, this rapport making in progress was best observed in her interaction with Oki-san, whom Hayashi-san had met only once before (whereas she had known the other two women for several months). In her conversation with Oki-san, whom Hayashi-san knew the least, use of the SJ addressee honorific affirmative form *-desu* and its variant *-desho(o)* was observed. It seems that both of them used politer forms of speech to indicate the appropriate social distance between them. At the same time, in order to create rapport, they retained dialectal features in their speech as well. Part of the interaction is shown in example (4).

(4) Hayashi-san = H, Oki-san = OW, Mr. Oki = OH

(Hayashi-san and I have just been invited to enter the room where the farmers keep cut roses cool. We all sit down to talk. It is a very humid, hot day in mid-August, and this room is the only cool place the family has.)

⌈11 H: *kondo soto ni <u>dete igu</u> to mata tsukareru* **desho**
⌊12 OH: *soo soo*(xxx)

13 H: *nde kon <u>nakaa</u> suzushiku tatte hausu n <u>nakaa</u> mata*(.)*mata*
⌈14   *mata sugoi atsui n da mon ne?*   *nn*
⌊15 OW: (1)*atsui <u>nante mon ja nee</u>   kurui soo*

16 H: *so kurui soo* **desho** *hontoni ne?*(.)*nanni mo shinai de ita tte*

17   *kuruisoo nan da mon <u>koa</u> hausu n naka ja naku tatte*
⌈18 H: *ijoo-<u>daa</u>-ne?*
⌊19 OW: *nn kotoshi wa ijoo* **desu** *yo ne?*

English Translation
⌈11 H: And then when you go outside, you get tired again, I bet.
⌊12 OH: yeah yeah

13   H: Even though this room is cool, the greenhouse is again
⌈14   extremely hot, isn't it?   yeah
⌊15   OW: It's far worse than hot   I almost go crazy
16   H: Yeah, I bet you almost go crazy, don't you?, really. Even if you don't do
17   anything you would go crazy, even if you aren't in a greenhouse . . . (so
             inside the greenhouse must be terrible)
⌈18   H: It is abnormal, I agree
⌊19   OW: It's unusually (hot) this year, don't you think?

This excerpt is near the beginning of the recording at the Okis' home. Hayashi-san and I, having moved from the car to the room, felt relieved to be in a cool place. We could tell that the Okis had been working in the heat for hours. Hayashi-san's focus was on sympathizing with Oki-san and at the same time applauding her hard work. In lines 11 and 16 Hayashi-san used the addressee honorific form *desho*, while in line 19 Oki-san used *desu*. However, the *desu* ending was not used at every possible place; in fact, plain forms were also used frequently in (4), as well as throughout the interaction. In SJ, the simple use of addressee honorifics is considered lower on the scale of politeness than other combinations of addressee and referent honorifics (Ogino 1986, Ide 1990). However, in the context here, where the use of the dialect with almost no honorifics is the norm of local interactions, the women's use of *desu* and *desho* stands out and indexes the distance between the speaker and addressee. At the same time, other dialectal elements such as the voicing of /k/ (as in *dete igu to* 'when [you] go outside' by Hayashi-san in line 11) and /ee/ in place of /ai/ (as in *atsui nante mon ja nee* 'it's far worse than hot' by Oki-san in line 15) contribute to their solidarity building.

The next segment comes from Hayashi-san's interaction with Nagano-san, whose household has just started growing *maitake* mushrooms. At this point, the Naganos are still deciding the best way of promoting their mushrooms in the market. Hayashi-san visited the Naganos to discuss the packaging, naming, and advertising of their new product. In example (5), one can see that Hayashi-san encourages Nagano-san by making positive comments as a consumer: younger people are interested in a healthy diet these days, and mushrooms would attract these people since they are low in calories and high in minerals. *Maitake* mushrooms are relatively new and not as common as *shiitake* mushrooms, and Hayashi-san points this fact out while emphasizing the *maitake*'s unique texture, which is harder than that of the *shiitake*.

The two women's speech exhibits ID's pitch-accent pattern, and without the formal endings of SJ it sounds casual. As a result of overlaps (lines 21 and 22; lines 23 and 24), as well as quick chime-in's with each other throughout the excerpt (but expecially lines 25 and 26), the interaction sounds lively and involved. It is as if Hayashi-san and Nagano-san are co-constructing a profile of *maitake* mushrooms by energetically and rhythmically throwing out their positive characteristics. By the end of their interaction, Nagano-san managed to come up with the copy she would use to market her mushrooms. It emphasized the mushrooms' unique texture and nutrition.

(5)   Hayashi-san = H, Nagano-san = NW
     20   H: *katai toko ga oishii ne mata ne*

```
⌈21                        oishii ne nn
⌊22   NW:   katai toko oishii ne          anooo mazegohan mo
⌈23   H:        shii kedomo         (xxx)      (xx ra)uken ne aa
⌊24   NW:   oi shii kedomoo(.)katai tokoo ga wakai hito dakara ne
⌈25   H:                              nn    hagire ga ii n da=
⌊26   NW:   (1) aa koshi ga aru n da yo ne anoo               =soo
```

English Translation

```
 20   H:    The hard parts are delicious, especially
⌈21                        delicious, yeah
⌊22   NW:   the hard parts are deli- cious  weeell, mixed rice [with maitake] is
⌈23   H:    -ty, but        (xxx)
⌊24   NW:   tasty, but the tough parts are [good] since [the targeted consumers are]
            young people [who like crisp food more than old people do]
⌈25   H:                              yeah  they're fresh and crisp
⌊26   NW:   (1) well, they (maitake) have good texture      well          right
```

In line 25, Hayashi-san uses the affirmative ending *hagire ga ii n **da*** 'it's fresh and crisp', which is considered masculine in SJ (Reynolds 1990) but not in ID.

To summarize, Hayashi-san employed two strategies in order to establish solidarity and empower the farm women, Hada-san, Oki-san, and Nagano-san. First, all the women's use of ID essentially without honorifics contributed to their establishing rapport and engaging in intimate yet task-oriented conversations. In their interactions, the adviser, Hada-san, and Nagano-san used dialect-dominant speech. Their speech contained virtually no "Japanese women's language" features but included a number of Ibaraki dialectal features, some of which are considered vulgar according to the rules of "Japanese women's language." Even in the conversation between the Advisor and Oki-san, who were more recent acquaintances, both utilized a mixture of SJ addressee honorifics and dialectal features simultaneously to maintain the socially appropriate distance (as relative strangers) and to establish rapport. Second, Hayashi-san made sure that it was the wife, instead of the husband, who was the representative to whom she came to talk, even though she included the husband in the conversation. By doing so, she successfully placed the wives in a more responsible, respected position than they have been traditionally accorded and she interacted with them as professionals. At the same time, the three farm women were by no means passive receivers of Hayashi-san's treatment. Instead, they were simultaneously empowering themselves, as well as being empowered, by actively voicing their professional selves in their discourse with her.

10.6.   Conclusion and implications

In this chapter, the discourse of an Agricultural Extension adviser and three women in a farming community in Ibaraki was analyzed. From the women's extensive use of dialectal features as well as the lack of morphological, phonological, and lexical features of "Japanese women's language" in their speech it is evident that we need to go beyond analyzing the presence or absence of "Japanese women's language" in Japanese women's language use. The use of "Japanese women's language" was not part of the speech repertoire of these four women. This finding is better understood when the relationship between regional dialects and SJ in Japan is historically reviewed. These women have always spoken in ID, with some elements of SJ mixed in depending on the context.

Though a small-scale study, this chapter suggests a crucial point in the field of language and gender. That is, gender may not always be the most salient category that can affect speakers. In order to understand how women speak, it is important to consider their regionality and occupation and other aspects of their identities, as well as the sociohistorical background of their linguistic resources. Regarding the four Ibaraki women's speech and lives, it is likely that they have more in common with other members of the rural population of Ibaraki or with other people engaged in agriculture elsewhere in Japan than with traditional Yamanote housewives. Indeed, the use of "Japanese women's language" is itself a regional phenomenon; "Japanese women's language" is the ideal shared by women of a certain socioeconomic background who reside in Tokyo or aspire to Tokyo values, including language use. Japanese women who have internalized the ideology of "Japanese women's language" may aspire to, negotiate with, or even reject "Japanese women's language." However, the speech of other women, for whom "Japanese women's language" is more fictive than real (cf. Inoue 2002 and chapter 3, this volume), may not even include "Japanese women's language." Nevertheless, thus far "Japanese women's language" has been treated as if it were the only speech style Japanese women should follow or resist. Part of the reason for this may be that even we scholars of language and gender have been deeply influenced by the social norm and gender identity associated with "Japanese women's language."

Of course, in order to confirm my observations more research needs to be conducted about women's and men's speech in various regions and occupations in Japan. There are still many questions to be answered regarding the relationship between dialects, SJ, and "Japanese women's language" and how or if gender difference is marked in various dialects.

I suspect that the gender ideology of "Japanese women's language" has not quite reached or, rather, has not been internalized by, locally centered people, including my study participants. At the same time, women and men of rural Ibaraki do understand what "Japanese women's language" features are supposed to index when they encounter these features on television or in novels. What kind of position, then, does "Japanese women's language" occupy in the language ideology and language use of these rural women and men of Ibaraki? Also, if there is a local gender-marking system in ID, how do female aspirers negotiate uses of the dialect's gender-preferred elements and "Japanese women's language"? To answer these questions requires a larger scale study than is possible in this chapter.

Notes

I thank the women and men in Ibaraki who helped me gather data for this research. My special appreciation also goes to Mary Bucholtz and the editors of this volume for their valuable comments.

1. The term *Japanese women's language* is ambiguous. For example, it may refer to any speech Japanese women use or to vaguely defined "feminine" speech. But throughout this essay, I use *Japanese women's language* to specifically refer to a set of morphological, phonological, and stylistic features that remind a Japanese native speaker of a stereotypical Tokyo woman.

2. But see chapter 15 for regional differences in men's use of sentence-final particles. Ogawa and [Shibamoto] Smith (1996) also deal with regionality in gay speech.

3. The degree of retention of a dialect differs from region to region, as well as from person to person. Kansai (e.g., Osaka, Kyoto) dialects preserve high ethnolinguistic vitality next to SJ in current Japanese society perhaps due to the region's history; Kansai dialects speakers tend to be proud of their dialect and use them even when they are outside their region. However, other speakers, including users of ID, tend to restrict their dialect use to within their own communities. See Inoue (1989) for surveys of various dialects.

4. However, Momoko Nakamura (2001) argues that users of "Japanese women's language," while being praised for their femininity, have also been subject to criticism that their speech is deviant from the standard (that is, standard male speech, which is often automatically subsumed under SJ).

5. All speakers' names that appear in this chapter are pseudonyms.

6. Despite Ibaraki's proximity to Tokyo, its dialect can be so distinct from SJ as to be unintelligible to SJ speakers, especially when the ID speaker is older, locally based, and working-class.

7. Strictly speaking, there is a difference between SJ and the Tokyo dialect, the former being the standard established for the mass media and education and the latter being the daily spoken variety of Tokyo residents. Contemporary Japanese living in regional Japan seem to be influenced by the "central" language at these two different levels (see Inoue 1994 and Sanada 1996, for example). However, it is beyond the scope of this chapter to differentiate these two levels or to develop a discussion on this matter.

8. Feature (c), vowel merger, is not indicated in the transcript for two reasons: the merger was not necessarily observed with all tokens of /i/ and /e/, and the degree of centralization was not uniform across occurrences. These variations are most likely due to the influence from SJ.

9. However, Irvine (1998) notes that class differences alone cannot sufficiently explain the existence of honorifics. In addition, this explanation leaves a question regarding ID. Mito, the Ibaraki prefectural capital, was where one of the three Tokugawa family branches was located during the Tokugawa Shogunate. In that sense, at least part of Ibaraki was "historically complex" between the seventeenth and the nineteenth century, though the dialect is said to be honorific-less. Further research is needed on this issue.

10. At the anecdotal level, I have heard people from different parts of the Kansai region (e.g. Osaka, Kyoto, and Nara) describing gender-differentiated features in their own dialects.

11. In fact, until they became amalgamated into one position a few years ago, advisers had two tracks: *noogyoo kairyoo-fukyuu-in* 'agricultural adviser' and *seekatsu kairyoo-fukyuu-in* 'life adviser', at the ratio of approximately 10:1. Hayashi-san was employed as the latter. On the one hand, the former position dealt with technology-related issues and was mostly occupied by males, who interacted with male members of farm families. On the other hand, the latter position dealt with issues to improve the quality of lives of these families, as discussed in this chapter. Like Hayashi-san, women mostly occupied the latter position, and its job was traditionally considered secondary to the former's.

12. Transcription conventions are:

?　　rising intonation

(xxx)　　unclear section that could not be transcribed

	=	latching
	(1)	number of seconds of pause
	(.)	micropause of less than one second
	boldface	analyzed features
	<u>underline</u>	dialectal features

⌈5 H: aaaaa   ccccc   temporal overlap. In this example, H utters 'aaaaa', followed
⌊6 OH: bbbbb   by OH's 'bbbbb', then H's 'ccccc'

References

Bucholtz, Mary (1999). Bad examples: Transgression and progress in language and gender studies. In M. Bucholtz, A. C. Liang, and L. A. Sutton (eds.), *Reinventing identities: The gendered self in discourse*, 3–24. New York: Oxford University Press.

Dore, Ronald P. (1978). *Shinohata: A portrait of a Japanese village*. Berkeley: University of California Press.

Gal, Susan. (1978). Peasant men can't get wives: Language change and sex roles in a bilingual community. *Language in Society* 7:1–16.

Haig, John H. (1990). A phonological difference in male-female speech among teenagers in Nagoya. In S. Ide and N. H. McGloin (eds.), *Aspects of Japanese women's speech*, 5–22. Tokyo: Kuroshio.

Hibiya, Junko (1988). A quantitative study of Tokyo Japanese. Ph.D. dissertation, University of Pennsylvania. Ann Arbor: University of Michigan.

Hunter, Janet (1993). *Japanese women working*. London: Routledge.

Ide, Sachiko (1990). How and why do women speak more politely in Japanese? In S. Ide and N. H. McGloin (eds.), *Aspects of Japanese women's language*, 63–79. Tokyo: Kuroshio

Inoue, Fumio (1989). *Kotobazukai shinfuukee: Keego to hoogen* (*New views on ways of speaking: Honorifics and dialects*). Tokyo: Akiyama Shoten.

——— (1994). *Hoogen-gaku no shinchihee* (*New horizon of dialectology*). Tokyo: Meiji Shoin.

Inoue, Miyako (2002). Gender, language, and modernity: Toward an effective history of "Japanese women's language." *American Ethnologist* 29(2): 392–422.

——— (in preparation). Vicarious language: The political economy of gender and speech in Japan. Book manuscript.

Irvine, Judith (1998). Ideologies of honorific language. In B. B. Schieffelin, K. A. Woolard, and P. V. Kroskrity (eds.), *Language ideologies: Practice and theory*, 51–67. New York: Oxford University Press.

Kanesawa, Naoto (1984). Ibaraki ken no hoogen (ID). In K. Iitoyo, S. Hino, and R. Sato (eds.), *Kanto chihoo no hoogen* (*Dialects of Kanto region*). Tokyo: Kokusho Kankokai.

Kindaichi, Haruhiko (1977 [1957]). *Nihongo* (*Japanese language*). Tokyo: Iwanami Shoten.

——— (1977). *Nihongo hoogen no kenkyuu* (*Study of Japanese dialects*). Tokyo: Tokyo-do Shuppan.

——— (1995 [1948]). Ikkee akusento ni tsuite no ichi koosatsu (A study of one-pattern accent). In F. Inoue, K. Shinozaki, T. Kobayashi, and T. Oonishi (eds.) (1995), *Kanto hoogen koo 1: Kanto ippan, Ibaraki ken, Tochigi ken* (*Dialects of Kanto region 1: Kanto region in general, Ibaraki prefecture, Tochigi prefecture*), 257–262. Tokyo: Yumani Shobo. ([=1948] *Kotoba* 7.)

Kondo, Dorinne (1990). *Crafting selves: Power, gender, and discourse of identity in a Japanese workplace*. Chicago: University of Chicago Press.

Labov, William (1972). *Sociolinguistic patterns*. Philadelphia: University of Pennsylvania Press.

Lebra, Takie Sugiyama (1993). *Above the clouds: Status culture of the modern Japanese nobility.* Berkeley: University of California Press.

Lee, Yeounsuk (1996). *"Kokugo" to yuu shisoo (The ideology of "the national language").* Tokyo: Iwanami Shoten.

Miyajima, Tatsuo (1961). Fukushima, Ibaraki, Tochigi. In Y. Endo, T. Hirayama, T. Okubo, and T. Shibata (eds.), *Toobu hoogen (Eastern dialects)*, 236–263. Tokyo: Tokyo-do Shuppan.

Miyake, Yoshimi (1995). A dialect in the face of the standard: A Japanese case study. In J. Ahlers, L. Bilmes, J. S. Guenter, B. A. Kaiser, and J. Namkung (eds.), *Proceedings of the Twenty-first Annual Meeting of the Berkeley Linguistics Society*, 217–225. Berkeley: Berkeley Linguistics Society.

Nakamura, Junko (1996). Ina hoogen ni okeru hoogen hoji no danjo-sa (Gender contrast in dialect retention in Ina dialect). *Nihongo Kenkyuu* 16: 25–38.

Nakamura, Momoko (2001). *Kotoba to jendaa (Language and gender).* Tokyo: Keiso Shobo.

Ogawa, Naoko, and Janet S. [Shibamoto] Smith (1996). The linguistic gendering of an alternative Japanese lifestyle: Speech variation in the gay communities of urban Japan. In R. Ide, R. Parker, and Y. Sunaoshi (eds.), *SALSA: Proceedings of the Third Annual Symposium about Language and Society*, 36, 28–40. Austin: University of Texas, Department of Linguistics.

Ogino, Tsunao (1986). Quantification of politeness based on the usage patterns of honorific expressions. *International Journal of the Sociology of Language* 58: 37–58.

Okamoto, Shigeko (1995). "Tasteless" Japanese: Less "feminine" speech among young Japanese women. In K. Hall and M. Bucholtz (eds.), *Gender articulated: Language and the socially constructed self*, 297–325. New York: Routledge.

——— (2000). The role of standard and non-SJ in conversations. Paper presented at the 2000 Annual Meeting of the American Association for Applied Linguistics, Vancouver, British Columbia.

Reynolds, Katsue Akiba (1990). Female speakers of Japanese in transition. In S. Ide and N. H. McGloin (eds.), *Aspects of Japanese women's language*, 129–146. Tokyo: Kuroshio.

Roberts, Glenda S. (1994). *Staying on the line: Blue-collar women in contemporary Japan.* Honolulu: University of Hawaii Press.

Sanada, Shinji (1991). *Hyoojungo wa ika ni seeritsu shita ka: Kindai nihongo no hatten no rekishi (How Standard Japanese has developed: History of the development of contemporary Japanese).* Tokyo: Sotakusha.

——— (1996). *Chiiki-go no seetai shiriizu: Chiiki-go no dainamizumu—Kansai (Regional variety series: Dynamism of regional varieties—Kansai region).* Tokyo: Ofu.

Sanada, Shinji, Katsumi Shibuya, Masataka Jinnouchi, and Seiju Sugito (1992). *Shakaigengogaku (Sociolinguistics).* Tokyo: Ofu.

Shibata, Takeshi (1980). Kyootsuugo (Common language); Hyoojungo (Standard language). In *Kokugo-gaku daijiten (Dictionary of the national language studies)*, 219–220, 729–730. Tokyo: Kokugo Gakkai.

Siegal, Meryl, and Shigeko Okamoto (1996). Imagined worlds: Language, gender and sociocultural "norms" in Japanese language textbooks. In *Proceedings of the Fourth Berkeley Women and Language Conference,* 667–678. Berkeley: Berkeley Women and Language Group.

Soorifu (ed.) (1993). *Josee no genjoo to shisaku: Kawaru kazoku to josee no seekatsu (Women's current situations and trials: Changing families and women's lives).* Tokyo: Okurasho.

Taguchi, Yoshio (1995[1944]). Ibaraki hoogen gohoo ni-san no koosatsu (A study of Ibaraki hoogen usage). In F. Inoue, K. Shinozaki, T. Kobayashi, and T. Oonishi (eds.) *Kanto hoogen koo 1: Kanto ippan, Ibaraki ken, Tochigi ken* (*Dialects of Kanto region 1: Kanto region in general, Ibaraki Prefecture, Tochigi Prefecture*), 295–306. Tokyo: Yumani Shobo. ([=1944] *Hoogen kenkyuu* 10.)

Trudgill, Peter (1974). *Sociolinguistics: An introduction to language and society.* Harmondsworth: Penguin.

Yamada, Tatsuya (1986). Hoogen to keego (Dialects and honorifics). In K. Iitoyo, S. Hino, and R. Sato (eds.), *Hoogen gaisetsu* (*Overview of dialects*), 181–204. Tokyo: Kokusho Kankokai.

11

HIDEKO ABE

Lesbian Bar Talk in Shinjuku, Tokyo

Two decades ago, the difference between sex (as biological, natural, physical, real, actual, unrefined) and gender (as social, fictitious, refined, forced) was presumed to be clear and obvious for language and gender researchers. However, the distinction between the two was questioned and challenged most powerfully by Butler, who claims that sex "by definition has been gender all along" (1990:8) and that gender is a discursive practice unfolding in an ongoing interaction and, thus, open to intervention and resignification. An important aspect of Butler's work is her claim that gender only exists in the service of heterosexism. Butler restructures gender as the performative effect of repeated acts, a cultural fiction, which can as such no longer privilege heterosexuality as the *real* or original sexuality at the expense of homosexuality (Jagose 1996). Ueno (1999:48) argues that one of queer theorists' contributions is to demolish the distinction between heterosexuality as norm/origin and homosexuality as deviation/imitation. Jagose defines *queer* as follows.

> Queer describes analytical models which dramatise incoherence in the allegedly stable relations between chromosomal sex, gender and sexual desire. Resisting that model of stability—which claims heterosexuality as its origin, when it is more properly its effect—queer focuses on mismatches between sex, gender and desires. Institutionally, queer has been associated most prominently with lesbian and gay subjects, but its analytic framework also includes such topics as cross-dressing, hermaphroditism, gender ambiguity and gender-corrective surgery. Demonstrating the impossibility of any 'natural' sexuality, it calls into question even such apparently unproblematic terms as 'man' and 'woman'. (1996:3)

In contrast to language and gender studies that have a relatively substantial history of methodological and theoretical development, language and sexuality studies are a new area of inquiry, provisionally called "queer" linguistics. Barrett argues that queer linguistics "provides a means for beginning to understand the ways in which people actually construct and produce markers of queer identities and deal with the ambiguity of identity categories and communities that are imagined differently by different community members" (1997:198).

In this chapter I look at how linguistic practice observed at lesbian bars in Tokyo is related to the construction of queer identities. I have chosen the lesbian bar community because it is the most concentrated place where lesbians gather and interact with one another on a personal level. My study does not attempt to describe how Japanese lesbians speak in general, but rather it discusses how lesbians construct their identities through a specific linguistic practice. This practice may be labeled masculine speech with noticeable linguistic variation by individual speakers in the same speech context.

11.1. Background

Japanese language and sexuality has been largely unexplored. Further, the limited number of studies (e.g., Maree 1997, Ogawa & [Shibamoto] Smith 1997, Valentine 1997) that have appeared are mainly focused on the speech of gay men (cf. chapter 5, this volume). There have been more studies on European languages, mainly English, and some of these focus on lesbian speech. Topics of lesbian-centered research cover (1) lexical variation (Kleinfeld & Warner 1997), (2) voice characteristics (Moonwomon-Baird 1997), (3) the language use of comic-book characters (Queen 1997), (4) coming-out stories (Wood 1997), (5) identity construction through language (Liang 1997, 1999; Neumann 1997), (6) language use in film (Queen 2000), (7) grammatical gender (Livia 1997, Pastre 1997), (8) language use in life stories (Moonwomon-Baird 2000), and (9) the textual analysis of personal ads (Livia 2000). These studies attempt to uncover different aspects of lesbian lives and their identities and promise an exciting future for research on language and sexualities.

While the field of language and sexuality has started producing many studies of private speech and of language in the media in recent years, we have seen a very limited number of studies on public speech, especially in gay/lesbian bars. Both Achilles' (1993 [1967]) and Read's (1980) studies of non-Japanese gay bars discuss the role and the significance of gay bars in providing a space for social interaction. So far, there are only a few studies on non-Japanese lesbian bars, all of which focus on how class-related differences play a role in bar-going habits as well as in ways of articulating lesbian identity (e.g., Chamberland 1993, Gilmartin 1996). The most recent study (Hankin 2002) analyzes how lesbian bars are represented in popular culture such as films. Barrett's (1997) study of gay identities and language use in bar settings discusses the speech of African-American drag queens and analyzes how they negotiate their overlapping identities by using code-switching strategies. As for Japanese gay bars, there are a few works (e.g., Ootsuka 1995, Sunagawa 1998), which emphasize the importance of gay bars as a crucial space for developing and maintaining one's gay identity. There are no studies of Japanese lesbian bars, although some popular women's magazines have published reports on a few, along with interviews with the owners. *Anise*, a lesbian and bisexual information magazine (*joohooshi*) that started in 1996 and ended in 1997, also discusses some lesbian bars. Another *joohooshi*, *Love Revolution* (AKIKO 2000), lists 10 lesbian bars in the Tokyo area. Few studies have focused on language use in either gay or lesbian bars.

11.2.   The goals of this study

This chapter focuses on the relationship between identity and language use observed among women at lesbian bars in Shinjuku, Tokyo. By examining specific linguistic behaviors and interactions at bars it attempts to demonstrate how "language *effects* gender" (Bucholtz 1999:6) and, in particular, how "masculine" power normatively associated with specific linguistic forms is negotiated differently by individual speakers. Here I use the word *power* not as an absolute or static term but as a relational and processual term. In other words, power should be understood as interactionally negotiated through submission to or resistance against force among participants (Foucault 1990). As Kramarae, Schultz, and O'Barr (1984:11) argue, regardless of the definition of power "the resources available to exert or resist influence are recurrent, similar, and—in societies at peace—chiefly *verbal*."

I chose a lesbian bar as a setting for ethnographic linguistic study because lesbians, in contrast to gays, have been generally underrepresented in Japanese gender studies. Watanabe (1990) argues that lesbianism in Japan has historically been marginalized and is much less well documented than male homosexuality. As Moonwomon-Baird puts it, "Lesbian practice is regarded as marked behavior, but goes unremarked much more than is true of gay male practice, even in this era of both friendly and hostile societal discourse on queers" (1997:202).

Specifically, this study discusses two issues: (1) naming and identity construction in discourse and (2) linguistic behavior and interaction at lesbian bars. In the first part of this chapter, I examine how certain terms of social categorization are used to differentiate one individual's identity from others and how the social spaces of lesbian bars help individuals construct, renew, or vitalize their identities. Then I discuss how lesbian speech at bars tends to contain extensive use of masculine forms with wide contextual and individual variation. As I will discuss later, these two phenomena are crucial to understanding the relationship between Japanese lesbian identities and linguistic practice.

11.3.   Method and data collection

Tokyo's Shinjuku Ni-choome 'the Second Block', an area as small as 300 meters by 400 meters, is often referred to as the world's largest gay town. It was formerly a district inhabited by Japanese female prostitutes who served American personnel during the Occupation after World War II (Treat 1999). According to a recent gay travel guide (Uminarikan 1998, cited by Sunagawa 1998), there are 217 gay bars in

Ni-choome.[1] By contrast, there are 12 lesbian bars in Ni-choome and one in San-choome 'the Third Block' in Tokyo, four in Osaka, and one each in Kyuushuu and Hokkaido.

The fieldwork for this study was conducted between September of 1999 and June of 2000 in the Shinjuku area of Tokyo. I visited lesbian bars almost every week, spending at least two to three hours as a customer and researcher at each bar. I also corresponded with employees via e-mail. In total, there are 13 lesbian bars in Shinjuku, and I visited 12 of them; I spent considerable time at some, and others I visited only once. Not all lesbian bars are the same; some target older middle-class professional women while others target younger nonprofessional women, both middle- and working-class. However, some bars have both types of women. All employees of the bars are lesbians.

Whenever I visited a bar for the first time, I arrived at opening time so that I could be the first customer and spend time alone with the owner or the manager of the bar to explain my research. This is when I asked for permission to take field notes. I was allowed to have a notebook in front of me and to make notes at any time. Oftentimes employees jokingly said to me, "*a mata nan ka kaiteru*" 'she's writing something again' while they were serving other customers. I conducted interviews with owners and employees but also interacted with other customers, all of whom knew of my research project. I did not tape-record interactions at bars, nor did I conduct interviews outside the bars. There are two reasons for not recording the interactions. The first is that there was always loud music playing at the bars, which would have made recording almost impossible. Second, and more important, the bar owners and employees did not agree to recording. The reason was clear. In most bars, women are anonymous and it was important that they be allowed to remain so. Tape-recording is one of the most important methods of collecting sociolinguistic data; in particular, it is crucial for analyzing phonological aspects of linguistic structure. Yet careful field notes "can provide important insights into the social use and significance of lexical, grammatical and rhetorical forms" (Gaudio 2001:40). Other means of text (such as e-mail) are also useful for examining language use, and I drew on these as well. My sources of data thus are (1) interviews, (2) field notes, (3) articles from magazines, and (4) e-mail messages.

11.4. Data analysis and discussion

11.4.1. Naming and identity construction in discourses at lesbian bars

The definition of the community served by lesbian bars turned out to be broader than I had expected. While some owners and employees described their businesses as places that catered only to a female clientele, some welcome *onabe* and *nyuu haafu* 'transsexual/transgendered people' and even gay male friends of customers or employees. Owners and employees generally assume that female clientele are homosexual or bisexual but welcome others. During my visit to one bar, I encountered a situation in which a *jooren* 'regular customer' brought her friend and introduced her to the owner and employees as a *nonke* 'straight'. It appears that a customer's sexuality has to be stated explicitly if she or he is straight.

Just as Sunagawa (1998) emphasizes the difference between a gay bar and a show pub in which there is an entertainment show by *nyuu haafu*, I found it crucial to differentiate between a lesbian bar and an *onabe* bar. The word *onabe* 'pan', which is parallel to *okama* 'pot', meaning male homosexuals, is often used to refer to lesbians in a broad sense, but the two words, lesbian and *onabe*, are not the same (cf. Valentine 1997), as is clearly demonstrated in example (1). In this example,[2] the manager (A) of a lesbian bar is talking about her sexuality.

(1) *Yoosuru ni jishoteki ni wa dooseeaisha tte koto ni narimasu ne. Onabe to chigau no wa, jibun no josee to yuu see o mitometa ue de, josee ga suki tte yuu.*

'Anyway, I am a homosexual by the dictionary definition. How I am different from *onabe* is that I accept my sex as female and like women'.

Another employee (B) at a different lesbian bar[3] contends that a lesbian is a woman who feels comfortable with her female body (in other words, with her biologically female sex) and who chooses a woman as a partner. Unlike straight women, however, her identity as a woman is constructed through a relationship with another woman. However, according to this employee, an *onabe* loves women and chooses a woman as a partner, but an *onabe's* social and emotional identity is male. Thus, both the concept of *onabe* and that of lesbian challenge the conventional heterosexual gender arrangement, yet her explanation remains restricted within the binary "woman"/"man."

The same employee (A) explains the difference between *onabe* and *rezu* (or *rezubian*) 'lesbians' in example (2).

(2) *Chigaimasu ne. Ishikiteki ni mo. Kore wa yoku iwareru n desu kedo, <u>onabe san</u> wa, <u>rezu no ko</u> to wa tsukiattari, anmari shinai n desu yo. Sore wa, <u>onabe san</u> wa jibun ga otoko to shite miraretai tte yuu no ga aru kara, onna o suki na <u>rezu no ko</u> to wa, tsukiaenai.*

'Yes, we are different. Consciously as well. People often say this—*onabe* do not date lesbians. Because they want to be seen as men, they cannot date a lesbian who likes women'.

It is significant that the speaker added *-san* 'Ms./Mr'. to *onabe* and *ko* 'child' to *rezu*. The former emphasizes the distance between the speaker and the referent, while the latter constructs an intimate or friendly relationship. This kind of identity construction through naming is also found in other interviews.

Onabe bars, then, are butch-type bars where staff members usually wear men's clothes and work as hosts. There are three *onabe* bars in Tokyo (Valentine 1997). Customers at *onabe* bars are usually half lesbians and half *nonke* 'straight women'. According to many employees of *rezubian* bars, these bars are places where customers, who may be *onabe* or lesbians, and employees are on equal terms, whereas in *onabe* bars employees are there to serve customers. They also suggest that customers who are tired of *onabe* bars may move on to host bars, where young straight men serve women.

Nine of the 13 lesbian bars accept only women, including heterosexuals, *onabe*, and *nyuu haafu*. In example 3, a manager (C) of another lesbian bar talks about her clientele.

(3) *Toriaezu, rezu no okyaku sama ga taihan nan desu kedo, rezu ja nai ko mo iru n desu ne. Rezu wa rezu de kakusazu ni, soo ja nai ko mo tanoshiku. Betsu ni itsu mo rezu no wadai bakkari tte wake nai kara. Dansee wa ne, watashi no hontoo ni goku shitashii homo no kata to ka, soo yuu hito dake desu ne. Yappari onna no ko ga dansee no me o ki ni shinai de kiraku ni nomeru tte koto de, kihonteki ni dansee wa dame desu. Onabe no ko to ka nyuu haafu no ko to ka kiraku ni asobi ni kite kureru shi, futsuu no onna no ko datte ii shi. Mattaku futsuu no otoko wa dame. Dono janru ga doo ka ja nakute, mainoritii de zenzen oorai. Soo soo, guroobaru na imi de nan de mo oorai.*

'Anyway, the majority of our customers are lesbians, but there are some who aren't. For lesbians, they don't have to hide their identity. Nonlesbians can have a good time here too. We don't talk only about lesbianism, you know. As for male customers, only a few close homosexual friends of mine can come here. As a rule, we don't allow male customers because we want to provide a place where women feel comfortable drinking without worrying about men's eyes. People who are *onabe* or *nyuu haafu* come here as well. Ordinary [meaning heterosexual] women are also welcome. But ordinary men are not welcome here. I'm not categorizing people, but as long as they are a minority, they're totally welcome. Yes, anybody in a global sense is welcome'.

Whereas speaker (A) in example (2) added *-san* to *onabe*, speaker (C) uses the term *ko* 'child/young person' (instead of *hito* or *kata*, two terms for "person"), as in *onabe no ko* 'a young *onabe*' and *nyuu-haafu no ko* 'a young *nyuuhaafu*'. This shift indicates that *onabe* are here treated as in-group members (customers). This use of *ko* is a reflection of the fact that the majority of customers are in their twenties (younger than the owners or employees) and also that employees want to sound more inclusive and intimate. The alternative words, *hito* or *kata*, are more formal and distant. Interestingly, the women I interviewed never use *ko* to refer to men; instead they use *dansei* 'men' or *otoko* 'men' or even *homo no kata* 'homosexuals'. Otherness is emphasized by nonuse of *ko*.

Another interesting usage is found in the term *futsuu* 'ordinary'. In example (3), speaker (C) uses the term *futsuu* to refer to heterosexuals. I was initially shocked to encounter this word, because I thought that the speaker meant that she considered herself and other lesbians not ordinary, although it is quite possible that by *futsuu* she meant "run-of-the-mill" or even "dull," and viewed being not *futsuu*, or being lesbian, in a positive light. However, the word *futsuu* is not always used for distinguishing lesbians from heterosexuals, as example (4) demonstrates. Here the manager of a lesbian bar, (A), uses the term *futsuu* when she is asked about the role and the function of such a bar.

(4) *Minna hontoo ni futsuu no renai o shite iru n desu yo ne. Naimenteki na bubun ga chigau tte yuu ka. Futokutei tasuu no hitobito ni yotte tsukuridasareta imeeji to yuu mono ga, henken o umidashita tte yuu no wa aru to omou. Shinjitsu o wakatte nai to yuu ka. Futsuu*

*no onna no ko demo, rezu baa tte donna tokoro na no ka na, mitai na kanji de kuru shi,
kite mireba, a, nan da futsuu no mono nan da mitai na. Onna no ko hitori de mo anshin
shite nomi ni kite kuremasu yo. Futsuu no onna no ko mo ippai kimasu. Shufu no hito
mo iru shi, kareshi ga iru kedo kuru ko mo imasu shi ne.*

'Lesbians have <u>ordinary</u> love relationships, you know. Internally, we are different. Some
people created the image of lesbians as different, which created prejudice, I think. They
don't know the real truth. <u>Ordinary</u> women come here because they're curious. Once
they come, they realize how <u>ordinary</u> we are. Girls can feel comfortable coming here on
their own to drink. Lots of <u>ordinary</u> women come here, including housewives and women
who have boyfriends'.

This manager emphasizes that lesbians have *futsuu* 'ordinary' love relationships. I
argue that the speaker characterizes lesbians' love relationships as *futsuu* because
she wants heterosexuals to be inclusive of her by thinking of her as ordinary. In other
words, she is not using this word to construct differences among customers but to
include people of both sexual orientations.

Example (5), from a conversation with the manager (D) of a different bar, underscores this point.[4]

(5) *Intaanetto mite kuru onna no ko to ka tte wari to booisshu na onna no ko to ka kitai
shite kuru ko mo iru kedo, soo yuu imi de wa, watashi ga kekkoo futsuu to yuu ka, gaiken
ga booishhu ja nai kara, sore o meate ni kita okyaku san ni wa warui ka na tte.*

'There are those who come here after seeing us on the internet, expecting that I'll be
boyish looking. In that sense, how should I put it? I'm pretty <u>ordinary</u> looking. I don't
have a boyish look. I feel kind of bad for customers who come expecting that'.

Here the word *futsuu* is used to contrast with boyish looks. By using *futsuu*, the speaker
D means to say that she is feminine looking. In other words, she wants to emphasize
that feminine as well as boyish types of lesbians are welcomed at her bar.

Identity thus is demonstrated through naming and lexical contrast. While in
example (3) the word *futsuu* contrasts with lesbian, example (4) treats the same word
as part of what it means to be a lesbian. In example (5), it distinguishes feminine
appearance from boyish looks. These three examples suggest the complexity and
situatedness of people's identities, as well as the rhetorical flexibility they have to
position themselves in different ways at different moments for different purposes.

11.4.2.   Linguistic behavior and interactions at bars

In the first part of this chapter, I examined how identities can be examined through
naming and lexical contrast. In this section, I discuss several linguistic features found
in interactions at lesbian bars among employees as well as between employees and
customers: (1) formal versus informal styles, (2) first-person pronouns, (3) second-
person pronouns, (4) commands and requests, and (5) sentence-final particles. These
features are chosen because these are the areas where the construction of gender differences is often observed and recognized.

11.4.2.1.   *Formal versus informal styles*

The first feature, formal versus informal style of speech, is mainly concerned with owners' and employees' approaches to language use at their own bars. At one end of the spectrum, I observed a striking difference between an owner and her employees whereby the former stayed in an informal style (e.g., using direct sentence endings) and the latter used more formal speech (e.g., distal sentence endings). However, both of them shifted their level of speech when talking to customers. Although it is often said that women use a more formal/polite style (Ide 1979), more than a few times I observed the exclusive use of direct style by employees while customers continued to use distal endings. I argue that the use of direct style by employees comes from their goal to create an atmosphere in which customers are brought into an inclusive group—a kind of performed friendliness that may nurture a strong sense of solidarity. For example, I observed one interaction between an employee in her early twenties and a customer in her thirties talking about relationships. It sounded as if a rude young brother was talking to his older sister, if judged by the protocols assumed to govern interpersonal communication in heterosexual-centered contexts. This employee stayed in direct style even when talking to her supervisor. It seems that she has made a conscious choice regarding her linguistic style at her workplace.

At some bars where owners hardly ever show up, the linguistic atmosphere feels much freer. In fact, one owner complained to me about the use of "bad" language at her bar on her day off (when her employee manages the bar). Thus, one may experience a completely different linguistic situation at the same bar from day to day.

11.4.2.2.   *First-person pronouns*

As with the contrast between formal and informal speech, the use of first- and second-person pronouns contributes to defining how speakers relate to one another at lesbian bars. I discuss first-person pronouns in this section and second-person pronouns in the following section.

Previous studies have claimed that the use of first- and second-person pronouns exhibits the most gender-differentiated characteristics of the Japanese language. Ide (1979) asserts that the first-person pronouns *watakushi* and *watashi* are used by both sexes, the forms *boku* and *ore* (standard) as well as *wagahai* and *washi* (nonstandard) are used exclusively by men, and the forms *atakushi* and *atashi* (standard) as well as *atai* and *uchi* (non-standard) are used by women. Kanamaru (1997) claims that *jibun* is also a masculine form. *Jibun* is a reflexive pronoun; its use as a personal pronoun is relatively old-fashioned and is often associated with men in sports or in militaristic groups such as the *jieetai* 'self-defense army' or the police force. It is clear that these options for first-person pronouns reflect the strong sense of an idealized form of women's and men's speech. However, the choice of personal pronouns is not as categorical as was once believed. Women in different parts of Japan may have different options and women in different parts of the age spectrum may use different forms (see chapter 10, this volume, for farm women's use of *ore* and chapter 14, this volume, for junior high school girls' use of *boku* and *ore*).

An example from the bisexual and lesbian magazine *Anise* (Hagiwara 1997) gives some insight into the use of first-person pronouns among lesbians, *onabe*, and transsexuals. Examples (6) through (9) are drawn from the magazine transcript of a panel discussion among six people, two self-identified female-to-male transsexuals (T1 and T2), two self-identified *onabe* (O1 and O2), and two self-identified lesbians (L1 and L2). They are talking about their gender.

(6)   T1: <u>*Boku*</u> *wa rezubian ga kirai nan ja nakute, rezu ikooru onna, jibun[5] ga onna ni mirareru no ga iya datta.*
      'It is not that I dislike lesbians, but lesbian means a woman. I didn't want to be perceived as a woman'.

      O2: <u>*Jibun*</u> *mo yoku rezu tte iwarete '<u>jibun</u> wa otoko nan da' tte tomodachi to kenka shimashita.*
      'I was also told that I'm a lesbian. I used to fight with my friends for saying that I'm a man'.

(7)   T2: <u>*Boku*</u> *wa nenrei ga agareba penisu ga haete kuru mon da to omotte ita n desu yo.*
      'I believed that once I got older, I would grow a penis'.

(8)   L1: <u>*Watashi*</u> *wa monogokoro tsuita toki kara, zutto onna no ko ga suki datta. Otoko to ka onabe ni naritai tte kimochi mo atta kedo, seken no hito wa otoko na no ka onna na no ka waketagaru n da yo ne. Ippan shakai de wa joshi toire ni wa hairenai shi.*
      'Ever since I was a child, I always liked girls. There was a time when I wanted to be a man or *onabe*. People want to categorize themselves into men or women. In this society, I can't use a public women's bathroom'.

      L2: <u>*Watashi*</u> *wa joshi toire ni hairu yo.*
      'I use a women's bathroom'.

(9)   O2: <u>*Jibun*</u> *mo danjo to ka kangaenai hoo nan desu yo.*
      'I tend not to think about if someone is a man or woman'.

The three groups of speakers use first-person pronouns distinctively; the transsexuals use *boku*, the *onabe* use *jibun*, and the lesbians use *watashi* almost uniformly. It is as if there is a rule for them to use a different personal pronoun depending on their own identity (at least in this context). Gender crossing reflected in this use of first-person pronouns has nothing to do with these women wanting to be men; instead, it is the appropriation of masculine resources.

The use of first-person pronouns shown in examples (6) through (9), however, does not mean that each speaker uses the same pronoun no matter what context s/he is in. Further analysis suggests that speakers negotiate gendered speech norms in each context. This negotiation becomes more apparent if we examine examples in which a speaker shifts the use of pronoun forms, which is frequently observed at lesbian bars. In fact, one of the participants in the panel discussion (L1) is an employee at a lesbian bar I often visited, where I observed her use of *jibun*. Moreover, I observed the use of several first-person pronouns at lesbian bars: *watashi, atashi, ore, washi,* and *jibun,* with the same speaker using multiple first-person pronouns depending on the context. One of the first questions I often asked at bars concerned the use of personal pronouns. Younger employees in their early twenties exclusively listed *jibun* 'oneself' (a form commonly considered masculine) as their favorite first-person pronoun. One employee explained that she uses the term because *watashi* and *atashi* exhibit too much femininity, but she does not want to use *boku* or other "masculine" first-person pronouns because she is not a man. She said that she refuses to *dooitsuka-suru* 'merge and identify' with men. An employee at a different bar argued, "Why do I need to use *boku*? I don't even like men." Her use of *jibun* is illustrated in example (10).

(10)   *Kutte nee, jibun wa. Nan da, nan ni mo nee jan.*

      'I haven't eaten. What! There's nothing left'.

    This employee was 21 years old and had been working at the bar for several months. Asked by her female supervisor if she had eaten something before coming to work, she replied, using *jibun*. During the course of the evening, this young employee maintained the use of *jibun* irrespective of whether she was talking to her coworkers or to customers. As she puts it, for her, *jibun* is the most neutral personal pronoun available.[6] The use of *jibun* was observed at all the bars in my study.

    However, at a bar down the street I observed a quite different interaction. The employee in example (11) was 20 years old and had been working almost a year. When I entered, there was nobody but her in the bar. We introduced ourselves and started talking about various things such as why she started working there and whether she enjoyed working at the bar. When I noticed her using *jibun* in our interaction, I asked the reason for her choice. Her answer was that she did not want to sound too feminine by using *watashi* or *atashi*. She added that *jibun* was her favorite term and that she did not use other "masculine" personal pronouns, unlike her boss, who uses *washi*. It is interesting to note that *washi* presents a more "masculine" nuance to her than *jibun*. However, her answer does not reflect her actual speaking practices. She and I had been talking alone for more than two hours when the telephone rang. The caller was a regular customer, whom this employee knew very well. The employee explained to me that there had been a party at the bar the night before during which this customer got drunk and did some crazy things that upset the employees and other customers, but the customer claimed that she did not remember anything. The employee did not believe she had forgotten. The employee's side of the conversation was as follows.

(11)   *Omee na, fuzaken na yo, ore oko-ru yo.*
      'Are you kidding? I'll get mad at you'.

    Jaa, A-san ni kiite mi na yo.
      'Then, ask A'.

    Anne, soo da yo, anta, minna ni meewaku kaketa n da kara.
      'You bothered everyone'.

    Ore sugee koshi itai mon. Koshi ni kita yo.
      'As for me, my lower back hurts. It really hurts'.

Here we see the employee's shift from *jibun* in her conversation with me to *ore* in her interaction with her customer. In the first instance of *ore*, the speaker is expressing her anger or frustration and thus is very emotionally involved. In the second instance, she is describing how much pain she has now thanks to the customer. The use of *ore* in this example as opposed to her previous use of *jibun* exhibits negotiation of multiple identity positions in relation to different contexts. For her, *jibun* is used in more formal settings of interaction, such as an interaction with a relatively new customer who is also a researcher, but *ore* is her preferred choice in more intimate and emotional contexts. It seems that since all the first-person pronouns (except the relatively formal ones such as *watakushi* and *watashi*) are normatively associated with either women or men, lesbians consider *jibun* the least gendered if one wants to be, literally, simply oneself (see also Maree 1997 for discussion of the use of *jibun* by *onabe*).

The use of *boku* is quite different. The speaker in example (12) is a lesbian customer in her mid thirties who works at a computer graphics company. She and I had been discussing the use of first-person pronouns for a while and I had noticed that she used *atashi* in our conversation. When I asked if she ever used different first-person pronouns, she answered by saying:

(12)   *Atashi* wa kyosee o haru toki, '*boku*' o tsuka-u.

'I (*atashi*) use I (*boku*) when [I] make a false show of power'.

She added that she uses *boku* in arguments at her workplace with her male boss, who may suspect that she is lesbian, and claims that this helps her situate herself at the boss's level. Here the speaker explicitly recognizes the forcefulness attached to "masculine" forms. She also expressed the belief that the "feminine" first-person pronoun, *atashi*, did not make her strong. However, in explaining the use of *boku* the speaker used the term *kyosee* 'false show of power', literally, *kyo* 'emptiness' + *see* 'power, force', which implies merely a superficial or even empty power.

These examples demonstrate that first-person pronouns are carefully and consciously chosen by each speaker at lesbian bars since they are one of the most obvious linguistic features generally associated with sex/gender.

11.4.2.3.   Second-person pronouns

Second-person pronouns are also considered highly gendered, but to a lesser degree than first-person pronouns. Many researchers identify two forms (*anata* and *anta*) for women and five or more forms (*anata, anta, kimi, omae, kisama, otaku,* and *temee*) for men (Ide 1979, Kanamaru 1997). However, actual uses of second-person pronouns do not necessarily conform to these gender classifications.[7]

I found two types of second-person pronouns at the bars I studied: *anta* and *omee*. The frequency of these two terms is not high, since speakers generally prefer to use nicknames or first names. *Anata* 'you', a more formal second-person pronoun, is almost never used. The use of *omee*, a very casual "masculine" second-person pronoun, is found among close friends at bars, between employees and customers, and between customers. In example (11), the speaker used both *anta* and *omee* in criticizing one of her customers. *Omee* is used to express the employee's extreme rage toward the customer (*omee na, fuzaken na yo*), whereas *anta* accompanies an attempt at persuasion (*soo da yo, anta, minna ni meewaku kaketa n da kara*). Thus, the shift between the two pronouns reflects the change in her emotional state.

The customer (in ex. 12) who uses *boku* in arguments with her boss also told me that she uses *omee* when she argues with close male friends, adding that *omee* has a certain forcefulness that cannot be expressed by *anta* or *omae*, a term that is stereotypically associated with male speakers. The speakers in examples (11) and (12) both assert that *omee* helps them argue more persuasively. Both speakers are manipulating the pragmatic meaning (forcefulness) attached to the term *omee*.

11.4.2.4. Commands and requests

Other linguistic forms that are often associated with gender roles are found in commands and requests. For instance, the use of bald imperative verb forms, such as *tabero* 'eat', is generally considered to indicate that the interlocutor is not in a superior position and also that the speaker is a man. This type of imperative is traditionally categorized as a "masculine" form (Martin 1975), and women are advised to avoid using it. For example, Tohsaku (1999:43) notes that this type of imperative form "sounds very blunt and harsh" and says that female speakers should not use it at all. In other words, women are culturally or ideally discouraged from using bald imperatives. Furthermore, Japanese language textbooks such as Tohsaku's reinforce this notion.

Despite this prescription, example (11) includes strong imperative forms. The first negative imperative, *fuzaken na* 'don't mess with me', can be articulated differently in different contexts, from the most formal *fuzakenai de kudasai*, to *fuzakenai de*, to the very informal *fuzakeru na*. The assimilation and reduction of *–ru* (in *fuzakeru na*) to *–n* (in *fuzaken na*) indexes even stronger roughness or toughness. As noted earlier, the speaker in this example is extremely angry and emotionally involved. The second imperative form, *kiite mi na yo* 'try to ask', is less strong than *kiite miro*.

Example (13) immediately continues the conversation in example (11).

(13)   *Chigau yo. Pantsu to bura wa tsukete ta yo.*
        'No, you were wearing your underpants and a bra'.

        Un, itte ta. "—no yaroo" tte. Dakara koi tte.
        'Yes, she was saying 'damn her'. So, come here'.

        Mada A san wa inai yo. Iru yo. Maa soo da to omou yo.
        'A isn't here yet. Yes, she's here. Well, I think so'.

        Soo yuu koto ja nai kedo ne. Okorareru yo, mata A san ni.
        'I don't think so. You'll be chewed out by A again'.

After the phrase—*no yaroo* 'damn her—', which is an extremely strong way to address someone, another strong imperative form, *koi*, is used.[8] This direct affirmative command form *koi* is normally used by men, as noted earlier, but it is used here to make a strong command.

11.4.2.5. Sentence-final particles

The last linguistic feature I discuss here is sentence-final particles, which are often studied in Japanese language and gender research (Uyeno 1971, McGloin 1997, Okamoto & Sato 1992, Okamoto 1995, Mastsumoto 1996, Abe 1999, 2000). The functions of such sentence-final forms have been identified as (1) indicating the speaker's emotions and attitudes such as doubt, caution, and confirmation (Martin 1975:914, Makino & Tsutsui 1986:45); (2) encouraging rapport between speech participants (Makino & Tsutsui 1986:45); (3) achieving a close monitoring of the feelings between speech participants (Maynard 1987:28); and (4) expressing one's own masculinity and/or femininity (Makino & Tsutsui 1986:49). Traditional gender classification of sentence-final particles suggests three types: (1) feminine forms, which are said to be predominantly used by female speakers (e.g., *wa* with a rising intonation, *na no/na no ne, kashira*); (2) masculine forms, used by male speakers (e.g., *zo/ze, da, da yo*); and (3) neutral forms, used by both women and men (e.g., *yo ne, ka na*). As Okamoto (1995) argues, the traditional classification should be understood as a reference point rather than a description of actual use.

The actual use of sentence-final particles at the lesbian bars bears this point out. The most frequently used sentence-final particles are *yo* and its variations such as *da yo* and *da yo ne*. For example, in (14) an employee and a few customers are chatting while looking at a magazine article, which describes an *onabe* bar.

(14)   Customer: *Kore otoko <u>da yo</u>, hakkiri itte.*
                      'This is a man, frankly speaking'.

         Employee: *Kurabete moraitaku nai ne.*
                      'I don't want you to compare me with this guy'.

The customer points out that the figure in the picture in the magazine looks like a man. She uses *da yo* in this utterance. As mentioned earlier, in the conventional classification, *da* + *yo* is regarded as a masculine form. Yet it seems that this form is used more commonly used by many women than it used to be (Abe 2000, chapter 13, this volume). Thus, it is possible that this form is neutral for this speaker.

Other conventional masculine forms are found in example (15). Here younger employees, who typically refer to themselves as *jibun*, are talking with some customers in their thirties. Two of them are trying to remove a spot from the surface of a toy.

(15)   Employee: *Kosutte mo torenee n <u>da</u>.*
                      'We can't get rid of it even by rubbing'.

         Customer :   *Nani ka iro ga chiga-u <u>zo</u>.*
                      'Hey, the color is somehow different!'

The employee uses *da*, a (moderately) masculine form, and the customer uses *zo*, which is often classified as strongly masculine. In addition, the "rough" negative form, *nee*, is used instead of *nai*. This use of *nee* was also observed at a different bar, as shown in example (10) earlier. There are two instances of *nee* in (10). Moreover, the speaker uses *kuu* 'to eat' instead of *taberu* 'to eat'. The latter is a standard form of the verb, while *kuu* suggests "masculine" speech. This speaker elsewhere uses the plain interrogative form *ka* (verb + *ka*) in *Ureshii ka* 'are you happy'? and *Nomu ka* 'do you want to drink'? another construction associated with "masculine" speech. This type of question form is usually considered too strong and rude for women to use.

In sum, these speakers are rejecting the forms that they feel are too feminine, while adopting masculine or neutral forms. Their use of masculine forms, however, does not mean that lesbians want to be identified as men, as the discussion on the difference between lesbian and *onabe* clearly demonstrates, nor is it simply the case of butch lesbians speaking like men. On the other hand, even though they may consider themselves women (also indicated earlier in their comparison of lesbians and *onabe*), they are not using stereotypical feminine forms. I argue, therefore, that their linguistic choices indicate that they are marking their difference in speech, which, they believe, supports their identities as lesbians. For instance, the use of direct/informal style and masculine sentence-final particles may be a way to create an intimate relationship among lesbians at the bars they frequent or to treat them as in-group members. Further, their use of *masculine* first-person pronouns may be an appropriation of men's resources, which enable them to express (real or imagined) powerfulness. In other words, some lesbians at bars recognize the assumed dominant power associated with *masculine* speech. It is also important to note that the same speaker may shift her speech style depending on the context. Recall, for example, that one speaker who used *jibun* "I" with me switched to *ore* "I" when talking to someone else. Shifts such as this indicate the speakers' negotiation of gendered identity in interaction.

11.6.   Conclusion

In this chapter, I have examined language use at lesbian bars in Tokyo. In the first part of the chapter, I have shown how lesbians use a variety of category names to identify themselves or distinguish themselves from others, from which I conclude that gender identities for these lesbians are not fixed, certain, or natural. Rather, they are constantly negotiated among themselves. In the latter part of the chapter, I analyzed characteristic speech styles observed at lesbian bars, in particular, the common use of linguistic features stereotypically associated with male speakers. I have argued that speakers use masculine speech styles in a complex way in order to express a variety of context-dependent meanings related to their lesbian identities and relationships. In sum, this study demonstrates that gender identities are not fixed, but negotiated and constructed through language use in interactions.

Notes

1. There are also quite a few gay bars in other parts of Tokyo, such as Shinbashi, where the first gay bar, Yanagi, was opened in 1950; there were 50 to 60 in other parts of Tokyo by 1960 (Sunagawa 1998).

2. This interview was taken from an article in a magazine called *Marumaru*, which specializes in introducing bars and men who work for the bars. (These bars are mostly in Shinjuku.)

A male reporter interviews many owners and managers of bars, including host, *onabe*, and lesbian bars. Four lesbian bar owners/managers are interviewed, which is shown in examples (1) through (5) (*Marumaru* 2000: 24–26).

3. She has been working for two years at the oldest lesbian bar. She is 21 years old.

4. Although this example is taken from a magazine interview, this manager and I visited at her bar quite often.

5. Here *jibun* is a reflexive pronoun, not a personal pronoun.

6. A similar explanation was given when I interviewed a cross-dresser who prefers the use of *watashi*. S/he told me that it was her/his conscious attempt to be neutral. S/he argues that many gay men use *atashi* or *atai*—which is often associated with women—but that s/he intentionally rejects these words because s/he does not want to be slotted into one of the binary categories of "women" or "men." S/he contends that *watashi* is a neutral first-person pronoun and is not as formal as *watakushi*.

7. *Kimi* is often used by female schoolteachers. I myself use it when talking to my former students or close male and female friends. The use of *omae* is much more common by male speakers, but it seems to be used by some women, particularly by speakers of some regional dialects.

8. This type of imperative is also found in Abe's (2000) study of women's speech, in which the speaker, a film director's wife, uses it 1.86% of the time.

References

Abe, Hideko (1999). Power negotiation between Japanese females and males. *Intercultural Communication Studies*: 8(1): 1–15.

———— (2000). *Speaking of power: Japanese women and their language*. Munich: Lincom Europa.

Achilles, Nancy (1993[1967]). The development of the homosexual bar as an institution. In H. Abelove, M. A. Barale, and D. M. Halperin (eds.), *Lesbian and gay studies reader*, 175–182. New York: Routledge.

AKIKO (2000). *Love Revolution* 2.

Barrett, Rusty (1997). The "homo-genius" speech community. In A. Livia and K. Hall (eds.), *Queerly phrased: Language, gender, and sexuality*, 181–201. New York: Oxford University Press.

Bucholtz, Mary (1999). Bad examples: Transgression and progress in language and gender studies. In M. Bucholtz, A. C. Liang and L. A. Sutton (eds.), *Reinventing identities: The gendered self in discourse,* 3–24. New York: Oxford University Press.

Butler, Judith (1990). *Gender trouble: Feminism and the subversion of identity*. New York: Routledge.

Chamberland, Line (1993). Remembering lesbian bars: Montreal, 1955–1975. *The Journal of Homosexuality* 25(3): 231–269.

Foucault, Michel (1990). *The history of sexuality: An introduction*. New York: Random House.

Gaudio, Rudolf P. (2001). White men do it too: Racialized (homo)sexualities in postcolonial Hausaland. *Journal of Linguistic Anthropology* 11(1): 36–51.

Gilmartin, Katie (1996). "We are not bar people": Middle-class lesbian identities and cultural spaces. *Journal of Lesbian and Gay Studies* 3: 1–51.

Hagiwara, Mami (ed.) (1997). Sexuality. *Anise 3*: 24–27.

Hankin, Kelly (2002). *The girls in the back room*. Minneapolis: University of Minnesota.

Ide, Sachiko (1979). *Onna no kotoba, otoko no kotoba* (*Women's language, men's language*). Tokyo: Nihon Keizai Tsushinsha.

Jagose, Annamaire (1996). *Queer theory: An introduction*. New York: New York University Press.

Kanamaru, Fumi (1997). Ninshoo daimeeshi/koshoo (Person pronouns and address terms). In S. Ide (ed.), *Joseigo no sekai (The world of women's language)*, 15–32. Tokyo: Meiji Shoin.

Kleinfeld, Mala S., and Noni Warner (1997). Lexical variation in the deaf community relating to gay, lesbian, and bisexual signs. In A. Livia and K. Hall (eds.), *Queerly phrased: Language, gender, and sexuality*, 58–84. New York: Oxford University Press.

Kramarae, Cheris, Muriel Schultz, and William O'Barr (eds.) (1984). *Language and power*. Beverly Hills: Sage.

Liang, A. C. (1997). The creation of coherence in coming-out stories. In A. Livia and K. Hall (eds.), *Queerly phrased: Language, gender, and sexuality*, 287–309. New York: Oxford University Press.

———(1999). Conversationally implicating lesbian and gay identity. In M. Bucholtz A. C. Liang, and L. A. Sutton (eds.), *Reinventing identities: The gendered self in discourse*, 293–312. New York: Oxford University Press.

Livia, Anna (1997). Disloyal to masculinity: Linguistic gender and liminal identity in French. In A. Livia and K. Hall (eds.), *Queerly phrased: Language, gender, and sexuality*, 349–368. New York: Oxford University Press.

——— (2000) Bi, androgyne S'abstenir: Lesbian community creation through the personals. Paper presented at the First International Gender and Language Conference, Stanford, CA.

Makino, Seiichi, and Michio Tsutsui (1986). *A dictionary of basic Japanese grammar*. Tokyo: Japan Times.

Maree, Claire (1997). Jendaa shihyoo to jendaa no imisee no henka: Eega *Shinjuku Boys* ni okero onabe no baai (Gender indexicality and semantic shifts in meanings: the case of an *onabe* in the documentary film *Shinjuku Boys*). *Gendai Shisoo* 25(13): 263–278.

Martin, Samuel (1975). *A reference grammar of Japanese*. New Haven: Yale University.

Marumaru (2000). Best spot. *Marumaru*: 24–26.

Matsumoto, Yoshiko (1996). Does less feminine speech in Japanese mean less femininity? In N. Warner, J. Ahlers, L. Bilmes, M. Oliver, S. Wertheim, and M. Chen (eds.), *Gender and belief systems: Proceedings of the Fourth Berkeley Women and Language Conference*, 455–467. Berkeley: Berkeley Women and Language Group.

Maynard, Senko Kumiya (1987). *Japanese conversation: Self-contextualization through structure and interactional management*. Norwood, NJ: Ablex.

McGloin, Naomi Hanaoka (1997). Shuujoshi (Sentence-final particles). In S. Ide (ed.), *Joseego no sekai (World of women's language)*. Tokyo: Meijishoin.

Moonwomon-Baird, Birch (1997). Toward the study of lesbian speech. In A. Livia and K. Hall (eds.), *Queerly phrased: Language, gender, and sexuality*, 202–213. New York: Oxford University Press.

——— (2000). Tales of lesbian times: A temporal template for the life story present. Paper presented at the First International Gender and Language Conference, Stanford, CA.

Neumann, Tina M. (1997). Deaf identity, lesbian identity: Intersections in a life narrative. In A. Livia and K. Hall (eds.), *Queerly phrased: Language, gender, and sexuality*, 274–286. New York: Oxford University Press.

Ogawa, Naoko, and Janet S. [Shibamoto] Smith (1997). The gendering of the gay male sex class in Japan: A preliminary case study based on *Rasen no Sobyoo*. In A. Livia and K. Hall (eds.), *Queerly phrased: Language, gender, and sexuality*, 402–415. New York: Oxford University Press.

Okamoto, Shigeko (1995). "Tasteless" Japanese: Less "feminine" speech among young Japanese women. In K. Hall and M. Bucholtz (eds.), *Gender articulated: Language and the socially constructed self*, 297–325. New York: Routledge.

Okamoto, Shigeko, and Shie Sato (1992). Less feminine speech among young Japanese females. In K. Hall, M. Bucholtz, and B. Moonwomon (eds.), *Locating power: Proceedings of the Second Berkeley Women and Language Conference*, 478–488. Berkeley:
Berkeley Women and Language Group.

Ootsuka, Takashi (1995). *Ni-choome kara uroko: Shinjuku gee sutoriito zakki-choo (Shinjuku
2-chome gay street note)*. Tokyo: Shooeisha.

Pastre, Genevieve (1997). Linguistic gender play among French gays and lesbians. In A. Livia
and K. Hall (eds.), *Queerly phrased: Language, gender, and sexuality*, 369–379. New
York: Oxford University Press.

Queen, Robin M. (1997) "I don't speak spritch": Locating lesbian language. In A. Livia and
K. Hall (eds.), *Queerly phrased: Language, gender, and sexuality,* 233–256. New York
and Oxford: Oxford University Press.

———— (2000). Language use in mainstream lesbian films. Paper presented at the First International Gender and Language Conference, Stanford, CA.

Read, Kenneth E. (1980). *Other voices: The style of a male homosexual tavern*. Novato, CA:
Chandler and Sharp.

Sunagawa, Hideki (1998). Sekushuaritii no saiteegi ni mukete (Toward the redefinition of
sexuality). Unpublished master's thesis, University of Tokyo.

Tohsaku, Yasu-Hiko (1999). *Yookoso: Continuing with contemporary Japanese*. Boston:
McGraw-Hill College.

Treat, John Whittier (1999). *Great mirrors shattered: Homosexuality, orientalism, and Japan*.
New York: Oxford University Press.

Ueno, Chizuko (1999). Gender studies: Gender trouble. *Gendaishisoo* 27(1): 44–77.

Uminarikan (ed.) (1998). *Otoko-gai mappu 98 nenban ([Gay] men's map of 1998)*. Tokyo:
Uminarikan.

Uyeno, Tazuko Y. (1971). A study of Japanese modality: A performative analysis of sentence particles. Unpublished Ph.D. dissertation, University of Michigan.

Valentine, James (1997). Pots and pans: Identification of queer Japanese in terms of discrimination. In A. Livia and K. Hall (eds.), *Queerly phrased: Language, gender, and sexuality*, 95–114. New York: Oxford University Press.

Watanabe, Mieko (1990). *Uuman rabingu (Women loving)*. Tokyo: Gendai Shokan.

Wood, Kathleen M. (1997). Narrative iconicity in electronic-mail lesbian coming-out stories. In A. Livia and K. Hall (eds.), *Queerly phrased: Language, gender, and sexuality*,
257–273. New York: Oxford University Press.

YUMIKO OHARA

Prosody and Gender in Workplace Interaction

Exploring Constraints and Resources in the Use of Japanese

12.1. Constraints and resources

Many previous studies of the Japanese language have made a distinction between the speech used by women and men (e.g., Ide 1979, Jugaku 1979, Shibamoto 1985, Shibatani 1990). One of the primary bases for this distinction has been the observation that the Japanese language includes certain gentler linguistic items that are used by women (e.g., the first-person pronoun *atashi* and the sentence-final forms *wa* and *no yo*) and certain rougher items that are used by men (e.g., the first-person pronoun *ore* and the sentence-final particles *zo* and *ze*). It is frequently assumed that it is socially unacceptable for women and men to cross these boundaries and use linguistic forms inappropriate for their gender. In other words, social expectations about language in Japan work as constraints that control, or at least influence, how women and men actually use language.

There is, however, a set of emerging studies that, primarily through empirical studies of actual language use, indicates that especially female speakers of Japanese are not actually as constrained in their use of language as previously thought (Inoue 1994, Okamoto 1995, Matsumoto 1996). Okamoto, for example, found that young women in conversations among friends were not averse to making use of the sentence-final particles *zo* and *ze* as well as "vulgar," strongly "masculine," and very informal lexical expressions (1995, 1996, 1997). These recent findings have, on the one hand, been used by researchers to challenge the female speech–male speech dichotomy in the Japanese language. Inoue (1994:322), for one, acknowledging "both tremendous social and contextual diversity of language use," points out that there is actually no empirically tested single set of speech patterns for all Japanese women and suggests that "Japanese women's speech" be treated as merely one particular representation of how Japanese women speak (see also chapter 1, this volume). On the other hand, these findings have led researchers to underscore the degree to which language serves as a set of resources that allows women (as well as all speakers of a language) to construct a variety of gendered identities according to different situations. In other words, instead of always and obligatorily using language according to social constraints, women are much freer than previously depicted to use various linguistic resources to project different images, which themselves may not necessarily conform to the cultural models of normative Japanese womanhood.

To be sure, research that has emphasized Japanese women's access to a wide range of linguistic resources, including those once deemed to belong strictly to men, does not deny the existence of gender-based constraints on language use. Still, recognition of the diverse speech styles adopted by Japanese women has prompted a significant shift in research focus. Rather than being viewed as strict followers of a predetermined code, "Japanese women's language," female speakers of Japanese have been recast as agents capable of using a variety of linguistic forms in innovative and resourceful ways that challenge or even resist tradition. As Matsumoto (1996:464) concludes, based on her study of women's speech both in contemporary magazine advertisements and in late nineteenth- and early twentieth-century Japan, young women's use of unconventional speech styles indicates not only "a greater role for speaker's agency than previously recognized" but also young women's ability to produce through their choice of language "resistance to the dominant ideology that frames the normative concept of femininity."

In this chapter, I attempt to shed further light on resources and constraints in the use of language by Japanese women and men by focusing on one particular aspect of language, namely, prosody. More specifically, I examine the voice pitch levels used by speakers of Japanese in their places of employment. Based on this chapter's examination of naturally produced speech by women and men, I contend that Japanese women are constrained in their pitch behavior, but at the same time I describe some of the ways that voice pitch functions as a resource that enables both the female and male employees to accomplish the speech activities that constitute their roles and relations at their workplaces. In particular, I show that a high-pitched voice can be used strategically by both female and male speakers of Japanese to emphasize specific aspects of their utterances. I describe the procedures used in this study in more detail in section 12.3, but I first explain in the next section the basis for using prosody to study gender in a specific linguacultural environment such as Japan.

12.2. Voice pitch and cultural assumptions: Making the connection

Traditionally, scholars in the fields of phonetics, communication, and speech have most frequently attempted to explain voice pitch variation in terms of human anatomy, physiology, physical and emotional states, age, or the structure of the language being spoken. However, some recent research has suggested that culture plays an important role in the production of voice pitch. For example, in some of my previous research (Ohara 1992, 1997, 1999), I measured the voice pitch levels of bilingual speakers of Japanese and English and discovered that the results of differences across language and gender could best be explained in terms of culture. Finding that the bilingual women produced higher fundamental frequency levels when speaking in Japanese than in English while the bilingual men did not vary their pitch across languages, I suggested that this difference could not be explained in terms of the structures of the languages, physiological differences, or variances in emotional or health states. Instead, I posited that the results were best understood in terms of sociocultural factors. Referring to previous research that has linked a high voice pitch to a woman's role in Japanese society (Loveday 1986), I argued that female speakers of Japanese were under cultural constraints that did not necessarily apply to men. More specifically, the claim was that these cultural constraints centered on expectations about femininity in Japanese society; one way Japanese women are expected to exert a feminine persona is through the use of a high-pitched voice.

These claims were supported by research that focused on the perception of voice pitch in Japanese (Ohara 1993, 1997; van Bezooijen 1995, 1996). Van Bezooijen (1995), for instance, in a comparative study of sociocultural aspects of pitch in Japan and the Netherlands, found a preference in Japanese culture for women's use of a high-pitched voice, while the Dutch culture preferred a low-pitched voice. In the same study she also observed a strong association between physical and psychological powerlessness (small, weak, indirect, modest, etc.) and a high-pitched voice. Her results, in other words, strengthen the argument for the existence of cultural expectations directly concerning female pitch behavior: If a higher-pitched voice is deemed more socially desirable, then many women may want to project socially desired images by using a high-pitched voice. That is, they may elevate their ptich in order to be heard as smaller, weaker, more indirect, and more modest.

Yet while this previous research has indicated imbalances in the voice pitch behavior of women and men in Japanese and, at the same time, suggested that gender norms and expectations in Japanese culture lead women to employ a high-pitched voice in order to explicitly express their femininity, there are two areas that require methodological refinement. First, most of my previous research (Ohara 1992, 1997, 1999), as well as the majority of research on voice pitch, has been based on data produced under laboratory conditions, with speakers reading isolated sentences into a tape recorder. In this study, by contrast, I move the research out of the laboratory and work with data that was tape-recorded in naturalistic settings. Because voice pitch, like other aspects of language such as syntax, phonology, and morphology, is something people use to express ideas, intentions, identities, and so on in real interactional encounters, this was deemed a necessary methodological move. Second, a method often used in previous research is to examine fundamental frequencies of speech samples. In the research reported here, in addition to this method I base my analysis of the naturalistic data on pitch extractions that actually show the flow of the pitch contours of the speakers' utterances. Only by attempting to place voice pitch within actual interactions and track how it changes and fluctuates as speakers engage in different speech acts will it be possible to gain a deeper understanding of what voice pitch means in human communication.

12.3.   Data and procedures

The analysis focuses on the speech of four native speakers of Japanese, two women and two men, who at the time of the study were working in businesses located in Honolulu, Hawaii. All four of the speakers were middle-class and in their mid-to-late thirties at the time of the study. The recordings took place over two two-week periods, one at the end of 1999 and the other at the beginning of 2000. During these intervals, the speakers were given a tape recorder and a microphone and asked to record their own interactions during their workday. For all of the recordings, the researcher was not present. A total of 15 hours of conversations was recorded, approximately 7 hours and 2 hours respectively for the two women and 4 hours and 2 hours respectively for the two men.

As a part of their interactions with customers, coworkers, business associates, and acquaintances, the four speakers typically performed and engaged in a number of different speech acts, including greetings, requests, apologies, posing and answering questions, negating prior utterances, and closings. In this chapter, in order to compare and contrast the pitch levels of the speakers across speech acts, I focus the analysis on two speech acts, requests and negation. These two speech acts were chosen because of the frequency with which they appear in the data. If gender differentiation in voice pitch levels is indeed a pervasive and fundamental feature of the Japanese language, then we would expect to see this differentiation in the accomplishment of very common actions, such as negation and requests, in Japanese social interaction.

With regard to requests, the analysis focuses specifically on those utterances in which the speakers told their interlocutors to "wait for a moment" (in Japanese, some variant of *chotto matte kudasai* 'Please wait for a moment').[1] Based on the perlocutionary force of the utterances, I categorized them together as one group, which I refer to as *requests*. Although *negation* is a category constituted by a wide variety of utterances, for example, negation of one's own previous statements (i.e., "I said *X* previously, but I was wrong. It's actually *Y*") and negation of statements produced by others (i.e., "What you said isn't true"), I consider in the analysis only one type, namely, negation of one's own previous statements. The reason for this choice is that these kinds of utterances are common in the data. While the speakers rarely directly negated statements made by customers, they often had to negate their own prior statements as a part of explaining things to customers (i.e., "I told you we could do *X* earlier, but actually it won't be possible to do *X*"). In addition, this kind of negation was not uncommon in interaction with acquaintances.

In order to consider the effects of context, I examine these two speech acts as they were produced to two different types of interlocutors, customers and acquaintances. The term *customer* is used to refer to buyers or potential buyers of the service provided by the company. *Acquaintance* refers to people whom the speakers themselves considered close friends, including some co-workers who were equal in rank to the speakers. For the purposes of the analysis, a total of 64 utterances, 32 requests and 32 negations, were first located within the 15 hours of recorded data. For each of the four speakers, 8 utterances per speech act were chosen, 4 that were made to customers and 4 made to acquaintances. The 64 utterances were first subjected to a fundamental frequency analysis that derived numerical values for the average, maximum, minimum, and standard deviation. Next, from the 64 utterances, the 16 most typical with respect to fundamental frequency values were chosen for a more detailed analysis that included examination of pitch extractions. This time, for each of the four speakers 4 utterances were chosen, 2 requests (1 to a customer and 1 to an acquaintance) and 2 negations (1 to a customer and 1 to an acquaintance).

12.4.   Results

The results are divided into three subsections. The first presents the findings of the fundamental frequency analysis for each of the 16 utterances chosen for further analysis. The second displays pitch extractions of some of the 16 utterances in order to point out similarities as well as differences across addressees, contexts, and the genders of the speakers. The third provides further details about the pitch extractions as well as additional extractions in order to highlight the relationship between prosodic patterns and the notion of emphasis.

For the sake of clarity, I have labeled the speakers A, B, C, and D, with A and B being the female speakers and C and D the males. In addition, I have used a code to indicate the interlocutor. The small letter *a* indicates acquaintance, and *c* signifies customer. Thus, the two symbols together, *Aa*, signify Speaker A's utterance directed to an acquaintance.

12.4.1.   Fundamental frequency analysis

This subsection presents the results of the fundamental frequency analysis of the 16 utterances that were most representative in terms of their fundamental frequency levels. Table 12.1 shows the results of the analysis for the eight requests. The utterance itself is shown in the last column on the right.

The numerical values show some noteworthy tendencies regarding the participants' gender. First of all, although the average pitch levels for the two female speakers, A and B, are considerably higher than those of speaker C, they are not necessarily higher than those of speaker D. This point would seem to contradict the previous findings that women use a higher pitched voice than those of men when speaking Japanese. In addition, a female speaker, B, used minimum pitch levels that were lower than those of male speaker D, another point where the numerical values seem to contradict previous findings. The only place where the fundamental frequency values display recognizable gender differentiation is across interlocutors. The female speakers used higher fundamental frequency levels when speaking to customers than they did when speaking to acquaintances, but the male speakers C and D did not show much variation across interlocutors. Moreover, the variation they did exhibit was not patterned, as the women's was. That is, both women had higher fundamental frequencies when addressing customers than when addressing acquaintances, but one of the male participants raised his voice pitch slightly when talking to customers, while the other participant employed a somewhat lower pitch when interacting with customers. The standard deviations show that for the female speakers fundamental

TABLE 12.1 Speakers' fundamental frequency levels when producing requests

Gender	Speaker	Average	Max.	Min.	sd*	Utterance
Female	Aa	217	277	167	35.39	*a chotto mattee* 'oh, please wait'
	Ac	260	352	174	49.84	*shoo shoo omachi* *kudasaimasee* 'please wait for a moment'
	Ba	166	221	116	30.38	*chotto mate chotto mate* 'wait a little; wait a little'
	Bc	202	365	133	61.91	*shoo shoo omachi itadakemasu ka* 'would you please wait for a moment?'
Male	Ca	130	166	115	19.78	*mateyooo* 'wait'
	Cc	139	169	106	17.24	*haai chotto matte kudasaai* 'yes, please wait for a moment'
	Da	218	260	160	39.36	*aa chotto matte* 'um, please wait'
	Dc	211	243	135	29.08	*hai ja sochira de matte kudasai* 'yes, please wait over there'

*The abbreviation *sd* stands for standard deviation, which indicates the degree to which fundamental frequency levels varied throughout the utterance.

frequencies varied more when they interacted with customers than when they interacted with acquaintances. Furthermore, Speaker B shows a greater variation across interlocutors than Speaker A. For the male speakers, the standard deviation figures do not vary much across interlocutors, especially for Speaker C.

Table 12.2 shows the fundamental frequency levels for each speaker when producing negations.

While the female speakers did show a pattern of elevated pitch when interacting with customers, some tendencies seen in negation, like those in requests, appear to contradict the results of previous studies. Especially for Speaker B, the average pitch level used when talking to an acquaintance is lower than the levels used by the two male speakers when they spoke with acquaintances. In addition, not only is Speaker B's maximum pitch level when speaking to an acquaintance lower than the two male speakers' maximum pitch, but also B's minimum pitch level with an acquaintance is nearly identical to those of the two male speakers.

Thus, speaking at a general level, the results would seem to be quite equivocal. On the one hand, it is difficult to conclude that Japanese women are under a general constraint to use high pitch levels if, under some conditions (such as speaking to acquaintances), at least some speakers (such as Speaker B in this study) are shown to use pitch levels equivalent to or even lower than those used by Japanese men. On the other hand, the fact that only the female speakers raised their voice pitch levels when speaking to customers would seem to suggest that their choice of pitch levels is not random. It would suggest that there was, at least when speaking to customers, some underlying motivation for employing a high-pitched voice. In order to enhance understanding of these results, I want to examine in more detail some of the requests and negations made by the speakers. To do so, I will present some of the pitch

TABLE 12.2 Speakers' fundamental frequency level when producing negation

Gender	Speaker	Average	Max.	Min.	sd	Utterance
Female	Aa	209	326	156	38.98	*anoo kooraru no hoo ano moobu ja nai hoo nee* 'um, the one that's coral, not the one that's mauve'
	Ac	241	405	169	50.98	*de ano tsuu ga anoo seezoo chuushi natte surii subete kawatteru n desu kedo* 'um, those labeled 2 were discontinued and have been all changed to 3'
	Ba	172	208	104	32.28	*namamono ja nai nihon no pantsu* 'it's not a raw food; it's a Japanese underwear'
	Bc	205	462	134	77.29	*aite ita n desu keredomo nihon no hoo kara yoyaku haitte shimaimashitee* 'it was vacant, but a reservation from Japan came in'
Male	Ca	185	235	105	24.13	*koko ni wa nai to omoun da kedo* 'I think we don't have it here'
	Cc	171	221	107	31.29	*are ima muryoo ja nai mitai desu nee* 'it seems that it isn't free now'
	Da	184	228	106	35.53	*chigau kapiolani ja nakute kapahulu datta yoo* 'it's wrong; it wasn't *kapiolani* but *kapahulu*'
	Dc	186	237	112	38.24	*igai nan desu kedo renzoku ja torenai desu nee* 'although it's unexpected, it cannot be reserved for consecutive days'

extractions of these 16 utterances. Examination of the pitch ranges and contours shown in the extractions makes it clear that the notions of constraints and resources are both applicable to the ways that the speakers employed voice pitch.

12.4.2.   Pitch extractions

The advantage of showing pitch extractions is that they make it possible to view the pitch contour and pitch range with which the utterances were produced. By showing in this subsection the pitch extractions for some of the utterances I hope to highlight differences—not easily seen in a purely numerical analysis—in the way that the female and male speakers produced their requests and negations.

Figure 12.1 shows the pitch extraction for A's request to an acquaintance. As the extraction shows, this utterance starts around 240 hertz, continues at that level a short while, and ends around 180 hertz.

Figure 12.2 shows the pitch extraction for A's request to a customer. As the extraction shows, the first segment of this utterance, *shoo shoo* 'a little', starts around

ARa

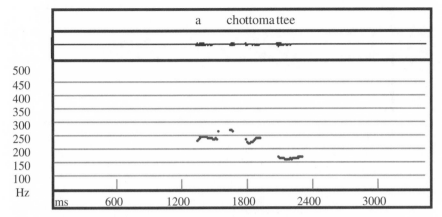

ARa

FIGURE 12.1 Pitch extraction of Speaker A's request to an acquaintance

280 hertz, rises to around 350 hertz and then ends at around 170 hertz. The pitch range used for this utterance is much larger than that for the utterance shown earlier in figure 12.1. This pattern, whereby a speaker used a much larger range of voice pitch levels to a customer than to an acquaintance, was also apparent in the pitch extractions for Speaker B's requests. It was not, however, observed in the extractions for the requests made by the two male speakers.

Figure 12.3 shows the pitch extraction for C's request to an acquaintance. As the extraction shows, this utterance starts around 110 hertz and then rises and finishes at around 160 hertz. Figure 12.4 shows the pitch extraction for C's request to a customer. The first part of this utterance, *haai* 'yes', is produced at around 160 hertz

ARc

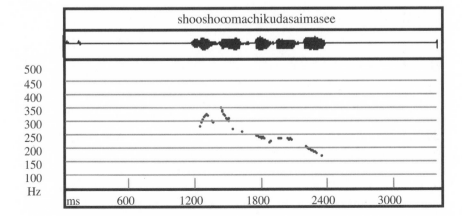

FIGURE 12.2 Pitch extraction of Speaker A's request to a customer

CRa

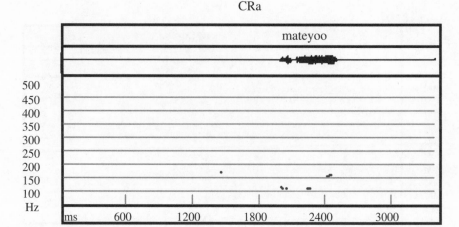

FIGURE 12.3 Pitch extraction of Speaker C's request to an acquaintance

and the latter part starts around 160 hertz and ends around 100 hertz. Unlike Speakers A and B, there is no considerable difference between the extractions of requests that are directed toward acquaintances and those directed toward customers. Although I will not take the space to show the extractions for Speaker D's requests, it can be noted that like Speaker C, there was little variance in the shape of the extractions of requests to acquaintances and customers.

Having presented some of the pitch extractions for the eight requests produced by the speakers, I now turn to the pitch extractions of the negations they uttered. Figure 12.5 shows the pitch extraction for B's negation to an acquaintance. As can be seen, the first part of this utterance, *namamono ja nai* 'it isn't a raw food', starts around

CRc

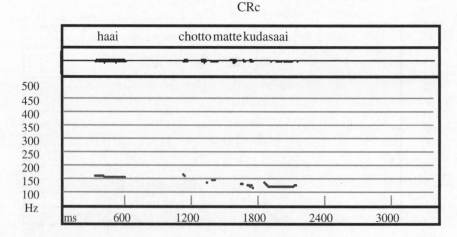

FIGURE 12.4 Pitch extraction of Speaker C's request to a customer

BNa

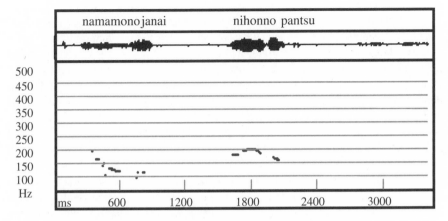

FIGURE 12.5 Pitch extraction of Speaker B's negation to an acquaintance

200 hertz and ends at about 130 hertz. The latter part begins at about 180 hertz, goes up until it reaches around 200 hertz, and then drops and ends around 160 hertz. Figure 12.6 shows the pitch extraction for B's negation to a customer.

The most striking feature of the utterance is the significantly high peak, over 450 hertz, within this segment. As the extraction shows, the utterance starts around 200 hertz, goes up to about 250 hertz, then goes down to around 150 hertz, next rises slightly to around 180 hertz, then rises dramatically to the highest peak of the utterance, 450 hertz, next falls to around 160 hertz, goes up again to about 260 hertz, and finally drops and ends around 150 hertz. Of the two female speakers, B's negation to a customer shows the larger range of voice pitch levels. However,

BNc

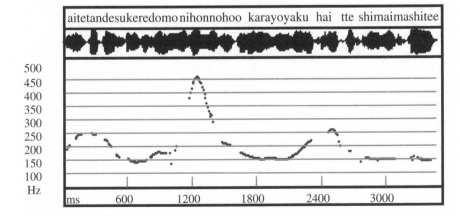

FIGURE 12.6 Pitch extraction of Speaker B's negation to a customer

like B, A's negation to a customer showed a larger range than did her negation to an acquaintance.

One of the most interesting aspects of the negation extractions is the pitch ranges used by men compared to women. Very similar to their use of pitch in requests, neither Speaker C nor D showed much variation in his pitch levels when producing negation to an acquaintance or to a customer. Here I show D's negation to an acquaintance (figure 12.7). This utterance starts around 180 hertz, rises to about 220 hertz, falls to around 120 hertz, then goes up again to about 200 hertz, and then falls and ends around 100 hertz. Figure 12.8 shows Speaker D's negation to a customer. As the extraction shows, this utterance starts at around 220 hertz, goes up to about 250 hertz, then declines to about 130 hertz, rises again to around 250 hertz, falls to approximately 140 hertz, and ends at around 100 hertz. The range of pitch levels, from 100 hertz to 250 hertz, is slightly more than the other three negations produced by the two male speakers but not nearly as large as the ranges produced by female speakers in the same situation. In the next subsection, I examine this and other pitch extractions in more detail, focusing especially on the connection between voice pitch and emphasis.

12.4.3.   Pitch contours and the concept of emphasis

As noted earlier, the results of the fundamental frequency analysis shown in section 12.4.1 are particularly striking because they seemingly make it difficult to argue that only the female speakers are subject to cultural constraints that lead them to employ high-pitched voices in order to explicitly express their gendered identity. Contrary to previous research which found that Japanese men basically do not alter their pitch across language or context, (Ohara 1992, 1993, 1997, 1999) the findings here, all based on naturally occurring conversations, demonstrate that the male speakers in this data did use different levels of voice pitch in constructing their utterances. In

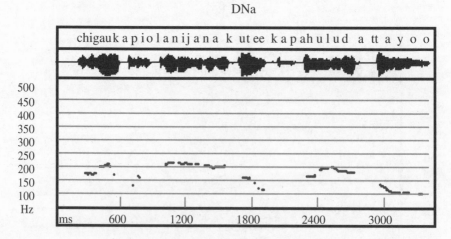

FIGURE 12.7 Pitch extraction of Speaker D's negation to an acquaintance

DNc

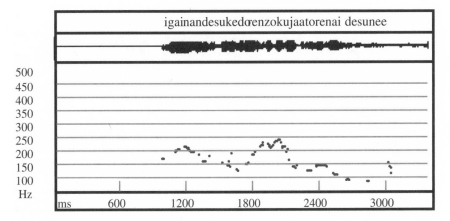

| igainandesukedœrenzokujaatorenai desunee |

FIGURE 12.8 Pitch extraction of Speaker D's negation to a customer

fact, as discussed, it was sometimes the case, especially in interaction with acquaintances, that the pitch levels used by the male speakers were higher than those used by one of the female speakers, Speaker B. Such results apparently make it impossible to say that there exist underlying social constraints that apply only to the women and not the men.

Yet before we begin to suggest that Japanese women and men use voice pitch in whatever way they like and that there are no apparent gender-differentiated cultural constraints concerning pitch behavior, it should be noted that the pitch extractions highlight an important point concerning the use of voice pitch in natural interaction. To demonstrate this point, it is necessary to observe some pitch extractions and examine at what points rises in pitch occurred. Figure 12.8 offers a good illustration of this point, and therefore, I discuss it here in further detail. It should first be noted that in making this negation the male speaker is responding to a customer about hotel room reservations. Since it is at the point where the word *renzoku* 'consecutively' is produced that the highest level of fundamental frequency occurs and since the word itself is constituted by a large range of voice pitch levels (from 150 to 250 hertz), it appears that the emphasis of the utterance *igai nan desu kedo renzoku ja torenai desu ne* 'although it is unexpected, it cannot be reserved consecutively' is on the term *renzoku* 'consecutively'. Thus, what this extraction seems to suggest is that sharp rises and falls in voice pitch can be used for emphasis; in other words, by raising voice pitch momentarily, a speaker can add emphasis to that particular part of an utterance. This phenomenon was also evident in the female speakers' speech. For example, in the following pitch extraction (figure 12.9), which shows a question posed by Speaker B to a customer, it can be seen that the speaker uses a rise and fall in pitch to repeat a term that is an especially important aspect of the utterance.

As the pitch extraction shows, Speaker B marks the term *pin nanbaa* 'PIN number' by raising its pitch level as well as by repeating it. Prior to this utterance, Speaker B had been having difficulty communicating with this particular customer. Despite

BQc

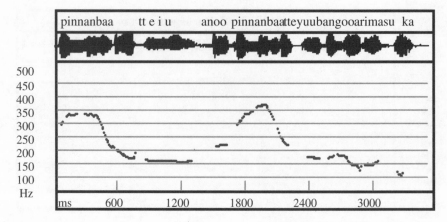

FIGURE 12.9 Pitch extraction of Speaker B's question to an acquaintance

Speaker B's attempt to explain how to make a phone call from the hotel room, the customer had failed to understand. Thus, since use of a telephone card with a PIN number is crucial to making a direct call, it is understandable that Speaker B emphasizes the term *pin nanbaa* 'PIN number' in this utterance.

A similar phenomenon can be seen in figure 12.6. This extraction, in which the utterance *nihon no hoo kara* 'from the Japanese side' receives an extremely high pitch, is another good example of high pitch as well as sharp rise and fall being used for emphasis. This utterance was made by Speaker B in response to a customer's question concerning the availability of a room. This is apparently a difficult task, since Speaker B in her earlier conversation with the customer had said that a room was available and in this particular utterance had to negate her earlier comment. The utterance of the segment *nihon no hoo kara* 'from the Japanese side' with an extremely high pitch and a sharp rise and fall, exceeding 450 hertz and with a range of over 300 hertz, emphasizes that it was a reservation from Japan that caused this misunderstanding.

The examples presented and discussed in this subsection indicate that at least part of the pitch variances seen in the data can be explained by recognizing that voice pitch can be used to emphasize certain aspects of speech. This point is further supported by the observation of a few instances in the data in which one of the male speakers, Speaker C, employed an extremely high pitch level that reached around or over 400 hertz. Figure 12.10 provides an illustration.

In this extraction, in which Speaker C was negating something said to him by his coworker, he uses a high pitch level, around 400 hertz, three times within this short segment. In particular, the word *kyaku* 'customer' starts around 240 hertz and ends at around 440 hertz, giving it a pitch range of 200 hertz. Similarly, it can be seen that another part of the utterance, *kureru ka yo anna no* 'would they give that kind of thing', starts around 240 hertz, then goes above 400 HZ, and ends up around

CNa2

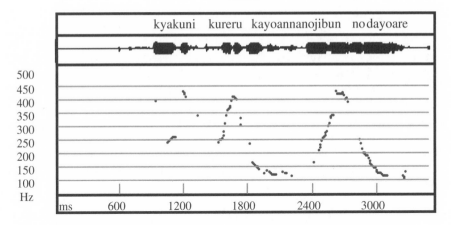

FIGURE 12.10 Pitch extraction of Speaker C's second negation to an acquaintance

130 hertz, showing a pitch range of close to 300 hertz within this rather short segment. The other part of this utterance, *jibun no da yo are* 'they're mine', hits 440 hertz with a range of over 300 hertz, almost as high as any utterance observed in this analysis, regardless of speaker gender. When we consider the fact that these utterances were made in response to a comment from the speaker's coworker that accused Speaker C of illicitly receiving special gifts from guests and trying to sell these items to her, we can understand how he, in his attempt to strongly deny the accusation, would want to emphasize certain parts of his negation by making use of the available resources, including a high-pitched voice. Indeed, this finding that voice pitch can be used for emphasis is in agreement with previous research on stress patterns in which the stressed or emphasized segment is found to be marked by high fundamental frequency or a rise or sharp fall (O'Shaughnessy 1987, Sugito, Inukai, & Sadanobu 1997).

12.5. Discussion

The idea that a high pitch level can be used by both women and men to accomplish an action such as emphasis is consistent with recent work on gender and language in Japanese that has stressed women's ability to use a variety of linguistic forms as resources for the construction of interaction and the projection of different gendered images. Just as this emergent set of research has stressed that the strict boundaries drawn between the language of women and men is not as rigid as once thought (Kobayashi 1993; Inoue 1994; Okamoto 1995, 1996, 1997; chapters 10–11, 13–15 this volume), the point made clear in the analysis—that high-pitched voice is not something that solely belongs in the predetermined domain known as "Japanese women's language"—provides further evidence for the claim that, because of the multiplicity of their functions, normatively gendered linguistic forms may serve as resources for speakers in social interaction (Ochs 1992, Trechter 1999). As the results of the analysis have demonstrated, high-pitched voice is a device that can be used by both women and men to create a certain effect, namely, emphasis.

The result that men also are shown at times to use a high-pitched voice as a resource is especially striking given the relative lack of attention accorded in previous research on Japanese to the language used by men. Although previous research that focused on the reading of isolated sentences in a laboratory has tended to describe the voice pitch levels used by Japanese men as being very narrow in range, the results of this study suggest that the men in this study, like the women, were dynamic users of language. In other words, as social actors who closely monitor the details of social interaction they were very capable of employing a high pitch at strategic points in the discourse, for example, when they needed to emphasize certain parts of their utterances.

And just as it is necessary to underscore how great a resource a high-pitched voice can be in interaction, by the same token, we would have to say the same for a low-pitched voice as well. Although previous research has said very little about women's capacity to use lower pitch levels, this study has not only shown that men sometimes use high-pitched voice, but it has also demonstrated that Japanese women utilize lower-pitched voices in some situations. In particular, Speaker B used voice pitch levels that were as low as levels used by the men when speaking to acquaintances.

However, while voice pitch can be seen as a resource available for pragmatic purposes to speakers of Japanese—both women and men—engaged in everyday conversational work, my findings do not by any means suggest that there are no gender-associated patterns of pitch usage. The results clearly indicate that the female speakers but not the male speakers varied their pitch levels considerably and systematically across interlocutors. More specifically, the results showed that the female speakers employed a considerably higher pitch when speaking to customers than when talking to acquaintances. This finding suggests, on the one hand, that high voice pitch was being used for the purpose of politeness. This suggestion is in accord with the observation made by Loveday (1986) that Japanese women are expected to use a high-pitched voice to make their utterances more polite. On the other hand, especially given the lack of variation in men's voice pitch according to interlocutor, this finding also suggests that the cultural constraint mentioned earlier might be at work: women are expected to use a high pitched voice to express femininity. In fact, we might say, based on this finding, that these cultural constraints are related not only to femininity but also to politeness (see Ohara 1999 for further discussion on pitch and politeness). In other words, even though in some circumstances, such as when talking to a close acquaintance, Japanese women might be culturally permitted to use a low-pitched voice, there are certain situations, for example, interactions with a customer, in which they are expected to use higher pitch levels to enhance the polite nature of their linguistic expressions.

To be sure, it needs to be emphasized, as Okamoto (chapter 2, this volume) has done, that politeness is a very situated phenomenon. Although some early research has suggested as a general principle that women are expected to be more polite than men when speaking in Japanese, more recent research has shown there to be many situations in which this is not the case (Okamoto 1996; chapters 2, 10, and 11, this volume). Accordingly, I do not want to suggest that women in all workplaces are expected to speak more politely to customers. Likewise, the results of this study do not necessarily mean that we should generalize too much and assume that a high-pitched voice in employee–customer interaction will always be utilized for politeness. Only further research can make it possible to understand how deep the relationship between voice pitch and politeness runs. Nonetheless, the results of this study, especially the fact that the women used higher-pitched voices when speaking to customers while men did not, would strongly suggest that in this particular situation—dealing with customers who were apparently very important to a particular business—women and not men face constraints such that they are expected to use a high-pitched voice to express politeness.

12.6. Conclusion

Using a phonetic analysis of naturalistic data, this chapter has paid tribute, in many ways, to the dynamic quality of voice pitch as it is actually used in social interaction. Like other aspects of language, it is a resource that is used by speakers, both women and men, to create specific effects and project certain images that are crucial to the construction and accomplishment of social interaction. At the same time, however, by focusing specifically on how voice pitch is connected to both gender and culture this chapter has supported the claim in previous research that women in Japan face cultural constraints that lead them to raise the pitch of their voice in order to project a feminine image. In particular, the results of the analysis in this chapter suggest that the link between voice pitch and femininity is mediated by a third concept, namely, politeness.[2] As the results showed, it was the female speakers and not the male speakers who consistently used a higher-pitched voice when speaking to customers than when speaking with acquaintances.

Because of my desire both to focus on speech activities actually performed by speakers in social interaction and to present pitch extractions of all the utterances examined, I was only able to examine in this chapter the speech of four speakers as they produced two speech acts. Still, the study presented here represents an improvement on previous laboratory results. By attempting to situate voice pitch within actual interactional encounters I was able to observe how some prosodic aspects were used by real people in real contexts. Moreover, by paying attention to context and observing how the employees used voice pitch to different interlocutors, customers, and acquaintances, I was able to describe the complex relationship that exists among gender, voice pitch, and the identities of participants in interaction. Especially when we attempt to understand how an aspect of language such as prosody interacts with gender in a specific cultural environment, the context of the interaction cannot be ignored. In addition, the methodological adjustments made in this study may facilitate our understanding of the speech not only of women but also that of men. Further analyses in a similar vein will make it possible to gain insight into the ways that both women and men use various pitch levels in various interactions. In the future, by continuing to examine naturally produced speech and considering social, cultural, and textual contexts it will be possible to gain a much deeper appreciation of what voice pitch means to human communication, including both how it serves people as a resource and how its production is subject to cultural constraints.

Notes

1. Although I call this category "request," the actual utterances seem to range from what might be considered a request to an order. For instance, an utterance such as *hai chotto matte kudasai* 'yes, please wait for a second' that is produced to a customer can be classified as a request without much dispute while a similar utterance to an acquaintance, *chotto mate chotto mate* 'wait for a little; wait for a little', can be said to be more of an order.

2. While I do not have space in this chapter to discuss politeness in more detail, it should be noted that the relationship among language, gender, and politeness has been a topic of extensive study (see, e.g., Lakoff 1975, Smith-Hefner 1988, Ide 1990, Holmes 1995).

References

Holmes, Janet (1995). *Women, men, and politeness*. London: Longman.

Ide, Sachiko (1979). *Onna no kotoba, otoko no kotoba* (*Women's language, men's language*). Tokyo: Nihon Keizai Tsushinsha.

———— (1990) How and why do women speak more politely in Japanese. In S. Ide and N. H. McGloin (eds.), *Aspects of Japanese women's language*, 63–79. Tokyo: Kuroshio.

Inoue, Miyako (1994). Gender and linguistic modernization: Historicizing Japanese women's language. In M. Bucholtz, A. C. Liang, L. Sutton, and C. Hines, (eds.), *Cultural performances: Proceedings of the Third Berkeley Women and Language Conference*, 322–343. Berkeley: Berkeley Women and Language Group.

Jugaku, Akiko (1979). *Nihongo to onna* (*The Japanese language and women*). Tokyo: Iwanami Shoten.

Kobayashi, Mieko (1993). Sedai to joseego: Wakai sedai no kotoba no "chuuseeka" ni tsuite (Generation and women's language: On "neutralization" on the speech of the young generation). *Nihongogaku* 12: 181–192.

Lakoff, Robin (1975). *Language and woman's place*. New York: Harper and Row.

Loveday, Leo (1986). *Explorations in Japanese sociolinguistics*. Amsterdam: John Benjamins.

Matsumoto, Yoshiko (1996). Does less feminine speech in Japanese mean less femininity? In N. Warner, J. Ahlers, L. Bilmes, M. Oliver, S. Wertheim, and M. Chen (eds.), *Gender and belief systems: Proceedings of the Fourth Berkeley Women and Language Conference*, 455–467. Berkeley: Berkeley Women and Language Group.

Ochs, Elinor (1992). Indexing gender. In A. Dutanti and C. Goodwin (eds.), *Rethinking context: Language as an interactive phenomenon*, 344–358. Cambridge, MA: Cambridge University Press.

Ohara, Yumiko (1992). Gender-dependent pitch levels: A comparative study in Japanese and English. In K. Hall, M. Bucholtz, and B. Moonwomon (eds.), *Locating power: Proceedings of the Second Berkeley Women and Language Conference*, 469–477. Berkeley: Berkeley Women and Language Group.

———— (1993). Koe no takasa kara ukeru inshoo ni tsuite (Images of voice pitch). *Kotoba* 14: 14–19.

———— (1997). Shakaionseegaku no kanten kara mita nihonjin no koe no takasa (Japanese pitch from a sociophonetic perspective). In S. Ide (ed.), *Sekai no joseego* (*Women's languages in the world*), 42–58. Tokyo: Meiji Shoin.

———— (1999). Performing gender through voice pitch: A cross-cultural analysis of Japanese and American English. In U. Pasero and F. Braun (eds.), *Performing and perceiving gender*, 105–116. Opladen: Westdeutscher Verlag.

Okamoto, Shigeko (1995). "Tasteless" Japanese: Less "feminine" speech among young Japanese women. In K. Hall and M. Bucholtz (eds.), *Gender articulated: Language and the socially constructed self*, 297–325. New York: Routledge.

———— (1996). Representation of diverse female speech styles in Japanese popular culture. In N. Warner, J. Ahlers, L. Bilmes, M. Oliver, S. Wertheim, and M. Chen (eds.), *Gender and belief systems: Proceedings of the Fourth Berkeley Women and Language Conference*, 575–588. Berkeley: Berkeley Women and Language Group.

———— (1997). Social context, linguistic ideology, and indexical expressions in Japanese. *Journal of Pragmatics* 28: 795–817.

O'Shaughnessy, Douglas (1987). *Speech communication: Human and machine*. Reading, MA: Addison-Wesley.

Shibamoto, Janet S. (1985). *Japanese women's language*. New York FL: Academic Press.

Shibatani, Masayoshi (1990). *The languages of Japan*. Cambridge, MA: Cambridge University Press.

Smith-Hefner, Nancy (1988). Women and politeness: The Javanese example. *Language in Society* 17(4): 535–554.

Sugito, Miyoko, Takashi Inukai, and Toshiyuki Sadanobu (1997). Bun no koozoo to purosodi (Sentence structure and prosody). In Onsee bunpoo kenkyuukai (Spoken Language Working Group) (ed.), *Bumpoo to onsee* (*Grammar and prosody*), 3–20. Tokyo: Kuroshio.

Trechter, Sara. (1999). Contextualizing the exotic few: Gender dichotomies in Lakhota. In M. Bucholtz, A. C. Liang, and L. A. Sutton (eds.), *Reinventing identities: The gendered self in discourse*, 101–22. Oxford: Oxford University Press.

van Bezooijen, Renée (1995). Sociocultural aspects of pitch differences between Japanese and Dutch women. *Language and Speech* 38(3): 253–266.

———— (1996). The effect of pitch on the attribution of gender-related personality traits. In N. Warner, J. Ahlers, L. Bilmes, M. Oliver, S. Wertheim, and M. Chen (eds.), *Gender and belief systems: Proceedings of the Fourth Berkeley Women and Language Conference*, 755–766. Berkeley: Berkeley Women and Language Group.

13

YOSHIKO MATSUMOTO

Alternative Femininity

Personae of Middle-aged Mothers

The origins of the common perceptions of femininity and of female roles within Japanese society have been illuminated in sociological and anthropological studies of Japanese women. For example, Lebra, describing the traditional socialization and discipline of young people in Japan, discusses an aspect of discipline that she labels "femininity training": training in manners and comportment according to the culturally standardized codes of propriety that were imposed upon young women (1984:42). According to her description, which is largely based on the prewar and wartime experience of women, the three dimensions of "femininity training" were "modesty," "elegance," and "tidiness." Women were trained to efface themselves in behavior that included posture, movement, and speech, and to portray elegance and tidiness in their handling of objects. With regard to speech according to Lebra, the prescription of modesty "demanded overall reticence, a soft voice, the polite and feminine style of speech, and avoidance of exposing the oral cavity" (1984:42).

There have been numerous studies with regard to the feminine style of speech, as discussed also in other chapters of this book (e.g., chapters 1 and 2). Such speech is purportedly manifested morphologically in the choice of sentence-final expressions, referential terms, and honorifics; these forms as used by women are seen as indicating softness, nonassertiveness, and politeness (e.g., Ide 1982, Shibamoto 1985, Mizutani & Mizutani 1987, Reynolds 1990, Shibatani 1990, Horii 1993). One common point in these previous considerations of gender indexing in Japanese is a focus on the conventional and stereotypical association between certain linguistic forms and the gender identity of the speaker. Specifically, such studies examined which forms are used in "women's language" and why, in light of Japanese cultural and historical background, they are regarded as characteristic of women.

The aspects of femininity that Lebra points out as the goals of femininity training evoke an image of traditional womanhood that is most associated with the Confucian ideology of *ryoosai kenbo* 'good wife, wise mother'. The concept of *ryoosai kenbo* has been described as an amalgamation of Confucian teaching on womanhood and the Western cult of domesticity, which developed in the mid-nineteenth to early twentieth centuries (e.g., Tamanoi 1990, Uno 1993). These ideologies assign to women the duties of subservience to men and of nurturance of family.

However, researchers have also noted signs of women's resistance to the dominant ideology (e.g., Tamanoi 1990; chapters 1–4, this volume), although such signs should be understood as symptomatic of incremental changes rather than as the start of an attitudinal revolution. Yet while such resistance may be incremental and fragile, it can gradually affect society, as noted by Rosenberger (1996). Other studies have shown that Japanese women in the last few decades have been given more opportunities to join the labor force (Fujimura-Fanselow & Kameda 1995) and have the potential to increase their status in the society (Iwao 1993). These studies suggest that women have a chance to choose not to adhere to the concept of femininity that has been the target of socialization training as described by Lebra.

Against the background of this social context, I discuss the language use of Japanese middle-aged women, especially mothers who do not work outside their homes. Among women, such stay-at-home mothers would appear to play the most traditional role and therefore could be expected to reflect more than others a traditional concept of femininity. In spite of their central position in forming the image of traditional femininity, the language of these middle-aged housewives and mothers has not been studied as much as that of professional women (e.g., [Shibamoto] Smith 1992). In this chapter, I analyze the real voices of such women, discuss the female personae conveyed in their speech, and consider whether and how these personae differ from (or are similar to) the stereotypical construction of femininity.

The examples discussed in this chapter are drawn from recordings collected during 1996–1997 that contain natural conversations of speakers, especially middle-aged (35-to-60-year-old) women. The analysis focuses particularly on one Japanese woman in her forties who is a mother of three teenagers. The data analyzed here is drawn from (1) a 120-minute recording of conversations of this woman with her fellow Parent Teacher Association committee members and (2) a 90-minute recording of conversations of the same speaker with fellow members of a women's amateur chanson group.

An analysis of the pragmatic and social meanings of the linguistic forms that the speaker and her interlocutors chose demonstrates that, contrary to the common and traditional assumption that middle-class middle-aged women's (especially mothers') speech is stable, gentle, and normatively feminine, expressions that are diverse in force and style are widely used throughout their conversations. This nonuniformity in style is observed even within an individual's utterances in the same speech situation. I suggest, based on this analysis, that the female personae that these middle-aged speakers portray diverge from the traditional norms of femininity that were inculcated in the femininity training described in Lebra (1984). As a result of such divergences, the femininity of Japanese women is seen to be not singular but multiple, encompassing alternative female personae that women can represent. The divergences also highlight the interaction between individual agentive choice and social constraints in constructing one's persona. (See also chapter 12, this volume.)

Two concepts useful in the following discussion are those of forceful and delicate stance. These stances can be conveyed linguistically or extralinguistically. Studies in linguistic pragmatics have shown that the same assertion, question, order, and so on, can be expressed forcefully or delicately depending on the speaker's intention or stance. In relation to the gender of the speaker, however, as exemplified by the femininity training mentioned earlier, women in Japan have been normatively expected to adopt a delicate stance, while men have been expected to be forceful. For those reasons, linguistic forms that pragmatically convey forceful stance, such as the sentence-final particle *zo*, which conveys one's determination and force, and the copula *da*, which conveys definiteness, have stereotypically been regarded as men's expressions, while expressions that convey a delicate stance, such as the sentence-final particle *wa*, which expresses a mild self-confirmation, and the use of an abbreviated request rather than the imperative (e.g., *yamete* . . . 'please stop' rather than the imperative *yamero* 'stop!'), have been labeled as women's expressions. In the following, I consider in more detail how these stances figure in conversations among middle-aged mothers.

13.1. Mixture of styles: The speech of middle-aged women

Example (1) is an excerpt of a 120–minute conversation among four women whose children attended the same public middle school in a middle-to-upper-middle-class residential neighborhood in Tokyo. The women were members of the local PTA Public Relations Committee and ranged in age from late thirties to early forties. They know one another relatively well, but more through their children and the PTA activities than privately. The main speaker, whom I refer to as Minako (M), was the oldest (43 years old at the time of the recording) in this group. The other speakers are referred to as Chie (C), Eri (E), and Fumiko (F).[1] The conversation took place in the course of a car trip to check a park on the outskirts of Tokyo where the school was planning to hold a sporting event. In the first excerpt, which was recorded while they were still on city streets, Minako was the driver and was unsure of the correct route. Single underlines indicate expressions that convey a forceful stance, while double underlines indicate speech that communicates a delicate stance.[2]

(1) 1 M: *chotto kotchi iketakke*
         :

     2 C: *. . . ki no oto ga sugoo(ku)*
     3 M: *a, yabbee, kore migi shika ikenai wa.*
     4 E: *a, honto da*
     5 M: *arararara*
     6 E: *minna ippoo-tsuukoo ni natchatte*

7   M: *kotchi hairitakunai n da yo na*
8   E: *ara, zutto da wa*
9   C: *koko n toko zutto soo nan desu yo, michi ga*
10 E: *a soo nan da yo ne*
11 M: *ura ikitai no yo ne, ura o*

1   M: I wonder if we can go this way
        :
2   C: ... the sound of trees was really terri(ble)
3   M: Oh, *damn*! I can only turn right here.
4   E: Oh, yeah, that's true
5   M: Dear, dear, dear
6   E: They became one-way
7   M: I don't want to go in here
8   E: Oh, all of them are
9   C: It's all like that around here; the roads are
10 E: Yeah, that's right, isn't it?
11 M: I want to take a back road, back road

One notable feature in the conversation in example (1) is that expressions that convey a forceful stance alternate with expressions that are delicate in force even within the same setting and topic of speech. The singly and doubly underlined sentence-final expressions and interjections in the example are salient in this regard.

Before we start examining the conversation in example (1) in detail, it is helpful to first consider elements whose pragmatic effect is to convey forceful or delicate stances. For example, one of the typical elements that bring about a delicate and attenuated force of speech is the pragmatic particle *wa*, which is used after a predicate, as can be seen in lines 3 and 8 in example (1). *Wa* was used historically as an exclamation, and it expresses as its core meaning the speaker's mild self-addressed confirmation about the propositional content of the sentence (Uyeno 1971, 1972; *Nihon kokugo dai-jiten* 1978).[3] Since it marks an utterance as addressed to oneself, the pragmatic force of an assertion with *wa*—in particular, its claim to the addressee's belief—is less intense than that which is conveyed by the absence of a particle or by the presence of more assertive particles such as *yo*, *ze*, and *zo*. When *wa* is uttered with a rising or sustaining intonation, as in all of the instances in example (1), the combination of intonation contour and core meaning of *wa* conveys an open-endedness that attenuates the speaker's assertion. For example, in the utterance in line 8, *ara, zutto da wa* 'Oh, all of them are', the sentence-final *wa* makes the utterance delicate and less intense.[4] Similarly, the interjection *ararara* 'dear, dear, dear' in line 5 and its core form *ara* 'oh' or 'oh, dear' in line 8 are relatively delicate or mild expressions of surprise.

In contrast to the delicate expressions discussed earlier, the interjection *yabbee* 'dangerous', in line 3 (an intensified version of a more common expression, *yabee*), although it has gained currency among young speakers, originated in gangsters' slang and expresses the strong feeling of the speaker about an unwanted situation. Another salient element that makes an utterance more forceful is the use of the copula *da*, which follows a noun or an adjective, as in lines 4, 7, and 10 of example (1). From a functional-linguistic (and pragmatic) point of view, the plain form copula *da* conveys as its modal function the speaker's certainty and definiteness toward the propositional content of the sentence (Teramura 1984, Konomi 1994). When the plain form *da* is used, the sentence conveys a stronger sense of assertiveness. For example, the utterance in line 4 *honto da* 'that's true' is more forceful than its counterpart without *da* as in *honto* 'true'. However, this forcefulness can be overridden when the copula is followed and attenuated by the particle *wa*, as in line 8, *zutto da wa* 'all of them are'.[5]

An alternating distribution of forceful and delicate expressions within a single context as observed in example (1) is interactionally interesting, but it deserves special attention in light of the normative and conventional association of the use of specific forms such as *wa* and *da* with the gender identity of the speaker. This conventional association is exemplified in example (2), which is an excerpt from a well-known textbook of Japanese for nonnative speakers that contrasts the differences between sentence-ending expressions in the informal or familiar speech of women and men. In this description, as shown in boldface, the use of the copula *da* is associated with men's speech while the pragmatic particle *wa* is associated with women's speech.

(2)   "In polite or formal speech, there is very little difference between men and women, but in familiar speech, there are some differences between the two."

Sentence Ending

Men usually say	**Women usually say**	[English glosses mine]
yokatta yo, yokatta ne	yokatta **wa** yo, yokatta **wa** ne	'(it) was good'
iku yo, iku ne	iku **wa** yo, iku **wa** ne	'will go'
ikanai yo, ikanai ne	ikanai **wa** yo, ikanai **wa** ne	'won't go'
soo **da** yo, soo **da** ne	soo yo, soo ne	'that's right'
soo **da**, soo **da**tta	soo da **wa**, so datta **wa**	'(it) is so, (it) was so'
ashita **da** yo, ashita **da** ne	ashita yo, ashita ne	'(it) is tomorrow'

(Mizutani & Mizutani 1977:150–151)

The association between the expressions illustrated here and gender identity, however, as argued by anthropological linguists and others, is not intrinsic to the language but is culturally mediated. For example, Ochs (1993), in discussing the indexicality of linguistic expressions, explains the conventional association between "female voice" and the Japanese pragmatic particle *wa*, which directly indexes delicate intensity. As explained by Ochs, this association is rooted in a complex of beliefs in Japanese culture about femininity and delicacy of expression. In other words, an affective disposition of delicacy is part of the preferred image of women, which both defines female voice and may motivate women's differential use of the form. For this reason, a delicate linguistic style has been normatively associated with female speakers and a forceful style with male speakers.

As exemplified in example (1), the extent of usage of forceful expressions by middle-class mothers raises questions about the functions and indexical meanings of such forms in addition to, and in contrast with, the well-studied association of delicate expressions with conventional female identity. It is not particularly plausible to consider, in the speech context of (1), that the variation in the expressions found there is motivated by the speakers' desire to indicate their alternating female and male identities. Further, although several studies and newspaper columns reported in the 1990s the increasingly frequent use by teenage girls and young women of forceful speech forms that were conventionally regarded as belonging to the realm of men's language (e.g., *Asahi Shimbun* 1992–1994; Uchida 1993; Okamoto 1995; Matsumoto 1996, 1999), it is not quite convincing to postulate that the speakers' identities are simply oscillating between youthful and adult.

I return to example (1) to consider this question by analyzing the stretch of conversation given there. I further discuss the issues by examining another excerpt of the same 120-minute conversation given in example (3) and an excerpt given in (7) from a conversation of the same main speaker, Minako, with another group of women.

Returning to example (1), Minako's (M's) use of the slang interjection *yabbee* 'damn' (lit., "dangerous") in line 3 can be interpreted as a clear indication of her frustration at not being able to keep the situation under control. On the one hand, her utterance in line 7 with *da* (*kotchi hairitakunai n da yo na* 'I don't want to go in here') can be understood similarly, that is, as a forceful expression used to express frustration. On the other hand, Eri's (E's) choice of *da* in lines 4 (*honto da* 'oh, yeah, that's true') and 10 (*soo nan da yo ne* 'that's right, isn't it?') does not seem to indicate such frustration. On the contrary, both utterances seem to express positive attitudes of agreement with or support for the other speakers. With the use of *da*, Eri's assertions are more definitive and convey a more forceful stance toward her expressions of agreement.

Interestingly, Eri uses an attenuated expression in line 8—*zutto da wa* 'all of them are'—observing and describing (seemingly to herself) the fact that the streets they are crossing are all one-way. Eri's choice between forceful and attenuated expressions may be explained according to the purposes of her speech act: forceful expressions are used when agreeing with others' opinions, while attenuated expressions are used to express her own view. We may further explain this by saying that Eri uses (at least) two strategies to convey her friendliness and thoughtfulness to others. One strategy is to give strong support to her interlocutor by making straightforward and forceful assertions. Another strategy is to show her concern for others by not pressing her own views and to convey friendliness in a more reserved manner. The first strategy, on the one hand, has been commonly associated with the communication style of men in informal settings and of some young women. The second strategy, on the other hand, has been associated with adult women as a choice or as a social constraint on their linguistic behavior (e.g., McGloin 1990, Mizutani & Mizutani 1987, Okamoto & Sato 1992). Eri seems to use these two strategies of indexing friendship effectively and to successfully create the persona of a supportive, friendly person who is versed both in recent trends and in tradition. She is apparently well liked among her peers and is seen as a pleasant person to be with.

In comparison to Eri, Minako's use of forceful and delicate expressions is not as clearly demarcated as Eri's. To express her feelings about the unwanted situations that she has been put in, Minako uses forceful expressions in lines 3 (*yabbee* 'damn') and 7 (*hairitakunai n da yo na* 'I don't want to go in here') but more delicate expressions in lines 5 (*arararara* 'dear, dear, dear') and 11 (*ikitai no yo ne* 'I want to take a back road'). Therefore, we cannot explain Minako's choices of expressions simply by linking them to different speech acts. A more plausible explanation of her choice is that Minako's speech pattern represents a more complex persona—one that is straightforward but delicate and recognizes the social constraints of being a "traditional" adult woman while attempting to avoid the "covert stigma" (Matsumoto 2002:345, 352) attached to traditional gender images. In this way, she balances and negotiates between the two (or more) different types of personae that she presents. What is common between these two mothers, however, is that neither one instantiates the traditional femininity associated with the stereotypical image of Japanese woman. Both represent (modern) alternatives to such beliefs.

We see more instances of variation in individual speakers' choices in example (3), an excerpt from the last part of the same 120-minute conversation that we saw in example (1). The broken underline indicates a trendy expression.

(3) 1   M: *are o hidari ni iku no?*
     2   E: *un, 412, un*
     3   F: *a! pikunikku rando tte kaite aru*
     4   E: *sono saki o sasetsu*
     5   F: *migi ga <u>sagamiko eki</u> **da** ne*
     6   M: <u>*oi oi*</u>
              :
     7   M: *nani ka o-mise mo roku ni <u>aitemasen koto yo</u>* (laughter)
     8   E: (laughter)
     9   F: *nee*
     10 M: *nanka shin to hora atchi-kotchi <u>shimatteru yo</u>. hora mada* (laughter)
     11   *koohii nomitakute mo <u>nomenai ja nai desu ka</u>, kore ja.*
     12 E, F (laughter)
     13 M: *nani ka attara <u>nomoo ne</u>, toriaezu, sagami p pikunikku rando ni hairu mae ni*
     14 E: *mada mada*
     15 F: *mada 10-ji dakara <u>aite nai ne</u>*
     16 E: <u>*aite nai ne*</u>. *makudonarudo mo nai shi tomerareru toko mo nai*
     17 M: <u>*nai yo*</u>
     18   *aa <u>waratchau yo ne</u>*
     19 E: *resuto hausu atte, yasumu toko nai no kashira. <u>komatchau wa ne.</u>*
     20 M: *demo <u>yokatta ne</u>, hayaku tsuite ne.*
     21 F: *nee. <u>suiteta ne</u>.*
     22 M: *suiteta suiteta.*
     23 F: *suitetara densha yori mo zutto <u>hayai n</u> **da** ne.*
     24 M: <u>*hayai* **wa** *yoo*</u>.

     1   M: Do we go left over there?
     2   E: Uh-huh, 412, uh-huh
     3   F: Ah! It says "Picnic Land."
     4   E: Make a left turn after that
     5   F: <u>Lake Sagami Station is on our right, isn't it?</u>
     6   M: <u>Hey, hey!</u>
              :

7	M:	It seems that <u>the stores are hardly open</u>. (laughter)
8	E:	(laughter)
9	F:	Yeah, right
10	M:	It's kind of quiet. Look, stores <u>are closed</u> here and there. Look, they're not yet open. (laughter)
11	M:	Even if we want to, <u>we can't have coffee</u>, can we? If it's like this
12	E, F:	(laughter)
13	M:	<u>Let's have coffee</u>, if there's any, one way or the other, before we get into Sagami p-, Picnic Land
14	E:	They're not open yet, not yet
15	F:	Since it's still 10 o'clock, <u>they aren't open, are they</u>?
16	E:	<u>They aren't open, are they?</u>. There isn't even a McDonald's, and there's no place to stop, either.
17	M:	<u>No</u>.
18		Oh, <u>this is something to laugh at, isn't it</u>?
19	E:	There's a rest area; I wonder if there's any place to rest. <u>I don't know what to do.</u>
20	M:	But <u>it's good</u> that we got here quickly, <u>isn't it</u>?
21	F:	Yeah; <u>the traffic was smooth, wasn't it</u>?
22	M:	It was; it was.
23	F:	When the traffic is smooth, driving a car is much <u>faster than a train, isn't it</u>?
24	M:	<u>It is faster</u>.

In this stretch of conversation, which was recorded close to their destination, the women were looking for a place to rest and have something to drink before their expedition at the park, Lake Sagami Picnic Land. As before, each speaker uses different linguistic strategies to convey stance and persona. Table 13.1 shows a comparison of the strategies used in this excerpt across the three speakers, Eri, Fumiko and Minako.

Eri, who is looking at a map and navigating, uses the same pattern of alternating expressions that we saw in example (1): when she agrees with someone, she uses more forceful expressions, as in line 16, *aite nai ne* (they aren't open, are they?), a repetition of what Fumiko (Speaker F) has just said, while less forceful expressions are chosen when she expresses her own thoughts and concern, as in line 19, *yasumu toko nai no kashira. komatchau wa ne* (I wonder if there's any place to rest. I don't know what to do).

TABLE 13.1 Types of expressions used by speakers

	Eri	Fumiko	Minako
Forceful expressions	1	5	6
Delicate expressions	1	0	2
Trendy expressions	0	0	1

Fumiko, however, uses no attenuated expressions regardless of the content of her utterances but most often compensates by adding the pragmatic sentence-final particle *ne(e)*, which gently invites the addressee's involvement. The persona that these expressions project may vary depending on the social background of the interpreter, but they generally give an image of someone who is wholesome and straightforward.

Minako's utterances again display a complex distribution of forceful and delicate expressions. Minako's utterances from lines 6 to 13 are of particular interest. *Oi oi* 'hey, hey!' in line 6 is a more forceful exclamatory attention getter than, for example, *chotto* (lit., 'a little') or *ara* ("oh" or "oh, dear"), which can be directed to oneself as well as to others. After a pause, Minako introduces in line 7 the new topic that the shops are hardly open, which is most likely to have prompted the exclamation *oi oi* in the previous line. She repeats this observation in line 10, using expressions that indicate a different attitude. The linguistic form in line 10 *shimatteru yo* 'the stores are closed' lacks the particle *wa* between the predicate and the assertive particle *yo*, and is therefore relatively forceful. In contrast, the main predicate *aitemasen* 'are hardly open' (rather than *aitenai*) in line 7 is in what is commonly termed the "polite form," unlike the majority of the utterances in this recording. What follows the polite-form predicate is the formal noun, or nominalizer, *koto* (lit., 'fact'), which functions to make the content of the preceding clause an established fact and has a distancing effect. In this sense, the emotional impact of the statement is lessened, and therefore its affective force is attenuated. Consequently, this form [predicate + *koto* + *yo*] can fit the traditional cultural norm of femininity and is known as one of the stereotypical old-fashioned forms of upper-middle-class female speech. It is likely that the speaker is aware of the connotations of the form and is using it ironically for humorous effect, as indicated by the laughter that follows the utterance and the overly clear pronunciation of the words.

Another contrastive set of expressions may be observed in lines 11 and 13. The contents of the two utterances are not exactly identical, but both concern the possibility of having coffee. The example in line 13, *nomoo ne* 'let's have coffee', indicates straightforward informal friendliness. The phrase used in line 11, *ja nai desu ka* "can we?: literally, 'isn't it the case that . . . ?' with a polite copula *desu* has recently caught the attention both of linguists and of speakers of Japanese (McGloin 1999, *Asahi Shimbun* 1992–1994) and is generally considered a trendy expression typically used by young people, probably as a polite expression of involvement. The use of such a trendy youthful expression also forms an interesting contrast with the old-fashioned expression *aitemasen koto yo* in line 7.

Except for this ironically used old-fashioned expression, which brings about a comical effect, none of the expressions used by the three speakers seems designed to create a special effect as an unexpected expression, although in their own ways all of the speakers use expressions that are different from those assumed to be used by middle-class mothers. Minako tends to take the lead in conversations more than others, but all the participants produce repetitions and agreements that indicate cooperation, which is generally associated in the literature with female speech styles (Coates 1996). The activities that the speakers are engaged in—driving to a place as PTA members, looking for a place to rest, and talking about these activities—do not seem peculiar in comparison to what mothers may normally do. We can thus conclude that the examples give us a glimpse—a slice of reality, as it were—of how middle-aged women in Tokyo talk among themselves, in contrast to the common cultural images of their speech.[6]

Minako, the main speaker in examples (1) and (3), has other groups of female friends, including a group of amateur chanson singers who are alumnae of a university chanson club and who perform concerts for themselves and with other similar alumnae /alumni groups. Where in the earlier conversation Minako, at age 43, was the oldest participant, here she is the youngest. Minako is one of the most prominent members of the group. Example (4) is an excerpt from a conversation recorded in a gathering of the group after a concert, in which Minako sang a solo. O (61 years old), P (52 years old), and Q (exact age unknown) are among the other women in the conversation. In this conversation we can observe a different choice of copula forms by Minako than in the earlier example, as well as contrastive uses of sentence-final forms between speakers O and P. The distancing copula form *desu*, rather than the more familiar form *da*, is indicated with wavy lines.

(4)	1	O:	*Okaasama suteki datta deshoo tte ittara, anoo.*
	2	P:	*soo itteta yo*
	3	O:	*soo ittemashita yo,⌈ soo itte irashita **wa** ee. suteki datta tte nee.*
	4	Q:	⌊*aa soo.*
	5	M:	*demo chotto utai-kata ga chigatta ne tte iwarechatta*
	6	O:	*aa soo*
	7	P:	*waaa*
	8	Q:	*heee*
	9	R:	*hontoo*
	10	O:	*yokuu⌈ja kiite ite ⌉kekkoo ne kiiterashita no nee*
	11	P:	⌊*yoku kiiteru n daa* ⌋
	12	M:	*kashi machigaeru na tte iwareru n desu yo, oboeteru n desu yo, kekkoo*
	13	P:	*sugoi nee*

1	O:	When I said, "Your mother was fabulous, wasn't she?" umm.
2	P:	They said so.
3	O:	They said so, ⌈ they said (honorific) so, yes. It was fabulous, right.
4	Q:	⌊Is that so.
5	M:	But they [my children] told me [lit., "I was told"] that the way I sang was a bit different
6	O:	Is that so?
7	P:	Wow.
8	Q:	Gee.
9	R:	Really?
10	O:	Well ⌈then they were listening ⌉fairly well, they were listening (honorific).
11	P:	⌊They were listening well ⌋
12	M:	"Don't make mistakes in the lyrics," they [my children] told me. They remember the lyrics fairly well.
13	P:	I'm amazed.

O and P have been friends with Minako for some time, but Minako notably uses the more polite and distancing copula *desu* in line 12. This may be on account of the age difference between M and the other participants and M's following or being constrained by the social expectations of linguistic behavior toward older individuals, especially O, who uses honorific forms, even in this informal context when talking to younger interlocutors.[7]

Another interesting point to note in this conversation is the contrast between O's and P's speech. O and P are both friendly to Minako, but their choices of expressions are divergent. Although both O and P are older (61 and 52, respectively), P uses more straightforward expressions that show camaraderie, similarly to E and F in earlier examples, while O uses more delicate expressions and honorific forms as well as the prosody characteristic of traditional women's speech, thereby creating the image of a stereotypical upper-middle-class female speaker. It is noteworthy that O uses such delicate and honorific expressions very consciously. In both lines 3 and 10, she first uses polite but nonhonorific form of expressions, *ittemashita* 'they said' and *kiite ite* 'were listening to the utterance' but repairs (repeating the same content while revising the form) to be more refined with the use of attenuated forms and honorifics. Interestingly, O, the speaker of this traditional style commonly associated with (upper-)middle-class housewives and not with working women, is the only participant who also works outside the home, albeit part-time: she is a home economics teacher at a private high school for girls. This fact confirms that style choice and job status do not directly correlate. O's deliberate use of a traditional style suggests a few things: She may be trying to prevent others from seeing her as less than middle-class—someone who works out of financial necessity. She may be trying to maintain the "ideal" style that she believes to be expected of someone of her background. As the only participant who was exposed to the prewar value system and education, she may still uphold in principle the traditional "good wife and wise mother" ideology, the aforementioned femininity training, and their associated linguistic behavior. Alternatively, O, who is also the head of the group, may have felt that, in order to successfully convey her compliments to Minako, she could indicate her respect by using honorifics to describe Minako's children's behavior. These do not exhaust all possible explanations. The excerpt in example (4) is therefore useful to illustrate again that women who share a similar background (e.g., age, class, education, and hobbies) do not necessarily choose the same strategies for presenting themselves.

13.2.   Conclusion: Alternative femininity and the presentation of a complex persona

We have observed multiple functions of linguistic expressions and the variability of female personae that are represented in the speech of middle-aged middle-class Japanese women, focusing primarily on mothers who do not work outside the home. In the data examined here, expressions of a forceful stance were used sometimes to display frustration but at other times to accommodate others' views and to be friendly. Expressions of a weaker and delicate stance were used to present the speaker's views in a friendly and deferential style and also perhaps to convey the speaker's delicacy.

Because forceful expressions have been associated with youth (both female and male) and delicate expressions with traditional women in Japan, it is likely that there were also times when the mothers' choices of expressions were motivated by the desire to portray themselves as current and anticonformist, or traditional and "classy" (see chapter 10, this volume, on class associations of Japanese women's language).

What these observations imply is that statements that present similar propositional, or semantic, content can be expressed with a variety of speech styles and forces, even in the same speech situation, to the same addressee, and sometimes by the same speaker. The only speaker in our data who could be characterized as upholding the traditional image of femininity in her language use and in her speech was the 61-year-old speaker O in example (4).

I should add in passing that the alternation between forceful and delicate stances is not necessarily limited to middle-aged mothers or other female speakers. Male Tokyo speakers have been known to use expressions perceived to be delicate such as those given in the column labeled as "Women usually say" in example (2). For example, I have observed the nonuse of the copula *da*, as in *kore niku yo* 'this is meat' and *soo yo* 'that's right' (but not the combination of particles *wa yo* or nonfalling intonation *wa* or *wa ne*).[8] Further study is necessary to delineate the distribution of such expressions and to discuss their implications, but it is important to note that the range of expressions that are in fact used by both female and male speakers is broader than in normative accounts.

The linguistically exhibited variability of female personae seems to generally reflect the societal situation since the 1980s and 1990s when, as briefly mentioned earlier, women in Japan were afforded more choices for their careers and lives. It is not surprising that an expansion in one's social (and career) domain should have as a corollary an expanded selection of available personae. What is particularly interesting here, however, is that most of the women in my data are mothers without even part-time jobs. Various interpretations can be given as to why mothers without outside careers should exploit linguistic choices to represent complex personae that differ from the traditional presentation of femininity. One possibility is that the traditional cultural belief about femininity is an ideological construct not reflected in reality. Another is that the social changes in recent years have affected even the paragons of the nurturing role model—mothers. Perhaps to some extent both explanations are true. Sociological studies on urban housewives show that they are becoming more regionally active with increased social participation outside the home through part-time jobs and volunteer activities (e.g., Imamura 1987, 1996; Fujimura-Fanselow & Kameda 1995). Such changes may have enabled the construction of the female personae that are seen linguistically in this study. At the same time, speakers have always been endowed with the ability to choose and construct their own personae based on aspects of their lives, including their past and current experiences that they wish to foreground, as well as on their awareness of and responses to cultural beliefs about femininity. As Eckert and McConnell-Ginet (1992) have argued, language use is a showcase of speakers' individual histories of previous experiences and engagements in various groups (or communities of practice) whose linguistic influences persist in their engagement in current activities and in the negotiation of their individual presentations of self.

Even within the limited selection of conversational samples that I examined here, the utterances of Minako exhibit a notable variety of expressions and stances. This variety may be explained by the way she has lived her life. Minako's past and current activities cut across several areas. She is active in the PTA at her son's school as well as in an amateur (or even half-professional) singing group. In college, she pursued a number of modern and traditional artistic as well as athletic interests. She married an athlete and educator and became the mother of one daughter and two sons, who are now in their teens. Minako's relatively broad current and past social network—although limited to a middle-class and mainly nonworking environment—seems congruent with her broad range of linguistic expressions.

The seemingly ambivalent style that embraces a range of stances provides the speakers in these examples with the opportunity to present themselves in a complex yet flexible fashion and allows them to negotiate their relationships with addressees in more varied ways. According to my data and previous studies, such a style is not prominent in younger women's speech[9] but may be a characteristic of at least some middle-aged speakers. It is not surprising that such a style is found among middle-aged women, who are old enough to have had a variety of experiences and social roles but young enough to feel affinity with the directness fostered in youth.

The examples cited in this chapter suggest that variations in linguistic style are part of the speaker's own linguistic repertoire rather than signaling the use of someone else's voice, such as a "male voice." When, Minako, for example, switches from one form to another, although the switch has a pragmatic and social effect, most of the time it does not seem to invite some sort of Gricean implicature (1975), which would result from a contextually unexpected choice of expressions.[10] The alternation among types of forms may be viewed as presenting a broad but coherent image of an individual speaker.

It should be noted here that not all middle-aged women draw from as wide a stylistic palette as Minako and Eri in the preceding examples. For example, Fumiko (ex. 3) and O and P (ex. 4) exhibit a consistent preference for one stance over another. Depending on their social backgrounds and interactional goals, some speakers may use predominantly delicate and attenuated expressions, some may favor more forceful expressions, some may choose to use conventionally gendered expressions, and some may employ a mixture of these. The examples presented here highlight this linguistic individuality among speakers who could all too often be categorized in terms of a single gender, age, class, or regional grouping.

I do not expect that the range of expressions shown in this chapter would in any way exhaust the possible personae that women can choose to present. It is conceivable that women of different age-groups and social backgrounds would exhibit other expressions and stances and therefore other types of femininity not discussed here.[11] For example, I considered in Matsumoto (1996) a cute, infantile feminine persona associated with younger married women as another alternative to the traditional Japanese expression of femininity. Echoing that earlier work, this study illustrates the multiplicity and complexity of female personae that language can represent. These works argue for the acknowledgment of the varieties of femininity at the outset of language and gender studies rather than consider femininity as a singular concept. While speakers recognize the cultural and social expectations and the constraints regarding their behavior, linguistic and otherwise, they still have room to negotiate among these conditions to represent themselves in multidimensional ways. Acknowledgment of the varieties of femininity and recognition of agentivity within the changing and not-very-clearly demarcated boundary of cultural and gender constraints should be a touchstone for our further studies in language and gender ideology and practice.

Notes

I would like to express my gratitude to the editors of this volume, Janet Shibamoto Smith and Shigeko Okamoto, and to Mary Bucholtz, the series editor, for their useful comments and suggestions. I am also indebted to the speakers who provided my data, especially "Minako," who kindly recorded her conversations. This chapter is a substantially revised version of a paper that I presented at the First International Gender and Language Conference in 2000 (Matsumoto 2002).

1. All the participants' names in this and other examples are pseudonyms.

2. Expressions that are labeled as "forceful" expressions and "delicate" expressions here were referred to as "so-called nonfeminine forms" and "feminine forms" (respectively) in my earlier paper (Matsumoto 1999) in accordance with the terms conventionally used in some of the recent studies in the area. I use more pragmatically oriented terms in this chapter because the focus of the discussion here is less to point out the discrepancy between the reality and the normative ideology of women's speech (as it was in my earlier work) and more to understand how women use linguistic devices to express a persona that transcends traditional conceptions of femininity.

3. As a consequence, *wa* cannot be used with a sentence that conveys meanings incompatible with the concept of confirmation, such as a sentence that conveys a question. The sentence *ii wa* ('good/OK Sentence-Final Particle') cannot mean "Is it OK?" but means "It's OK," and **ii ka wa* ('good/OK Question Particle Sentence-Final Particle') is ungrammatical.

4. My position here is that the same core pragmatic meaning is conveyed regardless of the intonation with which the sentence with *wa* is uttered, although I recognize that open-endedness is more clearly conveyed with a rising intonation and the combination of rising intonation with *wa* makes the utterance even less intense in force. There is a controversy over the function of intonation contour in relation to the meaning of *wa*, in particular as to which intonation contour indicates stronger emotion (Kitagawa 1977, McGloin 1990). My analysis here is based more on the core meanings of the particle proposed by Uyeno (1971) and *Nihon kokugo daijiten* (1978).

5. The particles *yo*, *na*, and *ne*, which are found in lines 7 and 10 (*hairitakunai n da yo na* 'I don't want to go in' and *soo nan da yo ne* 'that's right'), express assertiveness and involvement rather than delicacy.

6. A similar variety of forms is also found among middle-class middle-aged career women (see Matsumoto 1996), but I do not go into that issue in this chapter, as it is not the main concern here.

7. For further discussions and implications of mixed use of the *masu* form and plain forms, see Cook (1998). Minako here can be described as more aware of her "self-presentation" and "addressee deference" than in her other utterances earlier (Cook 1998:87).

8. Speakers of such forms of delicate stance can be perceived by speakers of non-Tokyo dialects as effeminate or as users of "women's language" (S. Iwasaki, S. Okamoto, personal communication).

9. This does not mean that younger women's speech totally lacks delicate expressions. In the data that I observed, such expressions are found in younger women's speech but are not as prevalent as in middle-aged women's speech.

10. I call this outcome an "interactional implicature" elsewhere (Matsumoto 1988).

11. See also other chapters in part II of this volume.

References

Asahi Shimbun (1992–4). Ima tookyoo-go wa (Tokyo-language now). Special weekly columns.

Coates, Jennifer (1996). Women talk: *Conversation between women women friends*. Oxford: Blackwell.

Cook, Haruko M. (1998). Situational meanings of the Japanese social deixis: The mixed use of the *masu* and plain forms. *Journal of Linguistic Anthropology* 8(1): 87–110.

Eckert, Penelope, and Sally McConnell-Ginet (1992). Communities of practice: Where language, gender, and power all live. In K. Hall, M. Bucholtz, and B. Moonwomon (eds.), *Locating power: Proceedings of the Second Berkeley Women and Language Conference*, 89–99. Berkeley: Berkeley Women and Language Group.

Fujimura-Fanselow, Kumiko, and Atsuko Kameda (eds.) (1995). *Japanese women: New feminist perspectives on the past, present, and future*. New York: Feminist Press.

Grice, H. Paul (1975). Logic and conversation. In P. Cole and J. L. Morgan (eds.), *Syntax and semantics 3: Speech acts*, 41–58. New York: Academic Press.

Horii, Reiichi (1993). Joseego no seeritsu (Establishment of women's language). *Nihongogaku* 12(5): 100–108.

Ide, Sachiko (1982). Japanese sociolinguistics: Politeness and women's language. *Lingua* 57: 357–385.

Imamura, Anne E. (1987). *Urban Japanese housewives*. Honolulu: University of Hawaii Press.

———. (ed.) (1996). *Re-imaging Japanese women*. Berkeley: University of California Press.

Iwao, Sumiko (1993). *The Japanese woman: Traditional image and changing reality*. New York: Free Press.

Kitagawa, Chisato (1977). A source of femininity in Japanese: In defense of Robin Lakoff's "Language and women's place." *Papers in Linguistics* 10: 275–298.

Konomi, Emiko (1994). The structure of the nominal predication in Japanese. Unpublished Ph.D. dissertation, Cornell University.

Lebra, Takie Sugiyama (1984). *Japanese women: Constraint and fulfillment*. Honolulu: University of Hawaii Press.

Matsumoto, Yoshiko (1988). Reexamination of the universality of face: Politeness phenomena in Japanese. *Journal of Pragmatics* 12: 403–426.

——— (1996). Does less feminine speech in Japanese mean less femininity? In N. Warner, J. Ahlers, L. Bilmes, M. Oliver, S. Wertheim, and M. Chen (eds.), *Gender and belief systems: Proceedings of the Fourth Berkeley Women and Language Conference*, 455–467. Berkeley: Berkeley Women and Language Group.

——— (1999). Japanese stylistic choices and ideologies across generations. In J. Verschueren (ed.), *Selected papers from the 6th International Pragmatics Conference*, vol. 1: *Language and ideology*, 352–364. Antwerp: International Pragmatics Association.

——— (2002). Gender identity and the presentation of self in Japanese. In S. Benor, M. Rose, D. Sharma, J. Sweetland, and Q. Zhang (eds.), *Gendered practices in language*. Stanford, CA: CSLI Publications.

McGloin, Naomi Hanaoka (1990). Sex difference and sentence-final particles. In S. Ide and N. H. McGloin (eds.), *Aspects of Japanese women's language*, 23–41. Tokyo: Kuroshio.

———— (1999). Pragmatic and discourse functions of the rhetorical negative question form, zyanai desu ka. In M. Muraki and E. Iwamoto (eds.), *Linguistics: In Search of the human mind*, 425–469. Tokyo: Kaitakusha.

Mizutani, Osamu, and Nobuko Mizutani (1977). *An introduction to modern Japanese*. Tokyo: Japan Times.

———— (1987). *How to be polite in Japanese*. Tokyo: Japan Times.

Nihon kokugo dai-jiten (The comprehensive dictionary of the Japanese language) (1978). Tokyo: Shogakkan.

Ochs, Elinor (1993). Indexing gender. In B. D. Miller (ed.), *Sex and gender hierarchies*, 146–169. Cambridge, MA: Cambridge University Press.

Okamoto, Shigeko (1995). "Tasteless" Japanese: Less "feminine" speech among young Japanese women. In K. Hall and M. Bucholtz (eds.), *Gender articulated: Language and the socially constructed self*, 297–325. New York: Routledge.

Okamoto, Shigeko, and Shie Sato (1992). Less feminine speech among young Japanese females. In K. Hall, M. Bucholtz, and B. Moonwomon (eds.), *Locating power: Proceedings of the Second Berkeley Women and Language Conference*, 478–488. Berkeley: Berkeley Women and Language Group.

Reynolds, Katsue Akiba (1990). Female speakers of Japanese in transition. In S. Ide and N. H. McGloin (eds.), *Aspects of Japanese women's language*, 129–146. Tokyo: Kuroshio.

Rosenberger, Nancy R. (1996). Fragile resistance, signs of status: Women between state and media in Japan. In A. E. Imamura (ed.), *Re-imaging Japanese women*, 12–45. Berkeley: University of California Press.

Shibamoto, Janet S. (1985). *Japanese women's language*. New York: Academic Press.

[Shibamoto] Smith, Janet S. (1992). Women in charge: Politeness and directives in the speech of Japanese women. *Language in Society* 21(1): 59–82.

Shibatani, Masayoshi (1990). *The languages of Japan*. Cambridge, MA: Cambridge University Press.

Tamanoi, Mariko Asano (1990). Women's voices: Their critique of the anthropology of Japan. *Annual Review of Anthropology* 19: 17–37.

Teramura, Hideo (1984). *Nihongo no shintakusu to imi (Japanese syntax and meaning)*, vol. 2. Tokyo: Kuroshio.

Uchida, Nobuko (1993). Kaiwa-koodoo ni mirareru seesa (Gender differences in conversation). *Nihongogaku* 12(6): 156–68.

Uno, Kathleen S. (1993). The death of "good wife, wise mother"? In A. Gordon (ed.), *Postwar Japan as history*, 293–322. Berkeley: University of California Press.

Uyeno, Tazuko Y. (1971). A study of Japanese modality: A performative analysis of sentence particles. Unpublished Ph. D. dissertation, University of Michigan.

———— (1972). Shuujoshi to sono shuuhen (Sentence-final particles and related issues). *Nihongo Kyooiku* 17: 62–77.

14

AYUMI MIYAZAKI

Japanese Junior High School Girls' and Boys' First-Person Pronoun Use and Their Social World

*Ndee, onna no ko ni kakomareteru tokii, nan to nakuu, **ore** tte icchau n da yo ne. Tte yuu kaa, "Aa, jibun ga otoko da ttara, kore zenbu jibun no onna na no ni naa" tte omottari suru toki **ore** nan da yo ne. Chotto kawatteru deshoo? . . . Atashi nee, nan daroo nee, nnn, dotchi katte yuu to, boseehonnoo yori moo, otoko no ko ga yowatchii onna no ko mamoritaku naru, ano kanji no hoo ga tsuyoi ka mo shinnai, boseehonnoo yori.*[1]

'And when I'm surrounded by girls, I'll say *ore* [a strongly masculine first-person pronoun]. Or when I imagine, "Ahh, if I were a boy, these girls would be all mine," I'll say *ore*. Aren't I strange? . . . I, I wonder, if I had to choose one, I'd say that I have more of a boy's instinct to protect weak girls than a maternal instinct'. (13-year-old girl)

***Ore** ga niau hito tte iru n desu yo. Tatoeba, supootsukee ga dekiru hito toka . . . **Ore** tte itte kimaru hito iru jan. Boku nanka zenzen kimannai jan.*

'*Ore* suits some people. For example, people who are good at sports . . . There are people who sound cool with *ore*. I wouldn't sound cool at all if I used *ore*'. (13-year-old boy)

In this chapter, I analyze diverse linguistic practices of Japanese junior high school students that go against the Japanese ideology of gender-divided language. In particular, I explore girls' and boys' untraditional first-pronoun usage, as demonstrated in the preceding comments of a girl who says that she uses the supposedly vulgar masculine first-person pronoun, *ore*, and of a boy who reports that he eschews this masculine pronoun. This chapter examines such linguistic practices by locating them within students' social world, namely, their peer-group relations, and within the power dynamics of their *gakkyuu*, the fundamental unit of Japanese schools.

From 1997 to 2001, I conducted a longitudinal ethnography of a largely middle-class public junior high school in a city that is an hour's train ride from Tokyo. The data for this study is drawn from observations of various classes and activities at school and interviews with students in individual and group settings when the students were in the seventh grade, the first year of junior high school (April 1998 to April 1999).

14.1. Beyond a direct linkage between gender and language

Many scholars (e.g., Shibamoto 1985, Ide & McGloin 1990, [Shibamoto] Smith 1992, Reinoruzu [Reynolds]-Akiba 1993, Ide 1997) have pointed out that, in the Japanese language, female and male speech diverges widely in self-reference and address forms, sentence-final particles, vocabulary, pitch range, and intonation. For instance, sentence-final particles, which signal speakers' various sentiments in conversation (e.g., McGloin 1990, 1997), directly index the gender of the speaker. Sentences that end with the particle *wa* are considered to belong to women's speech, while those that end with the particle *ze* are considered to belong to men's speech.

Another concrete example of this gendered framing is first-person pronouns—glossable as 'I' in English. Table 14.1 shows the variety of first-person pronouns within Standard Japanese.

As the table indicates, women and men are supposed to use different first-person pronouns: *atakushi* and *atashi* are for women; *boku* and *ore* are for men. Moreover, in women's speech there is no other-deprecatory first-person pronoun comparable to *ore* in men's speech. Women are expected to avoid the deprecatory level of pronoun use and to display a polite demeanor (Ide 1997:73–74).[2]

Many studies, however, including those in part III of this volume, have confirmed the existence of significant variation in the actual speech of Japanese women. Okamoto and Sato (1992) and Okamoto (1995, 1997), for instance, make it clear that gendered speech does not simply indicate the gender of the speaker. Analyzing the speech of Japanese women of various ages, these scholars observed that younger women tended to use traditional "masculine" speech more frequently than older women, although each age group exhibited wide variations. Sunaoshi (chapter 10, this volume) found that farm women in Ibaraki Prefecture frequently used *ore*, a first-person pronoun supposedly not available to women, during their product develop-

TABLE 14.1 Gender-marked first-person pronouns

	Men's Speech	Women's Speech
Formal	watakushi	watakushi
	watashi	atakushi
Plain	boku	watashi
		atashi
Deprecatory	ore	φ
		Ide (1997:73)

ment meetings. In Abe's study (chapter 11, this volume), young female employees at a lesbian bar used *jibun*, a first-person pronoun that is normally associated with men in sports or in militaristic groups.

Inoue (1994) calls into question the notion that a unified Japanese women's language has existed throughout Japanese history. Through the analysis of voices of female characters in early modern novels, Inoue demonstrates that "Japanese women's language" as it is characterized today does not flow from actual usage since time immemorial but was deliberately created in the process of Japan's modernization in the early twentieth century. The intensely researched gender division of the Japanese language, therefore, is an ideology of how Japanese speakers should speak, not rules that all Japanese speakers follow.

These findings coincide with gender and language studies in North American and Western European settings, where a number of scholars have recently stressed the need to examine seemingly direct and exclusive relationships between language and social attributes, such as the gender and social status of speakers (e.g., Bing & Bergvall 1996, Woolard 1998, Bucholtz 1999a), and have revealed, from ethnographic perspectives, how women and girls negotiate language ideologies of gender (e.g., Coates 1994, 1999; Mendoza-Denton 1994; Goodwin 1998, 1999; Bucholtz 1999b; Morgan 1999). Bucholtz's (1999b) ethnographic study, for instance, finds that a group of "nerdy" California high school girls resist the hegemonic ideology of femininity through creative linguistic practices such as punning. Morgan (1999), through analyzing how African-American girls and women actively participate in elaborate and skillful language games, opposes the idea that African-American vernacular culture is represented only by African-American boys and men and that femininity is represented only by middle-class European American girls and women. Goodwin (1998, 1999) observes that Latina girls playing hopscotch express strong disagreement by using their body movements and linguistic resources. Goodwin successfully challenges a series of earlier gender studies that dichotomized girls' and boys' play in terms of cooperation versus competition.

Based on these studies, this chapter explores similarly dynamic relationships between gender and language by examining Japanese girls' and boys' speech within its specific social and pragmatic context. Ochs (1992) argues that to untangle the seemingly direct connection between linguistic forms and gender one needs to examine the complex sets of pragmatic meanings that mediate them. The Japanese sentence-final particle *ze*, for instance, does not always suggest that the speaker is male, but the coarse intensity of this particle connects it to the image of masculinity. The sentence-final particle *wa*, in similar fashion, does not determine the female gender of its speaker; instead, its delicate intensity only indirectly constitutes its gender meaning. Agha (1993) also notes that linguistic forms, in this case the honorifics of Lhasa Tibetan, do not automatically encode social status. Rather, these honorifics signal deference entitlements in myriad ways and cannot be understood outside of their context. If someone says, "Mother went to the house," with the word *house* in an honorific form, the listener would not understand who is being deferred to: is it the mother, the owner of the house, or the builder of the house? The listener needs to understand the real-time occurrence of the events, discourses, and their contexts to make sense of how the linguistic form signals social status. Only by examining such

rich, complex constructions of local pragmatic meanings within a specific "community of practice" (Eckert & McConnell-Ginet 1992) are we able to understand the
connections between language and gender and other social categories.

The specific context explored in this chapter is the Japanese junior high school
class, called *gakkyuu* (or *kurasu*, from the English word *class*). The *gakkyuu* orga-
nizes its students differently from U.S. schools. *Gakkyuu* are composed of a group
of up to 40 students and one teacher who is in charge of the *gakkyuu*. From elementary school to high school, Japanese students belong to a *gakkyuu*. *Gakkyuu* are generally reorganized every one to two years; between reorganizations students cannot
switch *gakkyuu*.[3] Students in a *gakkyuu* spend most of their school life together in
the same classroom, follow the same curriculum, spend break time together, and
interact with one another in front of the lockers found in classrooms. Moreover, students in a *gakkyuu* share various nonacademic activities such as morning and after-
noon meetings, serving and eating lunch in the classroom, performing cleaning duties
together, preparing as a group for inter-*gakkyuu* competitions of chorus or sports,
and taking on numerous tasks such as organizing cleaning and lunch duties, organizing the classroom work assignments, checking attendance and reporting it to the
health office of the school, and taking care of handouts and bulletin boards. A *gakkyuu*
is therefore more than just a class; it is a *seekatsu kyoodootai* 'school community'
where tightly knit relationships form.

Students try to belong to a peer group within their *gakkyuu* not only because it
is important for their social lives in this closed community but also because both
academic and nonacademic activities are often organized around small groups of
students in a *gakkyuu*. In the school I studied, these small groups were usually composed of peer groups.[4] Students who do not belong to a peer group in their *gakkyuu*
have trouble finding their place on the daily or even hourly occasions in which a
gakkyuu divides itself into groups for performing activities. As a result, *gakkyuu*
become fields where students constantly negotiate their relationships, status, and
power.

Ethnographic methods allowed me to closely observe girls and boys who were
actively interacting and making sense of the meaning of gender, language, and identity in their *gakkyuu*. Based on such investigation, I analyze (1) what kinds of first-
person pronouns girls and boys actually use in their peer groups and how these
pronouns differ from the ideological map of feminine or masculine speech, (2) how
girls and boys form pragmatic meanings (Silverstein 1976) with respect to their first-
person pronoun uses, and (3) how these uses relate to students' relationships within
their *gakkyuu*.

Although previous studies of preadolescents and adolescents actively experiment-
ing with their speech and identity greatly contribute to reconsidering the fixed relationships between language and social categories, only a few studies (e.g., Ogbay
2000) have investigated them in great depth in a non-Western context. The Japanese
ideology of gendered language provides a pivotal point from which to explore the
ways individuals negotiate, struggle with, and resist their gender constraints. Such
negotiations in the social world of the *gakkyuu* in turn mirror intricate relations between individuals, groups, and the dominant ideology. As Woolard says, ideologies
of language "underpin not only linguistic form and use but also the very notion of

the person and the social group" (1998:3). Thus, I believe that the exploration of Japanese junior high school students' linguistic practices will contribute to a general theory of the complex interplay between human interactions and ideology.

14.2.   First-person pronoun uses of the girls and boys in Gakkyuu A

14.2.1.   Repertoires of first-person pronouns

Figure 14.1 shows a map of girls' and boys' peer-group relations and the first-person pronouns in a *gakkyuu* I studied, which I call Gakkyuu A. Small ovals in the diagram represent individual girls and small dotted ovals represent individual boys.[5] The forms of the first-person pronouns within each small oval represent the first-person pronoun most frequently used by the individual in question in informal settings such as when talking to friends.[6] The pronouns in the diagram are not drawn from students' own explanations but from my observations of students' actual use and from transcripts of group interviews. Larger ovals that surround these small ovals represent peer groups, ovals with unbroken lines with the letter *G* represent girls' groups, and dotted lines with the letter *B* represent boys' groups.

The masculine/feminine continuum at the top of the diagram compares the Japanese ideology of gendered first-person pronouns reflected in table 14.1 with students' interpretations of the four main pronouns they use. Although students' interpretations are by no means uniform, as I explain in the next section, the simple continuum nonetheless serves as a point of reference both for the dominant ideology of gendered first-person pronouns and for students' actual use of first-person pronouns shown in the diagram below the continuum.

According to table 14.1, girls should use *watashi* or *atashi*, an informal female pronoun, among friends. No girl in this *gakkyuu*, however, regularly used *watashi*, and many girls used *boku*, a plain male pronoun, or the other-deprecatory male pronoun *ore*. Many girls also used *uchi*, which does not even appear in table 14.1. *Uchi*, a word that originally meant "inside" or "home" seems to be a newly created first-person pronoun in the Tokyo area. Although I grew up in the city where the school is located, I had never heard of anybody using *uchi* as a first-person pronoun before I entered the research site. Of the seven mothers of students I interviewed in the year 2000, who were mostly in their forties, not one realized that such a first-person pronoun existed.

As table 14.1 shows, boys are supposed to use the plain form *boku* among friends. Most boys in Gakkyuu A, however, used *ore*, and only one boy used *boku* exclusively. One boy, who reported that he belonged to an otherwise all-girl group, often used *atashi*. Two boys regularly used forms other than the four main forms the students at the school used—*atashi*, *uchi*, *boku*, and *ore*. One boy used *washi*, which is considered to be a pronoun for old men. Another boy used *oresama* 'Mr. I' or 'the honorable I'.[7]

These descriptions of girls' and boys' first-person pronoun use demonstrate that the students did not always follow the gendered language ideology reflected in table 14.1. In fact, it is difficult to mark these untraditional linguistic practices as mere

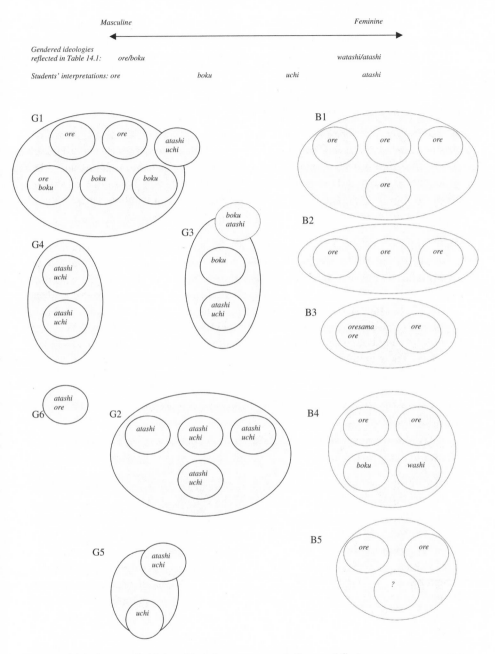

FIGURE 14.1 A map of girls' and boys' peer-group relations and first-person pronoun use in *Gakkyuu* A

deviations, since only 2 students out of 34 consistently followed the norm of gendered contexuality indicated in table 14.1—1 girl out of 17 used *atashi* exclusively, and 1 boy out of 17 used *boku* exclusively. These two students were the minority within the linguistic world of Gakkyuu A.

14.2.2. First-person pronouns within peer groups

According to my observations, and conversations and interviews with students, the girls and boys in Gakkyuu A divided themselves into different peer groups, each of which expressed different tendencies in the use of first-person pronouns and other nonlinguistic features. Peer-group cultures are by no means monolithic or simple, but in the following paragraphs I try to describe their salient features. The number of each group corresponds with the numbers in figure 14.1.

Girls' groups.   Group 1 was the group of girls whose first-person pronouns were most untraditional. The two core members of this group used *ore*, and three other members used both *ore* and *boku* or *boku* alone. There was also one girl who used *atashi* and *uchi*. This group had a distinctive subculture and language that both its members and other students considered *gehin* 'vulgar'. These girls invented dances to express their disdain for the skirts they had to wear as part of their school uniforms, and they composed erotic songs to express their strong interest in sex and sexuality. Their interest in their changing pubescent bodies also appeared in their subculture, as Aki, one of the core members of this group, shows in example (1).[8]

(1)   *Kinoo no yoru ore no shikyuu wa itteki mo dasanakatta . . . !* ***Ore*** *no shikyuu shiboridashitai...!*

'My [*ore no*] womb didn't produce a single drop of blood last night! I want to squeeze my (*ore no*) womb' . . . !

This statement certainly breaks with traditional Japanese constructions of feminine behavior and language. The content of the statement, Aki's disappointment at the sudden end of her menstrual period, is a taboo topic. Moreover, in producing this utterance, Aki used *ore*, a very masculine first-person pronoun.

This group of girls did not like the teacher in charge of their *gakkyuu* and resisted her strongly. One member in this group did not resist, however. This girl, who used *atashi* and *uchi*, belonged to the group because she and the core members participated in the ping-pong club together, but her attitudes toward school and the *gakkyuu* teacher differed from those of the other girls in this group. She later moved to Group 2.

Group 2 comprised four studious, pro-school girls who used *atashi*. All but one of these girls also used *uchi*. What differentiates these girls from the Group 1 girls is their attitude toward school. The girls in Group 2 diligently performed various *gakkyuu* tasks such as cleaning duties. They did not resist teachers and school rules, although they often complained about both within their group.

Group 3 was created when one girl who constantly used *boku* left Group 1 and formed a group with a girl who used mainly *atashi* and occasionally *uchi*. The social identities of Groups 3 and 4 fell somewhere between those of Groups 1 and 2. The girls in Group 3 were less resistant to the teacher than the girls in Group 1 but were not as accommodating to the rules or as active in official *gakkyuu* activities as the girls in Group 2. One boy who used *boku* and *atashi* considered himself to belong to this group.

Group 4 consisted of two girls who used *atashi* and *uchi*. These girls became closer because they belonged to the same sports club. Like the Group 3 girls, they did not oppose the teacher publicly but considered themselves to be less *otonashii* 'reticent' than Group 2 girls.

Group 5 had two members. One was a girl who constantly used *uchi*. She did not belong to any of the groups described earlier, and boys bullied her. Another girl who used *atashi* and *uchi*, and who was excluded from Group 2, interacted with other girls but reluctantly ended up forming a group with this unpopular girl.

Finally, "Group" 6 had only one member: a girl who was a loner and did not like belonging to a peer group. She used *atashi* and *ore*.[9]

Boys' groups.   Group 1 was a group of four boys who belonged to sports clubs, the Japanese equivalent of jocks (Eckert 1989). These boys always used *ore*. They were considered to be *undooshinkei ga ii* 'athletic', *kakkoii* 'cool', *ninki ga aru* 'popular', *ussai* 'noisy', and *tsuyoi* 'strong'. Three boys belonged to the soccer club and one to the track club.

There were three groups (2, 3, and 4) whose social identities fell between Groups 1 and 5. Group 2 consisted of three boys. These boys also used *ore* and belonged to sports clubs but did not get along with the boys in Group 1. One boy belonged to the soccer club with Group 1 boys, but he said he did not like to be with them because these boys, and one in particular, *shikiru* 'control too much' and are *jikochuushinteki* 'self-centered'. The other two boys belonged to the baseball club, whose members were considered weaker than those in the soccer club.

One boy in Group 3 used *ore* and the other boy used *oresama*, which as noted earlier can be translated as 'Mr. I', or 'the honorable I', and *ore*. These boys belonged to sports clubs but also drifted apart from the Group 1 boys.

The four boys who belonged to Group 4 used various first-person pronouns. Two boys used *ore*, one used *boku*, and the other used *washi*. Three boys belonged to the badminton club and one to the swimming club, which were considered less power-ful and athletic than most of the boys' sports clubs, though more powerful than the boys' ping-pong club. These boys were close to the Group 3 boys, with whom they often played role-playing games during break time.

There was also a group of three boys (Group 5) who were quiet and marginal in the *gakkyuu*. They shared an interest in playing the guitar. One boy rarely came to school. Because the subjects of sentences are often omitted in Japanese, it was diffi-cult to record which first-person pronouns these quiet boys used, but I heard two boys in this group using *ore* when speaking to each other.

Thus, different groups have different nonlinguistic characteristics, such as their attitudes toward school and the teacher (resistant, accommodating, etc.), their in-terests (sports, games, the body and sex, etc.), their positions in the *gakkyuu* (cen-tral, marginal, etc.), and their femininity or masculinity. The linguistic features of these groups were also a part of such subcultures (e.g., Eckert 1989, Mendoza-Denton 1994). Members of each group tended to use the same first-person pronouns or similar ones (*ore* and *boku*, or *atashi* and *uchi*). The first-person pronoun use of the girls and boys was influenced by that of the other students in the same peer groups. Girls in Group 1, for instance, used more masculine first-person pronouns than those in Group 2. First-person pronouns are thus in part products of group cultures.

It is important to note, however, that there were significant variations within groups with respect to girls' and boys' first-person pronoun uses. The complex interplay between individual and group identities is beyond the scope of this chapter (see Miyazaki 2002), but these intragroup variations in the students' pronoun uses testify to the negotiated distance between an individual and her or his group. For instance, the core members of girls' Group 1, on the one hand, used *ore*. The other three members, on the other hand, had been friends since elementary school and continued to use *boku*, their habitual pronoun. One of the three members, however, was influenced by the core members and often used *ore* with them, but the other *boku* girls were not so influenced. Thus, individual girls and boys do not completely follow the group norms of language, just as they do not always accommodate the gendered language ideology.

14.2.3. Metapragmatics of first-person pronoun use

In addition to investigating girls' and boys' use of first-person pronouns, I also examined the metapragmatics of such use—that is, how students themselves perceived, interpreted, and stereotyped their language use in the social world of peer-group relations. Inoue (1995) notes that speakers' interpretations and representations of language use can be an important resource in understanding speech as a social process. Similarly, Hanks (1993) says that although native metapragmatic discourses often diverge from actual usage, they are nonetheless essential because they serve as interpretive frames that guide everyday interactions.

Girls considered w*atashi*, a plain feminine first-person pronoun according to table 14.1, too formal to use in situations other than *sakubun* 'writing assignments' or presentations in class. Many girls regarded even *atashi*, a more informal pronoun than *watashi*, as too formal and too feminine to use in informal settings. Students' interpretations of *atashi*, however, are by no means uniform. The girl who used *atashi* exclusively explained that it is a normal girls' pronoun and that it has nothing to do with femininity. The use of *atashi* by a boy, however, was ridiculed and indexed as unusual, or *okama* 'homosexual/transsexual', by both girls and boys.

Uchi is regarded as less feminine and formal than *atashi* and is preferred by many girls for that reason. A number of girls also consider *uchi* a good pronoun to use among friends because it is shorter and easier to say than *atashi*.

Ore is considered to be the most masculine pronoun. Although it is usually classified as other-deprecatory, boys who used it did not necessarily attach such a connotation to it; they said that *ore* is just a pronoun for boys. One boy who constantly used *boku*, however, said that men fantasize about using *ore* and that only very cool men say *ore*. This boy did not think that he was cool enough to use *ore*, as he explains in the interview quoted at the beginning of this chapter. Another boy who used *boku* and *atashi* and who belonged to a girls' group also said that he did not use *ore* because it was for cool boys such as those in Group 1.

Boys' use of *ore* does not always arouse positive reactions in girls. Although one girl said that the speech of Group 1 boys sounds *imadoki* 'trendy', some girls said that *ore* sounds *erasoo* or *ibatteru* 'arrogant' and that *ore* users employ this form to try to cover up their inner weakness.

The use of *ore* by the resistant group of girls was received in various ways. When I asked about the use of *ore* by these girls in an interview, a Group 1 boy told me that these girls use *ore* "because they are *kichigai*" 'crazy'. In general, however, these girls' masculine speech, along with their behavior, was usually accepted with laughter. Some academic-oriented girls told me that these girls were problematic, but that they were so powerful that other students could not *sakarau* 'oppose' them.

Boku is considered less masculine than *ore* and often has negative connotations when used by boys: *boku* is for weak boys or for "mama's boys." In all six seventh-grade *gakkyuu* in the school, the groups of boys who used *ore* were regarded as stronger and more powerful than those who used forms other than *ore*. It is interesting that *boku*, a plain masculine pronoun, is denigrated in this way and is differentiated from *ore* on the basis of masculinity, strength, or power in the social world of the school. Girls' use of *boku*, however, generally did not trigger negative images. A girl who constantly used *boku* said that she used it simply because *uchi* is too feminine for her, to say nothing of *atashi*.

Thus, first-person pronouns index complex sets of meanings in the context of Gakkyuu A. Pronouns signal manifold pragmatic meanings not only regarding femininity and masculinity but also regarding many other factors such as power and solidarity and distance and intimacy (e.g., Brown & Gilman 1973, Friedrich 1979). Girls and boys actively make sense of and negotiate these myriad, sometimes contested meanings within and outside of their peer-group relations in the *gakkyuu*. These girls and boys have ways of making meaning by using the traditional gender-differentiated pronouns as well as others that fall outside the prescriptions of the dominant ideology. Within the context of this *gakkyuu*, girls' use of *ore*, which is supposed to be illegitimate, at times has positive meanings and boys' use of *ore*, which is supposed to be a normal masculine pronoun, is sometimes severely criticized.

It bears noting, however, that gender nonetheless plays a significant role in students' language negotiations. For instance, feminine pronoun use by a boy was indexed as unusual and discouraged among students. *Ore* and *boku* were differentiated in terms of desired masculinity. Although many girls received girls' use of *ore* positively, powerful boys perceived it as crazy. Moreover, although in this chapter I focus on pragmatic meanings among students in the *gakkyuu*, ideologies promoted by teachers and parents are an inseparable part of making meaning. These girls' teachers and parents often discouraged their masculine speech, which influenced girls' linguistic negotiations. This contrasts with boys' use of *ore*, which was rarely singled out for correction. In the next section, I turn to a "weak" boy, Taku, and his navigation of the sea of pragmatic meanings of first-person pronouns. Although my focus in this chapter is primarily on the dynamics of Gakkyuu A, I have chosen the following examples from another *gakkyuu* because they show well the field of gender and power in which an individual student negotiates meanings.

14.3. Example: Taku's negotiations of first-person pronouns

Taku, a student in Gakkyuu B, was a short, thin boy with eyeglasses who was always quiet in the *gakkyuu*. In this *gakkyuu*, a group of six boys, on the one hand, had the most power: they dominated classroom conversation, occupied the most space, and most effectively resisted the teacher in charge. Taku, on the other hand, along with two other boys, occupied the opposite pole of the power spectrum. One boy in the group told me in an individual interview that Taku was the boy least likely to join his *tsuyoi* 'strong' group.

All six boys in the powerful group used *ore*. One boy said that he had used *boku* in elementary school, at a time when he was weak, but that in junior high school, when he got close to Haruki, the leader of the group, he started using *ore*. Another boy, who was the weakest of the six, at one point used *oira*, which in urban areas has a funny, hillbilly connotation, and tried spreading it, but unsuccessfully.

Unlike the boys who used *ore*, Taku said in an interview with another powerless boy in his *gakkyuu*, Hide, that he changes his first-person pronouns *kanzen ni* 'completely' depending on the situation. Example 2 is Taku's own explanation of how he changes his first-person pronoun choices when he talks with Haruki.

(2) Taku = T, Hide =H, Interviewer = AM

1 T: *Eettoo, mazu,* (AM: Nn.).[10] *Konaka-kun* (Haruki's last name plus an honorific suffix) *mitai ni, kyooboo na hito no baai wa,* (H: . . .) ***boku*** *tutte . . .* (*AM: Nn.*)

(*H: . . .* ((whispering laughter))) *ojigi suru n desu. (H: Ojigi . . . no?)*

2 AM: *Heee.*

3 T: ((Turned to H)) *A, ojigi shinee na, yappa Konaka no baai dakan na. (H: Aa, soo da na . . .) Maa,* ***boku*** *tutte owari ni shite, de.* ×××

4 *De, Uchida-kun* (Hide's last name plus an honorific suffix) *mitai ni yasashii hito wa,* (*H: . . .*) (*AM: Nn*) *nanka, nanka, nanka,* ***ore*** *tutte mo okonnasoo dakaraa. (AM: Nn.)*

5 *Ne! Uchida!*

1 T: Well, first, (AM: Nn.) to violent people like Konaka-kun (Haruki's last name plus an honorific suffix), (H: . . .) I use ***boku*** (AM: Nn.) (H: . . . ((whispering laughter))) and bow to him. (H: Bow . . . ?)

2 AM: Hmm.

3 T: ((Turned to H)) No, I don't bow to him; after all, it's just Konaka. (*H: Oh, that's right . . .*) Well, I just say ***boku*** and . . .

4 To somebody who's nice like Uchida-kun (Hide's last name plus an honorific suffix), (H: . . .) (AM: Nn) well, I guess, ***ore*** wouldn't upset him. (AM: Nn)

5 Right, Uchida?

Taku explains that he uses *boku* to Haruki, the powerful boy in his *gakkyuu*, but *ore* in front of Hide, whom he considers his equal. When I asked Taku which was easier for him, he answered, "*Ore* is easier to say, but when I'm in front of Konaka-kun I chicken out and end up using *boku*." Taku added that *ore* sounds *erasoo* 'arrogant' and that if he uses it in front of the strong boys, he feels that they might try to get revenge on him. Thus, Taku was aware that his status in the *gakkyuu* affected his personal pronoun choices.

Right after Taku explained to me that he would use *boku* and bow to Haruki, he turned to Hide, who had just murmured the question *Ojigi . . . no*? 'Bow?'. In response, Taku and denied what he had just said, that is, that he would bow to Haruki (line 3). When Taku spoke to Hide, his speech suddenly shifted in a strongly masculine direction: he omitted the honorific suffix on Haruki's name and employed strongly masculine forms such as *shinee na* and *dakan na*.[11] This shift reinforces Taku's assertion that his use of gendered forms depends on audience.

The powerful boys in Taku's *gakkyuu* lend further support to this assertion. When I interviewed these six boys about their personal pronoun use, they said that they unconsciously said *ore*. In example (3) I asked further.

(3)   Haruki = H, Aiki = A, Shigeki = S, Yuji = Y, B = Bunta, Masa = M, Interviewer = AM

6   AM: *Tatoeba saa*, Konaka-kun (Haruki's last name plus an honorific suffix) *ga* **boku** *to ka ittara imeeji awanai?*

7   H: ***Ore** iwanai.*
            [   ]

8   A?:   *. . . daro?*

9   H: ***Ore** iwanee yo.*

10   A?:   *Awanee yo.*
            [   ]

11   Y?:   *Nanka Katchan* (the nickname of a boy in another class) *mitai jan.*

12   H: ***Ore** iwanee yo.*

13   B: *Kami no ke ga Katchan jan.*
                    [   ]

14   H: ***Ore boku** tte iwanee yo.*

15   AM: *E,* **boku** *tte doo yuu no?*
                    [   ]

16   A: *Ichiban au no wa nee Taku..*
                                [   ]

17   S: (To H) *Ima itta ja nee ka.*

18   Y: *Taku ka.*

19   AM: *Aa, aa soo, Taku-kun* **boku** *tte yuu yo ne.*
            [   ]

20   B: *Taku wa, seekaku ga Taku mitai dattara,* **boku** *tte . . .*
                                            [   ]

21   Y: *Taku wa nan ka saa,*
            joshi no mae dato **ore** *tte to ka ittete saa, koko made kuru to saa =*
                            [   ]

22   S: *Taku kimochiwarui.*

23 Y: = *boku* (in a high, small voice) *ttu n da yo ne.*

24 H: *Nakanishi* (the last name of a girl who is in the same *gakkyuu*) *kiratteru,*
        kiratte n desho.
                    [ ]

25 M: *Aa! Ano saa, ano shine tte yatsu desho?*
                                        [   ]

26 H: *Soo soo.*

27 B: *E? Nani?*

28 M: *Furareta no.*

6   AM: For example, if Konaka-kun (Haruki's last name plus an honorific suffix)
        said **boku**, would it be strange?

7   H: I (*ore*) wouldn't say **boku**.
        [   ]

8   A?:   . . . isn't it?

9   H: I (*ore*) wouldn't say it.

10 A?:   It wouldn't fit.
        [   ]

11 Y?:   It sounds sort of like Katchan.

12 H: I (*ore*) wouldn't say it.

13 B: (Your?) hairstyle is like Katchan's.
                            [   ]

14 H: I (*ore*) wouldn't say **boku**.

15 AM: What is **boku** like?
                [   ]

16 A: The person **boku** fits best is Taku.
                                    [   ]

17 S: (To H) You just said it (**boku**).

18 Y?:   Ah, Taku.

19 AM: Ah, yeah, Taku-kun says **boku**. That's right.
                [   ]

20 B: Taku says **boku** because of his character.
                                        [   ]

21 Y: Taku says *ore* in front of girls,
        but in front of us, =
        [   ]

22 S: Taku's weird.

23 Y: = he says **boku** (in a high, small voice).

24 H: Nakanishi (the last name of a girl who is in the same *gakkyuu*) hates him,
        right?
                [   ]

25 M: Ah!
        That one, (she told him,) "I hope you die!" Right?
                                        [   ]

26 H: Yeah.

27 B: What?

28 M: Taku was dumped by her.

This interview excerpt shows that Taku's fear of the strong boys was not unfounded. In this interview, they characterized him as *kimochiwarui* 'weird' (line 22) and made fun of him for being rejected by a girl he liked (lines 24–28). From these boys' perspective, *boku* fits Taku's character (lines 16 and 20), but *ore*, which indexed masculinity, arrogance and coolness in the pragmatic world of the school, does not. They also made fun of Taku for saying *boku* in a high-pitched, frightened voice in front of them (lines 21 and 23) and for using *ore* in front of girls (line 21). This accusation indicates the power differences between these boys and Taku: they themselves unconsciously and freely used *ore* to every classmate, whereas Taku did not enjoy such freedom because of the strong boys' pressure and intimidation. The way the strong boys and Taku refer to each other in these interviews provides additional evidence of power differences. Taku, on the one hand, called the powerful boys by their last names plus the honorific suffix *-kun*; the powerful boys, on the other hand, called Taku by his first name without any suffix, despite the fact that I used the honorific in my question to them. Haruki's group formed a powerful group culture represented by strongly masculine, fast-paced speech, including the first-person pronoun *ore*, thereby setting the terms of desired masculinity in Gakkyuu B and excluding Taku in the process.

Taku had to face such power dynamics in his *gakkyuu* every day. He was fully aware of his situation and chose to shift his pronouns in front of the strong boys. Taku's personal history also seemed to affect his choice. Some girls informed me that he had been severely bullied in elementary school; one girl suggested this might have given him some bitter lessons in keeping a low profile. Hide's pronoun choice, however, provided an interesting contrast to Taku's. Hide did not modulate his speech in front of the strong boys, although he, too, was on the powerless side of social relationships in the *gakkyuu*. Hide boasted to me, "I could say *ore* even in front of the principal." His persistence with *ore* may relate to the kind of identity he hoped to construct. Hide explained that he himself was *memeshii* '[a] sissy', by which he meant that he was cowardly and easily frightened, had an *amae no seishin* 'the habit of being indulged', and acted like a girl, although he wanted to change himself into a *otokorashii* 'manly' person. Hide's steady expression of his desired identity, even in front of Haruki's group, however, came at a cost. The strong boys bullied him, often physically. In the interview, Hide told me that when one of the strong boys kicked the back of his leg he could not hold back tears. Such *ijime* 'bullying' has long been a serious problem in Japanese education.

Taku chose a path different from Hide's, although he, too, wanted to use *ore* and express the masculine side of his identity. The teacher in charge of their *gakkyuu* told me that the strong boys generally left Taku alone because he was harmless to them, but that Hide's challenge to them resulted in bullying. Taku avoided being bullied by altering his speech and attitude and by making himself harmless in front of the strong boys. He repressed the part of his identity that could be expressed through *ore* and reserved it for occasions such as conversations with Hide. In the interview with Hide, Taku could constantly use *ore*, raise many topics of conversation he was interested in, such as action movies and plastic models, or freely interrupt Hide. Taku's relationship with Hide allowed him to construct a different aspect of his identity, one that he could not express in front of Haruki. Taku's and Hide's negotiation of their speech and identity[12] provides us with an example of the complex interplay between individuals' language, identity, and social world. These boys, as well as the girls and boys in Gakkyuu A, offer a valuable perspective on the linguistic dynamics of language, power and gender.

14.4. Conclusions

I draw three conclusions from my analysis of first-person pronoun use within the junior high school *gakkyuu*. First, gender as a fixed category cannot explain the complex personal pronoun use of the students I studied. Girls and boys variously went along with, contested, and continually negotiated the ideology of gendered language in their daily *gakkyuu* interactions. Indeed, their negotiations often went beyond the traditional grammar chart in table 14.1 that represented this language ideology. Some girls used *ore* and *boku*, and one boy used *atashi*. Some girls created new pronouns, such as *uchi*, which is not as feminine as *atashi*.

Second, students' first-person pronoun use is deeply embedded in the specific context of the *gakkyuu*. Students construct complex sets of pragmatic meanings about their own and others' use of first-person pronouns. Each student brings both individual and group perspectives to the *gakkyuu* arena, creating a dynamic, changing assemblage of meanings around gender, power, relationships, and identity. Nonlinguistic and linguistic meanings fuse in this arena when, for example, girls convey a taboo topic with a masculine pronoun and are positively received by other girls or when a plain masculine pronoun, *boku*, is imbued with various negative meanings regarding power and masculinity. Thus, rich, lively processes for making meaning sway students' speech away from the rigid traditional grammar chart.

Third, and finally, however, it is important to note that a student is not a completely free agent, just as she or he is not an inactive object whose language is automatically molded by language ideology. Although girls' and boys' first-person pronouns are often at odds with the traditional language ideology, gender ideology nonetheless affected the complex mass of pragmatic meanings of such pronouns. Girls' masculine pronoun use, for instance, was at times well received but at other times dismissed as crazy. A boy's feminine first-person pronoun use was ridiculed and sometimes severely punished. Girls and boys continually have to negotiate their speech and identity in a complex field of gender and power, such as when Taku suppressed his desire to express the masculine side of his identity in front of the strong boys.

The processes of creating actual speech and its meanings in a specific community reach far beyond the imagination of the fixed, dichotomous picture of traditional gender ideology. Such complex, contradictory, and unexpected processes can be understood only by following the naturally occurring linguistic practices of a specific community. Ethnographic methods are best suited to capturing such richly contextualized processes.

Notes

I appreciate the excellent guidance of the editors of this book, Shigeko Okamoto and Janet S. Shibamoto Smith, and the series editor, Mary Bucholtz. I also would like to thank Profs. Sara

Lawrence-Lightfoot, Marcyliena Morgan, and Miyako Inoue for their continued guidance regarding this topic. The Japan Society for the Promotion of Science and the Tokyo Women's Foundation provided financial support for the research described here. Special thanks go to the girls, boys, and teachers who generously shared their lives with me.

1. Transcription conventions are as follows:
.   end of intonation unit; falling intonation
?   end of intonation unit; rising intonation
. . .   omission of material by the author
[ ]   beginning and end, respectively, of overlapping utterances
=   places between utterances with no gaps, or to link different parts of a single speaker's utterance
. . .   sounds that are inaudible or in doubt
(( ))   description of quality of talk and activity related to talk

2. The level of formality is said to differ between the genders. In Japanese, as in many other languages, speakers are expected to use different language levels depending on the formality of context and social relationship (e.g., Kondo 1990, Dunn 1996). *Watashi* indicates a formal level for men but not necessarily for women; women's *watashi* sounds plainer than men's *watashi* (Kondo 1990). Women, on the one hand, are said to use *watashi* or *atashi* among friends or in other informal settings. Men, on the other hand, are usually said to use *watashi* only in formal settings, such as when talking to superiors or older persons, or in an official setting. This shows that women are expected to use more formal forms than men.

3. In elementary school, one teacher teaches all subjects to the *gakkyuu*, but in junior high and high school various teachers enter the *gakkyuu* classroom to teach their subject of specialization.

4. These groups are at times arranged according to lottery, other times according to the class roster. One teacher told me that in another school he himself allocated students into groups in ways that he thought would maximize educational outcomes.

5. Group formations underwent both dramatic and slight changes over the year. Figure 14.1 captures peer-group relations in the middle of the academic year.

6. The first-person pronouns listed here are the first-person pronouns the students used regularly in their peer groups but do not completely exhaust their playful and creative practices. I observed many students occasionally using forms of first-person pronouns other than those listed in the diagram—for instance, when girls who regularly used *ore* or *boku* occasionally used *atashi* to make fun of femininity. In addition, students reported that they and their *gakkyuu* mates sometimes used pronouns other than those I observed. These are not included in the diagram.

7. There were many girls and boys at the school who creatively used pronouns other than the four main ones. For instance, some girls used *atai*, *oira* (as noted earlier), their full names (e.g., "Miyazaki Ayumi is sleepy"), their first names (e.g., "Ayumi is going home"), and their first names plus the informal suffix -*chan* ("Ayumi-*chan* doesn't want to study!"). There was even a girl with worldly pretensions who used the pronoun *mii*, which comes from the English pronoun *me*. *Atai*, as well as *oira*, has a funny, hillbilly connotation in urban areas. One girl explained to me that her friend's use of *atai* conjures up images of a middle-aged woman selling *dango* 'sweet rice cake balls' in the Edo period. Self-referring with the suffix –*chan* has a childish connotation.

8. The names of the girls and boys that appear in this essay are all pseudonyms.

9. She reported that she had used *ore* in preschool, when she always played with boys, but when she entered elementary school her girlfriends discouraged her from using *ore*. Scared of being different from everybody else, she started using *atashi* and tried not to use *ore* throughout

her elementary school years, although *ore* popped out whenever she talked to her preschool friends. When she was a seventh grader (the first year of junior high school), she started using *ore* more often, as she explains in the quotation at the beginning of this chapter. After this academic year, her use of *ore* increased over her junior high school years; by the time she was a ninth grader (her final year of junior high school), she used *ore* more often than *atashi*.

10. In a Japanese conversation, listeners generally interject sounds such as "hmm" and "nn" more often than English speakers would. In addition, Hide often made almost inaudible backchanneling sounds. I put these small sounds in parentheses, instead of giving each sound its own line.

11. According to McGloin (1990), the sentence-final particle *na* is characteristically used by men, along with *zo* and *ze*, and signals strong insistence. Taku also used *shinee* instead of its regular verb form, *shinai*. The phonological form *ee* instead of *ai* or *oi* is also considered to be strongly masculine (Okamoto & Sato 1992, Okamoto 1995).

12. In the following year, when Taku became an eighth grader, however, he started to challenge Haruki fiercely, and by the end of the ninth grade (the final year of junior high school) Taku succeeded in using *ore* in front of him and other strong boys. Taku told me that he was not afraid of Haruki anymore. Haruki admitted to me that Taku had become much stronger and, in fact, almost like an equal.

References

Agha, Asif (1993). Grammatical and indexical convention in honorific discourse. *Journal of Linguistic Anthropology* 3(2): 131–163.

Bing, Janet M., and Victoria L. Bergvall (1996). The question of questions: Beyond binary thinking. In V. L. Bergvall, J. M. Bing, and Alice F. Freed (eds.), *Rethinking language and gender research: Theory and practice*, 1–30. London: Longman.

Brown, Roger, and Albert Gilman (1973). The pronouns of power and solidarity. In P. P. Giglioli (ed.), *Language and social context*, 252–282. Harmondsworth: Penguin.

Bucholtz, Mary (1999a). Bad examples: Transgression and progress in language and gender studies. In M. Bucholtz, A. C. Liang, and L. A. Sutton (eds.), *Reinventing identities: The gendered self in discourse*, 3–24. New York: Oxford University Press.

——— (1999b). "Why be normal"? Language and identity practices in a community of nerd girls. *Language in Society* 28(2): 203–223.

Coates, Jennifer (1994). Discourse, gender, and subjectivity: The talk of teenage girls. In M. Bucholtz, A. C. Liang, L. A. Sutton, and C. Hines (eds.), *Cultural performances: Proceedings of the Third Berkeley Women and Language Conference*, 116–132. Berkeley: Berkeley Women and Language Group.

——— (1999). Changing femininities: The talk of teenage girls. In M. Bucholtz, A. C. Liang, and L. A. Sutton (eds.), *Reinventing identities: The gendered self in discourse,* 123–144. New York: Oxford University Press.

Dunn, Cynthia D. (1996). Style and genre in Japanese women's discourse. Unpublished doctoral dissertation, University of Texas, Austin.

Eckert, Penelope (1989). *Jocks and burnouts: Social categories and identity in the high school.* New York: Teachers College Press.

Eckert, Penelope, and Sally McConnell-Ginet (1992). Think practically and look locally: Language and gender as community-based practice. *Annual Review of Anthropology* 21: 461–490.

Friedrich, Paul. (1979). Structural implications of Russian pronominal usage. In A. S. Dil (ed.), *Language, context, and the imagination*. Stanford, CA: Stanford University Press.

Goodwin, Marjorie. H. (1998). Games of stance: Conflict and footing in hopscotch. In S. Hoyle and C. T. Adger (eds.), *Kids talk: Language practices of older children*, 23–46. New York: Oxford University Press.

——— (1999). Constructing opposition within girls' games. In M. Bucholtz, A. C. Liang, and L. A. Sutton (eds.), *Reinventing identities: The gendered self in discourse*, 389–409. New York: Oxford University Press.

Hanks, William F. (1993). Metalanguage and pragmatics of deixis. In J. A. Lucy (ed.), *Reflective language: Reported speech and metapragmatics*, 127–158. Cambridge, MA: Cambridge University Press.

Ide, Sachiko (ed.) (1997). *Joseego no sekai (The world of women's language)*. Tokyo: Meiji Shoin.

Ide, Sachiko, and Naomi Hanaoka McGloin (eds.) (1990). *Aspects of Japanese women's language*. Tokyo: Kuroshio.

Inoue, Miyako (1994). Gender and linguistic modernization: Historicizing Japanese women's language. In M. Bucholtz, A. C. Liang, L. A. Sutton, and C. Hines (eds.), *Cultural performances: Proceedings of the Third Berkeley Women and Language Conference*, 322–333. Berkeley: Berkeley Women and Language Group.

——— (1995). A woman manager and "local" metapragmatics in a Tokyo corporate office. In R. Ide, R. Parker, and Y. Sunaoshi (eds.), *SALSA: Proceedings of the Third Annual Symposium about Language and Society—Austin*, vol. 36, *Texas Linguistic Forum*, 41–48. Austin: University of Texas, Department of Linguistics.

Kondo, Dorinne (1990). *Crafting selves: Power, gender, and discourse of identity in a Japanese workplace*. Chicago: University of Chicago Press.

McGloin, Naomi Hanaoka (1990). Sex difference and sentence-final particles. In S. Ide and N. H. McGloin (eds.), *Aspects of Japanese women's language*, 23–41. Tokyo: Kuroshio.

——— (1997). Shuujoshi (Sentence-final particles). In S. Ide (ed.), *Joseego no sekai (The world of women's language)*, 33–41. Tokyo: Meiji Shoin.

Mendoza-Denton, Norma (1994). Language attitudes and gang affiliation among California Latina girls. In M. Bucholtz, A. C. Liang, L. A. Sutton, and C. Hines (eds.), *Cultural performances: Proceedings of the Third Berkeley Women and Language Conference*, 478–486. Berkeley: Berkeley Women and Language Group.

Miyazaki, Ayumi (2002). Relational shift: Japanese girls' nontraditional first-person pronouns. In S. Benor, M. Rose, D. Sharma, J. Sweetland, and Q. Zhang (eds.), *Gendered practice in language*, 355–374. Stanford, CA: CSLI Publications.

Morgan, Marcyliena (1999). No women, no cry: Claiming African American women's place. In M. Bucholtz, A. C. Liang, and L. A. Sutton (eds.), *Reinventing identities: The gendered self in discourse*, 27–45. New York: Oxford University Press.

Ochs, Elinor (1992). Indexing gender. In A. Duranti and C. Goodwin (eds.), *Rethinking context: Language as an interactive phenomenon*, 335–358. Cambridge, MA: Cambridge University Press.

Ogbay, Sarah (2000). The social and linguistic construction of identities of girls and boys in Eritrea urban. Paper presented at the First IGALA Conference, Stanford University, Stanford, CA.

Okamoto, Shigeko (1995). "Tasteless" Japanese: Less "feminine" speech among young Japanese women. In K. Hall and M. Bucholtz (eds.), *Gender articulated: Language and the socially constructed self*, 297–325. New York: Routledge.

——— (1997). Social context, linguistic ideology, and indexical expressions in Japanese. *Journal of Pragmatics* 28(6): 795–817.

Okamoto, Shigeko, and Shie Sato (1992). Less feminine speech among young Japanese females. In K. Hall, M. Bucholtz, and B. Moonwomon (eds.), *Locating power: Proceedings of the*

Second Berkeley Women and Language Conference, 478–488. Berkeley: Berkeley Women and Language Group.

Reinoruzu [Reynolds]-Akiba, Katsue (ed.) (1993). *Onna to nihongo (Women and the Japanese Language)*. Tokyo: Yushindo.

Shibamoto, Janet S. (1985). *Japanese women's language*. New York: Academic Press.

[Shibamoto] Smith, Janet S. (1992). Women in charge: Politeness and directives in the speech of Japanese women. *Language in Society* 21(1): 59–82.

Silverstein, Michael (1976). Shifters, linguistic categories, and cultural description. In K. Basso and H. Selby (eds.), *Meaning in anthropology*, 11–55. Albuquerque: University of New Mexico Press.

Woolard, Kathryn A. (1998). Introduction: Language ideology as a field of inquiry. In P. V. Kroskrity, B. B. Schieffelin, and K. A. Woolard (eds.), *Language ideologies: Practice and theory*, 3–47. New York: Oxford University Press.

15

CINDI STURTZ SREETHARAN

Japanese Men's Linguistic Stereotypes and Realities

Conversations from the Kansai and Kanto Regions

There is very little empirical research into how men of any society use language at the everyday, local level (but see Coates 2003; Johnson & Meinhof 1997). This is certainly true in the Japanese case. The lack of investigation into Japanese men in general and their language use in particular may give the impression that any Japanese man on the street can stand as representative of the generic Japanese male and that the language style he uses is both known and normatively spoken by all Japanese men.

This chapter emphasizes the diversity among Japanese men's linguistic practices. I propose an alternative account based on ethnographically collected speech data of how individual men negotiate their own ideas of normative or stereotypical masculinity in expressing their identities through language. I examine casual conversations of men from two regions—Kanto and Kansai. Specific features considered for investigation include sentence-final particles and discourse strategies. My analysis will show that men use stereotypically masculine sentence-final particles infrequently, and that even when they do, they use them in both ideology-consistent and other ways to further particular discourse goals.

15.1. Background

15.2.1 Men, masculinity, and language in Japan

The literature on gender and speech styles in Japanese is very large. This literature can be divided into two categories: research that deals with formal linguistic differences (phonological, morphological, lexical, syntactic, etc.) and research that deals with interactional or discourse differences (backchannels, interruptions, emotional expressivity, etc.). The former are more numerous than the latter.

Using self-report surveys and prescriptive usage rather than empirical investigation, the bulk of the studies on women's and men's differential use of formal linguistic features report that women and men are thought to use different sets of first- and second-person pronouns and sentence-final particles (SFPs) (e.g., Ide 1993, Kanamaru 1993). Other research claims that Japanese men use polite forms of verbs less frequently than women do and use a higher frequency of verb endings that are blunt, assertive, and direct (e.g., Ide 1982, Reynolds 1985, Shibamoto 1987). Men are also associated with reduced phonological forms such and *dekee* (< *dekai* 'big') and *umee* (< *umai* 'delicious') (Ide 1982).

Previous studies have provided fairly clear differences between SFPs that women and men use. McGloin (1990), Reynolds (1985), and Uchida (1993), among many others, report that Japanese men use a set of SFPs that index aggression, authority, masculinity, or intimacy, depending on interlocutor and context of interaction. Specifically, McGloin (1990) asserts that the SFPs *zo* and *ze* are used exclusively by men and are typically characterized as strongly masculine. *Zo*, however, is considered the most imposing of SFPs, conveying insistence, authority, aggressiveness, and a status higher than one's interlocutor. While McGloin's examples appear to derive from prescriptive usage or native speaker intuition, it is important that she relates the pragmatic meanings of SFPs to gender.

Uchida (1993), based on actual speech data of SFPs used by university students in the Tokyo area, finds that *ze* and *yo na* are used exclusively by men; however, she concludes that the SFPs used by women and men are becoming neutralized with regard to gender differentiation.

Investigations that address the interactional aspects of Japanese language and gender have found men to exhibit less pitch variation (Ohara 1992, chapter 12, this volume), to use a smaller and less emotionally charged lexicon (Shigemitsu 1993, Uchida 1993), to use fewer backchannels and tag questions (Kurozaki 1987, Horiguchi 1991), and to interrupt their conversational partners more frequently than women (Shigemitsu 1993, Uchida 1993).

Neither the structural nor the discursive-interactional studies of gender differences in Japanese have been linked to larger issues of language ideology, masculinity, identity, or region, although they have been linked to femininity (cf. Shibamoto 1987, Okamoto & Sato 1992, Inoue 1996). However, it has been frequently noted that Japanese speakers have notions of what it means to "talk like" a woman or man. Inoue (1996) and Okamoto (1995, chapter 2, this volume) both note that women and men recognize idealized forms of Japanese and provide numerous examples of popular (often negative) commentary about women's failure to use Japanese women's language. Specific linguistic features that trigger these responses need to be further investigated (but see chapter 12, this volume); nevertheless, it is evident that Japanese women and men have linguistic ideological positions concerning the particular language forms that they hear and use (cf. Silverstein 1979).

Ethnographic and historical documents on Japanese men indicate that prior to the Meiji era (1868–1912), the *bushidoo* warrior with his topknot and two swords was the image of manliness; after 1868, a new man emerged, an updated samurai, now showing off his masculinity by being enterprising and entrepreneurial (see Kinmonth 1981). The *bushidoo* warrior ideals had not been replaced but rather "re-dressed," literally, in more stereotypical Western fashion and ideologically transformed into a "company warrior" or "entrepreneurial *samurai*" (Vogel 1979). Characterizations of Japanese men as strong, silent, dependable, and so on are also abundant in popular culture materials (e.g., novels, films, songs, and commercials; cf. Davis 1996). However, systematic research on masculinity in Japan, in which the portrait of the "masculine man" is emerging, is very recent.

More recent ethnographic accounts of Japanese men note that to be masculine in Japan is to be hardworking and useful (Fujieda 1995, Gill 1999); it is to be strong and dependable on the outside (Ito 1996, Seko 2000) and yet soft on the inside (Yorifuji 1998). A masculine man excels at sports and is *tsuyoi* 'strong' at drinking alcohol (Toyoda 1997, Seko 2000); he is rhetorically adept (Rosenberger 1994) and yet paradoxically lacks eloquence (Iwao 1993, Yamada 1997).

Descriptions of Japanese men as silent, taciturn, or at least verbally restrained are not uncommon. Donahue (1998) notes that a Japanese man who is verbally serious and unexpressive has been traditionally more highly valued than one who is effusive and verbally outgoing. Similarly, Loveday claims that in formal settings of social equality between males Japanese men "take a low profile linguistically, understating, being terse, presenting an unemotional, self-restrained exterior" (1986:95). Seward comments that "Japanese men emphasize the masculinity of their speech by adopting a deep-voiced, guttural mode of speaking which is often accompanied by stern faces and stiff postures" (1968:111).

These studies give insight into different social (and sometimes sociolinguistic) behaviors that men are expected to exhibit but are limiting because they do not delineate the specific behavioral or linguistic strategies available to individual men to construct "hardworking," "strong and dependable" yet "soft-on-the-inside" selves as well as to examine how individual men deal with the ideologies of normative behavior in specific social contexts.

15.1.2 Regionality, language, and men

Until quite recently, much English language scholarship on modern Japan has focused on the Tokyo area. Japan has typically been assumed to be homogeneous at many levels, including ethnicity, class, and language, and scholarship on Japan focuses on the characteristics of the middle class in Tokyo or Kanto, part of the eastern region of Japan. However, as is increasingly recognized, a rich diversity of Japanese identities exists and proliferates.

Kansai, part of the western region of Japan, is as representative of urban Japanese people as Kanto, albeit in a slightly different way. Historically, Kanto's population was largely samurai families, while merchants were limited to the *shitamachi* 'downtown' regions (Otani 1994). Although it is currently a large commercial center, it is better known for its administrative function and political power. This is in con-trast to Osaka, which has been historically and continues today to be a major com-mercial center of Japan, enjoying strong economic power. Kansai, in particular Osaka, is one of the main regions that dictate popular culture trends to the rest of the nation; it is the area responsible for karaoke and most of Japan's TV comedy entertainment (*manzai*) (Sugimoto 1997).

The dialect of the Kansai region is popular throughout Japan; it is considered one of the two prestige varieties used in Japan (the other being Tokyo "standard"; see, e.g., Miyake 1995, Kunihiro, Inoue, & Long 1999). Scholars report that Kansai residents "do not hesitate to speak openly and publicly in their own language[s]"[1] (Sugimoto 1997:59); moreover, young people strive to mimic the dialect of Kansai in lieu of their own "Tokyo language," or Standard Japanese (SJ) (Onoe, Kasai, & Wakaichi 2000). The dialect is particularly loved at "home," that is, in the Kansai region itself. While the Tokyo dialect is described as monologue-esque (*monoroogu muki*; Sato 2000:65), the dialect of the Kansai region is said to be *shitashimi yasui* 'friendly/familiar/affectionate' and to have the ability to bind speakers together (Peng 2000).

Images of men specific to Kansai are difficult to obtain, at least in the research literature. Kansai natives are described as *isogashii* or *sewashinai* 'busy' and always in a hurry (Otani 1994). This image of hurriedness is matched linguistically by Peng's description of the Kansai dialect as being spoken quickly, at a fast tempo (2000:75). Whether this "hurried" image is particular to men is not clear, but images of Kansai residents certainly provide alternative gendered identities to draw upon rather than just the strong, silent, and slow *sarariiman* 'company man' of Tokyo found in popu-lar literature. We are left to wonder how ordinary Kansai men talk and how they might utilize linguistic expressions of masculinity.

15.2. This study

This chapter, then, examines theories of masculinity and of linguistic difference as they are instantiated in different regions of Japan. I maintain that masculinity, like language, is a dynamic force that interacts and manifests itself differently across speakers, spaces, and contexts. I do not assume that all Kansai men talk like the men in my data, nor that these men talk this way at all times. Rather, I hope to begin to make empirical inroads into potential links or connections between speech styles, masculinity, and regionality.

I analyze the conversations of men from the Kanto and Kansai regions to find out how—or whether—they express masculinity through particular linguistic features or discourse strategies, and whether there are regional or situational differences in the way they use these features and strategies. Rather than the term *Kansai dialect*, I use the more specific term *Hanshinkan dialect* (HKD) to refer to the variety spoken by Osaka and Kobe speakers. The Osaka and Kobe area in the Kansai region is commonly re-ferred to as Hanshin, a Sino-Japanese term (*Han* refers to Osaka and *Shin* to Kobe), and its dialect is called Hanshinkan dialect, although exactly what should be included in this dialect has been debated (e.g., Wada & Kamata 1992, Hirayama 1997).

15.3. Methods

15.3.1. The conversations

The main data analyzed in this chapter comes from three conversations (approximately 70 minutes each): two from the HKD area and one from Kanto. The HKD conversations used in this chapter are part of a larger corpus of data (comprising over 45 hours of conversation) collected during my field research in the Kansai area of Japan, including Kobe and Osaka, from July 1998 through January 2000. The Kanto conversation is taken from the Shibamoto Smith Japanese Conversation Corpus, comprising data collected in the late 1970s by Janet S. Shibamoto (as reported in Shibamoto 1985). In each case of data collection, the participants knew the researchers were interested in language use but were not guided toward discussions of language.

All HKD data was recorded on a MiniDisc portable recording device; I was not present for any of the recordings. After being introduced (via a third party) to one man, I would then explain my research to him and, if he agreed to help, would ask him to gather one or two friends together to talk. I provided my contact with a recorder and recording instructions. I encouraged the men to have their conversations anywhere they felt comfortable talking informally. The Kanto conversation was recorded on a Sony TC-800A open reel recorder with an attached microphone. The investigator was present during this recording; however, based on the informality of the forms used, the conversations were judged to "sound natural" by native speakers of Japanese (Shibamoto 1985:74).

All of the men were in the career stage of their lives[2] and, at the time of each recording, all were employed by Japanese companies. The Kanto conversation has three participants and takes place in the men's company lunchroom. The three men—Shibata, Mihara, and Kawamura[3]—are each 34 years of age and are coworkers. The Kobe conversation has four participants and takes place in a local *okonomiyaki-ya*, a shop that sells a pizza-pancake kind of food found throughout Japan. The four men, like their Kanto counterparts, are co-workers; they are Sato (42 years old), Yamada (38 years old), Honda (45 years old), and Nakayama (29 years old). Despite their slightly disparate ages, they are a closely knit group and have attended one another's weddings. The Osaka conversation has two participants—Tanaka (40 years old) and Honda, who also appeared in the Kobe conversation. It takes place in Honda's company office. The men have been friends for a long time and often join each other on both private and company sporting excursions. They are coworkers, although in different sections of the same company.

Each conversation was transcribed and coded for a variety of features; in this chapter I examine the use of SFPs as discourse strategies. SFPs were chosen because the recent findings by Inoue (1996), Okamoto (1996, 1998), and Ogawa and [Shibamoto] Smith (1997) raise questions about how speakers actively use SFPs to subvert or conform to traditional or stereotypical notions of gender.

One additional HKD conversation is analyzed later, but not with respect to SFPs. In this conversation, I focus on the use of highly marked stereotypical masculine linguistic practices, including phonological, lexical, and morphological features. This conversation is by two men—Ito and Kado—from the Kawachi region of Osaka

Prefecture. The Kawachi dialect is stereotypically associated with rough or rude speech and, perhaps consequently, with male speech. Both Ito and Kado are 67 years old and retired. Ito's son is married to Kado's daughter. Thus, Ito and Kado have known each other for as long as their children have been married, about 15 years, and frequently interact via their children and grandchildren.

15.3.2.   Stereotypically gendered categories of SFPs

The SFPs identified in this chapter are based on previous studies of SFPs and on grammar texts (cf. Fujiwara 1982, 1985, 1986; Komatsu 1988; Okamoto & Sato 1992; Kawashima 1999). Table 15.1 shows stereotypical gender categorizations of SFPs; each category has two subcategories, HKD and SJ.

The categorizations for SJ are based on the vast literature on this topic (e.g., Kawaguchi 1987, Okamoto & Sato 1992); the categorizations for HKD are based on a less vast and perhaps a less strictly academic literature (e.g., Kamata 1979; Fujiwara 1982, 1985, 1986; Makimura 1984; Wada & Kamata 1992; Yamamoto 1995; Hirayama 1997). Thus, it is important to note that for both HKD and SJ the categorizations are ideological or prescriptive in nature.

While it is not always possible to separate dialect usage cleanly from SJ, the men from Hanshin display quite typical HKD features at the lexical and morphological levels. However, they also use SJ; the usage is highly mixed at the morphological, lexical, and syntactic levels. Following are examples of two HKD features drawn from my data. Because this chapter focuses on masculinity, examples 1 and 2 are only of those SFPs that are associated with stereotypically masculine gender. (For explanation of those HKD SFPs that are considered to be neutral with regard to gender see, e.g., Hirayama 1997.)

(1)   [HKD] *moratteru no kai?*
     (cf. [SJ] *moratte iru no ka?*)
          'Do you receive it'?

TABLE 15.1 Stereotypical gender categorization of sentence-final particles in Standard Japanese and Hanshinkan dialect

	Strongly masculine	Moderately masculine	Neutral	Moderately feminine	Strongly feminine
HKD	yan ke jai	ga na; wai; kai	ya n(ai)(ka) de; non nen/ten (na) shi; de ne; na	ya wa	
SJ	zo ze na	da yo; kai ka na; mon na VB/ADJ + yo na sa; VB/ADJ+ yo ja n; ke	VB/ADJ + yo ne VB/ADJ + ne wa↓ Q no↑	mon/o NOM + ne VB/ADJ + no↓	kashira VB/ADJ + no(yo)(ne) VB/ADJ + wa(yo)(ne) NOM + na no(yo) NOM + yo; wa↑

VB = verb; ADJ — adjective; NOM = nominal form; Q = question; ↓↑arrows indicate falling or rising intonation.

The form *kai*, equivalent to the interrogative final particle *ka* in SJ, is considered to be masculine in both SJ and HKD; it is used to express strong opposition to something said by an interlocutor (Makimura 1984, Kawashima 1999).

(2) [HKD] *mainichi, nikkee o yomu no? erai ga na*
    (cf. [SJ] *mainichi, nikkee o yomu no? rippa ja nai ka*)
        'You read the *Nikkei* [Japanese Economic Newspaper] every day? That's amazing, isn't it!'

The ending *ga na* is an emphatic equivalent of the SJ form *ja nai ka* 'isn't it?'. It is considered stereotypically masculine in HKD (Makimura 1984).

15.4.   Results and discussion

15.4.1.   Quantitative analysis

Not all of the SFPs listed in table 15.1 were used within the segments under investigation. The subset of SFPs included in my analysis is shown in table 15.2.

Table 15.3 presents the distribution of SFPs according to their gender categories. The neutral count and percentage do not include the absence of SFPs, which is normally considered neutral; the percentage is calculated against the total SFPs possible.[4]

There are some notable differences across the conversations. First, I examine the conversation of the Kanto men. They use neutral forms most frequently (40%), followed by masculine forms (22%), and feminine forms the least (9.1%). The form *da yo* is considered to be moderately masculine, at least ideologically (see table 15.1). However, it is used rarely by the Kanto speakers (4 times, or 2.3%). Likewise, the standard strongly masculine SFP *na* is used only 9 times (8%) by the Kanto speakers. *Zo* and *ze*, two of the strongly masculine forms, are never used. Rather, the neutral form *ne* is overwhelmingly the SFP of choice. The Kanto men do make use of the relatively masculine SFP adjective/verb + *yo* and other moderately masculine forms (29 times, or 17%). Among feminine forms, the moderate forms ADJ/VB + *no*((4%) and NOM + *ne* (3.4%) were most favored.

Turning to the Osaka conversation next, we see a slightly different pattern emerging. These speakers overwhelmingly use neutral SFPs (49%—with 27% in SJ and 22% in HKD). They split the rest of their SFP usage equally into moderately mascu-

TABLE 15.2 SFPs used in the analysis

	Strongly masculine	Masculine	Neutral	Feminine	Strongly feminine
HKD		ga na kai	ya n(ai)(ka) wa ↓; de na; nen/ten		
SJ	na	kai; da yo ADJ/VB + yo sa	ADJ/VB + yo ne ~TE/ADJ/VB + ne wa ↓; Q no↑	mon/o NOM + ne ADJ/VB . no↓	ADJ/VB + no ne ADJ/VB + no yo NOM + yo

TABLE 15.3 Percentage of stereotypical gendered SFPs used in each conversation

	Kaato	Osaka	Kobe
Strongly masculine	9 (5.0%)	0	0
Moderately masculine	29 (17.0%)	9 (4.4%)	36 (13.0%)
Neutral	70 (40.0%)	101 (49.0%)	119 (43.3%)
Moderately feminine	13 (7.4%)	9 (4.4%)	8 (3.0%)
Strongly feminine	3 (1.7%)	0	6 (2.2%)
Total			
Masculine	38 (22.0%)	9 (4.4%)	36 (13.0%)
Feminine	16 (9.1%)	9 (4.4%)	14 (5.2%)
Neutral	70 (40.0%)	101 (49.0%)	119 (43.3%)

line SFPs and moderately feminine forms (4.4% in each case, all in SJ). They make use of neither the strongly masculine nor the strongly feminine SFPs.

Finally, looking at the Kobe speakers we find that they also use neutral forms most frequently (43.3%); they use masculine forms 13% of the time (all moderately masculine, with 10.5% in SJ and 2.5% in HKD) and feminine forms 5.2% of the time (3% moderately feminine and 2.2% strongly feminine, all in SJ).

The speakers' patterns of SFP use do not conform to one another; more crucially, they do not correspond to those described in the literature for male speakers. Japanese men, at least those in my data, are not taking advantage of SFPs as a place to index their gender. Overwhelmingly, all speakers from each region use neutral SFPs with a much higher frequency than they use moderately or strongly masculine ones. Further, they occasionally use feminine particles.

While no speakers use strongly and moderately masculine forms frequently, the Kanto speakers have a much higher usage (22%) than either the Osaka (4.4%) or the Kobe speakers (13%). Further, gendered forms used by Osaka and Kobe speakers are primarily SJ forms. These findings may be partially explained by the fact that the ideology of gendered language has been more prominent in SJ than in other dialects.

15.4.2.   Qualitative analysis

While it is true that these men do not use masculine SFPs the majority of the time, it is important to investigate the contexts in which they are using these forms. The following examples illustrate how masculine SFPs are qualitatively used by both SJ speakers and HKD speakers.[5]

(3)   *da yo*   *iya nai nai, dakara komaru n **da yo***   [CT, Mihara, #13]
                'Uh, no, no [it doesn't], that's why it's a problem!'

(4)   *da yo*   *marukkiri onaji **da yo***   [CT, Mihara, #43]
                'They are exactly the same'.

In examples (3) and (4), Mihara uses the stereotypically masculine sentence final form *da yo*. The participants in the Tokyo conversation are discussing accents (*namari*) in Japan. Shibata states that he is originally from Iwate Prefecture (in the northeast of Japan) but that he does not find Iwate to be known for an accent nor does he have an accent himself.[6] Upon his saying this, Mihara responds with example (3), a complaint that Shibata's lack of accent is a problem, and laughter by all speakers follows. Mihara here seems to be using the masculine form *da yo* to express his complaint in a direct and forceful manner. The complaint here is not a serious one; it is a kind of banter only allowable when the appropriate degree of intimacy obtains. Its humorously forceful expression is indexing friendship or solidarity rather than a serious, forceful complaint.

In example (4), Mihara again uses *da yo*. The men are still discussing dialect variation within Japan and how it correlates with gender differences in speech. Mihara mentions that his wife is from Fukushima, where the regional dialect (according to Mihara) does not exhibit gender differences. Mihara says that *minna onaji yoo ni shabetteru kedo* 'everyone talks the same', to which Kawamura says *dakedo onaji ja nai↓* 'but they're not the same' with falling intonation. Mihara responds with example (4), confirming that, indeed, the language that women and men in the Fukushima region speak is exactly the same. In this case, I suggest that Mihara is using the masculine form *da yo* to make a strong disagreement, which in turn may index his expert knowledge and authority, because he thinks he is most knowledgeable about the Fukushima dialect, the dialect of his wife, and because he originally established the topic of regional dialects and has contributed more to this topic than the other two speakers. Consequently, when Kawamura opposes Mihara's statement, he linguistically points to himself as the expert by using the stereotypical masculine form of authority: *da yo*.

I turn now to how HKD speakers use stereotypically masculine SFPs within the context of their conversations. Examples 5 and 6 involve the forms *ga na* and *kai*.

(5) *kai*   *ee n **kai** na*   [CK, Sato, #82]
             'That's good, isn't it'.

(6) *ga na*   *ee kotcha **ga naa***   [CK, Honda, #192]
             'That's nice, isn't it?' (sarcastically)

Examples (5) and (6) occur during a discussion of the free gifts that one is offered in exchange for signing up for newspaper home delivery. Yamada begins the topic by saying that recently someone came by his home offering the newspaper *Yomiuri Shimbun* free for one year if he signed up for a three-year delivery contract. Sato responds with example (5). Yamada continues his topic by naming the items he has received in the past (cookware and salad oil), noting that he has gotten over 10,000 yen in goods from these "deals." Nakayama joins in the conversation, saying that he is "unable to run out of dishwashing liquid" even though he tells the sales representatives not to bring it. At this point, Honda sarcastically utters (6), "That's nice, isn't it?"

In these examples, Sato and Honda listen, give minimal responses, and offer some kind of evaluation that utilizes stereotypical masculine final forms to index their sympathy and support for the two complaining men. The support is not to be confused with nurturing; it is "manly" strong support, and this "manliness" is indexed through the final forms and the dialect itself. The dialect bolsters the camaraderie and friendship ties that the men have with one another.

In all cases, the men creatively and deftly use stereotypically masculine SFPs. They are not using these final forms necessarily to jockey for position, establish a position of authority, or show status; they are joking and giving support as well as showing authority. It seems that the men are aware of the stereotypical functional values of these final forms given their use of them, albeit infrequently, in an ideological fashion.

Although the men in these conversations do not seem to be relying heavily upon SFPs as a resource for marking masculine linguistic behavior, this does not necessarily mean that they are not or do not know how to be masculine. Other linguistic sites need to be investigated to identify other potential places where men do gender work, if, in fact, they do. What follows is a brief excerpt taken from a conversation between two men from the southern part of Osaka. These men, like those whose conversations are analyzed earlier, do not use SFPs as a place to mark their masculine gender (Sturtz 2000). However, in example (7) they indicate that they are capable of using highly stylized stereotypical masculine linguistic features such as trilled /r/ and rough command forms to enact masculinity. This excerpt underscores the need for further investigation of other potential sites of gender work.

In this conversation, Ito and Kado are talking about how today's young people have no manners and do not learn to say "thank you," "excuse me," "I am sorry," and other mannered formulas properly. They focus on the failure to say "excuse me" when people collide with one another on foot or bicycle. At this point, Kado invites Ito to join him in the performance of a bicycle accident. In the excerpt given here, the two men display their ability to negotiate and manage conflict in a situationally proper, manly manner—that is, through vulgar, crude, and rough speech.[7]

(7)   K: *soohoo ga hashittemashite, gashan-tto yarimashita. taoremashita. <aita!>*

I: *<mazu> watashi wa **"omae nani shitton nen"** to yuu koto o mazu yaru deshoo na.*

K: *soo deshoo na.*

I: ***"omae nani shitton nen"** to*

K: ***"ware"** maa, warui kotoba desu to **"warre** [trilled r] **nan ya sono hashirikata wa"** t-to*

I: *sono hashirikata wa nan ya, to yuu koto de ·**"omae aho chau ka"** yuu kotoba ga, mazu, dete kuru deshoo na, ee.*

K: ***"yarre** [trilled r] **sonna supiido dashiyagatte, sonna ni hashitorru kara ataru n ya nai ka"** to*

I: *un, **"ataru n ya nai ka"** to yuu*

K: ***"mae mite hashire! doko muitotten?"***

I: *un, soo yuu kotoba deshoo na.*

English Gloss:

K: We both are riding our bikes, *Gasshan!* [sound of bikes colliding], we collide and fall down. *<aita!>* [sound of shock/anger]

I: <at the least> I would say, at the least, "**What the hell are you doing**?!"

K: Yeah, that's right, isn't it.

I: "What the hell are you doing?!" [I would say]

K: The word "*ware*" [you] is bad, but, "**Hey asshole, you drive too fast; what kind of fucked-up bike riding is that [you're doing]**" [I would say]

I: I'd say, "**What kind of bike riding is that**?!" and at least something like "**You're a fool/asshole!**" would probably come out [of my mouth].

K: "**If you speed that much and ride your bike, that's why you hit me!**"

I: uh-huh, "**You'll hit someone**," you'd say

K: "**Look in front of you when you ride! Where the hell were you looking**?!"

I: Yeah, that's the kind of words we would use, right.

In this conversation, Kado overtly invites Ito to participate in a role play of two bikes colliding. Kado trills his /r/ sounds, which is not typical of the phonology of either SJ or HKD but rather is stereotypically associated with working-class male speakers or with TV gangsters. Moreover, prescriptively nongeminated forms are geminated (for example, *shitton* 'doing'). There appears potentially to be a correlation between rude or gruff speech and "hyper-geminated" forms; further research across more speakers is necessary to confirm this hypothesis. The boldface segments exhibit stereotypical masculine speech style in their forms—that is, the verbs are marked neither for politeness nor for honorifics; in other words, the style is rude, coarse, and quite rough. For example, in "*Mae mite **hashire!**" 'Look in front [of you when you] ride!', the verb *hashiru* 'ride' (lit., 'run') is in the command form of *hashire*; there is no mitigation of the on-record rebuke. The pronouns are stereotypically strongly masculine forms; for example, the crude masculine second-person pronoun ***warre*** is used. The overall style is unelaborated and very curt. In short, this metalinguistic discussion is filled with boorish, vulgar, and rude utterances.

The conversation that precedes and follows the bicycle accident role play does not make use of these extreme stereotypical masculine styles, but this metalinguistic demonstration gives a clear indication that these men are capable of producing stereotypical masculine styles, and of judging under what circumstances such styles are appropriate and, indeed, effective.

15.5.   Conclusion

The SFPs used and the way that they are used by the men in Kanto and HK are different not only from one another but also from what would be expected from traditional gendered classifications of SFPs (as seen in table 15.1). My findings challenge the idea that there is a single *danseego* 'Japanese men's language', or (male) "Standard Japanese." None of the men in any of the conversations ever called upon the most marked SFPs available to them, such as *zo* and *ze*. The moderately masculine form *da yo* was used by the Kanto speakers only a few times and never by the HKD speakers. This suggests that the traditional gendering of SFPs is ideological and that in reality (at least in ordinary conversations) male speakers do not resort to the exclusive or frequent use of masculine forms to express stereotypical (or old-fashioned) masculinity.

It is clear, however, that men can use language to create and inhabit specific stances (e.g., camaraderie, support, authority, anger, vulgarity, gangster-associated identity). Examples (3) through (6) show that the men are able to use the stereotypically masculine final particles both beyond and within their ideological uses. By using the forms variously to enact a joking or an authoritative context, the men show how these final forms can be used as creative as well as presupposing indexes (Silverstein 1976). Furthermore, in example (7), Kado and Ito use rude and rough language in an imaginary conversation to show how to be angry in appropriate situations. Although this is hardly surprising, heretofore men (Japanese or otherwise) have rarely been awarded recognition of this linguistic "prowess."

Large differences were not observed across the Kanto and Kansai regions of Japan. While it is true that Kanto speakers use more traditionally masculine final forms, all speakers produce neutral forms (including the absence of an SFP) much more than any gendered form available to them. The HKD speakers do favor dialect final forms somewhat over equivalent SJ forms. It is not that the SJ forms are not available to the HKD speakers (as is easily seen by the high use of other SJ forms), but it is possible that for HKD speakers, SJ forms index something more than "just stereotypical masculinity." Using the SJ forms to create or display camaraderie, for instance, may not be effective for HKD speakers.

This chapter has been a preliminary study only. Regionality still needs much more attention (but see chapter 10, this volume). Class distinctions and identification also demand much more consideration, for both female and male speakers. In order to get an encompassing picture of what is going on with Japanese men's linguistic practices, we must look across regions, class, genders, and ages to identify and begin to sustain an understanding of how men and their dynamic identities are arrayed across Japanese real space.

Notes

I would like to thank Janet S. Shibamoto Smith and Shigeko Okamoto for their careful and valuable comments. This research was supported by the Kobe College Corporation Graduate Fellowship and the National Science Foundation.

1. I add the plural *languag*[es] here to recognize the variation within the Kansai dialect.
2. Plath (1989), Skov and Moeran (1995), and Traphagan (2000) suggest that life stage stratification is quite salient in Japanese society.
3. All of the names that appear in this chapter are pseudonyms.
4. The neutral total for the Osaka and Kobe speakers represents the combined total of SJ and HKD. The Osaka speakers used 56 (27%) SJ forms and 45 (22%) HKD forms, totaling 49% combined; the Kobe speakers used 62 (23%) SJ forms and 57 (20.3%) HKD forms, totaling 43.3% combined. All gendered SFPs produced by the HKD speakers from Osaka were SJ, although Kobe speakers occasionally used an HKD-gendered SFP.
5. The information in brackets includes the conversation (C = Conversation, O/K/T = Osaka/Kobe/Tokyo), the speaker's name and the clause number from the conversation.
6. Although from Iwate Prefecture, Shibata has lived in Tokyo for several years and exhibits Tokyo dialect throughout the conversation.

7. Square brackets indicate author's note, angled brackets (< >) indicate overlap, of the words within, and boldface text indicates metalinguistic speech under discussion. The translations are mine, done with help from male native speakers of HKD.

References

Coates, Jennifer (2003). *Men talk: Stories in the making of masculinities.* Oxford: Blackwell.
Davis, Darrell (1996). *Picturing Japaneseness: Monumental style, national identity, Japanese film.* New York: Columbia University Press.
Donahue, Ray (1998). Japanese culture and communication: Critical cultural analysis. Lanham, Md.: University Press of America.
Fujieda, Mioko (1995). Ehon ni miru onna (no ko) zoo, otoko (no ko) zoo (Images of women (girls) and men (boys) in picture books). In T. Inoue, C. Ueno, and Y. Ehara (eds.), *Hyoogen to media (Expression and media),* 173–192. Tokyo: Iwanami Shoten.
Fujiwara, Yoichi (1982). *Hoogen bunmatsushi "bunmatsu joshi" no kenkyuu (Research on dialectal sentence-ending particles "sentence-final particles"),* vol. 1. Tokyo: Shun'yodo.
——— (1985). *Hoogen bunmatsushi "bunmatsu joshi" no kenkyuu,* vol 2. Tokyo: Shun'yodo.
——— (1986). *Hoogen bunmatsushi "bunmatsu joshi" no kenkyuu,* vol. 3. Tokyo: Shun'yodo.
Gill, Tom (1999). Yoseba no otokotachi (Men of the *yoseba*). In Y. Nishikawa and M. Ogino (eds.), *Kyoodoo kenkyuu: Danseeron (Collaborative research on men),* 17–43. Kyoto: Jinbun Shoin.
Hirayama, Teruo (1997). *Osaka-fu no kotoba (Osaka Prefecture's language).* Tokyo: Meiji Shoin.
Horiguchi, Sumiko (1991). Aizuchi kenkyuu no gendankai to kadai (The issues and stages of *aizuchi* research). *Nihongogaku* (10): 31–41.
Ide, Sachiko (1982). Japanese sociolinguistics: Politeness and women's language. *Lingua* 57: 357–385.
——— (1993). Sekai no joseego, Nihon no joseego: Joseego kenkyuu no shintenkai o motomete (Women's language of the world, women's language of Japan:Searching for new developments in women's language research). *Nihongogaku* 12(6): 4–12.
Inoue, Miyako (1996). The political economy of gender and language in Japan. Unpublished Ph.D. dissertation, Washington University, St. Louis, MO.
Ito, Kimio (1996). *Danseegaku nyuumon (Introduction to men's studies).* Tokyo: Sakuhinsha.
Iwao, Sumiko (1993). *The Japanese woman: Traditional image and changing reality.* New York: Free Press.
Johnson, Sally, and Ulrike Hanna Meinhof (eds). (1997). *Language and masculinity.* Oxford: Blackwell.
Kamata, Ryoji (1979). *Hyogoken hoogen bunpoo no kenkyuu (Research on the grammar of Hyogo-ken dialect).* Tokyo: Sakura Hosha.
Kanamaru, Fumi (1993). Ninshoo-daimeeshi, koshoo (Personal pronouns and address terms). In S. Ide (ed.), *Joseego no sekai (The world of women's language),* 15–32. Tokyo: Meiji Shoin.
Kawashima, Sue (1999). *A dictionary of Japanese particles.* New York: Kodansha.
Kawaguchi, Yoko (1987). Majiriai danjo no kotoba: Jittai choosa ni yoru genjoo (The intersecting speech of men and women: The current situation as assessed by survey). *Gengo Seekatsu* 429: 34–39.
Kinmonth, Earl (1981). *The self-made man in Meiji Japanese thought: From samurai to salary man.* Berkeley: University of California Press.

Komatsu, Hisao (1988). Tokyogo ni okeru danjosa no keeshiki: Shuujoshi o chuushin to shite (The form of gender differences in Tokyo dialect: Centering on the sentence-final particles). *Kokugo to Kokubungaku* 65(11): 94–106.

Kunihiro, Tetsuya, Fumio Inoue, and Daniel Long (1999). *Takesi Sibata: Sociolinguistics in Japanese contexts*. Berlin: Mouton de Gruyter.

Kurozaki, Yohei (1987). Danwashinkoojo no aizuchi no unyoo to kinoo (The function of *aizuchi* to the advancement of conversation). *Kokugogaku* 150: 15–28.

Loveday, Leo (1986). *Explorations in Japanese sociolingusitics*. Amsterdam: John Benjamins.

Makimura, Shiyo (1984). *Osaka kotoba jiten* (*Dictionary of the Osaka language*). Tokyo: Kodansha.

McGloin, Naomi Hanaoka (1990). Sex difference and sentence-final particles. In S. Ide and N. H. McGloin (eds.), *Aspects of Japanese women's language*, 23–41. Tokyo: Kuroshio.

Miyake, Yoshimi (1995). A dialect in the face of the standard: A Japanese case study. In J. Ahlers, L. Bilmes, J. S. Guenter, B. A. Kaiser, and J. Namkung (eds.), *Proceedings of the 21st Annual Meeting of the Berkeley Linguistics Society*, 217–225. Berkeley: Berkeley Linguistics Society.

Ogawa, Naoko, and Janet S. [Shibamoto] Smith (1997). The gendering of the gay male sex class in Japan: A preliminary case study based on *Rasen no Sobyoo*. In A. Livia and K. Hall (eds.), *Queerly phrased: Language, gender, and sexuality*, 402–415. New York: Oxford University Press.

Ohara, Yumiko (1992). Gender-dependent pitch levels: A comparative study in Japanese and English. In K. Hall, M. Bucholtz, and B. Moonwomon (eds.), *Locating power: Proceedings of the Second Berkeley Women and Language Conference*, 469–477. Berkeley: Berkeley Women and Language Group.

Okamoto, Shigeko (1995). "Tasteless" Japanese: Less "feminine" speech among young Japanese women. In K. Hall and M. Bucholtz (eds.), *Gender articulated: Language and the socially constructed self*, 297–325. New York: Routledge.

——— (1996). Indexical meaning, linguistic ideology, and Japanese women's speech. In *The Proceedings of the Twenty-second Annual Meeting of the Berkeley Linguistics Society*, Berkeley: Berkeley Linguistics Society, 290–30.

——— (1998). The use and non-use of honorifics in sales talk in Kyoto and Osaka: Are they rude or friendly? *Japanese/Korean Linguistics* 7: 141–157.

Okamoto, Shigeko, and Shie Sato (1992). Less feminine speech among young Japanese females. In K. Hall, M. Bucholtz, and B. Moonwomon (eds.), *Locating power: Proceedings of the Second Berkeley Women and Language Conference*, 478–488. Berkeley: Berkeley Women and Language Group

Onoe, Keisuke, Seiji Kasai, and Kooji Wakaichi (2000). Interview: Osaka no kotoba, Osaka no bunka (Osaka language, Osaka culture). *Gengo* 29(1): 14–39.

Otani, Kooichi (1994). *Osaka Gaku* (*The study of Osaka*). Tokyo: Shinkosha.

Peng, Fei (2000). Gaikokujin kara mita Osaka kotoba (Osaka language from the perspective of a foreigner). *Gengo* 29(1): 73–79.

Plath, David (1989). Arc, circle, and sphere: Schedules for selfhood. In Y. Sugimoto and R. Mouer (eds.), *Constructs for understanding Japan*, 67–93. London: Kegan Paul International.

Reynolds, Katsue Akiba (1985). Female speakers of Japanese. *Feminist Issues* 5: 13–46.

Rosenberger, Nancy (1994). Indexing hierarchy through Japanese gender relations. In J. Bachnik and C. Quinn (eds.), *Situated meaning: Inside and oustide in Japanese self, society, and language*, 88–112. Princeton, NJ: Princeton University Press.

Sato, Makoto (2000). Osakaben no seeshin (The spirit of Osaka dialect). *Gengo* 29(1): 60–65.

Seko, Koji (2000). *Koo yuu otoko ni naritai (I want to be a man like that)*. Tokyo: Chikuma Shobo.

Seward, Jack (1968). *Japanese in action*. New York: Weatherhill.

Shibamoto, Janet S. (1985). *Japanese women's language*. New York FL: Academic Press.

——— (1987). The womanly woman: Manipulation of stereotypical and non-stereotypical features of Japanese female speech. In S. Philips, S. Steele, and C. Tanz (eds.), *Language, gender, and sex in comparative perspective*, 26–49. New York: Cambridge University Press.

Shigemitsu, Yuka. (1993). Kaiwa no pataan (Conversational patterns). *Nihongogaku* 12(6): 135–140.

Silverstein, Michael (1976). Shifters, linguistic categories, and cultural description. In K. Basso and H. Selby (eds.), *Meaning in anthropology*, 11–56. Albuquerque: University of New Mexico Press.

——— (1979). Language structure and linguistic ideology. In P. R. Clyne, W. Hanks, and C. L. Hofbauer (eds.), *The elements: A parasession on linguistic units and levels*, 193–247. Chicago: Chicago Linguistic Society.

Skov, Lise, and Brian Moeran (1995). Introduction: Hiding in the light: From Oshin to Yoshimoto Banana. In L. Skov and B. Moeran (eds.), *Women, media, and consumption in Japan*, 1–74. Honolulu: University of Hawaii Press.

Sturtz, Cindi (2000). Being and becoming (Japanese) men at 67. Paper presented at the 99th Annual Meeting of the American Anthropological Association, San Francisco, CA.

Sugimoto, Yoshio (1997). *An introduction to Japanese society*. Cambridge, MA: Cambridge University Press.

Toyoda, Masayoshi (1997). *Otoko ga "otokorashisa" o suteru toki (When men throw away "masculinity")*. Tokyo: Asuka Shinsha.

Traphagan, John (2000). Reproducing elder male power through ritual performance in Japan. *Journal of Cross-Cultural Gerontology* 15: 81–97.

Uchida, Nobuko (1993). Kaiwa-koodoo ni mirareru seesa (Sex differences seen in conversational patterns). *Nihongogaku* 12(6): 156–168.

Vogel, Ezra (1979). *Japan as No. 1: Lessons for America*. Cambridge, MA: Harvard University Press.

Wada, Minoru, and Ryoji Kamata (1992). *Hyogo no hoogen, rigen (Hyogo's dialect and slang)*. Kobe: Kobe Shimbun Sogo Shuppan Senta.

Yamada, Haru (1997). *Different games, different rules: Why American and Japanese misunderstand each other*. New York: Cambridge University Press.

Yamamoto, Toshiharu (1995). *Osakaben no ruutsu o saguru*. In NHK Osakaben Project (ed.), *Osakaben no sekai (The world of Osaka dialect: Searching for the roots of Osaka dialect)*, 54–63. Tokyo: Keidoo Shoin.

Yorifuji, Kazuhiro (1998). *Ii otoko mitsuketa! (I found a good man!)* Tokyo: Kaneko Shobo.

INDEX

romance novels (*see* romance fiction)
teyo-dawa novels, 68
nyooboo kotoba 'court women's language',
    10, 24, 31, 44, 83–84, 86, 89

O'Barr, William, 207
objectivism in linguistic research, 31
occupation and language use, 46, 200
Ochs, Elinor, 51, 161, 244, 258
Ogawa, Naoko, 33, 92, 96, 201
Ohara, Yumiko, 15, 32, 151–152, 222–237
Okamoto, Shigeko, 3–17, 32, 38–54, 94,
    126, 150, 188, 217, 222, 236, 257,
    276
onomatopoeic words and cute femininity,
    153
onee kotoba 'older sister speech', 96–97,
    99, 101
onnarashii kotoba 'feminine speech'. *See*
    femininity
onnarashisa 'womanliness', 24, 27, 50–53,
    83. *See also* femininity
Otsuma, Kotaka, 82, 87
Ozaki, Koyo, 67

Peak, Lois, 119
peer group relations
    power dynamics in, 257, 282–284
    within a *gakkyuu* 'class', 259–264
performance
    burikko performance (*see burikko*)
    gender performance, 148, 150, 154,
        205
    performative strategy (*see* strategy)
    subversive linguistic performance (*see*
        practice)
personal pronouns
    gender and the use of first-person
        pronouns, 16, 27, 33, 79, 83, 93, 96–
        107, 120–124, 193, 211–215, 256–
        270
    gender and the use of second-person
        pronouns/references, 26, 79, 120–121,
        123–124, 215–216
politeness and gender, 3, 9, 15–16, 28, 38–
    53, 62, 87, 98, 197, 236–238, 249–
    250. *See also* femininity *and*
    honorifics
Povinelli, Elizabeth, 114

power
    as a relational and processual term, 207
    expressions of, 16
    hegemonic power, 23
    masculine power, 213, 218
    modern power, 60, 62
    power dynamics, 257, 282–284
practice
    discursive practice and identity
        construction, 6, 12, 135, 205
    distinction between ideology and
        linguistic practice, 7, 38, 53
    semiotic practice and construction of
        gender, 12, 113
    subversive linguistic/discourse practice,
        8, 24, 26–27, 132, 136
pragmatic meanings of (gendered)
    linguistic forms, 14–16, 32, 61, 215–
    218, 223–236, 240–253
pronouns. *See* personal pronouns
prosodic features,
    high-pitched voice and femininity, 4, 15,
        27, 32, 148, 151–152, 156, 158–159,
        161, 223–224, 227, 232–233, 237
    high-pitched voice and politeness, 151,
        236
    nasality and cute femininity, 153
    pragmatic meanings of voice-pitch
        levels, 223–235

queer. *See* sexuality

Radway, Janice A., 115–116
Read, Kenneth, 206
Reehoo yookoo 'Essentials of etiquette'.
    See education of women
reference terms. *See also* personal pronouns
    gender and the use of, 30, 92, 119–120,
        196, 208–211
    gender and the use of self-reference
        terms, 4, 10, 14–15, 33, 93–107, 120–
        124, 211–215
regional dialects
    gender and speakers of, 33, 52–53, 187–
        188, 200
    Hanshinkan dialect (*see* Kansai dialect)
    hoogen bokumetsu undoo 'dialect
        extermination movement', 188
    Ibaraki dialect (*see* Ibaraki dialect)